CONTENTS

W9-CDM-480

PART I

Intellectual Freedom and Libraries: An Overview

PART II

Library Bill of Rights

PART III

Protecting the Freedom to Read

PART IV

Intellectual Freedom and the Law

PART V

Preparing to Preserve and Protect Intellectual Freedom

PART VI

Working for Intellectual Freedom

PREFACE

This manual is designed to answer practical questions that confront librarians in applying the principles of intellectual freedom to library service. It is our hope that every librarian will keep this volume close at hand as a convenient reference work. If, for example, a librarian wants to know what the American Library Association (ALA) can do to help resist censorship of library materials, how to handle complaints, or how to write an appropriate letter to legislators, help can be found in this volume. If the problem is complex—for example, the development of a materials selection program—practical guidelines on how to tackle the problem are offered.

Part 1 of the manual explains the meaning of intellectual freedom in library service and how today's broad concept of intellectual freedom evolved from opposition to book censorship. It also includes an overview of today's issues and the challenges they present, ranging from the Internet to privacy and confidentiality. Part 2, "*Library Bill of Rights*," and part 3, "Protecting the Freedom to Read," present the texts and historical development of ALA's intellectual freedom policies and guidelines and give concrete examples of problems librarians can expect to encounter or should anticipate in formulating policy for their own institutions. The Interpretations of the *Library Bill of Rights* in part 2 are arranged in alphabetical order, and the policies and guidelines in part 3 are organized by broad topic area.

New to this edition of the manual are "Privacy," an Interpretation of the *Library Bill of Rights* (part 2); "Confidentiality and Coping with Law Enforcement Inquiries" and "Guidelines for Developing a Library Privacy Policy" (part 3); "Minors' First Amendment Rights to Access Information," "Public Libraries and the Public Forum Doctrine," and "Privacy and Confidentiality in Libraries" (part 4), as well as historical information about the Code of Ethics (part 3). A new appendix, "Navigating the OIF Website," and a glossary have also been added. To accommodate this new material, several articles from the previous edition, as well as some original new material prepared in conjunction with this seventh edition, can now be found on the ALA website, http://www.ala.org/ala/oiof/iftoolkits/ifmanual/intellectual.htm. It is suggested that you check the website regularly to find the latest news on these evolving issues, as well as to monitor changes in ALA policies.

Applying the principles and guidelines in this manual cannot ensure that the rights of librarians and users will never be challenged or that difficulties will not arise. But adhering to these principles in every library is absolutely essential if librarians and users are to enjoy the full benefit of freedom of expression under the First Amendment.

JUDITH F. KRUG, Director
Office for Intellectual Freedom

ACKNOWLEDGMENTS

Special thanks and appreciation to Candace D. Morgan, who served as project director for this seventh edition. Besides updating, editing, writing, and rewriting portions of the manual, Candace revised the overall arrangement of this edition to provide better access to both the existing and the new information it provides. Beverley Becker and Don Wood, staff members of the Office for Intellectual Freedom, contributed articles and provided invaluable assistance and support throughout the revision process. Their work since the sixth edition was published brought this seventh edition into existence.

INTRODUCTION

Censorship reflects a society's lack of confidence in itself. It is a hallmark of an authoritarian regime.

Justice Potter Stewart, dissenting
Ginzberg v. United States

Intellectual freedom can exist only where two essential conditions are met: first, that all individuals have the right to hold any belief on any subject and to convey their ideas in any form they deem appropriate, and second, that society makes an equal commitment to the right of unrestricted access to information and ideas regardless of the communication medium used, the content of the work, and the viewpoints of both the author and the receiver of information. Freedom to express oneself through a chosen mode of communication, including the Internet, becomes virtually meaningless if access to that information is not protected. Intellectual freedom implies a circle, and that circle is broken if either freedom of expression or access to ideas is stifled.

Intellectual freedom is freedom of the mind, and as such, it is both a personal liberty and a prerequisite for all freedoms leading to action. Moreover, intellectual freedom, protected by the guarantees of freedoms of speech and press in the First Amendment, forms the bulwark of our constitutional republic. It is an essential part of government by the people. The right to vote is alone not sufficient to give citizens effective control of official actions and policies. Citizens also must be able to take part in the formation of public opinion by engaging in vigorous and wide-ranging debate on controversial matters. Censorship can only stifle this debate, thus weakening government by the people. In the words of Thomas Paine:

> He that would make his own liberty secure must guard even his enemy from opposition; for if he violates this duty he establishes a precedent that will reach to himself.[1]

Intellectual freedom is not only the bulwark of our constitutional republic but also the rallying cry of those who struggle for democracy worldwide. The metaphorical circle of intellectual freedom has expanded to global proportions over the past two decades with the advent of potent new communications technologies and the growing international recognition of the Universal Declaration of Human Rights, Article 19 of which declares the right of all people to freedom of expression. As the free flow of information transcends national boundaries, it becomes increasingly clear that prohibitions on freedom of expression in one country will inhibit the freedom of those in many other countries around the world. In an age of multinational media corporations, international computer links, global telecommunications, and the World Wide Web, we can no longer think simply in local terms. Promoting and defending intellectual freedom requires "thinking globally and acting locally."

The American Library Association (ALA) has recognized the importance of global thinking in an Interpretation of the *Library Bill of Rights* titled "The Universal Right to Free Expression." Recognizing the crucial role that free access to information plays in the international arena and the international effects of restrictions imposed on the creation, distribution, and receipt of information and expression, this Interpretation acknowledges free expression as a basic human right. ALA also has recognized for many years the right of individuals to be free from governmental intimidation in the exercise of their right to free expression. The Policy on Government Intimidation was adopted February 2, 1973, and last amended June 30, 2004.

A multitude of new challenges to intellectual freedom have arisen over the past two decades. Significant changes in political, social, and economic conditions both before and after the terrorist attacks on September 11, 2001, have had a powerful effect on librarians' ability to defend intellectual freedom.

Librarians recognize that the threats we face from terrorism today are significant. We were shocked and saddened by the events of September 11 and are concerned about the possibility of future terrorist attacks. However, we are also deeply concerned that provisions of the USA PATRIOT Act, as well as related legislation and law enforcement practices, are significantly eroding the right to receive information free from fear of intrusion, intimidation, or reprisal. The most recently adopted Interpretation of the *Library Bill of Rights*,

"Privacy," explains how the long-standing principles of intellectual freedom apply to issues related to privacy and confidentiality in the library. The Intellectual Freedom Committee has also developed a Privacy Tool Kit, including questions and answers to assist librarians with these issues.

Now more than ever, librarians need to be mindful of the special role libraries play as centers for uninhibited intellectual inquiry. Librarians have taken upon themselves the responsibility to provide, through their institutions, all points of view on all questions and issues of our times, and to make these ideas and opinions available to anyone who needs or wants them, regardless of age, background, or views. These statements should sound familiar; they are basic principles outlined in the *Library Bill of Rights*, which serves as the library profession's interpretation of the First Amendment to the U.S. Constitution.

The freedom of expression guaranteed by the First Amendment and Article 19, and the corollary to that freedom, the freedom to read, are uniquely fulfilled by the library. Any person, regardless of station, can have access to materials and information. Although libraries are widely recognized as the repositories of civilization, in order to guarantee that the freedom to read has substance, libraries also must acquire and provide information without prejudice or restriction. It is this latter point that gives the *Library Bill of Rights* and its guidance for professional librarianship special importance.

Intellectual freedom cannot bring itself into existence. Librarians must apply the principles of intellectual freedom to activities undertaken daily—materials selection, reference service, reevaluation, protection of confidential patron information, and most important, collection building. It is in acquisition and its product, the collection, that intellectual freedom must be reflected.

The role of the library as governed by the *Library Bill of Rights* cannot be filled by any other societal institution. Newspapers provide information, but it is perforce abridged and can reflect the prejudices of an editor or publisher. Schools educate but according to a program designed to fit the many; one attends school under conditions devised and imposed by administrators and educators. It is in the library, and in the library alone, that self-directed learning, to the limits of one's abilities and to the limits of what is known, can take place.

No one—least of all the librarian—should underestimate the importance of this role. If its significance has been overlooked by many, including librarians, perhaps it is because some librarians have been neither vigorous in the application of these principles nor imaginative in the provision of library services. With the application of the principles of intellectual freedom, with vision and imagination, librarians can—and do—measure up to their unique task.

NOTE

1. Thomas Paine, *Dissertation on First Principles of Government*.

CONTRIBUTORS

Beverley Becker is associate director of the ALA Office for Intellectual Freedom.

Deborah Caldwell-Stone is deputy director of the ALA Office for Intellectual Freedom. She is also an attorney and an instructor for the Office for Intellectual Freedom's Lawyers for Libraries Training Institute. Prior to joining ALA, she was an appellate litigator practicing before state and federal courts in Illinois.

Theresa Chmara is a partner in the Washington, D.C., office of Jenner & Block. She has served as counsel to the Freedom to Read Foundation for fifteen years. She is on the steering committee of the Lawyers for Libraries program and was an instructor at Lawyers for Libraries I and II, as well as six regional training programs held in Washington, D.C., Chicago, San Francisco, Dallas, Boston, and Atlanta. She frequently speaks to library groups around the country and currently serves on the board of the American Booksellers Foundation for Free Expression.

Larra Clark is the ALA manager of media relations. She joined ALA in 2000 after working almost ten years in nonprofit public affairs, media relations, and print journalism in Chicago and Arizona. She also is currently pursuing her master's degree in library science through the distance education program at the University of Illinois Urbana–Champaign.

Judith F. Krug is the director of the ALA Office for Intellectual Freedom and is executive director of the Freedom to Read Foundation, the First Amendment legal defense organization for libraries and librarians.

Daniel Mach is a partner in Jenner & Block's Washington, D.C., office. He is a member of the firm's Appellate and Supreme Court and Media and First Amendment Practices. He has represented and counseled, among others, the American Library Association, the Freedom to Read Foundation, the American Booksellers Association Foundation for Free Expression, and the Liberty Project on a variety of First Amendment and other constitutional issues.

Candace D. Morgan recently retired after forty years as a librarian in public, state, special, and academic libraries. She is currently a trainer, consultant, and adjunct faculty member for the Emporia State University School of Library and Information Management and the Portland State University Hatfield School of Government.

Evelyn Shaevel, currently assistant to the executive director of the Medical Library Association, has served as executive director of ALA's Young Adult Services Division, as director of marketing for ALA Publishing, and has worked in both a school library and a public library.

Linda K. Wallace, principal with Library Communications Strategies, based in Chicago, is a former journalist and director of the American Library Association's Public Information Office.

Don Wood is the program officer/communications for the ALA Office for Intellectual Freedom.

PART I

Intellectual Freedom and Libraries
An Overview

1
Intellectual Freedom
An Enduring and All-Embracing Concept

CANDACE D. MORGAN

Libraries are directly and immediately involved in the
conflict which divides the world, and for two reasons;
first, because they are essential to the functioning of a
democratic society; second, because the contemporary
conflict touches the integrity of scholarship, the freedom
of the mind, and even the survival of culture, and librar-
ies are the great symbols of the freedom of the mind.
Franklin D. Roosevelt
ALA Bulletin 36 (January 1942): 2

The First and Fourth Amendments to the U.S. Constitution are integral to American librarianship. They are the basis of the concept librarians call intellectual freedom. Intellectual freedom accords to all library users the right to seek and receive information on all subjects from all points of view without restriction and without having the subject of one's interest examined or scrutinized by others.

The role of libraries in America today is shaped by our constitutional legacy. The importance of intellectual freedom as a part of that legacy can be traced to the circumstances surrounding the founding of our country. Most, if not all, other nations in the world were founded based on a defined territory, a religious authority, a common culture or ethnicity. Unlike these nations the United States was invented from an idea—and that idea was liberty.

A desire for liberty motivated individuals to take great risks to colonize the New World. The meanings of "liberty" to the colonists were myriad, including

freedom to worship as one wishes;

freedom to express ideas without government sanction;

freedom to make individual choices about how to live one's life;

freedom from intrusions into one's private life by the government or other people;

opportunity to improve one's quality of life without regard to one's religion, politics, economic status, or other arbitrary distinctions; and

living in a participatory democracy based on majority, rather than authoritarian, rule.

The definition of "liberty" has never been free of controversy. As Eric Foner has described it,

> American freedom was born in revolution. During the struggle for independence inherited ideas of liberty were transformed, new ones emerged, and the definition of those entitled to enjoy what the Constitution called "the blessings of liberty" was challenged and extended. The Revolution bequeathed to future generations an enduring yet contradictory legacy.[1]

After the Revolutionary War was won, the Articles of Confederation were adopted as the instrument of government. The drafters of the Articles were so intent upon avoiding the tyranny of a strong centralized government and protecting the rights of the states that they designed a government that was inefficient, ineffective, and incapable of exercising the vision and creativity essential for the survival and growth of the new nation. For example, the government under the Articles was unable to collect taxes to support troops, to defend against foreign attacks, or to resolve interstate conflicts, many of which disrupted commerce between the states. And so the founders went back to the drawing board to draft a constitution.

Librarians often assume that the constitutional legacy for our profession and for the institution of the public library is solely the Bill of Rights. In fact, the founders did not leave the protection of liberty to the Bill of Rights. The body of the Constitution was also designed with liberty in mind.

The precipitating factors for the War of Independence included inadequate representation of the colonies in the British Parliament, the imposition of a number of new taxes, and trade regulations that favored British interests over American. These actions were regarded by the colonists as unauthorized seizure of authority by the king and British government. Majority rule, therefore, is an important part of our constitutional legacy. The body of the Constitution includes provisions to preserve majority rule and to guard against usurpation of that rule. Among those provisions are separation of powers, checks and balances, federalism, representative government, and popular elections.

The main body of the Constitution also contains some guarantees of individual liberties, including the prohibition of religious tests for office holding (Article VI), the guarantee that each citizen has the privileges and immunities of the citizens of the several states (Article IV, Section 2), and the guarantee of a republican form of government in each state (Article IV, Section 4). Separation of powers and checks and balances reduce the possibility of the abuse of liberty by requiring the action of both executive and legislative branches and allowing for review by the judicial branch. In addition, these constitutional provisions usually work to slow down government action, making it easier for those adversely affected to bring attention to possible injustices.

However, the delegates to the various state conventions that were convened to ratify the Constitution expressed the opinion that these protections were not enough. As a result, the framers promised that once the Constitution was adopted, a prime order of business for the First Congress would be consideration of amendments to the Constitution to protect individual liberties. The product of this was the Bill of Rights.

The Bill of Rights is by far the most effective protection of individual rights against abuse by either government excesses or the influence of a tyrannous majority. James Madison and Thomas Jefferson were both concerned about the threat to individual liberties by abuse of power. In a letter to Jefferson on October 17, 1788, Madison expressed the following opinion:

> In our Governments the real power lies in the majority of
> the Community, and the invasion of private rights is

> *chiefly* to be apprehended, not from acts of Government
> contrary to the sense of its constituents, but from acts in
> which the Government is the mere instrument of the
> major number of the constituents. This is a truth of great
> importance.[2]

Jefferson was concerned about legislative abuse. Responding to Madison in a letter on March 15, 1789, he stated, "The tyranny of the legislatures is the most formidable dread at present, and will be for long years."[3]

Madison's concerns led him to be one of the principal authors of the Bill of Rights, the first ten amendments to the U.S. Constitution. Jefferson was in Paris during the drafting and adoption of the Bill of Rights. His letters on the topic, however, are considered to have been a major influence in their development.

In summary, freedom is the value most cherished by Americans. Constitutional provisions to protect freedom from the threats of usurpation, incompetence, and tyranny of the majority have created a constitutional legacy for libraries. The importance of the Bill of Rights for that legacy is clearly expressed by Madison in his letter to Jefferson on October 17, 1788:

> What use then it may be asked can a bill of rights serve
> in popular Governments? I answer the two following
> which though less essential than in other Governments,
> sufficiently recommend the precaution. 1. The political
> truths declared in that solemn manner acquire by
> degrees the character of fundamental maxims of free
> government, and as they become incorporated with the
> national sentiment, counteract the impulses of interest
> and passion. 2. Altho' it be generally true as above stated
> that the danger of oppression lies in the interested
> majorities of the people rather than in usurped acts of the
> Government, yet there may be occasions on which the
> evil may spring from the latter sources; and on such, a
> bill of rights will be a good ground for an appeal to the
> sense of the community.[4]

A description of our constitutional legacy cannot be complete without a discussion of expectations for the role of citizens of this new regime. Both Thomas Jefferson and James Madison felt strongly that an informed and educated citizenry is the best defense again a despotic or tyrannous government. They believed that free-dom of inquiry and speech are essential to the search for truth. For truth to emerge, erroneous ideas must also be available for the peo-ple to examine and discuss. The marketplace of ideas must be free and unfettered and, most of all, not restricted by government action.[5] The founders also believed that an educated citizenry is essential to the preservation of freedom and democracy. These prin-ciples, a fundamental part of our historical legacy, are best captured in the following two quotations by Jefferson and Madison:

> If a nation expects to be ignorant and free, in a state of civilization, it expects what never was and never will be. The functionaries of every government have propensities to command at will the liberty and property of their con-stituents. There is no safe deposit for these but with the people themselves; nor can they be safe with them with-out information. Where the press is free, and every man is able to read, all is safe. (Thomas Jefferson in a letter to Colonel Yancy, January 16, 1816)[6]

> A popular government, without popular information or the means of acquiring it, is but a Prologue to a Farce or a Tragedy or perhaps both. Knowledge will forever gov-ern ignorance; and a people who mean to be their own Governors, must arm themselves with the power knowl-edge gives. (James Madison in a letter to William T. Barry, August 4, 1822)[7]

In summary, the Bill of Rights serves both to protect individual liberties (private purpose), which includes the pursuit of happiness, and to support an informed, educated citizenry with access to the open dialogue necessary for democracy (public purpose).

What does this constitutional legacy have to do with libraries? The public library is the only government agency with a core mis-sion that encompasses both the private and the public purposes of the Bill of Rights. This constitutional legacy means that libraries must balance the requirements of majority rule and citizen partici-pation with the mandate to protect minority rights.

Other types of publicly funded libraries, including public school, college, and university libraries; state libraries; and special libraries in governmental agencies, also are covered by the First Amendment. However, the framework of intellectual freedom within which they operate varies because their missions are more limited in scope than the missions of public libraries.

The First Amendment does not directly apply to privately funded libraries. However, because our constitutional legacy is based on the historical circumstances of this country's founding, the principles of intellectual freedom create an ethical framework for libraries that are not subject to the constitutional mandate. Librarians in privately funded libraries should use this framework to advocate for providing access to as broad a range of information as is possible within their library's mission.

Below is a summary of the framework of intellectual freedom by type of library, based on articles available on the American Library Association website (www.ala.org/ala/oif/iftoolkits/ifmanual/intellectual.htm).

Public Libraries

The public library exists primarily to provide access to information on all subjects, from all points of view, to all people who live in the geographic area served by the library, regardless of race, nationality, ethnic origin, religion, income, age, or any other arbitrary classification. The individual library user exercises free choice about whether she seeks information or library materials for educational, recreational, informational, cultural, political, job-related, or other reasons. Public libraries are committed to protecting the privacy of library users and keeping each individual's use of the library confidential.

The public library also serves a public purpose as the source for the information and knowledge necessary for a viable democracy. The highest duty of library boards or governing bodies, librarians, and library staff is to protect and nurture the constitutional system and the values established by our constitutional legacy. For additional information, see Gordon M. Conable, "Public Libraries and Intellectual Freedom," http://www.ala.org/ala/oif/iftoolkits/ifmanual/publiclibraries.htm.

School Library Media Centers

As the first library that many children and young adults are introduced to and use on a continuing basis, school library media programs play a vital role in promoting intellectual freedom.

School library collections support the curriculum as well as the intellectual growth, personal development, individual interests, and recreational needs of students. The Supreme Court has ruled that books cannot be removed based on the ideas the books express but has permitted removal of books if officials were motivated by concerns that the books were "educationally unsuitable" or "pervasively vulgar" (see "Minors' First Amendment Rights to Access Information," part 4, section 2).

Private school libraries are not subject to the First Amendment. However, school library media specialists should be advocates for the educational importance of providing students with the opportunity to learn about opposing viewpoints in order to prepare them to support their own beliefs. Robert Harris's "Why Christians Should Examine All the Wares in the Marketplace of Ideas," http://www.virtualsalt.com/wares.htm, discusses the importance of this approach. Harris's viewpoint can be applied to a school based on any religious or private mission. For additional information, see Dianne McAfee Hopkins, "School Library Media Centers and Intellectual Freedom," http://www.ala.org/ala/oif/iftoolkits/ifmanual/schoollibrary.htm, and Doug Johnson, "Lessons School Librarians Teach Others," *American Libraries* 35, no. 11 (December 2004): 46–48, http://www.ala.org/ala/oif/iftoolkits/ifmanual/lessonsschoollibrariansteachothers.pdf.

Academic Libraries

The mission of a college or university library is based upon the particular institution's mission and purpose. The First Amendment applies only to publicly supported colleges and universities. The principles of academic freedom and freedom of inquiry, however, apply to all institutions of higher learning and their libraries. As stated in the Principles on Academic Freedom and Tenure of the American Association of University Professors:

> Institutions of higher education are conducted for the common good. . . . The common good depends upon the free search for truth and its free exposition. Academic freedom is essential to these purposes and applies to both teaching and research. Freedom in research is fundamental to the advancement of truth.[8]

Legal scholar Rodney Smolla applies this framework to the mission of the academic library:

> It is worth saying a word about private acts of censorship aimed at private-sector libraries, such as libraries at private universities. The decision by a private university to engage in censorship is not, of course, subject to the restraints of the First Amendment at all, because the Constitution places restrictions only on government. Borrowing on notions of academic, artistic, and scientific freedom, surely the nation's great private institutions of learning and culture ought to operate as if the First Amendment applied to them. The fabric of society's intellectual and cultural life is a tightly knit weave of private and public institutions. An open society committed to free expression as a transcendent value will be committed to principles of artistic and scholarly freedom in private universities, museums, theaters, and libraries as well as public institutions, encouraging the free flow of information among all of them. The life of the mind should not be cramped by the artificial distinctions of law.[9]

In the twenty-first-century academic library, the concept of intellectual freedom has broadened to include such library issues as fee-based services, donor restrictions on manuscript collections, reference interviews, and purchasing politically incorrect materials, not to mention the Internet's impact. The Internet, now a major vehicle for scholarly communication, has raised important First Amendment issues on college campuses—including the problem of explicit content offensive to some and campus network-use policies that sometimes conflict with the *Library Bill of Rights*. For additional information, see Barbara M. Jones, "Academic Libraries and Intellectual Freedom," http://www.ala.org/ala/oif/iftoolkits/ifmanual/academiclibraries.htm.

Federal Libraries

The federal library community is composed of a variety of libraries comparable in type to those in the library community as a whole.

Federal libraries range from the one-of-a-kind Library of Congress to small school libraries on Native American reservations and to specialized libraries serving executive agencies.

Federal libraries have censorship problems just like other libraries, but these are seldom brought to the attention of the library profession or the public. Many federal librarians feel that there is no problem with censorship in government libraries. Others do not agree. Most of them do agree that positive steps should be taken to help prevent possible censorship.

Even though federal libraries differ in many respects, they do have some things in common: (1) they must function according to a number of federal laws and regulations; (2) their mission is usually dictated by the agency to which they belong; and (3) given that they are supported by federal taxes, they are answerable, directly or indirectly, to all U.S. citizens. Since many federal libraries are contracted out to private vendors, it is important that the federal officials legally responsible for seeing that the libraries function as federal entities be involved in developing the libraries' policies. Because federal libraries are important information links in the decision-making process of the U.S. government, and because citizen access to information about that process is crucial to the preservation of a free society, federal libraries must be protected from censorship. For additional information, see Bernadine Abbott Hoduski, "Federal Libraries and Intellectual Freedom," http://www.ala.org/ala/oif/iftoolkits/ifmanual/federallibraries.htm.

State Library Agencies

State library agencies, as institutions, vary from state to state. Most state library agencies have responsibility for promoting library development and coordinating interlibrary cooperation. In some states, the agency is responsible for maintaining a collection, either to serve state government or to serve the residents of the state. Whatever the state library structure may be, the state library agency usually assumes the responsibility of fostering the free exchange of information and ideas.

State libraries help local libraries prepare to handle challenges. In addition, many state libraries maintain relationships with active and supportive intellectual freedom committees of their state's library association. Such committees can provide assistance and links to a statewide network of supporters of intellectual freedom who are willing to come forward in a crisis.

The state library agency plays a pivotal role in the development of library services and in influencing state law and policy to ensure that citizens have the best possible access to information. This access will, in turn, help preserve our democratic society as we now know it and will allow citizens to participate fully in the society. For additional information, see Diana Young, "State Library Agencies and Intellectual Freedom," http://www.ala.org/ala/oif/iftoolkits/ifmanual/statelibrary.htm.

Privately Funded Special Libraries

The mission or purpose of a special library is to support the research and requests of its specific clientele. Examples of special libraries include corporate libraries, medical libraries, museum libraries, and law libraries. The resources in a special library are unique to the focus of the population it serves and are usually inaccessible to the general public.

Privately funded special libraries are not subject to the First Amendment. However, creativity and intellectual inquiry are critical to the survival and progress of corporations, small businesses, and other private institutions. Librarians in these institutions are in a position to advocate that policies supporting intellectual freedom are in the best interests of the organization within the framework of its institutional mission.

NOTES

1. Eric Foner, The Story of American Freedom (New York: W. W. Norton, 1998), 3.
2. James Madison, *Writings* (New York: Literary Classics of the United States, 1999), 421.
3. Thomas Jefferson, *Writings* (New York: Literary Classics of the United States, 1984), 944.
4. Madison, *Writings*, 421–22.

5. William Lee Miller, *The Business of May Next: James Madison and the Founding* (Charlottesville: University Press of Virginia, 1992), 270–73.

6. Martin A. Larson, *Jefferson: Magnificent Populist* (Greenwich, CT: Devin-Adair, 1984), 251.

7. Madison, *Writings*, 790.

8. American Association of University Professors, "1940 Statement on Academic Freedom Tenure with 1970 Interpretive Comments," http://www.aaup.org/statements/Redbook/1940stat.htm.

9. Rodney A. Smolla, "Freedom of Speech for Libraries and Librarians," *Law Library Journal* 85 (1993): 78.

2

ALA and Intellectual Freedom
A Historical Overview

JUDITH F. KRUG

A t the outset, two myths can be dispelled; namely, that intellectual freedom in libraries is a tradition and that intellectual freedom has always been a major, if not the major, part of the foundation of library service in the United States. Both myths, assumed by many librarians, are grounded in the belief that librarians support a static concept of intellectual freedom. Nothing, however, could be further from the truth.

The attitude of librarians toward intellectual freedom has undergone continual change since the late-nineteenth century when, through the American Library Association (ALA), the profession first began to approach such issues with the semblance of a unified voice. ALA, however, has never endorsed a uniform definition of *intellectual freedom*. Instead, through the Council (the ALA's governing body), the Intellectual Freedom Committee (IFC), and the Office for Intellectual Freedom (OIF), ALA has promoted a variety of principles aimed at fostering a favorable climate for intellectual freedom, but without the limits imposed by a rigid definition. This approach has permitted a broad definition capable of meeting librarians' needs as they arise.

The seeds of the general definition of intellectual freedom were sown in the movement against censorship of published materials and grew into a strong, central trunk from which many branches of ALA and intellectual freedom have continued to spring. One branch concerns the library user's access to all of the materials in a library collection. Another pertains to the librarian's professional practice, particularly selecting and making available all published materials to all library users and protecting the confidentiality of patron records to ensure that every individual may use the library freely and without fear of reprisal. At stake also is the librarian's personal intellectual freedom: participation in the democratic process, the right to free expression, and the right to pursue a chosen lifestyle without fear of negative professional repercussions. Yet another aspect of intellectual freedom encompasses the library as an institution and its role in social change and education. Of particular importance is the question of advocacy versus neutrality. Can a library committed to intellectual freedom and to providing materials that represent all points of view also support one point of view?

Each of these branches in turn has sprouted a plethora of twigs and, viewed in its entirety, the tree makes anything other than an issue-oriented approach nearly impossible. Consequently, the profession's stance on intellectual freedom has sometimes lagged behind that of society at large; most often it has paralleled public opinion; and, occasionally, it has anticipated changes in taste, mores, and social issues, and has taken positions in advance of the rest of the citizenry.

Censorship of Published Materials

The catalyst spurring librarians to take the initial steps toward supporting intellectual freedom was the censorship of specific publications. "Censorship" in this context means not only deletion or excision of parts of published materials but also efforts to ban, prohibit, suppress, proscribe, remove, label, or restrict materials. Opposition to these activities emanated from the belief that freedom of the mind is basic to the functioning and maintenance of democracy as practiced in the United States. Such democracy assumes that educated, free individuals possess powers of discrimination and are to be trusted to determine their own actions. It assumes further that the best guarantee of effective and continuing self-government is a thoroughly informed electorate capable of making real choices. Denying the opportunity of choice, for fear it may be used unwisely, destroys freedom itself. Opposition to censorship derives naturally from the library's historical role as an educational institution providing materials that develop individuals' abilities, interests, and knowledge. Censorship denies the opportunity to choose from all possible alternatives and thereby violates intellectual freedom. The library profession has aimed to ensure every individual's freedom of the mind so that society as a whole benefits. Even in this central area, however, the professional position has fluctuated, being influenced by such factors as taste, quality, responsibility, morality, legality, and purpose.

One early incident concerning censorship, involving a substantial number of librarians, occurred in 1924 when the Librarians' Union of the American Federation of Labor reported that the Carnegie Libraries fostered "a system under which only books approved in a certain manner may be placed on Carnegie Library shelves and that amounts to censorship and is so intended."[1] The ALA Executive Board considered the union's charges and offered to enlist volunteers to investigate the claims. Apparently, however, the union did not act upon the offer, and the matter was not considered further by the Executive Board.

In 1929, the Association indicated its future approach to censorship when the ALA Executive Board studied a proposed federal tariff bill and opposed prohibiting the import of materials "advocating or urging treason, insurrection, or forcible resistance to any law of the U.S. . . . or any obscene book, paper, etc."

The Board's opposition was based

> on the grounds that this clause creates an effective censorship over foreign literature, will ban many of the classics on modern economics, will keep out material relating to revolution in foreign countries, will indirectly stop the reprinting of such books by our own publishers, and is a reflection upon the intelligence of the American people by implying that they are so stupid and untrustworthy that they cannot read about revolutions without immediately becoming traitors and revolutionaries themselves; and because the question of social policy is withdrawn from the ordinary courts and placed in the hands of officials primarily chosen for their special qualifications in dealing with the administrative details of tariff laws.[2]

Ironically, just four years later, when the Executive Board received a letter requesting that the Association "take some action in regard to the burning of books in Germany by the Hitler regime, the matter was "considered briefly but it was the sense of the meeting that no action should be taken."[3]

In 1934, the Association recorded its first protest against the banning of a specific publication, "*You and Machines*," a pamphlet by William Ogburn. Prepared for use in Civilian Conservation Corps camps under a grant from the American Council on Education, the pamphlet was denied circulation by the camps' director, who believed it would induce a philosophy of despair and a desire to destroy existing economic and political structures. Initially, the ALA president and executive secretary wrote a joint letter to President Franklin D. Roosevelt stating that "[governmental] censorship on a publication of this character written by a man of recognized authority is unthinkable."[4] Later the Board discussed the banning further and appointed a committee to draft another letter for approval by the ALA Council. The result was a formal request that President Roosevelt "make it possible for the U.S. Commissioner of Education and the Education Director of the Civilian Conservation Corps to direct the educational policies to be operative in these camps and to make available the reading matter essential in a modern program of education."[5]

These examples illustrate the Association's wavering position and reflect the ambivalent attitude of the profession as a whole regarding censorship. A review of library literature reveals relatively few articles on intellectual freedom prior to the 1930s, and many of the articles that did appear supported censorship and only quibbled over the degree and nature of it. Typical was the opinion of ALA president Arthur E. Bostwick, whose inaugural address at the 1908 Annual Conference included these remarks:

> "Some are born great; some achieve greatness; some have greatness thrust upon them." It is in this way that the librarian has become a censor of literature. . . . Books that distinctly commend what is wrong, that teach how to sin and how pleasant sin is, sometimes with and sometimes without the added sauce of impropriety, are increasingly popular, tempting the author to imitate them, the

> publishers to produce, the bookseller to exploit. Thank
> Heaven they do not tempt the librarian.[6]

Given the multiplicity of professional attitudes toward censorship of print materials, it is not surprising that censorship of nonprint media was once viewed as completely outside the concerns of
the profession. For example, as late as 1938, the ALA Executive
Board believed it was inappropriate to protest when the Federal
Communications Commission forced a radio station to defend its
broadcast of Eugene O'Neill's *Beyond the Horizon*.[7]

The Association's basic position in opposition to censorship
finally emerged in the late 1930s, when John Steinbeck's *The Grapes
of Wrath* became the target of censorship pressures around the country. It was banned from libraries in East St. Louis, Illinois; Camden,
New Jersey; Bakersfield, California; and other localities. Whereas
some objected to the immorality of the work, most opposed the
social views advanced by the author.

ALA's initial response to the pressures against *The Grapes of
Wrath* was the adoption in 1939 of the *Library's Bill of Rights*, the pre-
cursor of the present *Library Bill of Rights*, the profession's basic policy statement on intellectual freedom involving library materials
(see *Library Bill of Rights*, part 2, section 1).

In 1940, one year after adoption of the *Library's Bill of Rights*, the
Association established the Intellectual Freedom Committee, or
IFC. (Originally called the Committee on Intellectual Freedom to
Safeguard the Rights of Library Users to Freedom of Inquiry, the
Committee's name was shortened by Council action in 1948 to
Committee on Intellectual Freedom and inverted through usage to
Intellectual Freedom Committee.) The 1940 charge to the IFC was
"to recommend such steps as may be necessary to safeguard the
rights of library users in accordance with the Bill of Rights and the
Library's Bill of Rights, as adopted by Council."[8] Although the IFC's
role has varied, its main function has been to recommend policies
concerning intellectual freedom, especially—but not limited to—
matters involving violations of the *Library Bill of Rights*. Although its
original statement of authority referred only to library users, in reality the IFC became active in promoting intellectual freedom for
librarians and patrons as well. Its diversified role was recognized
and formalized in 1970, when the Council approved a revised statement of authority:

To recommend such steps as may be necessary to safeguard the rights of library users, libraries, and librarians,
in accordance with the First Amendment to the United
States Constitution and the *Library Bill of Rights* as
adopted by the ALA Council. To work closely with the
Office for Intellectual Freedom and with other units and
officers of the Association in matters touching intellectual freedom and censorship.[9]

The original *Library's Bill of Rights* focused on unbiased book
selection, a balanced collection, and open meeting rooms. It did not
mention censorship or removal of materials at the behest of groups
or individuals. Over the years, however, the document has been
revised, amended, and interpreted, often in response to specific situations with general implications. The first change, a 1944 amendment against banning materials considered "factually correct," was
occasioned by attacks on *Under Cover*, an exposé of Nazi organizations in the United States, and *Strange Fruit*, a novel about interra-
cial love. The reference to "factually correct" was later dropped, but
the directive against removal of materials remained. Opposition to
censorship of nonprint media was amended to the document in
1951 because of attacks on films alleged to promote communism. To
combat the suppression of communist materials or other allegedly
subversive publications, the Association issued its Statement on
Labeling (renamed "Labels and Rating Systems" in 2005; see part 2,
section 2.13), which stated that designating materials subversive is
subtle censorship, because such a label predisposes readers against
the materials. Responding to pressures against materials about civil
rights activities, a 1967 amendment to the *Library Bill of Rights*
warned against excluding materials because of the social views of
the authors. In its 1971 Resolution on Challenged Materials, the
Association counseled libraries not to remove challenged materials
unless, after an adversary hearing in a court of law, the materials
were judged to be outside the protection of the First Amendment
(see "Challenged Materials," part 2, section 2.5).

Changing circumstances necessitate constant review of the
Library Bill of Rights and often result in position statements to clarify the document's application (see "*Library Bill of Rights: Interpretations*," part 2, section 2). The present *Library Bill of Rights* was
last revised in 1980. Its interpretive documents were systematically

reviewed and updated in 1980, 1981, 1982, 1989, 1991, 1994, 1999–2000, and most recently in 2004–5. The newest Interpretation is "Privacy," adopted by the ALA Council in June 2002.

Taken together, these documents recognize and explain that censorship of any materials, in any guise, eventually affects the library. The *Library Bill of Rights*, therefore, provides principles upon which libraries may stand to oppose censorship and promote intellectual freedom. Referring directly to censorship practices, the *Library Bill of Rights* states that no library materials should be "excluded because of the origin, background, or views of those contributing to their creation" and that materials should not be "proscribed or removed because of partisan or doctrinal disapproval."

On its face, the profession's view of intellectual freedom is a pure one, based on a strict reading of the First Amendment to the U.S. Constitution, which states, "Congress shall make no law . . . abridging freedom of speech, or of the press." Within the limits defined by the U.S. Supreme Court (for example, the legal doctrines governing obscenity, child pornography, harmful to minors, defamation, and fighting words), the position relies on the extension of First Amendment principles via the Fourteenth Amendment to the states and their agencies, including publicly supported libraries. (Some state constitutions actually provide greater protection for free speech than does the First Amendment as interpreted by the U.S. Supreme Court, but no state is permitted to provide less protection for these fundamental rights.) In actual practice, the purist position sometimes gives way to compromises by individual librarians, resulting in the removal, labeling, or covert nonselection of certain materials.

If followed by librarians and governing bodies, however, the Association's policy statements provide an effective means of helping to prevent library censorship. Ideally, application of these policies to materials selection, circulation practices, and complaint handling establishes the library as an indispensable information source for individuals exercising their freedom of inquiry.

Free Access to Library Materials

Access to library collections and services is another concern of the profession. For intellectual freedom to flourish, opposition to censorship of materials is not enough. Free access to materials for every member of the community must also be ensured. ALA first recognized this in the 1939 *Library's Bill of Rights*, which included a proviso that library meeting rooms be available on equal terms to all groups in the community regardless of the beliefs and affiliations of their members.

Another policy on free access emerged from a study of segregation made by the Association's Special Committee on Civil Liberties during the late 1950s. One result of the study was a 1961 amendment to the *Library Bill of Rights* stating that "the rights of an individual to the use of a library should not be denied or abridged because of his race, religion, national origins, or political views." This amendment was broadened in 1967, when "social views" and "age" were incorporated to emphasize other areas of potential discrimination. "Age" was included to resolve a long-standing debate on the right of minors to have access to libraries on the same basis as adults. It should be noted that the addition of "age" illustrates one instance in which the library profession acted well in advance of public opinion.

In 1971, at the urging of the Task Force on Gay Liberation of the Social Responsibilities Round Table, the Association recommended that libraries and ALA members strenuously combat discrimination in serving any individual from a minority, whether it be an ethnic, sexual, religious, or any other arbitrary classification. In 1980, the *Library Bill of Rights* was revised to encompass all discrimination based on "origin, age, background, or views." Interpretations of the *Library Bill of Rights* addressing specific issues that fall under these deliberately broad categories include "Access for Children and Young People to Videotapes and Other Nonprint Formats" (renamed "Access for Children and Young Adults to Nonprint Materials" in June 2004), "Access to Resources and Services in the School Library Media Program," "Free Access to Libraries for Minors," "Economic Barriers to Information Access," and "Access to Library Resources and Services regardless of Gender or Sexual Orientation." All of these Interpretations are presented and discussed in part 2.

Privacy and Confidentiality

Another aspect of the library patron's access to materials was broached in 1970, when the Internal Revenue Service requested permission from several libraries to examine circulation records to determine the names of persons reading materials about explosives and guerrilla warfare. The Association responded by developing its Policy on Confidentiality of Library Records, urging libraries to designate such records as confidential and accessible only "pursuant to such process, order, or subpoena as may be authorized under the authority of, and pursuant to, federal, state, or local law relating to civil, criminal, or administrative discovery procedures or legislative investigatory power" (see part 3, section 5.1). The rationale of the policy was that circulation records are purely circumstantial evidence that a patron has read a book and that fear of persecution or prosecution may restrain users from borrowing any conceivably controversial materials, for whatever purpose.

The question of library records and the confidentiality of relationships between librarians and library users arose again in 1971 regarding the "use of grand jury procedure to intimidate anti–Vietnam War activists and people seeking justice for minority communities." In response, the Association asserted "the confidentiality of the professional relationships of librarians to the people they serve, that these relationships be respected in the same manner as medical doctors to their patients, lawyers to their clients, priests to the people they serve," and that "no librarian would lend himself to a role as informant, whether of voluntarily revealing circulation records or identifying patrons and their reading habits" (see part 3, section 5.6, "Policy on Governmental Intimidation").

In late 1987 it was disclosed that Federal Bureau of Investigation (FBI) agents were visiting libraries in what are best described as fishing expeditions. Agents generally first approached library clerks and solicited information on the use of various library services (e.g., interlibrary loan, database searches) by "suspicious-looking foreigners" and, in some instances, asked to see the library's circulation records.

A public confrontation between the IFC and the FBI eventually ensued. The IFC stressed the inextricability of First Amendment and privacy rights, as well as the fact that the FBI was requesting that librarians violate not only a professional ethic but also the law in thirty-eight states and the District of Columbia. (As of this writing, there are confidentiality laws in forty-eight states and the District of Columbia and opinions from two attorneys general supporting confidentiality.) The FBI refused to back away from what it characterized as a program (the Library Awareness Program) to alert librarians to the possibility that libraries were being used by foreign agents as places to recruit operatives, that librarians themselves were sometimes targeted for approach by foreign agents, and that valuable material was being stolen by these agents and their operatives. The IFC emphasized, in congressional testimony and in the media, the principle of open access to publicly available information and the central role of libraries in this society as providers of that access.

In the fall of 1989, through a Freedom of Information Act (FOIA) request, ALA obtained documents from the FBI in which 266 individuals, all of whom had in some way criticized the Library Awareness Program, were identified as subjects of FBI index checks. These documents also suggested that the Library Awareness Program covered parts of the country other than New York City alone, as previously claimed by the FBI.

Early in 1990, ALA wrote to President George Bush, then to FBI Director William Sessions and to the relevant House and Senate committees, urging that the Library Awareness Program be discontinued and that the files of the 266 individuals be released to them and expunged from FBI records. Director Sessions responded in March 1990, defending the program and denying that any investigation of the 266 had taken place, claiming that index checks were administrative and not investigative in nature. Subsequently, individuals were urged to make their own FOIA requests, but only one person who filed such a request later reported receiving any information from the FBI.

In addition, ALA filed yet another FOIA request, which was denied, as was the appeal of that denial, on the grounds that the FBI was in litigation with the National Security Archive (NSA) over the same issue. The FBI promised to give ALA any information released to the NSA and eventually did so. Nevertheless, ALA reserved the right to bring suit against the FBI for denying its right of appeal and obstructing a legitimate attempt to gain information under the Freedom of Information Act.

The FBI has never publicly abandoned the Library Awareness Program and may still be conducting it. For more information on current issues with the FBI, see http://www.ala.org/ala/oif/ifissues/fbiyourlibrary.htm.

Federal agencies are not alone in attempting to make use of library-patron records. Local law enforcement officials, journalists, students, parents, fund-raisers, marketing professionals, civil litigants, and politicians have been known to seek borrowing records, registration data, mailing lists, and other information about library patrons. In 1990, a library director in Decatur, Texas, challenged one such attempt in court and won an important victory for library confidentiality policies. In *Decatur Public Library v. District Attorney's Office of Wise County*, the district attorney, investigating a child-abandonment case, subpoenaed the records of all libraries in Wise County, requesting the names, addresses, and telephone numbers of all individuals who had checked out books on childbirth within the previous nine months, the titles they borrowed, and the dates the materials were checked out and returned.[10] The police had no evidence indicating that the person who abandoned the child might have borrowed library books or otherwise used the library. They were simply conducting a fishing expedition.

The director of the Decatur Public Library refused to comply with the subpoena and, with the help of the city attorney, filed a motion to quash it on behalf of the library's patrons. On May 9, 1990, Judge John R. Lindsey ruled in favor of the library and quashed the subpoena. His decision recognized the library's standing to assert a constitutional privilege on behalf of its unnamed patrons and clients, affirmed a constitutional right of privacy available to patrons, and held that the state was unable to demonstrate a compelling governmental objective under its police powers or other legitimate function of government to warrant intrusion of those rights.

In 1995, the issue of library-user confidentiality again reached the courts in connection with a lawsuit brought by a tobacco company, Brown and Williamson, against the University of California. The company alleged that the University of California at San Francisco library possessed in its collection documents stolen from the company that purportedly showed that the tobacco industry had known of a link between smoking and cancer for many years and had failed to disclose it. The documents had previously been leaked to the press and discussed in congressional hearings at the time the lawsuit was filed. The lawsuit sought not only the return of the documents but also a list of all library patrons who had access to them and a description of the nature of those users' research and publications.

ALA's sister organization, the Freedom to Read Foundation (see below and part 6, section 1, "Free People Read Freely: Knowing Where to Go for Help"), identified the case as one of extreme importance, with the potential to set a positive precedent in favor of First Amendment protection for library-user privacy, and filed an amicus brief explaining the crucial link between library confidentiality and First Amendment rights. Although the case ultimately was resolved without reaching the confidentiality issue, the fact that a request for library-user records was made as part of the lawsuit indicates the breadth of circumstances in which a threat to confidentiality may arise.

Through the Association's various position statements, the profession has established a code of free access to services and materials for all library users. Opposed to using the library as a means of intimidating patrons, the profession strives to enhance the intellectual freedom of the library user by providing not only all materials requested but also free and equal access to all materials without fear of recrimination for pursuing one's interests.

The Librarian and Intellectual Freedom

Although the profession, through ALA, formulates policies to help ensure a climate favorable to intellectual freedom, the individual librarian is the key to achieving the end result. Adherence to the *Library Bill of Rights* by individual librarians is the only means of effecting the profession's goals. Consequently, the concept of intellectual freedom also considers the individual librarian's intellectual freedom, both in pursuit of professional responsibilities and in personal life. Several agencies within or closely affiliated with ALA, accordingly, encourage and protect the librarian's commitment to the principles of intellectual freedom. In relation to support for intellectual freedom, the Code of Ethics of the American Library Association, passed by the ALA Council in June 1995, specifically states, "We uphold the principles of intellectual freedom and resist all efforts to censor library materials."

From 1940 until 1967, most such activities were centered in the Intellectual Freedom Committee. For many years, it not only recommended policies but also directed a variety of educational efforts, including collecting and publicizing information about censorship incidents, sponsoring censorship exhibits at conferences, conducting preconferences on intellectual freedom themes, and planning complementary programs to further the Association's goals regarding intellectual freedom.

Office for Intellectual Freedom

One of these complementary programs is the Office for Intellectual Freedom, established in December 1967. The OIF evolved finally from a 1965 preconference on intellectual freedom held in Washington, D.C. That meeting recommended establishing an ALA headquarters unit to conduct and coordinate the Association's intellectual freedom activities and to provide continuity for the total program. The goal of the OIF is to educate librarians and the general public about the importance of intellectual freedom, relieving the IFC of this task and allowing it to concentrate on developing policy. The OIF serves as the administrative arm of the Intellectual Freedom Committee and bears the responsibility for implementing ALA policies on intellectual freedom, as approved by the Council. The philosophy of the Office for Intellectual Freedom is based on the premise that if librarians are to appreciate the importance of intellectual freedom, they must first understand the concept as it relates to the individual, the institution, and the functioning of society. Believing that with understanding comes the ability to teach others, the OIF maintains a broad program of informational publications, projects, and services.

The premier OIF publication is the bimonthly *Newsletter on Intellectual Freedom.* The OIF prepares special educational materials, for instance, the Banned Books Week Resource Kit and others, as need dictates. In addition, the OIF works closely with ALA Editions (part of Publishing) to develop books. Recent ALA titles have included *Libraries, Access, and Intellectual Freedom: Developing Policies for Public and Academic Libraries,* by Barbara M. Jones (1999); *Libraries and Democracy: The Cornerstones of Liberty,* by Nancy Kranich (2001); *Hit List for Young Adults 2: Frequently Challenged Books,* by Teri S. Lesesne and Rosemary Chance for the Young Adult Library Services Association (2002); *Libraries, the First Amendment, and*

Cyberspace: What You Need to Know, by Robert S. Peck (2000); *Teaching Banned Books: Twelve Guides for Young Readers,* by Pat R. Scales (2001); and *Speaking Out! Voices in Celebration of Intellectual Freedom,* by Ann K. Symons and Sally Gardner Reed (1999). The OIF also distributes documents, articles, brochures, and all ALA policy statements concerning intellectual freedom in print and on the Web. As part of its information program, the OIF maintains and distributes a banned books exhibit. The exhibit is available for display at national, state, and local conferences, workshops, seminars, and other meetings.

The Office for Intellectual Freedom advises and consults with librarians confronting potential or actual censorship problems. For example, it responds with appropriate assistance to telephone and written requests about materials that have drawn the censorial efforts of an individual or group in the community. Another means of assistance established in 1994 is the Intellectual Freedom Action Network (see part 6, section 1, "Free People Read Freely: Where to Go for Help"), a group of concerned volunteers who have identified themselves as willing to stand up in support of intellectual freedom when controversy comes to their area and to alert the OIF to the activities of censorship pressure groups in their communities. The OIF coordinates the Action Network, calling upon its members when necessary to write letters, attend meetings, or provide moral support to librarians fighting challenges in their localities.

The OIF also coordinates the Intellectual Freedom Committee's relations with other organizations having similar concerns. These include the intellectual freedom committees of the ALA divisions and the state library associations' intellectual freedom committees. Close contact with nonlibrary organizations—such as the Association of American Publishers, the American Booksellers Association, the American Civil Liberties Union, the Media Coalition, and the National Coalition against Censorship—is also maintained.

Intellectual Freedom Round Table

As ALA's intellectual freedom program developed, the need for an organizational forum through which individual ALA members could participate in intellectual freedom activities according to their varying levels of interest began to be felt. At the 1973 Annual

Conference in Las Vegas, the Intellectual Freedom Round Table (IFRT) was organized as the Association's membership-activity program for intellectual freedom. The activities of the Round Table supplement the OIF's education program and offer opportunities for ALA members to become active in the Association's intellectual freedom efforts.

The IFRT sponsors three intellectual freedom awards. The annual State and Regional Achievement Award, given by the IFRT since 1984, was revised in 1991. Formerly presented to a state intellectual freedom committee, the award has been expanded to include "state educational media association intellectual freedom committee[s], state intellectual freedom coalition[s], legal defense fund[s] or other such group that has implemented the most successful and creative state intellectual freedom project during the calendar year. The award also may be presented for ongoing or multiyear projects." The IFRT established the John Phillip Immroth Memorial Award for Intellectual Freedom, given annually in memory of the cofounder and first chairperson of the Round Table, "to honor notable contributions to intellectual freedom and demonstrations of personal courage in defense of freedom of expression."

Biennially, the IFRT sponsors the Eli M. Oboler Memorial Award, presented for the best published work in the area of intellectual freedom.

Program of Action in Support of the Library Bill of Rights

Soon after adoption of the *Library Bill of Rights* and establishment of the Intellectual Freedom Committee, the profession realized that more than just information sources were needed to foster the practice of intellectual freedom in libraries. Some members called for a "policing" effort to publicize censorship problems and bring pressure upon authorities to correct conditions conducive to censorship. As early as the 1948 ALA Annual Conference in Atlantic City, Robert D. Leigh, director of the Public Library Inquiry, addressed the Council and recommended that "some responsible group" be created to investigate reports of library censorship, make public reports of investigations, give possible aid to professionals who become victims of censorship, and in extreme cases, exercise "a professional boycott against the libraries of censoring authorities."[11]

Some of Leigh's recommendations were debated for nearly twenty years before a national resolution of the problems began to emerge. As a first substantive step, in 1969 the Association adopted its Program of Action in Support of the *Library Bill of Rights*.

The first Program of Action, developed by the IFC and approved by the Council, created a mechanism whereby complaints about censorship incidents were reported to the Office for Intellectual Freedom and acted upon by the Intellectual Freedom Committee. Such complaints were studied by the OIF and the IFC to determine whether they involved intellectual freedom problems within the scope of the *Library Bill of Rights*. If the complaint fell under the Program of Action, the Office for Intellectual Freedom and the Intellectual Freedom Committee attempted to mediate, arbitrate, or provide appropriate assistance to effect a just resolution of the problem. If these means failed, one prerogative of the Committee was to establish a fact-finding team to investigate further. After such an investigation, the team reported its findings to the IFC for review. Further substantive action required a recommendation by the IFC to the ALA Executive Board. Under a sanctions policy adopted in 1971, the IFC could recommend publication of a summary of the report, publication of the entire report, or various other sanctions against groups or individuals violating the spirit of the *Library Bill of Rights*. The ALA Executive Board made the final disposition of the Intellectual Freedom Committee's recommendations.

From 1969 to 1971, in response to requests for action, three fact-finding projects were undertaken by the IFC. The first major case was brought by Joan Bodger. An extensive investigation explored Bodger's charge that she had been fired from the Missouri State Library because of her public support of intellectual freedom. She had written a letter to a local newspaper protesting the suppression of an underground newspaper. The IFC concluded that her allegations were correct and recommended publication of the complete report in *American Libraries*, vindicating Bodger and deploring the actions of the Missouri State Library Commission that resulted in her firing.

The other two requests for action also entailed fact-finding studies, but those studies led the Intellectual Freedom Committee to find that it could not support charges contained in the complaints. Reports summarizing the two cases were published in *American*

Libraries.[12] The three complaints investigated under the Program of Action made it clear that cases involving intellectual freedom also might raise issues of tenure, academic status, ethical practices, and a variety of other matters. The difficulty of focusing only on intellectual freedom increased in late 1970 when a complaint was received from J. Michael McConnell, who was denied a position at the University of Minnesota library shortly after his well-publicized application for a marriage license to marry another male. Charging that the university discriminated against him because of his homosexuality, McConnell appealed to the IFC, claiming his case fell under the Program of Action. To support his claim, he cited the 1946 ALA Statement of Principles of Intellectual Freedom and Tenure for Librarians, which asserts, "Intellectual freedom precludes partisan political control of appointments and makes it possible for librarians to devote themselves to the practice of their profession without fear of interference or of dismissal for political, religious, racial, marital or other unjust reasons."

The IFC did not dispute McConnell's claim that his case fell under the scope of the 1946 policy statement. It disagreed, however, that the case came within the jurisdiction of the Program of Action, because that mechanism dealt only with violations of the *Library Bill of Rights*. The Committee attempted to resolve the problem by rewriting the Program of Action to allow jurisdiction over all ALA policies on intellectual freedom. The revision, completed during a special December 1970 meeting of the IFC, was to come before the Council for approval in January 1971. At its midwinter meeting, however, the Committee again revised the document to include all ALA policies on intellectual freedom and tenure. It was then pointed out that both the Library Administration Division (LAD) and the Association of College and Research Libraries (ACRL) claimed vested interests in investigations, particularly those involving tenure of academic librarians. The complex jurisdictional problems resulted in an appeal to ALA president Lillian Bradshaw to take steps immediately to develop a central investigatory agency for the entire Association. Moving swiftly, President Bradshaw appointed a membership group representing various interests. In June 1971, the group presented the Program of Action for Mediation, Arbitration, and Inquiry to the Council, which adopted it and rescinded the first Program of Action.

The new Program of Action established the Staff Committee on Mediation, Arbitration, and Inquiry (SCMAI), which functioned somewhat as the IFC had under the old document. In addition to intellectual freedom problems, however, the new committee handled cases involving tenure, professional status, fair employment practices, ethical practices, and due process as set forth in ALA policies. In June 1990, the SCMAI was replaced by the Standing Committee on Review, Inquiry, and Mediation (SCRIM). Lack of funding caused the SCRIM to cease operation on September 1, 1992.

Freedom to Read Foundation

The Intellectual Freedom Committee, the Office for Intellectual Freedom, and the Intellectual Freedom Round Table are the primary agencies for establishing and promoting the Association's positions on questions involving intellectual freedom. In addition, the Intellectual Freedom Action Network supports these positions and responds to controversies on the local level. The element in the Association's program in support and defense of intellectual freedom that takes the most aggressive, proactive role, however, is the Freedom to Read Foundation (FTRF).

Incorporated in November 1969, FTRF was ALA's response to librarians who increasingly wanted defense machinery to protect their jobs from jeopardy when they undertook to challenge violations of intellectual freedom. Another primary objective in establishing the Foundation was to have a means through which librarians and other concerned individuals and groups could begin to set legal precedents for the freedom to read. The Foundation was created outside the structure of ALA, and to ensure its full freedom to act with vigor in the legal arena, it remains legally and financially independent. But the Foundation is closely affiliated with ALA through the ex officio membership of ALA officers on its board of trustees. The Foundation's executive director also serves as director of the ALA Office for Intellectual Freedom.

A program of education on the importance of, and the necessity for a commitment to, the principles of intellectual freedom requires assurance that such commitment will not result in reprisals, such as legal prosecution, financial loss, or personal damage. The FTRF attempts to provide that assurance through financial and legal assistance and legal challenges to restrictive legislation, thereby helping to create a favorable climate for intellectual freedom. Through the provision of financial and legal assistance, the Foundation attempts to negate the necessity for librarians to make the difficult choice between practical expediency (that is, keeping a job) and upholding principles, such as in selecting materials for library collections. Through its various projects and grants, the Foundation hopes to establish those principles enunciated in the *Library Bill of Rights* as legal precedents rather than mere paper policies. For more information on the FTRF, including on past and current First Amendment court cases, see http://www.ftrf.org/.

Established by the Freedom to Read Foundation but now formally independent, the LeRoy C. Merritt Humanitarian Fund was created in 1970. The Merritt Fund was established by the Foundation's board of trustees in recognition of individuals' need for subsistence and other support when their positions are jeopardized or lost as a result of defending intellectual freedom. This special fund offers short-term, immediate assistance even prior to the development of all pertinent facts in a particular case, whether or not legal action has been taken.

In the combined forces of the Intellectual Freedom Committee, the Office for Intellectual Freedom, the Intellectual Freedom Round Table, the Intellectual Freedom Action Network, and the Freedom to Read Foundation, along with the LeRoy C. Merritt Humanitarian Fund, the library profession has available a complete program to support the practice of intellectual freedom.

The Librarian and Personal Intellectual Freedom

The profession, however, has not yet achieved the same success in a closely related area, that of the librarian's personal rather than professional intellectual freedom. The question of what support should be given to librarians who suffer professionally because of personal beliefs and actions has been approached in individual cases but has not been fully resolved.

One of the first signals that librarians could be penalized for their personal beliefs came in the late 1940s with the advent of loyalty oaths and loyalty programs designed to ferret out communists and subversives. The Intellectual Freedom Committee faced the loyalty issue with its Policy on Loyalty Programs, first adopted by the Council in 1948 and revised in 1951. When another case arose in Florida in 1969, the Policy on Loyalty Programs was reexamined and again revised. The last revision, adopted by the Council in July 1992, states in part the following:

> The American Library Association protests conditions of employment predicated on inquiries into library employees' thoughts, reading matter, associates, or memberships in organizations. The Association also protests compulsory affirmations of allegiance as a condition of employment in libraries and calls on libraries not to impose loyalty tests or oaths as conditions of employment.[13]

In 1969, another incident arose involving a librarian who lost his position because of actions, based on personal beliefs, taken in his capacity as a private citizen. T. Ellis Hodgin was fired as city librarian of Martinsville, Virginia, shortly after he joined a lawsuit challenging the constitutionality of a religious education course taught in the city school his daughter attended. He had also been active in civil rights efforts. Hodgin's situation sparked a controversy among librarians, resulting in a recommendation from the Intellectual Freedom Subcommittee of the Activities Committee on New Directions for ALA (ACONDA):

> The scope of intellectual freedom encompasses considerably more than just the freedom to read. Support must also be rendered to the librarian who is fired for sporting a beard, for engaging in civil rights activities, etc., etc. And he should not have to claim "poverty" in order to receive it.[14]

The recommendation, however, was not approved as part of the final ACONDA report. Some concerned librarians responded to Hodgin's plight by organizing the National Freedom Fund for Librarians (NFFL), which collected several thousand dollars to aid him. (When the NFFL disbanded in 1971, its cash balance was sent to the LeRoy C. Merritt Humanitarian Fund.)

Hodgin also appealed to the Freedom to Read Foundation for assistance to defray the financial hardship he suffered when he lost his position. In June 1970, the Foundation's executive committee awarded him $500

> for having suffered in his defense of freedom of speech as a result of which he lost his position as a librarian. Inasmuch as it is the obligation of the librarian to protect free speech and a free press through his work as a librarian, it is then particularly appropriate that, when he is deprived of his job because of his own exercise of free speech, the Freedom to Read Foundation assist him in the defense of his freedom.[15]

A second grant of $500 was made to Hodgin in January 1971 for the specific purpose of perfecting an appeal to the U.S. Supreme Court of his suit for reinstatement.

The limits of intellectual freedom were again debated by the profession when the previously mentioned case of J. Michael McConnell arose in 1970. The Intellectual Freedom Committee found that McConnell's rights "under the First Amendment have been violated" because he met reprisals for freely expressing his sexual preference.[16] On that basis the LeRoy C. Merritt Humanitarian Fund granted $500 to help defray financial hardship occasioned by his inability to find another job.

The question of how far librarians are willing to extend the scope of intellectual freedom for the benefit of their colleagues was raised anew by the case of Utah librarian Jeanne Layton. In September 1979, Layton was dismissed from her position as library director in Davis County after she refused to comply with requests to remove the novel *Americana*, by Don DeLillo, from library shelves. The following month she filed suit to regain her job.

The suit was supported from the beginning by the Freedom to Read Foundation, but it soon became clear that the legal battle would be a lengthy and very costly one. Both the Intellectual Freedom Committee and the Freedom to Read Foundation designated the case a priority for 1980. The Utah Library Association rallied librarians and others statewide in support. At the 1980 ALA Annual Conference in New York, the Freedom to Read Foundation announced that it would match two dollars for every dollar contributed to Jeanne Layton's defense from June 27, 1980, to December 31, 1980, up to a limit of $10,000 in matching funds. The response was, in the words of Foundation president Florence McMullin, "nothing short of overwhelming." When the challenge expired, $6,024 had been received, of which $5,000 was matched "two for one" by the Foundation. Moreover, Jeanne Layton won her suit and regained her job, and one of her main antagonists was defeated for reelection to the county commission.

Although the question of how far librarians will go to support colleagues in defense of intellectual freedom will always be resolvable only on a case-by-case and issue-by-issue basis, the response to Layton's courageous stand surely indicates that in general the library profession takes its responsibilities on this front seriously indeed.

The Library and Advocacy for Social and Political Issues

Each aspect of intellectual freedom in libraries that has been discussed to this point has involved either library users and their access to all published materials or librarians and their practice of professional or personal intellectual freedom.

One last branch of intellectual freedom remains to be examined, that being the library as an institution and the nature of its role in social change and education. Continually debated within the profession and the American Library Association, the issue has been summarized as neutrality versus advocacy. In essence, the question is, can libraries, as institutions, advocate social or political causes and still maintain their image as providers of views representing all sides of all questions?

Whenever the question is raised, it initiates further queries. For example, what constitutes advocating a cause—biased book selection, biased displays, or a prejudicial assignment of library meeting rooms? For that matter, what constitutes a cause—peace, ecology, democracy? If a library sponsors a display of books on peace, in order to maintain neutrality must it also sponsor a display on war? The questions are complex, and the answers have shown no uniformity whatsoever. The American Library Association itself has vacillated on the main issue, reaching only a partial resolution in the late 1960s and the early 1970s.

At the 1969 Annual Conference in Atlantic City, the membership and the Council debated whether or not the Association should take a public stand opposing the war in Vietnam or opposing deployment of an antiballistic missile system (ABM). It was argued that because political and moral issues are so deeply entangled with education and library issues, institutions such as ALA and libraries are obligated to take such positions.

Those who opposed such positions argued in favor of neutrality on questions not directly related to libraries. They argued that intellectual freedom for those librarians opposed to the majority view would be violated if the Association attempted to take stands on social and political issues. They further maintained that they had tradition on their side, given that the Association had always declined to take a stand on issues not directly related to libraries. That argument, of course, was incorrect. The Association had previously taken stands in some instances and refused to do so in others.

In June 1921, for example, the ALA Council espoused a very decided position on the question of disarmament after the First World War. In a strong resolution, the Council stated the following:

> WHEREAS, The members of the American Library Association had full demonstration of the pain and pinch that belongs to war and the increased cost of all necessities, both personal and professional, caused thereby; and

> WHEREAS, The exigencies of international conditions brought about by the cost of war is appalling from every standpoint; and

> WHEREAS, We believe the example of the United States in this matter will be followed by the other nations;

> THEREFORE BE IT RESOLVED, That the American Library Association urge upon the president of the United States and Congress the initiative of a movement leading to a reduction of armament at the earliest possible moment; and be it further

> RESOLVED, That a request be made by the members of the American Library Association to their individual congressman for such action and that a record be made of the replies.[17]

However, in 1928, when faced by a request from the American Civil Liberties Union that ALA adopt "one or more resolutions on civil liberty," the ALA Executive Board declined, saying the Association "does not take actions on questions outside the library and bibliographic field."[18] That was similar to the philosophy that prevailed in 1969, when the Vietnam and ABM resolutions failed to pass the Council. The question arose again, though, at the 1970 and 1971 Midwinter Meetings and Annual Conferences. After a great deal of debate, the Council voted at its 1970 Annual Conference in Detroit to "define the broad social responsibilities of ALA in terms of the willingness of ALA to take a position on current critical issues with the relationship to libraries and library service clearly set forth in the position statements."[19]

In line with this policy, a carefully reworded resolution opposing the war in Vietnam was adopted by the Council one year later:

> WHEREAS, The stated objective of the American Library Association is the promotion and improvement of library service and librarianship; and
>
> WHEREAS, Continued and improved library service to the American public requires sustained support from the public monies; and
>
> WHEREAS, The continuing U.S. involvement in the conflict in Southeast Asia has so distorted our national priorities as to reduce substantially the funds appropriated for educational purposes, including support for library services to the American people; and
>
> WHEREAS, Continued commitment of U.S. arms, troops, and other military support has not contributed to the solution of this conflict;
>
> BE IT THEREFORE RESOLVED, That the American Library Association calls upon the president of the United States to take immediately those steps necessary to terminate all U.S. military involvement in the present conflict in Southeast Asia by December 31, 1971, and to insure the reallocation of national resources to meet pressing domestic needs.[20]

With approval of the Vietnam resolution, the Association seemed to give broader interpretation to the old "library and bibliographic field." However, this more permissive interpretation still did not resolve the more basic question of whether libraries themselves should follow the course of neutrality or advocacy.

The contradiction was further focused in July 1974, when ALA endorsed the Equal Rights Amendment (ERA). ALA's support for ERA went much further than its opposition to U.S. military involvement in Southeast Asia. In 1977, the Council voted not to hold conferences in states that had not ratified the amendment. In June 1978, the Council endorsed the ERA Extension Resolution and, at the 1979 Midwinter Meeting, established an ERA task force charged with assisting and consulting with "ALA Chapters in carrying out the commitment to passage of the Equal Rights Amendment in ways best suited to the individual states."[21]

The Association justified this active support of the proposed amendment by noting the support already expressed by other professional associations "by reason of its beneficial implications for all persons in the American society," and, more specifically, by considering the support an outgrowth of ALA's policy requiring equal employment opportunity in libraries, adopted at the 1974 Midwinter Meeting. The resolution in support of ERA noted that "women constitute 82 percent of the library profession." Hence, it was argued, "equal employment required support of equal rights for women."[22] None of the operative resolutions on ERA addressed themselves to the content of library collections. Opponents of the amendment and pro-ERA advocates of ALA neutrality, however, were quick to argue that library users "have a right to expect the library to furnish them with uncensored information on both sides of this and all other issues. Adoption of advocacy positions and participation in boycotts cannot help but strike a blow at the public's confidence in the fair-mindedness and even-handedness of librarians."[23]

Yet another aspect of the advocacy-versus-neutrality conundrum was addressed by the Association in 1987 at its Annual Conference in San Francisco. David Henington, director of the Houston Public Library, brought to the IFC for its response and assistance an antiapartheid ordinance passed and implemented by the city of Houston. This ordinance required that all city agencies obtain certification from suppliers of goods and services that they had no affiliates in, and did no business with, the Republic of South Africa.[24] Henington asserted that this requirement was causing serious acquisition problems for the library. Major information services such as the New York Times Company, the *Wall Street Journal*, and leading publishers refused to sign such certificates. Some refused because they had reporters in South Africa, one religious group because it had missionaries there, and others on principle, in the belief that the free flow of information both into and out of South Africa must be defended and enlarged for the sake of those struggling to dismantle the apartheid system there. Because it did not have a copy of the ordinance in hand and because it had received reports of similar ordinances elsewhere, the IFC voted to explore the matter further.

Two ALA members decided that the issue should be taken to the membership at that Conference, and they presented a resolution at the membership meeting. The resolution stressed the intellectual freedom implications of this policy and asked that ideas and information be exempted from the laudable goal of enforcing economic sanctions against South Africa for its abhorrent apartheid system. A heated encounter ensued between the presenters and other supporters of the resolution and those who saw it as supportive of apartheid and, therefore, racist. The resolution was resoundingly defeated.

At the 1988 Annual Conference in New Orleans, the membership adopted a resolution reaffirming its commitment to Article 19 of the Universal Declaration of Human Rights: "Everyone has the right to freedom of opinion and expression; this right includes freedom to hold opinions without interference and to seek, receive and impart information and ideas through any media regardless of frontiers."

Measuring the Profession's Response

The foregoing discussion illustrates that anything other than an issue-oriented definition of intellectual freedom is impossible. At the present time, the profession uniformly disdains censorship of published materials, print or nonprint. The attitude toward user access is somewhat uniform but contains a great deal of dissent on the question of access for minors to all the materials in a library collection. On the question of the librarian's professional practice of intellectual freedom, there is near agreement that every effort should be made to encourage and protect this aspect of librarianship. The librarian's personal intellectual freedom, on and off the job, presents some points of agreement, but major areas of dissent still exist. The same is true in the area of institutional neutrality versus advocacy.

One conclusion from a review of the history, status, and future of intellectual freedom in libraries is that the American Library Association's positions and programs provide one of the few gauges for measuring the profession's response to the problems of defining, promoting, and defending the concept. ALA's evolving position reflects the steady emergence of a philosophy within the entire library community. Although that philosophy exhibits some loose ends, its core grows firmer, based on a history of trial and error and forced response to a continually changing social climate. The philosophy is young, too young to be rooted in tradition, but gradually it has gained recognition as the substance of the total philosophy shaping library service in the United States.

At the 1990 Midwinter Meeting, ALA was asked to review and support an Association of American Publishers (AAP) report on the effect of book boycotts in South Africa titled "The Starvation of Young Black Minds: The Effect of Book Boycotts in South Africa," which recommended that the boycott on books and other educational materials be discontinued.

The Intellectual Freedom Committee reported no existing ALA policy upon which to base recommendations regarding the AAP report, and at the 1990 Annual Conference proposed a new Interpretation of the *Library Bill of Rights*, initially called "The Free Flow of Information," to address free expression issues raised in the global arena. The resolution was adopted by the Council at the 1991 Midwinter Meeting as "The Universal Right to Free Expression: An Interpretation of the *Library Bill of Rights*" (see part 2, section 2.18). At the same time, the Council adopted Article 19 of the Universal Declaration of Human Rights as official ALA policy. This action superseded a 1988 ALA membership resolution reaffirming its commitment to Article 19, which read, "Everyone has the right to freedom of opinion and expression; this right includes freedom to hold opinions without interference and to seek, receive and impart information and ideas through any media regardless of frontiers."

Simultaneously with the 1990 AAP request, the Social Responsibilities Round Table (SRRT) proposed Guidelines for Librarians Interacting with South Africa. The Intellectual Freedom Committee responded with a memorandum on guidelines for librarians interacting with South Africa in which the Committee recommended that the guidelines be rewritten to address, among other matters, the intellectual freedom concerns absent from the text. The ALA Council declined to adopt the guidelines as written, following which a motion carried to refer the guidelines back to the IFC, the International Relations Committee (IRC), and the Committee on Professional Ethics. At the 1991 Midwinter Meeting, these committees returned a joint recommendation that no further action be taken until the guidelines were rewritten. The Council then referred the document to the Executive Board.

The subject of including books and informational materials in the sanctions against South Africa was never revisited in light of the new policy, The Universal Right to Free Expression. Subsequently, with the elimination of apartheid in South Africa and progress toward democratic majority rule, the issue was defused.

Another issue to raise the advocacy-versus-neutrality controversy was the war in the Persian Gulf. At the 1991 Midwinter Meeting, the Council passed a resolution condemning the war. This action provoked strong protest from parts of the ALA membership, many of whom believe the Association should not involve itself in matters of public policy not directly related to library interests and concerns. Many members had loved ones serving in the armed forces in the Persian Gulf region at the time. Also at the 1991 Midwinter Meeting, the new policy The Universal Right to Free Expression was inaugurated with the passage of two resolutions calling for the "exemption of publications and other informational materials from sanctions" levied by the United States and by the United Nations against Iraq and Kuwait.

The passage of The Universal Right to Free Expression opens new vistas to librarians concerned about intellectual freedom. With the exponential growth in global communications and publications, it will be possible for American librarians to act in support of their colleagues and counterparts in countries where intellectual freedom principles are under fire—China, Turkey, Syria, Saudi Arabia, Guatemala, El Salvador, Kenya, and many others. Conversely, librarians facing censorship attempts in the United States may benefit from the experience and support of those in other countries who have endured far greater challenges.

The Association revisited the debate over advocacy versus neutrality, or library-related and nonlibrary-related matters, with its decision to withdraw the 1995 Midwinter Meeting from the city of Cincinnati, where voters had repealed a gay rights ordinance. Many ALA members felt it would be outrageous to sponsor a meeting in a city that had withdrawn legal protection from discrimination for their gay colleagues. Others felt that ALA was compromising its intellectual freedom principles by taking a political position that implied official disapproval of the opinions of Cincinnati's voters and could have the effect of jeopardizing, in the mind of the library-using public, librarians' neutrality in the provision of information from all points of view on homosexuality and other controversial subjects.

The latest example of controversy concerning ALA's response to an advocacy issue concerns access to information in Cuba. After much discussion over several years at various levels of the organization, ALA Council adopted the conclusions of the "International Relations Committee and Intellectual Freedom Committee Report on Cuba" on January 14, 2004, relating to matters of access to information in Cuba.

In the conclusions, ALA (1) joined the International Federation of Library Associations and Institutions (IFLA) in its deep concern over seventy-five political dissidents who were arrested and given long prison terms in spring 2003; (2) supported IFLA's call for the elimination of the U.S. embargo that restricts access to information in Cuba and for lifting travel restrictions that limit professional exchanges; and (3) supported IFLA in urging the Cuban government to eliminate obstacles to access to information imposed by its policies and in advocating an investigative visit by a special rapporteur of the United Nations Commission on Human Rights. Such a visit should give special attention to freedom of access to information and freedom of expression, especially in the cases of those individuals recently imprisoned and the reasons for and conditions of their detention. For more information on the complex and controversial issue, see http://www.ala.org/ala/iro/iroactivities/alacubanlibraries.htm.

Undoubtedly, as threats to free expression at home and abroad become more complex and interwoven, the line separating advocacy from neutrality will be crossed many times. Following the best of democratic traditions, a healthy debate on the library's role in the issues of the moment must be encouraged.

NOTES

1. American Library Association, Minutes of Executive Board Meetings 3 (September 29, 1924): 20.
2. American Library Association, Minutes of Executive Board Meetings 5 (January 1, 1930): 11.
3. American Library Association, Minutes of Executive Board Meetings 6 (October 15, 1933): 214.
4. American Library Association, Minutes of Executive Board Meetings 7 (December 27, 1934): 89.
5. Ibid., 48–49.
6. Arthur E. Bostwick, "The Librarian as Censor," *ALA Bulletin* 2 (September 1908): 113.
7. American Library Association, Minutes of Executive Board Meetings 10 (October 5, 1938): 48.
8. "Cincinnati Proceedings—Council," *ALA Bulletin* 34 (August 1940): P-37.
9. American Library Association, *Handbook of Organization, 1971–1972* (Chicago: American Library Association, n.d.), 13.
10. *Decatur Public Library v. District Attorney's Office of Wise County*, No. 90-05-192, 271st Judicial District Court; Wise and Jack Counties, Texas; (Letter Opinion) Judge John R. Lindsey.
11. Robert D. Leigh, "Intellectual Freedom," *ALA Bulletin* 42 (September 1948): 369.
12. Judith F. Krug and James A. Harvey, "Intellectual Freedom," *American Libraries* 1 (May 1970): 433; and "ALA Report: Proceedings and Findings Pertaining to a Request for Action Submitted by Robert E. Scott," *American Libraries* 2 (March 1971): 316–17.
13. "Loyalty Oaths," http://www.ala.org/ala/oif/statementspols/otherpolicies/loyaltyoaths.htm.
14. American Library Association Activities Committee on New Directions for ALA, "Final Report and Subcommittee Reports, June 1970," 53.
15. "Hodgin Appeal Rests with U.S. Supreme Court," *Freedom to Read Foundation News* 1 (Fall 1971): 5.
16. David K. Berninghausen, "Report of the Intellectual Freedom Committee to Council, Dallas, June 25, 1971," *American Libraries* 2 (September 1971): 891.

17. *ALA Bulletin* 15 (July 1921): 169.

18. American Library Association, Minutes of Executive Board Meetings 4 (May 29, 1928): 142.

19. *American Libraries* 1 (July–August 1970): 674.

20. "Resolution on Southeast Asia Conflict," *American Libraries* 2 (September 1971): 826.

21. American Library Association, news release, September 1979.

22. ALA Council Minutes, 1974, 335.

23. Terence L. Day, Chairman, Neill Public Library Board of Trustees, letter to the editor, *Chicago Tribune*, January 21, 1979.

24. The Houston City Council subsequently voted to exempt both the public library and the city zoo from the requirements of the ordinance.

3

Challenges and Issues Today

EVELYN SHAEVEL, BEVERLEY BECKER,
and
CANDACE D. MORGAN

A democratic society operates best when information flows freely and is freely available, and it is the library's unique responsibility to provide open and unfettered access to that information. With information available and accessible, individuals have the tools necessary for self-improvement and participation in the political process. An essential part of this responsibility is ensuring that the information is not limited because of the format in which it is found, be it a book, a video, a compact disc, or a website on the Internet.

Unfortunately, libraries must frequently confront and deal with objections to free access to library materials, most often raised by those who believe that unlimited access to information and ideas causes harm to the individual or society, and sometimes both. These objections currently center upon four major issues: (1) access to the Internet, (2) the right of youth to access library materials, (3) the privacy of library patrons and the confidentiality of patrons' records, and (4) access to government information.

Because the challenges these issues present to libraries and librarians are continually evolving, it is important to know about the issues and to be aware both of the laws and court decisions that govern the library's provision of materials and services to its patrons and of those patrons' rights. Frequently updated sources of information about challenges and legal issues can be found on the websites maintained by the Freedom to Read Foundation (http://www.ftrf.org/) and the American Library Association's Office for Intellectual Freedom (http://www.ala.org/alaorg/oif/). It is also important to regularly consult with your library's legal counsel, who will be able to provide detailed information about any state or local laws that affect your provision of library services.

The Internet

The Internet may well be the most significant technological innovation of the twentieth century, rivaling the printing press for the changes it is bringing to communications, commerce, and the availability of information. Through the Internet, one may find a vast array of news, ideas, opinions, and entertainment, all easily accessible to anyone with a computer and a modem. By supplying access to the World Wide Web, libraries can now provide their patrons with information resources unimagined only a few decades ago. With just a click of a mouse, patrons are free to choose among the thousands of websites, newsgroups, and databases, selecting for themselves the materials that best suit their desire for information or entertainment.

But the Internet's wealth of information and the ease with which it is accessed raise concern for some persons, who argue that the Internet provides too much access, especially for children. These parties fear that children may find or look for websites that contain sexually explicit material or that children may come across information and ideas deemed objectionable by a particular religious or political community. Some even believe that such unlimited access is harmful for adults as well. Acting on these fears, they campaign for the use of filtering software in public libraries, believing that the harms that arise from censorship are minor in comparison to the harms they believe will arise when a patron views material they deem inappropriate.

The American Library Association does not recommend the use of filters that block access to constitutionally protected speech on computers located in public libraries. In its groundbreaking opinion in *Reno v. American Civil Liberties Union*, the Supreme Court declared that the Internet, as a medium of communication, deserves the First Amendment's highest protection and that persons using the Internet enjoy the same rights to publish information and receive information as do those who use the print media. These rights extend to minors, who also enjoy the right to receive information that is constitutionally protected for them. The use of filters in ways that block access to constitutionally protected speech compromises not only these constitutional freedoms but also the core values of librarianship, which esteem a person's right to read and hear ideas without limitation and regardless of income, status, or age.

In December 2000, Congress enacted the Children's Internet Protection Act (CIPA). This act requires that public and school libraries that wish to receive certain federal discounts or grants for Internet access (e-rate discounts, Library Services and Technology Act [LSTA] or Elementary and Secondary Education Act [ESEA] grants) must certify that they have in place a policy of Internet safety that includes the use of technology protection measures, that is, filtering or blocking software that protects against access to illegal visual depictions accessible through the Internet.[1]

In June 2003, the Supreme Court in *United States v. American Library Ass'n.*, found CIPA to be constitutional. This decision was based upon the solicitor general's statement during oral argument that CIPA does not require libraries to block access to constitutionally protected speech because adults can request that filtering be disabled without specifying any reason for the disabling request.

The newly revised Interpretation of the *Library Bill of Rights* "Access to Electronic Information, Services, and Networks" (part 2, section 2.2) provides a policy framework for decisions related to Internet access regardless of whether a library is CIPA compliant or not. (For more information on the issues related to CIPA compliance, see "Public Libraries and the Public Forum Doctrine," part 4, section 1.) The IFC also has developed questions and answers about this Interpretation, available at http://www.ala.org/ala/oif/statements pols/statementsif/interpretations/qandaaccesselectronic.htm.

Rather than relying on an imperfect and robotic technology, ALA believes that education offers the best means of addressing the issue of Internet safety for both children and adults. Libraries that offer classes to teach children how to play and learn safely and effectively on the Internet not only ensure a positive experience for their young patrons but also equip them with lifelong learning tools with which to evaluate and deal with the wide range of material found on the World Wide Web. Similar classes for parents and other adults on netiquette, search engines, and the use of the Internet as a means of communicating with others about special interests such as genealogy, cooking, and travel familiarize adult patrons with the utility and worth of this technology and assist them to become online guides and resources for their children.

Additionally, libraries that develop Internet use policies can address the fears of those who dread even inadvertent exposure to material they deem inappropriate while effectively protecting their patrons' right to access information and right to privacy. Written policies can emphasize the library's support for the principles of intellectual freedom and its respect for the diversity of its community while at the same time establishing that the library does not condone the use of its computers to access materials that are obscene or otherwise illegal. The use of time limits, terminal placement, privacy screens, and education classes can further support the library's mission while addressing community needs.

For more information on this topic, see "Libraries and the Internet" (part 4, section 3). Much more detailed and frequently updated information can be found in OIF's Libraries and the Internet Tool Kit, http://www.ala.org/oif/iftoolkits/internet/.

Rights of Youth

Whether it is Harry Potter books, R-rated videos, or sexually explicit material on the Internet, most efforts to censor or remove materials from libraries arise when some citizens seek to limit young people's access to information in order to protect their moral and emotional development. Such campaigns can focus on materials with violent content or information about sex, the occult, or alternative religions or lifestyles, or they can center on classic works that are perceived as racist, sexist, homophobic, or hostile to certain ethnic or religious groups. Unfortunately, many people do not understand or refuse to accept that with some exceptions minors have First Amendment rights and enjoy the same rights to read and receive information in the library as do adult patrons.

Accordingly, the American Library Association believes strongly that young people are entitled to freely access ideas and information, subject only to limitations imposed by their parents or guardians. Indeed, "Free Access to Libraries for Minors: An Interpretation of the *Library Bill of Rights*" specifically states, "The American Library Association opposes all attempts to restrict access to library services, materials, and facilities based on the age of library users." Limiting access to books, videos, compact discs, or the Internet does not protect the young from the complex and challenging world that confronts them but can deprive them of information that is important to them or even vital for their learning and development as maturing persons. ALA believes, therefore, that teaching young people how to evaluate information, how to think critically about the information they do receive, and how to make decisions about the materials they view offers the best protection for them. Fostering the individual youth's discernment and curiosity ensures that we are preparing future citizens who are able to participate fully in our democracy and think for themselves. Ultimately, the role of the librarian is to guide and advise young people on how to find and use the best available material for their information needs. Any decisions on whether to limit access to materials are most appropriately made by the child's parents, who are best equipped to know and understand their child's intellectual and emotional development. For more discussions of this topic, see "Minors' First Amendment Rights to Access Information" (part 4, section 2) and "Minors' Rights to Receive Information under the First Amendment," http://www.ala.org/ala/ourassociation/othergroups/ftrf/ftrfinaction/jennerblockmemo/minorsrightreceive.htm.

Privacy and Confidentiality

Privacy is the bedrock foundation for the individual's constitutional right to freely read and receive ideas, information, and points of view. Only when individuals are assured that their choice of reading material does not subject them to reprisals or punishment can they fully enjoy their freedom to explore ideas, weigh arguments, and decide for themselves what they believe.

In 2002, the ALA Council adopted a new Interpretation of the *Library Bill of Rights* on privacy (part 2, section 2.16) to provide libraries and librarians with a framework for dealing with this core principle of intellectual freedom. The Interpretation states:

In a library (physical or virtual), the right to privacy is the right to open inquiry without having the subject of one's interest examined or scrutinized by others. Confidentiality exists when a library is in possession of personally identifiable information about users and keeps that information private on their behalf. Everyone (paid or unpaid) who provides governance, administration, or service in libraries has a responsibility to maintain an environment respectful and protective of the privacy of all users.

This responsibility extends not only to the patron's personal information, but also to database search records, circulation records, and other materials that identify a person's use of library materials, activities, or facilities.

The most significant current issues affecting privacy and confidentiality in the library relate to the nation's reaction to the terrorist attacks on September 11, 2001. The response of the federal government has included the passage of the USA PATRIOT Act and the Homeland Security Act ; the 2002 revision of the Attorney General's Guidelines on General Crimes, Racketeering Enterprise and Terrorism Enterprises Investigations (http://www.usdoj.gov/olp/generalcrimes2.pdf); as well as various programs to profile and identify potential terrorists by collecting and linking data from multiple public and private sources. These and other related initiatives in response to the threat of terrorism have had a chilling effect on freedom of speech, inquiry, and association. As the ALA Council Resolution on the USA PATRIOT Act and Related Measures That Infringe on the Rights of Library Users describes it:

> Certain provisions of the USA PATRIOT Act, the revised Attorney General Guidelines to the Federal Bureau of Investigation, and other related measures expand the authority of the federal government to investigate citizens and non-citizens, to engage in surveillance, and to threaten civil rights and liberties guaranteed under the United States Constitution and Bill of Rights; and
> ... The USA PATRIOT Act and other recently enacted laws, regulations, and guidelines increase the likelihood

that the activities of library users, including their use of
computers to browse the Web or access e-mail, may be
under government surveillance without their knowledge
or consent.

It is important for librarians to understand the legal basis for
protecting the confidentiality of library use. The Fourth Amendment protects "the right of the people to be secure in their persons,
houses, papers, and effects, against unreasonable searches and
seizures." It has taken judicial interpretation to clarify the circumstances under which legal protection may be provided for personally identifiable information given to governmental agencies and
other institutions. The test most often used by the courts to determine whether a right to privacy may exist looks to whether a person has exhibited an actual expectation of privacy and the expectation is one that society is prepared to recognize as "reasonable."

In *Katz v. United States,* the United States said that "the person's
general right to privacy—his right to be let alone by other people—
is like the protection of his property and of his very life, left largely
to the law of the individual states." This is why the privacy of
library records is addressed in state law or in the opinions of state
attorneys general.

Librarians must act in ways that foster the confidence of library
users that information about their library use will be kept confidential. Failure to do this may eventually erode the expectation of privacy in the library to the point that society no longer recognizes this
expectation as reasonable. At that point, the legal basis for the confidentiality of library records could be threatened.

More information on this topic, including privacy concerns
raised by the use of radio frequency identification (RFID) technol-
ogy in libraries, can be found in "Privacy and Confidentiality in
Libraries" (part 4, section 4). Frequently updated information on
this topic is available on the OIF website, including Questions and
Answers about Privacy and Confidentiality and Privacy Tool Kit.
These and other related resources may be found at http://www.ala
.org/ala/oif/statementspols/privacypages.html. See also the ALA
Washington Office website, http://www.ala.org/ala/washoff/
WOissues/issues.htm#govinfo.

Access to Government Information

Access to government information is fundamental to democracy. Legitimacy requires informed consent of the governed and an informed populace. This idea is firmly rooted in the history of the United States. The framers of the Constitution intended that government should operate in secret only "when it would be fatal and pernicious to publish the schemes of government."[2]

Libraries are the means by which all individuals in this country have free access to information produced by the government. When access to government information is restricted or removed, libraries are unable to accomplish this very important aspect of their mission. Federal and state document depository systems as well as freedom of information laws provide the means for libraries to acquire the publications and reference information necessary to provide library users with government information.

In response to national security concerns, all levels of government have taken actions to restrict access to information of possible use to terrorists, radically shifting the balance between the public's need to access government information and national security concerns. Types of information upon which restrictions have been placed include critical infrastructure information, "sensitive but unclassified" information, and presidential records. In addition, the federal government has become increasingly resistant to responding to Freedom of Information requests. For more about concerns related to government information, see http://www.ala.org/ala/washoff/WOissues/governmentinfo/improvingaccess.htm#posit.

NOTES

1. Specifically, CIPA requires that the blocking or filtering technology must protect access for both adults and minors to visual depictions that are obscene or child pornography and for minors (not yet seventeen years of age) to visual depictions that are harmful to minors.
2. J. Marshall, *Debates in the Several State Conventions on the Adoption of the Federal Constitution* . . . , vol. 3, revised and arranged by Jonathan Elliot (Philadelphia: J.B. Lippincott, 1901), 233.

PART II

Library Bill of Rights

I

Library Bill of Rights
The Policy

The American Library Association affirms that all libraries are forums for information and ideas, and that the following basic policies should guide their services.

I. Books and other library resources should be provided for the interest, information, and enlightenment of all people of the community the library serves. Materials should not be excluded because of the origin, background, or views of those contributing to their creation.

II. Libraries should provide materials and information presenting all points of view on current and historical issues. Materials should not be proscribed or removed because of partisan or doctrinal disapproval.

III. Libraries should challenge censorship in the fulfillment of their responsibility to provide information and enlightenment.

IV. Libraries should cooperate with all persons and groups concerned with resisting abridgment of free expression and free access to ideas.

V. A person's right to use a library should not be denied or abridged because of origin, age, background, or views.

VI. Libraries which make exhibit spaces and meeting rooms available to the public they serve should make such facilities available on an equitable basis, regardless of the beliefs or affiliations of individuals or groups requesting their use.

Adopted June 18, 1948, by the ALA Council; amended February 2, 1961; June 27, 1967; January 23, 1980; inclusion of "age" reaffirmed January 23, 1996. http://www.ala.org/ala/oif/statementspols/statementsif/librarybillrights.htm.

HISTORY

Library Bill of Rights

The *Library Bill of Rights* constitutes the American Library Association's basic policy on intellectual freedom. The document derives from a statement originally developed by Forrest Spaulding, librarian of the Des Moines Public Library, and adopted by that library on November 21, 1938, as the *Library's Bill of Rights*:

> Now when indications in many parts of the world point to growing intolerance, suppression of free speech, and censorship, affecting the rights of minorities and individuals, the Board of Trustees of the Des Moines Public Library reaffirms these basic policies governing a free public library to serve the best interests of Des Moines and its citizens.
>
> I. Books and other reading matter selected for purchase from public funds shall be chosen from the standpoint of value and interest to the people of Des Moines, and in no case shall selection be based on the race or nationality, political, or religious views of the writers.
>
> II. As far as available material permits, all sides of controversial questions shall be represented equally in the selection of books on subjects about which differences of opinion exist.
>
> III. Official publications and/or propaganda of organized religious, political, fraternal, class, or regional sects, societies, or similar groups, and of institutions controlled

by such, are solicited as gifts and will be made available
to library users without discrimination. This policy is
made necessary because of the meager funds available
for the purchase of books and reading matter. It is obvi-
ously impossible to purchase the publications of all such
groups and it would be unjust discrimination to purchase those of some and not of others.

   IV. Library meeting rooms shall be available on equal
terms to all organized nonprofit groups for open meetings to which no admission fee is charged and from
which no one is excluded.

The document approved by the ALA Council at the 1939
Annual Conference in San Francisco as the *Library's Bill of Rights*
retained the spirit of the Des Moines Public Library policy but differed from the original in several respects. The principal differences
concerned Articles II, III, and IV of the Des Moines policy. In Article
II, reference to equal representation "in the selection of books on
subjects about which differences of opinion exist" was changed to
"fair and adequate" representation. This change recognized the
impossibility of equal representation in terms of numbers of vol-
umes on a particular subject. Article III of the Des Moines policy
was completely deleted because it dealt with the individual budget,
needs, and purposes of a specific library. As such, it was inappropriate for a document to be applied nationwide.

   Article IV of the Des Moines policy, concerning the use of
library meeting rooms, was revised extensively before approval by
the Council. An introductory phrase establishing the library as "an
institution to educate for democratic living" was added, and references to "nonprofit groups" and "admission fee" were deleted. The
resulting article broadened the sense of the original by stating that
library meeting rooms be available "on equal terms to all groups in
the community regardless of their beliefs or affiliations." As
adopted by the ALA Council, the revised *Library's Bill of Rights* read
as follows:

   Today indications in many parts of the world point to
   growing intolerance, suppression of free speech, and censorship affecting the rights of minorities and individuals.
   Mindful of this, the Council of the American Library

Association publicly affirms its belief in the following basic policies which should govern the services of free public libraries.

I. Books and other reading matter selected for purchase from the public funds should be chosen because of value and interest to people of the community, and in no case should the selection be influenced by the race or nationality or the political or religious views of the writers.

II. As far as available material permits, all sides of questions on which differences of opinion exist should be represented fairly and adequately in the books and other reading matter purchased for public use.

III. The library as an institution to educate for democratic living should especially welcome the use of its meeting rooms for socially useful and cultural activities and the discussion of current public questions. Library meeting rooms should be available on equal terms to all groups in the community regardless of their beliefs or affiliations.

The three-point declaration approved by the Council was recommended by the Association to governing boards of individual libraries for adoption. ALA could not force individual librarians and boards to take specific action, but this policy statement, as all other Association recommendations and statements, provided a guide.

For five years, the *Library's Bill of Rights* stood without change. In 1944, the Intellectual Freedom Committee, chaired by Leon Carnovsky, recommended that Article I of the document be amended to include the statement "Further, books believed to be factually correct should not be banned or removed from the library simply because they are disapproved of by some people." Approved by the ALA Council on October 14, 1944, the amendment proclaimed for the first time the Association's position regarding the banning or removal of materials. The addition, however, also introduced the phrase "factually correct," which was later to be a source of controversy, debate, and change.

Four years later, with David K. Berninghausen as chair, the Intellectual Freedom Committee recommended a broad revision of the *Library's Bill of Rights* and called for a considerable expansion of the document's scope. Its introductory passage was pared to a precise statement of the Association's purpose: "The Council of the American Library Association reaffirms its belief in the following basic policies which should govern the services of all libraries." By 1948, there was no longer the pre–World War II need to point out "growing intolerance, suppression of free speech, and censorship affecting the rights of minorities and individuals." In the developing cold war, those factors justifying the 1939 policy were even more evident, and it was recognized that the remedies stated in the *Library's Bill of Rights* were necessary to protect free library service in times of peace as well as of crisis.

Article I was prefaced by the phrase "As a responsibility of library service." Intellectual freedom was thus clearly related to the process of materials selection and, moreover, highlighted by being designated a "responsibility." Reference to purchase from the public funds was deleted, thereby extending application of the policy to all library materials, not just those acquired through purchase. Whereas the 1939 document stated that selection should not be influenced by the race, nationality, or political or religious views of writers, the revision more explicitly said that no materials by any authors should be excluded on those grounds.

The first part of Article II was changed to effect a smoother reading, but there were no substantive alterations. However, the 1944 amendment concerning "books believed to be factually correct" was changed to "books . . . of sound factual authority" and the word "banned" was replaced by "proscribed." Despite their seeming slightness, these subtle changes in the second part of the article actually enlarged the scope of the policy.

A totally new Article III recognized the need of libraries to challenge "censorship of books urged or practiced by volunteer arbiters of morals or political opinion or by organizations that would establish a coercive concept of Americanism." A new Article IV recognized the libraries' responsibility to cooperate with "allied groups . . . in science, education, and book publishing in resisting all abridgment of the free access to ideas and full freedom of expression." Article III of the 1939 document, concerning the use of library meeting rooms, became Article V of the new policy. Although the wording was altered, no change was made in the intent.

The entire recommended revision was adopted by the ALA Council on June 18, 1948. In effect, it was a completely different document from its predecessor, the 1939 bill. The new bill's scope and possible applications were broadly expanded, establishing its national significance. For the first time, the policy mentioned censorship, and also for the first time, the Association declared the responsibility of libraries to challenge censorship—alone and with allied organizations. As adopted by the Council, the newly entitled *Library Bill of Rights* read as follows:

> The Council of the American Library Association reaffirms its belief in the following basic policies which should govern the services of all libraries.
>
> I. As a responsibility of library service, books and other reading matter selected should be chosen for values of interest, information and enlightenment of all the people of the community. In no case should any material be excluded because of race or nationality, or the political or religious views of the writer.
>
> II. There should be the fullest practicable provision of material presenting all points of view concerning the problems and issues of our times, international, national, and local; and books or other reading matter of sound factual authority should not be proscribed or removed from library shelves because of partisan or doctrinal disapproval.
>
> III. Censorship of books, urged or practiced by volunteer arbiters of morals or political opinion or by organizations that would establish a coercive concept of Americanism, must be challenged by libraries in maintenance of their responsibility to provide public information and enlightenment through the printed word.
>
> IV. Libraries should enlist the cooperation of allied groups in the fields of science, of education, and of book publishing in resisting all abridgment of the free access to ideas and full freedom of expression that are the tradition and heritage of Americans.
>
> V. As an institution of education for democratic living, the library should welcome the use of its meeting rooms

for socially useful and cultural activities and discussion of current public questions. Such meeting places should be available on equal terms to all groups in the community regardless of the beliefs and affiliations of their members.

Although the text of the 1948 document remained unchanged until 1961, its application was broadened in 1951. On the recommendation of the Intellectual Freedom Committee, with the endorsement of the Audio-Visual Board, the Council unanimously resolved that "the *Library Bill of Rights* shall be interpreted as applying to all materials and media of communication used or collected by libraries." The statement, appended as a footnote to all printings of the *Library Bill of Rights* until June 27, 1967, resulted from a Peoria, Illinois, case of attempted censorship by the American Legion and a local newspaper. The Peoria Public Library was pressured to remove the films *The Brotherhood of Man*, *Boundary Lines*, and *Peoples of the U.S.S.R.* All three films appeared on the ALA Audio-Visual Committee's 1947 list of films suggested for purchase by small libraries. The Educational Film Library Association urged ALA to combat censorship of library film collections, but some librarians contended that the *Library Bill of Rights* applied only to print on paper. The Council resolved the problem by its action of February 3, 1951. That same year, in response to efforts to suppress allegedly subversive publications, the Council also adopted the first interpretive statement on the *Library Bill of Rights*, the "Statement on Labeling" (renamed "Labels and Rating Systems" in 2005). Additional interpretive statements on a wide variety of issues were to follow in subsequent years (see part 2, section 2).

In 1961, another major addition to the *Library Bill of Rights* was approved by the Council. From 1948 through February 1961, the library profession had studied the problem of segregation in libraries. A study made by the Association's Special Committee on Civil Liberties recommended that a new article be added to the *Library Bill of Rights* stating that "the rights of an individual to the use of a library should not be denied or abridged because of his race, religion, national origins, or political views." The recommendation was approved by the Council on February 2, 1961. The new statement became Article V, and the old Article V, concerning use of meeting rooms, became Article VI. The revised *Library Bill of Rights* read as follows:

> The Council of the American Library Association reaffirms its belief in the following basic policies which should govern the services of all libraries.
>
> I. As a responsibility of library service, books and other reading matter selected should be chosen for values of interest, information and enlightenment of all the people of the community. In no case should any book be excluded because of the race or nationality or the political or religious views of the writer.
>
> II. There should be the fullest practicable provision of material presenting all points of view concerning the problems and issues of our times, international, national, and local; and books or other reading matter of sound factual authority should not be proscribed or removed from library shelves because of partisan or doctrinal disapproval.
>
> III. Censorship of books, urged or practiced by volunteer arbiters of morals or political opinion or by organizations that would establish a coercive concept of Americanism, must be challenged by libraries in maintenance of their responsibility to provide public information and enlightenment through the printed word.
>
> IV. Libraries should enlist the cooperation of allied groups in the fields of science, of education, and of book publishing in resisting all abridgment of the free access to ideas and full freedom of expression that are the tradition and heritage of Americans.
>
> V. The rights of an individual to the use of a library should not be denied or abridged because of his race, religion, national origins or political views.
>
> VI. As an institution of education for democratic living, the library should welcome the use of its meeting rooms for socially useful and cultural activities and discussion of current public questions. Such meeting places should be available on equal terms to all groups in the community regardless of the beliefs and affiliations of their members.

By official action of the Council on February 3, 1951,
the "Library Bill of Rights" shall be interpreted to apply
to all materials and media of communication used or collected by libraries.

On June 27, 1967, almost thirty years after its origin, the *Library
Bill of Rights* underwent its second thorough revision. The need for
change was made explicit during a special preconference, sponsored by the Intellectual Freedom Committee with Ervin Gaines as
chair, held prior to the 1965 Midwinter Meeting in Washington, D.C.
The primary target in the text was the phrase "of sound factual
authority," introduced into Article I in 1944, and revised and trans-
ferred to Article II in 1948. Criticism of the phrase arose when a
librarian in Belleville, Illinois, used it to exclude a Protestant publication that he, being Catholic, described as lacking "sound factual
authority."

In their discussion of the Belleville situation, the preconference
participants determined that some of the most profound and influ-
ential publications in our culture lack the element of "sound factual
authority" and that the phrase itself could easily be abused to
thwart the intent and purpose of the *Library Bill of Rights*. It was
apparent that the phrase also could effectively hold the Association
from defending fiction or any of those great works that start from
philosophical premises but have nothing to do with fact.

Along with recommending that the troublesome phrase be
dropped, the Intellectual Freedom Committee asked that several
other textual changes be made. In Articles I and V, the Committee
suggested adding the word "social" because of the far-reaching
results of the civil rights movement. In Article IV, the Committee
recommended eliminating the phrase "that are the tradition and
heritage of Americans" because it was both redundant and nation-
alistic. The Committee further recommended that the reference in
Article IV be expanded beyond the groups in science, education,
and book publishing to reflect the wider context in which librarians
and the Association actually operated.

It was also recommended that Article VI, concerning the use of
meeting rooms, be amended to include the phrase "provided that
the meetings be open to the public." This amendment clarified the
Association's position regarding the use of library meeting rooms

by private groups with restricted attendance. The enlarged scope of the text led the IFC to recommend that "library materials" be substituted for "reading matter," thus making the footnote of 1951 regarding nonprint materials unnecessary.

By the time the Intellectual Freedom Committee's proposed changes came before the Council in 1967, a preconference on intellectual freedom and the teenager had recommended that young people be given free access to all books in a library collection. Accordingly, the Committee included with its previous suggestions the recommendation that Article V include the word "age."

On June 28, 1967, the Council adopted all of the Intellectual Freedom Committee's recommendations. The revision was a statement very different from its 1939 progenitor. Whereas the original document concerned itself primarily with unbiased book selection, a balanced collection, and open meeting rooms, the new version went much further. It recognized that censorship of any materials and in any guise eventually *affects* the library. It therefore provided libraries with principles for opposing censorship and promoting intellectual freedom in the broadest sense. The 1967 revision of the *Library Bill of Rights* read as follows:

> The Council of the American Library Association reaffirms its belief in the following basic policies which should govern the services of all libraries.
>
> I. As a responsibility of library service, books and other library materials selected should be chosen for values of interest, information and enlightenment of all the people of the community. In no case should library materials be excluded because of the race or nationality or the social, political, or religious views of the authors.
>
> II. Libraries should provide books and other materials presenting all points of view concerning the problems and issues of our times; no library materials should be proscribed or removed from libraries because of partisan or doctrinal disapproval.
>
> III. Censorship should be challenged by libraries in the maintenance of their responsibility to provide public information and enlightenment.

IV. Libraries should cooperate with all persons and groups concerned with resisting abridgment of free expression and free access to ideas.

V. The rights of an individual to the use of a library should not be denied or abridged because of his age, race, religion, national origins or social or political views.

VI. As an institution of education for democratic living, the library should welcome the use of its meeting rooms for socially useful and cultural activities and discussion of current public questions. Such meeting places should be available on equal terms to all groups in the community regardless of the beliefs and affiliations of their members, provided that the meetings be open to the public.

Yet the document, though thoroughly refined, was still not above criticism. During the following decade, questions were raised about its silence with respect to sex discrimination and institutional censorship in college and research libraries, while its unqualified references to "the community" and to "public" meeting rooms made it appear as a document for public libraries only. Moreover, the profound changes in American society that took place in the late 1960s and early 1970s virtually mandated further changes. Hence, in January 1980, the *Library Bill of Rights* underwent a third major revision, the product of nearly three years of careful review.

The initial impetus for revision came in 1977 with a request from the Committee on the Status of Women in Librarianship that the *Library Bill of Rights* be revised to reject sex discrimination in library services and to eliminate sex-linked pronoun usage from the document itself, which the Intellectual Freedom Committee agreed to act upon as part of an overall reassessment of the document. The subsequent review process involved unprecedented, broad participation from all sectors of the library community.

At the 1978 Midwinter Meeting, the Intellectual Freedom Committee asked a subcommittee of its own members to prepare a new draft. At the 1978 Annual Conference, the Committee received a report from the subcommittee and conducted a membership hearing on the revision process. At the 1979 Midwinter Meeting, a draft *Library Bill of Rights* was approved for distribution and sent for comment to all ALA councilors, divisions, round tables, and committees, and to all chapter intellectual freedom committees, journals, and bulletins. The draft was also published in the national library press. Comments received were then reviewed at the 1979 Annual Conference, where the Committee also held another open hearing. Shortly after the close of this conference, a new draft was approved by mail and circulated by the IFC to all councilors and ALA units and the library press. Final comments were reviewed by the Committee at the 1980 Midwinter Meeting, where Frances C. Dean, its chair, submitted the final revision to the Council.

In addition to eliminating the use of sex-linked pronouns, the Committee recommended revision of the preamble to state explicitly the role of libraries in maintaining intellectual freedom. Libraries are described in the revision as "forums for information and ideas," employing the word "forum" to indicate that the library should be open to any opinion or view. During discussion of this revision, it was suggested that the library be defined as in Article VI, as "an institution of education for democratic living." This formulation was rejected because it could imply support for the idea that libraries should censor all materials that it deems antidemocratic.

"Democracy," strictly speaking, means "rule by the majority." From the standpoint of intellectual freedom, the library's role in our society is not based on the principle of majority rule but on the principle embodied in the First Amendment, that minority points of view have a right to be heard, no matter how unpopular with, or even detested by, the majority.

In Article I, the Intellectual Freedom Committee recommended the elimination of verbiage that seemed to detract from clarity and simplicity of expression, and the modification of the word "community" to read "the community the library serves," inasmuch as many libraries serve a special public, such as a specific academic or school community. The Committee further recommended replacing the word "author" with the phrase "those contributing to their creation" because the originators of many library materials are today referred to by other terms.

In Article II, the Committee recommended adding that libraries have an obligation to provide information and diverse points of view on historical as well as current issues. In Article III, stylistic changes, as well as elimination of the modifier "public," were suggested. The meaning of "public" in the article's context placed an obligation on nonpublic libraries that such libraries insist they do not have.

The revision of Article V was marked by considerable debate about whether a general statement affirming the rights of all individuals to library use could serve the same function as a more detailed list of all those specific conditions or factors that might lead to infringement of this right. Considering that explicitly designating one or more factors as discriminatory might risk excluding other grounds not specifically mentioned, either by oversight or by inability to predict the future, and judging the so-called laundry list approach to be stylistically unwieldy, the Committee recommended instead a general statement condemning discrimination according to origin, background, or views. The Committee recommended, however, retaining specific reference to age, because a suitable generic term that would readily be recognized as inclusive of this factor could not be found.

Finally, Article VI was revised to take into account differences among types of libraries and to eliminate any implication that libraries might censor materials and exclude programs on the grounds that they contain antidemocratic ideas or are not socially useful. The revision laid firm emphasis on the principle of equitable and nondiscriminatory application of rules and regulations governing meeting rooms and exhibit space while permitting libraries broad flexibility in formulating such rules and regulations according to the dictates of their widely varied situations.

On January 23, 1980, the Council adopted the recommendations of the Intellectual Freedom Committee. The resulting document constitutes the present *Library Bill of Rights*.

At the 1988 Annual Conference, the Minority Concerns Committee recommended, and the Council approved, that "the *Library Bill of Rights* be reviewed to include the concepts of freedom of access to information and libraries without limitation by language or economic status." During its initial review of this Council action at the 1989 Midwinter Meeting, the Intellectual Freedom Committee suggested that a revision of the Interpretations be undertaken first to address explicitly and immediately the issues raised by the Minority Concerns Committee. The *Library Bill of Rights* would then be reassessed in light of the revised Interpretations. Thus began a review process that resulted in the reworking of all but one of the then-extant Interpretations and the addition of a new Interpretation: "The Universal Right to Free Expression" (see part 2, section 2.18).

During the process of reviewing the Interpretations, concerns regarding gender and sexual orientation also were brought to the attention of the Committee. When review of the existing Interpretations was complete, the Intellectual Freedom Committee considered the *Library Bill of Rights* itself in light of the revised Interpretations and the request of the Minority Concerns Committee. The IFC concluded not only that revision of the basic document was unnecessary but also that it would be unwise to open a document that had stood the test of time to the laundry-list approach. To address concerns relating to economic status and fees for library service, the Committee recommended adoption of a new Interpretation, "Economic Barriers to Information Access." To address the issues of equity of service and access and representation in the collection for gays, bisexuals, and lesbians, which had been raised during the process of review, the Committee recommended adoption of another new Interpretation, "Access to Library Resources and Services Regardless of Gender or Sexual Orientation." The new Interpretations were adopted by the ALA Council in 1993.

As a further response to concerns that the wording of the *Library Bill of Rights* may be interpreted to exclude groups of individuals not specifically mentioned, the Committee adopted the following statement:

> In the *Library Bill of Rights* and all of its Interpretations, it is intended that: "origin" encompasses all the characteristics of individuals that are inherent in the circumstances of their birth; "age" encompasses all the characteristics of individuals that are inherent in their levels of development and maturity; "background" encompasses all the characteristics of individuals that are a result of their life experiences; and "views" encompasses all the opinions and beliefs held and expressed by individuals.

In 1994, in response to a rapidly changing information environment and the need for guidance expressed by many librarians about how to apply the *Library Bill of Rights* to electronic access to information, the Committee began work on a new Interpretation called "Access to Electronic Information, Services, and Networks." As part of the development process, the Committee sponsored a hearing at the 1995 Midwinter Meeting in Philadelphia to receive testimony and observations from librarians working in different library settings on the issue of access to information via electronic means. Meeting in Chicago in March 1995, the IFC prepared a draft Interpretation that was circulated to all ALA units for comments. A revised draft was presented to the ALA Council at the 1995 Annual Conference in Chicago. After concerns were raised on the floor of Council about the effect of some of the language relating to fees and nondiscriminatory access, particularly in academic library settings, the draft was sent back to the IFC for additional consideration. A new version of the Interpretation was distributed prior to the 1996 Midwinter Meeting. The document was further refined at the 1996 Midwinter Meeting, and the Council adopted it on January 24, 1996.

During the discussion of the Interpretation it became clear that although there was general agreement that the *Library Bill of Rights* and its Interpretations apply to the provision of access to electronic information, it is extremely difficult to produce a document that directly addresses each type of library and library service. As a result, the Office for Intellectual Freedom developed Questions and Answers: Access to Electronic Information, Services, and Networks: An Interpretation of the *Library Bill of Rights*, which was finalized in June 1997 (see part 2, section 2.2).

At the 1996 ALA Midwinter Meeting, the Board of Directors of the American Library Trustee Association (ALTA) voted to reaffirm the inclusion of "age" in the *Library Bill of Rights* because of challenges that might result in restricting access to libraries and library materials to children and young adults. The American Library Trustee Association brought a request to the Council to reaffirm the inclusion of "age." The motion was passed by the ALA Council on January 24, 1996, by acclamation.

The latter part of the twentieth century was marked by growing concerns about the erosion of personal privacy in light of advancing technology. ALA had consistently taken a strong stand on patron privacy, adopting the Policy on Confidentiality of Library Records in 1971 and the Policy concerning Confidentiality of Personally Identifiable Information about Library Users in 1991. To assist libraries in implementing these policies the IFC developed Suggested Procedures for Implementing "Policy on Confidentiality of Library Records" (1983) and Guidelines for Developing a Library Privacy Policy (2003).

At the 1999 Annual Conference, ALA Council resolved that the Library and Information Technology Association be asked to examine the impact of new technologies on patron privacy and the confidentiality of electronic records. The Task Force on Privacy and Confidentiality in the Electronic Environment was formed at the 2000 Midwinter Conference, with broad participation from across ALA.

In July 2000, ALA Council approved the Final Report of the Task Force on Privacy and Confidentiality in the Electronic Environment and referred it to the IFC for review. The recommendations contained therein were

> that ALA revise its policy statements related to "Confidentiality of Library Records" (rev. 1986), and "Concerning Confidentiality of Personally Identifiable Information about Library Users" (1991), in order to specifically and appropriately incorporate Internet privacy;
>
> that ALA develop model privacy policies, instructional materials, and privacy "best practices" documents for libraries; and
>
> that ALA urge that all libraries adopt a privacy statement on web pages and post privacy policies in the library which cover the issues of privacy in Internet use as accessed through the library's services.

In its report to Council, the IFC responded to this referral by saying, "The Intellectual Freedom Committee gladly accepts Council's charge to review the recommendations. IFC has been reviewing and will continue to monitor the appropriateness of all ALA policies regarding privacy and confidentiality and will address all three recommendations in our Midwinter Meeting report to Council."

At the 2001 ALA Midwinter Meeting, the IFC established a standing Privacy Subcommittee, which was charged to monitor ongoing privacy developments in technology, politics, and legislation and to identify needs and resources for librarians and library users.

At its 2001 spring meeting, the IFC returned to Council's original request to consider developing an Interpretation of the *Library Bill of Rights* on privacy. Initial work began on a draft Interpretation at that time and continued through the 2001 Annual Conference and the Committee's 2001 fall meeting. In its deliberations, the Committee members thought carefully about the implications of the events of September 11, 2001, on privacy issues. They sought to develop the Interpretation for lasting impact, knowing that privacy had been of importance to libraries prior to those events.

The ALA Council adopted "Privacy: An Interpretation of the *Library Bill of Rights*" on June 19, 2002, at the ALA Annual Conference in Atlanta, Georgia. Recognizing the complexity of the issues related to privacy and confidentiality in libraries, the IFC also developed Questions and Answers on Privacy and Confidentiality for local libraries to use when they are developing their own privacy policies.

Although there is little doubt that future developments will mandate yet further revision or the development of additional interpretive statements, the *Library Bill of Rights* is by no means a product of hasty work, and as its history proves, it remains a vibrant statement of principle and a useful guide to action for librarians in all library settings.

2

Library Bill of Rights
Intrepretations

Although the articles of the *Library Bill of Rights* are unambiguous statements of basic principles that should govern the service of all libraries, questions do arise concerning application of these principles to specific library practices. For example, a 1951 Peoria, Illinois, case involving certain films in the public library required the Association to clarify the application of the *Library Bill of Rights* to nonprint materials. A recommendation by the Intellectual Freedom Committee and the Audio-Visual Board resulted in the ALA Council's adding an interpretive footnote explaining that the *Library Bill of Rights* applies to all materials and media of communication used or collected by libraries.

During the 1971 Annual Conference in Dallas, the Intellectual Freedom Committee considered censorship cases that clearly called for interpretations of the *Library Bill of Rights* to define its application to certain practices. Believing that frequent revisions, amendments, or additions of footnotes weaken the document's effectiveness, the Committee resolved instead to develop statements to be called Interpretations of the *Library Bill of Rights*. The Committee said further that certain documents already in existence should be designated Interpretations of the *Library Bill of Rights*.

After the Council adopted the 1980 revision of the *Library Bill of Rights*, the Intellectual Freedom Committee undertook the first systematic review of all the Interpretations. The initial purpose of this review was to make all policies consistent with both the letter and the spirit of the revised *Library Bill of Rights*. As the process developed, however, the goals became more sweeping. Important gaps in policy were filled, and, taken as a group, the Interpretations were remolded into a unified general guide to application of the *Library Bill of Rights*. Not only were most policies thoroughly rewritten or amended, but also new Interpretations were formulated and outdated or inadequate material eliminated. As with the 1980 revision of the *Library Bill of Rights*, the IFC sought and received extensive comments from ALA councilors, units, and chapters to whom all drafts were circulated. The process of revision was completed at the 1982 Annual Conference in Philadelphia.

In response to a 1988 Minority Concerns Committee report recommending a revision of the *Library Bill of Rights* to ensure protection against discrimination in library services based on language or economic status, the Intellectual Freedom Committee began the second comprehensive review of the Interpretations. The IFC agreed that each Interpretation would be considered separately and recommended to the Council for adoption upon completion of any necessary revisions. The process resulted in the revision of all but one Interpretation; the addition of two new Interpretations, "The Universal Right to Free Expression" and "Economic Barriers to Information Access"; and the rescission of an Interpretation no longer deemed relevant. Indirectly, the process spurred the development of two other new Interpretations, "Access to Library Resources and Services regardless of Gender or Sexual Orientation" and "Access to Electronic Information, Services, and Networks."

In line with the ongoing practice of periodic review, the IFC carefully reviewed all of the Interpretations in 1999–2000, especially in regard to the applicability to the Internet. As a result of the review, Council approved updates to three Interpretations: "Access to Library Resources and Services regardless of Gender or Sexual Orientation," "Library-Initiated Programs as a Resource," and "Restricted Access to Library Materials."

At the 2003 Midwinter Meeting, the IFC began a review of the Interpretation "Meeting Rooms" in light of controversy involving the use of library meeting rooms by the white-supremacist group World Church of the Creator. After this review, which included an open forum at the 2003 Annual Conference, the IFC determined that the ALA policy remained a strong statement of professional commitment that needed no changes.

At their spring 2004 meeting, the IFC initiated a review of all *Library Bill of Rights* Interpretations as well as the various policies, guidelines, and statements that are included in the *Intellectual Freedom Manual*. The Committee identified eight Interpretations and three policies for revision. Seven Interpretations and one policy were edited for grammar and the accuracy of references.

During its work on the Interpretations and policies identified for revision the Committee reviewed each one to ensure that it begins and ends with strength and clarity, that the first and last paragraphs support each other, that the order of the paragraphs makes sense and reflects relative importance, and that the entire document supports the library profession's philosophy and principles of intellectual freedom. In addition, the Committee attempted to use language that is both specific enough to be practical and general enough to avoid being immediately outdated. Committee members agreed to continue to develop and update guidelines and question-and-answer documents to address the more rapidly changing aspects of intellectual freedom issues.

In response to concerns about the impact of the digital divide on access to information, the Committee expanded "equal access" to "equal and equitable access" whenever it was appropriate to do so. When asked to explain this change, Committee chair Nancy Kranich provided an example of the importance of including both terms:

> The SEC [Securities Exchange Commission] had one reading room in the old days to read all those filings. Everyone had *equal* access to the reading room in New York City, but it wasn't *equitable* access for those who had to pay to come to New York City. It is important to include *equitable* because *equal* is not about the digital divide and *equitable* is; it is crucial to remind people that the digital divide still exists.

At the 2004 Annual Conference, after circulating proposed changes to ALA units, liaisons, and chapters, and discussing all comments received, the IFC presented Council with recommendations for changes in the following Interpretations and policies:

- The title "Access for Children and Young People to Videotapes and Other Nonprint Formats" was changed to "Access for Children and Young Adults to Nonprint Materials" to keep the Interpretation from becoming outdated as a result of technology and terminology changes.

- The title "Access to Library Resources and Services regardless of Gender or Sexual Orientation" was changed to "Access to Library Resources and Services regardless of Sex, Gender Identity, or Sexual Orientation" to more accurately describe the applicability of the Interpretation. Appropriate passages in the Interpretation were revised to reflect this change.

- "Exhibit Spaces and Bulletin Boards" was changed for clarity concerning the option of limiting the use of space to library-related activities.

- "Free Access to Libraries for Minors," concerning the rights of minors, was strengthened, including the addition of a reference to the legal basis for those rights. The section on the responsibility of parents was revised to include a statement from Libraries: An American Value.

- Policy on Governmental Intimidation was changed for inclusion and clarity.

- The Freedom to Read statement was changed to include censorship or suppression based on concerns about safety or national security. The word "citizens" was changed to "others," "individuals," or "Americans" as appropriate. In addition, two references to censors that were unnecessary for the message of the statement were removed.

- "Restricted Access to Library Materials" was edited for clarity and conciseness.

- A new first paragraph was added to Policy concerning Confidentiality of Personally Identifiable Information about Library Users. It consisted of the definitions of privacy and confidentiality from "Privacy: An Interpretation of the *Library Bill of Rights*." The remaining paragraphs were reordered for strength and clarity.

At the 2005 Midwinter Meeting, the IFC completed its review of policies by recommending to Council changes in the following Interpretations and policies:

- "Access to Electronic Information Services and Networks" was changed for clarity, logical organization, and consistency of terminology. References were added to support the right to receive information as a corollary right of freedom of speech and the right of minors to receive constitutionally protected information. Three new paragraphs were added to bring the Interpretation up-to-date.
- At the request of the AASL Board, throughout "Access to Resources and Services in the School Library Media Program," the term "school library media professional" was replaced with "school library media specialist." The description of the scope of collection resources was expanded from resources supporting the curriculum to include "materials that support the intellectual growth, personal development, individual interests, and recreational needs of students."
- The title of "Statement on Labeling" was changed to "Labels and Rating Systems," which more accurately reflects the scope of the Interpretation. Wording was added to distinguish between viewpoint-neutral directional aids and labels designed to prejudice attitudes or restrict access. The Committee acknowledged that many questions remain about how this Interpretation applies to the content of online library catalogs with enhanced content, including book jackets and access to book reviews and recommended reading lists. To answer these questions and others that may arise, the Committee agreed to develop a question-and-answer document.

Following are those documents designated by the Intellectual Freedom Committee as Interpretations of the *Library Bill of Rights*, along with background statements detailing the philosophy and history of each. For convenience and easy reference, the documents are presented in alphabetical order. These documents are policies of the American Library Association, having been adopted by the ALA Council.

2.1
Access for Children and Young Adults to Nonprint Materials

An Interpretation of the
Library Bill of Rights

Library collections of nonprint materials raise a number of intellectual freedom issues, especially regarding minors. Article V of the *Library Bill of Rights* states, "A person's right to use a library should not be denied or abridged because of origin, age, background, or views."

The American Library Association's principles protect minors' access to sound, images, data, games, software, and other content in all formats such as tapes, CDs, DVDs, music CDs, computer games, software, databases, and other emerging technologies. ALA's "Free Access to Libraries for Minors: An Interpretation of the *Library Bill of Rights*" states:

> The "right to use a library" includes free access to, and unrestricted use of, all the services, materials, and facilities the library has to offer. Every restriction on access to, and use of, library resources, based solely on the chronological age, educational level, literacy skills, or legal emancipation of users violates Article V.
>
> . . . [P]arents—and only parents—have the right and responsibility to restrict access of their children— and only their children—to library resources. Parents who do not want their children to have access to certain library services, materials, or facilities should so advise their children. Librarians and library governing

bodies cannot assume the role of parents or the functions of parental authority in the private relationship between parent and child.

Lack of access to information can be harmful to minors. Librarians and library governing bodies have a public and professional obligation to ensure that all members of the community they serve have free, equal, and equitable access to the entire range of library resources regardless of content, approach, format, or amount of detail. This principle of library service applies equally to all users, minors as well as adults. Librarians and library governing bodies must uphold this principle in order to provide adequate and effective service to minors.

Policies that set minimum age limits for access to any nonprint materials or information technology, with or without parental permission, abridge library use for minors. Age limits based on the cost of the materials are also unacceptable. Librarians, when dealing with minors, should apply the same standards to circulation of nonprint materials as are applied to books and other print materials except when directly and specifically prohibited by law.

Recognizing that librarians cannot act in loco parentis, ALA acknowledges and supports the exercise by parents of their responsibility to guide their own children's reading and viewing. Libraries should provide published reviews and/or reference works that contain information about the content, subject matter, and recommended audiences for nonprint materials. These resources will assist parents in guiding their children without implicating the library in censorship.

In some cases, commercial content ratings, such as the Motion Picture Association of America (MPAA) movie ratings, might appear on the packaging or promotional materials provided by producers or distributors. However, marking out or removing this information from materials or packaging constitutes expurgation or censorship.

MPAA movie ratings, Entertainment Software Rating Board (ESRB) game ratings, and other rating services are private advisory codes and have no legal standing ("Expurgation of Library

Materials"). For the library to add ratings to nonprint materials if they are not already there is unacceptable. It is also unacceptable to post a list of such ratings with a collection or to use them in circulation policies or other procedures. These uses constitute labeling, "an attempt to prejudice attitudes" ("Labels and Rating Systems"), and are forms of censorship. The application of locally generated ratings schemes intended to provide content warnings to library users is also inconsistent with the *Library Bill of Rights*.

The interests of young people, like those of adults, are not limited by subject, theme, or level of sophistication. Librarians have a responsibility to ensure young people's access to materials and services that reflect diversity of content and format sufficient to meet their needs.

Adopted June 28, 1989, by the ALA Council; amended June 30, 2004.
http://www.ala.org/Template.cfm?Section=interpretations&Template=/
ContentManagement/ContentDisplay.cfm&ContentID=89578.

HISTORY

Access for Children and Young Adults to Nonprint Materials

In January 1989, the IFC examined the Interpretation "Circulation of Motion Pictures and Video Productions" in response to urgings from the ALA youth divisions and to the Minority Concerns Committee's request for a review of the *Library Bill of Rights* to ensure that it provided for equitable access without regard to language or economic status. The IFC concluded that a new Interpretation was necessary to address fully the issue of minors' access to videos and to provide similar guarantees for nonprint materials resulting from new technologies.

The Committee also sought to provide clearer guidelines for librarians, emphasizing the importance of parent—not librarian—responsibility for guiding a child's viewing or choice of other library materials, opposing the use of cost-based restrictions to inhibit minors' access to materials, and rejecting the imposition of private rating systems and the unapproved editing of films or other copyright materials for classroom use.

The new draft Interpretation was presented to the Committee at the June 1989 ALA Annual Conference. After discussion with representatives from the youth divisions and the Professional Ethics Committee, which resulted in minor editorial changes, the Interpretation was adopted and recommended to the Council. On June 28, 1989, the Council adopted "Access for Children and Young People to Videotapes and Other Nonprint Formats" in place of the former "Circulation of Motion Pictures and Video Productions." The latter was then rescinded by the Council.

As part of the periodic review of all of the Interpretations, this Interpretation was reviewed by the IFC in 1999–2000. No changes were recommended.

As part of the 2004–5 review of Interpretations the title was changed to "Access for Children and Young Adults to Nonprint Materials" to be inclusive of current as well as future changes in formats for nonprint materials. The Interpretation was edited for clarity and grammar, and the second paragraph was moved to the end to strengthen the statement. In light of repetitive federal and state efforts to enact legislation restricting minors' access to the Internet and video games as well as a continuing stream of challenges to materials for children and young adults in both public and school libraries, a new paragraph was added:

> Lack of access to information can be harmful to minors. Librarians and library governing bodies have a public and professional obligation to ensure that all members of the community they serve have free, equal, and equitable access to the entire range of library resources regardless of content, approach, format, or amount of detail. This principle of library service applies equally to all users, minors as well as adults. Librarians and library governing bodies must uphold this principle in order to provide adequate and effective service to minors.

The statement that lack of access to information can be harmful to minors was inspired by Judge Posner's defense of minors' First Amendment rights in *American Amusements Machine v. Kendrick*:

> Now that eighteen-year-olds have the right to vote, it is obvious that they must be allowed the freedom to form their political views on the basis of uncensored speech before they turn eighteen, so that their minds are not a blank when they first exercise the franchise. And since an eighteen-year-old's right to vote is a right personal to him rather than a right to be exercised on his behalf by his parents, the right of parents to enlist the aid of the state to shield their children from ideas of which the parents disapprove cannot be plenary either. People are unlikely to become well-functioning, independent

minded adults and responsible citizens if they are raised in an intellectual bubble.

[Shielding] children right up to the age of 18 from exposure to violent descriptions and images would not only be quixotic, but deforming; it would leave them unequipped to cope with the world as we know it. Maybe video games are different. They are, after all, interactive. But this point is superficial, in fact erroneous. All literature (here broadly defined to include movies, television, and the other photographic media, and popular as well as highbrow literature) is interactive; the better it is, the more interactive.

2.2
Access to Electronic Information, Services, and Networks

An Interpretation of the
Library Bill of Rights

Introduction

Freedom of expression is an inalienable human right and the foundation for self-government. Freedom of expression encompasses the freedom of speech and the corollary right to receive information.* Libraries and librarians protect and promote these rights by selecting, producing, providing access to, identifying, retrieving, organizing, providing instruction in the use of, and preserving recorded expression regardless of the format or technology.

The American Library Association expresses these basic principles of librarianship in its Code of Ethics and in the *Library Bill of Rights* and its Interpretations. These serve to guide librarians and library governing bodies in addressing issues of intellectual freedom that arise when the library provides access to electronic information, services, and networks.

Libraries empower users by providing access to the broadest range of information. Electronic resources, including information available via the Internet, allow libraries to fulfill this responsibility better than ever before.

Issues arising from digital generation, distribution, and retrieval of information need to be approached and regularly

---

* *Martin v. Struthers*, 319 U.S. 141 (1943); *Lamont v. Postmaster General*, 381 U.S. 301 (1965); Susan Nevelow Mart, "The Right to Receive Information," 95 *Law Library Journal* 2 (2003).

reviewed from a context of constitutional principles and ALA policies so that fundamental and traditional tenets of librarianship are not swept away.

Electronic information flows across boundaries and barriers despite attempts by individuals, governments, and private entities to channel or control it. Even so, many people lack access or capability to use electronic information effectively.

In making decisions about how to offer access to electronic information, each library should consider its mission, goals, objectives, cooperative agreements, and the needs of the entire community it serves.

The Rights of Users

All library system and network policies, procedures, or regulations relating to electronic information and services should be scrutinized for potential violation of user rights.

User policies should be developed according to the policies and guidelines established by the American Library Association, including Guidelines for the Development and Implementation of Policies, Regulations and Procedures Affecting Access to Library Materials, Services and Facilities.

Users' access should not be restricted or denied for expressing or receiving constitutionally protected speech. If access is restricted or denied for behavioral or other reasons, users should be provided due process, including, but not limited to, formal notice and a means of appeal.

Information retrieved or utilized electronically is constitutionally protected unless determined otherwise by a court of law with appropriate jurisdiction. These rights extend to minors as well as adults (Free Access to Libraries for Minors; Access to Resources and Services in the School Library Media Program; Access for Children and Young People to Videotapes and Other Nonprint Formats).*

---

* *Tinker v. Des Moines Independent Community School District*, 393 U.S. 503 (1969); *Board of Education, Island Trees Union Free School District No. 26 v. Pico*, 457 U.S. 853, (1982); *American Amusement Machine Association v. Teri Kendrick*, 244 F.3d 954 (7th Cir. 2001), *cert. denied*, 534 U.S. 994 (2001).

Libraries should use technology to enhance, not deny, access to information. Users have the right to be free of unreasonable limitations or conditions set by libraries, librarians, system administrators, vendors, network service providers, or others. Contracts, agreements, and licenses entered into by libraries on behalf of their users should not violate this right. Libraries should provide library users the training and assistance necessary to find, evaluate, and use information effectively.

Users have both the right of confidentiality and the right of privacy. The library should uphold these rights by policy, procedure, and practice in accordance with Privacy: An Interpretation of the *Library Bill of Rights*.

Equity of Access

The Internet provides expanding opportunities for everyone to participate in the information society, but too many individuals face serious barriers to access. Libraries play a critical role in bridging information access gaps for these individuals. Libraries also ensure that the public can find content of interest and learn the necessary skills to use information successfully.

Electronic information, services, and networks provided directly or indirectly by the library should be equally, readily and equitably accessible to all library users. American Library Association policies oppose the charging of user fees for the provision of information services by libraries that receive their major support from public funds (50.3 Free Access to Information; 53.1.14 Economic Barriers to Information Access; 60.1.1 Minority Concerns Policy Objectives; 61.1 Library Services for the Poor Policy Objectives). All libraries should develop policies concerning access to electronic information that are consistent with ALA's policy statements, including Economic Barriers to Information Access: An Interpretation of the *Library Bill of Rights*, Guidelines for the Development and Implementation of Policies, Regulations and Procedures Affecting Access to Library Materials, Services and Facilities, and Resolution on Access to the Use of Libraries and Information by Individuals with Physical or Mental Impairment.

Information Resources and Access

Providing connections to global information, services, and networks is not the same as selecting and purchasing materials for a library collection. Determining the accuracy or authenticity of electronic information may present special problems. Some information accessed electronically may not meet a library's selection or collection development policy. It is, therefore, left to each user to determine what is appropriate. Parents and legal guardians who are concerned about their children's use of electronic resources should provide guidance to their own children.

Libraries, acting within their mission and objectives, must support access to information on all subjects that serve the needs or interests of each user, regardless of the user's age or the content of the material. In order to preserve the cultural record and to prevent the loss of information, libraries may need to expand their selection or collection development policies to ensure preservation, in appropriate formats, of information obtained electronically. Libraries have an obligation to provide access to government information available in electronic format.

Libraries and librarians should not deny or limit access to electronic information because of its allegedly controversial content or because of the librarian's personal beliefs or fear of confrontation. Furthermore, libraries and librarians should not deny access to electronic information solely on the grounds that it is perceived to lack value.

Publicly funded libraries have a legal obligation to provide access to constitutionally protected information. Federal, state, county, municipal, local, or library governing bodies sometimes require the use of Internet filters or other technological measures that block access to constitutionally protected information, contrary to the *Library Bill of Rights* (*ALA Policy Manual*, 53.1.17, Resolution on the Use of Filtering Software in Libraries). If a library uses a technological measure that blocks access to information, it should be set at the least restrictive level in order to minimize the blocking of constitutionally protected speech. Adults retain the right to access all constitutionally protected information and to ask for the technological measure to be disabled in a timely manner. Minors also retain the right to access constitutionally protected information and, at the minimum, have the right to ask the library or librarian to provide access to erroneously blocked information in a timely manner. Libraries and librarians have an obligation to inform users of these rights and to provide the means to exercise these rights.*

Electronic resources provide unprecedented opportunities to expand the scope of information available to users. Libraries and librarians should provide access to information presenting all points of view. The provision of access does not imply sponsorship or endorsement. These principles pertain to electronic resources no less than they do to the more traditional sources of information in libraries (Diversity in Collection Development).

Adopted January 24, 1996, by the ALA Council; amended January 19, 2005. http://www.ala.org/ala/oif/statementspols/statementsif/interpretations/ accesselectronic.htm.

---

   * "If some libraries do not have the capacity to unblock specific Web sites or to disable the filter or if it is shown that an adult user's election to view constitutionally protected Internet material is burdened in some other substantial way, that would be the subject for an as-applied challenge, not the facial challenge made in this case." *United States, et al. v. American Library Association*, 539 U.S. 194 (2003) (Justice Kennedy, concurring). See also Questions and Answers on Access to Electronic Information, Services, and Networks: An Interpretation of the *Library Bill of Rights*, http:// www.ala.org/ala/oif/statementspols/statementsif/interpretations/ qandaaccesselectronic.htm.

HISTORY

Access to Electronic Information, Services, and Networks

At the 1994 Annual Conference in Miami Beach, the Intellectual Freedom Committee discussed its response to a document titled "Principles for the Development of the National Information Infrastructure," which had been developed by several ALA divisions and other library organizations as a unified statement of the library community's hopes with regard to development of the national information superhighway. The Committee endorsed the concept of the draft but found many areas of concern, including wording that suggested an acceptance of fees for access to electronic information and distinctions between library service based upon the type or the format of information to be provided. An atmosphere of urgency about issuing a statement on the subject of the national information infrastructure pervaded the 1994 conference. Bills on the subject were pending before Congress. Nevertheless, the Intellectual Freedom Committee felt that ALA's basic intellectual freedom policies were being swept aside, at least to some degree, in the rush by many library organizations to become players in the discussions taking place in Washington on the structure of the national information superhighway. It was the compound effect of these concerns, coupled with an increasing volume of requests for guidance from librarians in the field, that solidified the Intellectual Freedom Committee's determination to develop a new Interpretation of the *Library Bill of Rights*, "Access to Electronic Information, Services, and Networks." An IFC subcommittee was appointed at the 1994 Annual Conference to prepare a first draft; at the same time, the

Committee agreed to sponsor open hearings on the subject at the 1995 Midwinter Meeting in Philadelphia.

Both before and during the hearing, the Committee received comment and testimony from librarians representing a broad variety of types of libraries and library services, expressing their concerns and questions about access to electronic information. The Committee itself also identified several areas of concern, not the least of which was the definition of "electronic communication." For example, is the Internet a public forum, or is it not? Are parts of it public forums and parts of it not? Other areas of concern included privacy and confidentiality, attribution or lack thereof of articles and information appearing on the Internet, flaming and hate speech, punishment by cutting off information or user accounts, fees, children's access, content and diversity, collection development, language, disability, and restriction of newsgroups. Recognizing the breadth of issues that needed to be addressed and the urgency of the need, the Committee decided to hold a special meeting to work on and produce a draft Interpretation for circulation prior to the 1995 Annual Conference.

The Committee met in Chicago on March 3–5, 1995. An intensive weekend of work resulted in a draft document that was circulated broadly to ALA's Council and Executive Board, all of the divisions and round tables, chapter intellectual freedom committees, and all other interested librarians. It also was posted on the Office for Intellectual Freedom's list, ALAOIF, and comments were invited from all participants.

At the 1995 Annual Conference in Chicago, as a result of additional comments, the sections on equity of access and the rights of users were changed to clarify the Committee's intent that fees not be charged for electronic information services and that services be provided in a nondiscriminatory manner.

The revised draft was circulated to all ALA units meeting at the conference. It was endorsed by the Public Library Association and the American Association of School Librarians. Other units, particularly the Association of College and Research Libraries, expressed strong reservations about the draft, especially about its principles on fees and equity of access. In light of these concerns, the draft was sent back to the IFC for additional work. At the 1996 Midwinter

Meeting, the IFC presented a revised Interpretation to the Council. It was adopted on January 24, 1996.

No changes were made in the Interpretation during the 1999–2000 review. The Interpretation was reviewed again during the 2004–5 cycle. A revised policy was recommended to Council at the 2005 Midwinter Meeting after comments were received from a number of ALA units and individual members. In addition to general editing for grammar, clarity, and logical order, one paragraph was removed and three new paragraphs were added. Changes included:

Introduction
- The original first paragraph was no longer needed and was removed.
- As a result of a comment the Committee received, a footnote was added to support the concept that the right to receive information is a necessary corollary to the right of free speech.
- A new paragraph was added concerning the responsibility of libraries to "empower users by providing access to the broadest range of information."
- The fourth paragraph was revised to stress the importance of continual monitoring of current issues related to electronic information in light of ALA policies and current judicial interpretations.
- The list of specific reasons why individuals may "lack access or capability to use electronic resources" in the fifth paragraph was eliminated to broaden the statement.

Rights of Users
- A statement concerning the rights of minors, previously in the introduction, was moved to the fourth paragraph in this section.
- In the first sentence of the fifth paragraph a more concise and direct statement, "Libraries should use technology to enhance, not deny, access to information," replaced "Although electronic systems may include distinct property rights and security concerns, such elements may not be employed as a subterfuge to deny users' access to information."

- The revised last sentence of the fifth paragraph, "Libraries should provide library users with the training and assistance necessary to find, evaluate, and use information effectively," reflects the growing importance of information literacy in libraries.
- In the final paragraph in this section, concerning confidentiality and privacy, the sentence "Users should be advised, however, that because security is technically difficult to achieve, electronic transactions and files could become public" was removed because of its vagueness. Specific security issues become outdated quickly and are best discussed in question-and-answer documents.

Equity of Access

- The first paragraph in this section is new. It describes the library's role in bridging the information access gap for all individuals who face serious barriers to access for whatever reason.
- The second paragraph was not changed. However, the Resolution on Access to the Use of Libraries and Information by Individuals with Physical or Mental Impairment was added to the list of references to ALA policy to clarify that the need for equitable access includes persons who face barriers to access as a result of physical or mental impairment.

Information Resources and Access

- The second and third paragraphs in this section combined three paragraphs from the original Interpretation. The statement "Information retrieved or utilized electronically should be considered constitutionally protected unless determined otherwise by a court with appropriate jurisdiction" was moved from this section to "Rights of Users."
- The IFC added a new fourth paragraph in response to the U.S. Supreme Court's 2003 decision finding the Children's Internet Protection Act (CIPA) to be constitutional because libraries can provide access to constitutionally protected information that a filter may block by unblocking erroneously blocked information for minors and allowing

adults to request that the filter be disabled in a timely manner. This paragraph is based on recognition that some state legislatures, municipal governments, or library governing bodies are requiring CIPA compliance. It is not intended to encourage libraries to become CIPA compliant.

2.3

Access to Library Resources and Services regardless of Sex, Gender Identity, or Sexual Orientation

An Interpretation of the
Library Bill of Rights

American libraries exist and function within the context of a body of laws derived from the United States Constitution and the First Amendment. The *Library Bill of Rights* embodies the basic policies that guide libraries in the provision of services, materials, and programs.

In the preamble to its *Library Bill of Rights*, the American Library Association affirms that *all* libraries are forums for information and ideas. This concept of *forum* and its accompanying principle of *inclusiveness* pervade all six Articles of the *Library Bill of Rights*.

The American Library Association stringently and unequivocally maintains that libraries and librarians have an obligation to resist efforts that systematically exclude materials dealing with any subject matter, including sex, gender identity, or sexual orientation:

- Article I of the *Library Bill of Rights* states that "Materials should not be excluded because of the origin, background, or views of those contributing to their creation." The Association affirms that books and other materials coming from gay, lesbian, bisexual, and/or transgendered presses, gay, lesbian, bisexual, and/or transgendered authors or other creators, and materials regardless of format or services dealing with gay, lesbian, bisexual, and/or transgendered life are protected by the *Library Bill of Rights*. Librarians are obligated by the *Library Bill of Rights* to endeavor to select materials without regard to the sex, gender identity, or sexual orientation of their creators by using the criteria identified in their written, approved selection policies (ALA policy 53.1.5).

- Article II maintains that "Libraries should provide materials and information presenting all points of view on current and historical issues. Materials should not be proscribed or removed because of partisan or doctrinal disapproval." Library services, materials, and programs representing diverse points of view on sex, gender identity, or sexual orientation should be considered for purchase and inclusion in library collections and programs (ALA policies 53.1.1, 53.1.9, and 53.1.11). The Association affirms that attempts to proscribe or remove materials dealing with gay, lesbian, bisexual, and/or transgendered life without regard to the written, approved selection policy violate this tenet and constitute censorship.

- Articles III and IV mandate that libraries "challenge censorship" and cooperate with those "resisting abridgement of free expression and free access to ideas."

- Article V holds that "A person's right to use a library should not be denied or abridged because of origin, age, background or views." In the *Library Bill of Rights* and all its Interpretations, it is intended that: "origin" encompasses all the characteristics of individuals that are inherent in the circumstances of their birth; "age" encompasses all the characteristics of individuals that are inherent in their levels of development and maturity; "background" encompasses all the characteristics of individuals that are a result of their life experiences; and "views" encompasses all the opinions and beliefs held and expressed by individuals. Therefore, Article V of the *Library Bill of Rights* mandates that library services, materials, and programs be available to all members of the community the library serves, without regard to sex, gender identity, or sexual orientation. This includes providing youth with comprehensive sex education literature (ALA Policy 52.5.2).

- Article VI maintains that "Libraries which make exhibit spaces and meeting rooms available to the public they serve should make such facilities available on an equitable basis, regardless of the beliefs or affiliations of individuals or groups requesting their use." This protection extends to all groups and members of the community the library serves, without regard to sex, gender identity, or sexual orientation.

The American Library Association holds that any attempt, be it legal or extra-legal, to regulate or suppress library services, materials, or programs must be resisted in order that protected expression is not abridged. Librarians have a professional obligation to ensure that all library users have free and equal access to the entire range of library services, materials, and programs. Therefore, the Association strongly opposes any effort to limit access to information and ideas. The Association also encourages librarians to proactively support the First Amendment rights of all library users, regardless of sex, gender identity, or sexual orientation.

Adopted June 30, 1993, by the ALA Council; amended July 12, 2000; June 30, 2004. http://www.ala.org/ala/oif/statementspols/statementsif/interpretations/accesslibrary.htm.

HISTORY

Access to Library Resources and Services regardless of Sex, Gender Identity, or Sexual Orientation

The American Library Association held its 1993 Midwinter Meeting in Denver, Colorado, two months after that state had adopted a constitutional amendment repealing legislation protecting the civil rights of gays and lesbians. The amendment, Colorado Constitutional Amendment 2, was one of several such initiatives that sprang up in Western and Pacific Northwestern states in 1992 and reappeared persistently, despite being struck down as unconstitutional in courts or being turned back by voters. Thus, it was in an atmosphere of intolerance and discrimination against individuals based on their sexual orientation that a proposed resolution on gender, sexual orientation, and the *Library Bill of Rights* came before the ALA Council. Specifically, the resolution directed that Article V of the *Library Bill of Rights* be amended to add the words "gender" and "sexual orientation" after the word "age," with the amended section to read thus: "A person's right to use the library should not be denied or abridged because of origin, age, gender, sexual orientation, background, or views." The proposed resolution was referred to the Intellectual Freedom Committee for review and recommendation.

The IFC became concerned with the impulse and momentum for amending the *Library Bill of Rights*, pointing out the long-standing laundry-list problem in Article V, which sometimes led to the assumption that any characteristic not specifically listed is thereby excluded. The 1980 revisions to the *Library Bill of Rights* deliberately broadened the language of Article V to cover all possibilities, and in response to a request of the Minority Concerns Committee in 1989 to review the *Library Bill of Rights* to ensure that it addressed language and economic status, the Intellectual Freedom Committee declined to amend the document. It opted instead to incorporate those concerns into revisions of Interpretations. In addition, amending the *Library Bill of Rights* would mean that thousands of libraries across the country that had adopted the document as part of their operating principles and practices would need to readopt a revised version. Ordinarily, this would be a matter of routine. The repressive national atmosphere at the time, however, aroused concern that the process of adopting a revised version of the *Library Bill of Rights* would invite vigorous assault by conservative pressure groups that had identified the document as a target and had worked in various localities to secure its removal from local library policy.

Faced with these concerns, the Intellectual Freedom Committee elected to present a substitute resolution reaffirming that the *Library Bill of Rights* did include gender and sexual orientation. In her report to Council, Intellectual Freedom Committee chair Candace Morgan explained:

> We took this action for several reasons: first, our Association's commitment to nondiscrimination with regard to gender and sexual orientation has always been part of the meaning of all Articles of the *Library Bill of Rights*, not just Article V; second, terminology in the *Library Bill of Rights*, particularly in Article V, is deliberately broad to prohibit discrimination targeted at any class of individuals on the basis of arbitrary distinctions; third, we have frequently been asked to add language to Article V, and we have refused to do so in the belief that the addition of specific classifications implies that other classes not explicitly included are therefore excluded; and fourth, this organization has never, in our memory, amended the *Library Bill of Rights* without broad distribution for comment from all divisions and other interested bodies.

The Council accepted the Intellectual Freedom Committee's substitute resolution. At that same Midwinter Meeting, the IFC also recommended, and the Council adopted, a more generic Resolution on Gay Rights and Materials, designed to be useful and immediately available in localities where antigay initiatives were springing up with regularity.

In addition to adopting these two resolutions, however, the Council directed the Intellectual Freedom Committee to bring to the 1993 Annual Conference in New Orleans specific language to revise the *Library Bill of Rights* to address the issue of sexual orientation.

In New Orleans, the Committee's concerns about revising the *Library Bill of Rights* were as strong as they had been at the Midwinter Meeting. Battles over maintaining the current version of the *Library Bill of Rights* had just been fought in both North Carolina and Nevada. Given the atmosphere of attack on the *Library Bill of Rights* already evident in many communities, the Committee believed the wiser course would be to present a very strongly worded Interpretation of the *Library Bill of Rights* to the Council for its adoption. Such an Interpretation would state specifically that the document already covers gays, lesbians, and anyone else, with regard to both their access to materials and the necessity of maintaining collections that contain materials by and about homosexuals. The Council had directed that language to amend the *Library Bill of Rights* be prepared, however. The Intellectual Freedom Committee was faced with the dilemma of responding to the Council's directive despite strong reservations about the approach to the problem that the Council apparently wanted to take. In addition to proposed language to revise the *Library Bill of Rights*, a draft Interpretation on gender and sexuality was prepared and circulated to all ALA units prior to the Annual Conference, soliciting response on this approach to the issue. The draft, and the approach of adopting an Interpretation rather than amending the *Library Bill of Rights* itself, was enthusiastically received and endorsed by a number of ALA's divisions and committees, including the Association for Library Service to Children, Public Library Association, American Library Trustee Association, Young Adult Library Services Association, the Committee on Professional Ethics, and the Intellectual Freedom Round Table. Given that response, Intellectual Freedom Committee chair Candace Morgan explained in her 1993 Annual Conference Report to Council that the Committee had decided—with the support of the above-named divisions, committees, and round table—to recommend the option of adopting an Interpretation only and leaving the *Library Bill of Rights* as is. Morgan acknowledged in her report:

There is no question that materials by and about gays, lesbians, and bisexuals, and on the subject of homosexuality in general, are at the top of the agenda of organized pressure groups that are attacking libraries all over the country for including such materials in their collections. There is also no question that gays, lesbians, and bisexuals themselves are the victims and the targets of unprecedented attacks aimed at codifying discrimination against homosexuals into law. Finally, there is no question that the library profession's commitment to intellectual freedom and the responsibility of libraries and librarians to protect and defend access to information from all points of view, requires including materials in libraries on homosexuality to serve the needs of all library users, including gays, lesbians, and bisexuals. This commitment to free expression also mandates that we take positive action to protect the rights of access for all persons regardless of sexuality, gender, or age.

Morgan went on to explain that, ironically, the *Library Bill of Rights* had recently come under attack in Nevada and North Carolina by opponents of intellectual freedom because those opponents assumed that the document, unamended, already protected materials by, about, or of interest to gays, lesbians, and bisexuals. The battles to protect the *Library Bill of Rights* in state and local policy had been hard fought and narrowly won. Many of the fighters, including public and school librarians in many other states, reported that in the current climate of attacks on the freedom to read, adopting a newly amended *Library Bill of Rights* would be politically impossible. Believing that the document would be useless to the profession if not incorporated into local library policy, Morgan explained the Committee's strong belief that it would be unwise to initiate an opportunity to exclude the document from local policy by forcing local libraries to consider readopting an amended version. Issuing an Interpretation for governing bodies and librarians would guide their understanding of the *Library Bill of Rights* as it was already incorporated in policy. Finally, Morgan explained the laundry-list problem, in which revision of Article V of the *Library Bill of Rights* to include specific characteristics renders it vulnerable to requests that a long list of characteristics be added and creates the implication that any characteristic not explicitly included is, therefore, excluded. One of the first comments the Intellectual Freedom Committee received when the possibility of revision to include gender and sexual orientation was announced was that if disability was not currently covered, as a move to amend implied, the word "ability" should be included to cover mental, emotional, or physical conditions. Health, race, national origin, and language were also suggested as additions to the list. The Committee itself added "financial status" to the language for the proposed amendment because, at the time, it was still considering a request of the Minority Concerns Committee to address economic status and language in the *Library Bill of Rights* while simultaneously working on a proposed Interpretation to do just that.

The Intellectual Freedom Committee's reasoning was persuasive, and the Council rejected amendments to the *Library Bill of Rights*. Instead, it adopted a new Interpretation of the *Library Bill of Rights*, "Access to Library Resources and Services regardless of Gender or Sexual Orientation," which makes absolutely clear that censorship of material based on sexuality, or discrimination against library users based on gender or sexual orientation, is and always has been totally inappropriate and violative of the *Library Bill of Rights*.

As part of its overall review of all of the Interpretations in 1999–2000, the IFC proposed removal of references to terms of sexual orientation in the belief that terms can become dated or offensive, or both. The Committee also affirmed that all materials—regardless of format or services—are protected by the *Library Bill of Rights* and referenced ALA policy 52.5.2, Sex Education Materials in Libraries, in the Interpretation. On July 12, 2000, the ALA Council adopted the Interpretation as amended.

This Interpretation was revised again during the 2004–5 policy review process. The title was changed to "Access to Library Resources and Services regardless of Sex, Gender Identity, or Sexual Orientation" to more accurately describe the applicability of the Interpretation. The text was revised to reflect the title change. Council adopted the amended Interpretation on June 30, 2004.

2.4

Access to Resources and Services in the School Library Media Program

An Interpretation of the *Library Bill of Rights*

The school library media program plays a unique role in promoting intellectual freedom. It serves as a point of voluntary access to information and ideas and as a learning laboratory for students as they acquire critical thinking and problem-solving skills needed in a pluralistic society. Although the educational level and program of the school necessarily shapes the resources and services of a school library media program, the principles of the *Library Bill of Rights* apply equally to all libraries, including school library media programs.

School library media specialists assume a leadership role in promoting the principles of intellectual freedom within the school by providing resources and services that create and sustain an atmosphere of free inquiry. School library media specialists work closely with teachers to integrate instructional activities in classroom units designed to equip students to locate, evaluate, and use a broad range of ideas effectively. Through resources, programming, and educational processes, students and teachers experience the free and robust debate characteristic of a democratic society.

School library media specialists cooperate with other individuals in building collections of resources appropriate to the needs and to the developmental and maturity levels of students. These collections provide resources that support the mission of the school district and are consistent with its philosophy, goals, and objectives. Resources in school library media collections are an integral component of the curriculum and represent diverse points of view on both current and historical issues. These resources include materials that support the intellectual growth, personal development, individual interests, and recreational needs of students.

While English is, by history and tradition, the customary language of the United States, the languages in use in any given community may vary. Schools serving communities in which other languages are used make efforts to accommodate the needs of students for whom English is a second language. To support these efforts, and to ensure equal access to resources and services, the school library media program provides resources that reflect the linguistic pluralism of the community.

Members of the school community involved in the collection development process employ educational criteria to select resources unfettered by their personal, political, social, or religious views. Students and educators served by the school library media program have access to resources and services free of constraints resulting from personal, partisan, or doctrinal disapproval. School library media specialists resist efforts by individuals or groups to define what is appropriate for all students or teachers to read, view, hear, or access via electronic means.

Major barriers between students and resources include but are not limited to imposing age or grade level restrictions on the use of resources; limiting the use of interlibrary loan and access to electronic information; charging fees for information in specific formats; requiring permission from parents or teachers; establishing restricted shelves or closed collections; and labeling. Policies, procedures, and rules related to the use of resources and services support free and open access to information.

The school board adopts policies that guarantee students access to a broad range of ideas. These include policies on collection development and procedures for the review of resources about which concerns have been raised. Such policies, developed by persons in the school community, provide for a timely and fair hearing and assure that procedures are applied equitably to all expressions of concern. School library media specialists implement district policies and procedures in the school.

Adopted July 2, 1986, by the ALA Council; amended January 10, 1990; July 12, 2000; January 19, 2005. http://www.ala.org/ala/oif/statementspols/statementsif/interpretations/accessresources.htm.

HISTORY

Access to Resources and Services in the School Library Media Program

During the early 1950s, as the anticommunist reaction of McCarthyism swept across the United States, school librarians and school curriculum planners were affected no less than people in journalism, entertainment, and government. Schools were coerced to ban works that were alleged to contain "un-American" thinking. The issue of selecting school library materials was raised during the meeting of the Board of Directors of the American Association of School Librarians (AASL) during the 1953 ALA Annual Conference in Los Angeles. Sue Hefley, chair of the school libraries discussion group at the second Conference on Intellectual Freedom (held at Whittier College, June 20–21), reported on her group's consensus concerning the need for a policy statement on the matter of selection. In response to Hefley's report, the board voted

> that a committee be appointed to consider the advisability of preparing a statement on book selection in defense of liberty in schools of a democracy, and in considering this problem to make use of the excellent statement prepared at the Conference on Intellectual Freedom. Furthermore, that this committee make recommendations as to what further action AASL should take in this matter.[1]

In preparation for the AASL meeting at the 1954 Annual Conference in Minneapolis, the Committee on Book Selection in Defense of Liberty in Schools of a Democracy submitted a draft for a *School Library Bill of Rights*. At the 1955 Midwinter Meeting, the AASL officially accepted the *School Library Bill of Rights*, and on July 8, 1955, it was adopted by the ALA Council.

In the years following the adoption of the *School Library Bill of Rights*, ALA's *Library Bill of Rights* underwent several basic changes. (For full discussion, see part 2, section 1, "*Library Bill of Rights*: History.") Because of changes in the *Library Bill of Rights*, affirmed by the *School Library Bill of Rights* of 1955, as well as changes in the conception of the range of materials to be provided by libraries, the AASL Board of Directors appointed a committee in 1968 to consider revising the 1955 *School Library Bill of Rights*.

At the 1969 ALA Annual Conference in Atlantic City, the revised *School Library Bill of Rights* was brought before the AASL Board of Directors. Making only minor corrections, the board voted to accept the revised version:

> The American Association of School Librarians reaffirms its belief in the *Library Bill of Rights* of the American Library Association. Media personnel are concerned with generating understanding of American freedoms through the development of informed and responsible citizens. To this end the American Association of School Librarians asserts that the responsibility of the school library media center is:
>
> To provide a comprehensive collection of instructional materials selected in compliance with basic written selection principles, and to provide maximum accessibility to these materials;
>
> To provide materials that will support the curriculum, taking into consideration the individual's needs, and the varied interests, abilities, socioeconomic backgrounds, and maturity levels of the students served;
>
> To provide materials for teachers and students that will encourage growth in knowledge, and that will develop literary, cultural, and aesthetic appreciation, and ethical standards;
>
> To provide materials which reflect the ideas and beliefs of religious, social, political, historical, and ethnic groups

and their contribution to the American and world heritage and culture, thereby enabling students to develop an intellectual integrity in forming judgments;

To provide a written statement, approved by the local boards of education, of the procedures for meeting the challenge of censorship of materials in school library media centers; and

To provide qualified professional personnel to serve teachers and students.

It soon became clear, however, that the existence of two documents with very similar titles could be a source of confusion. Moreover, with the 1967 amendment of the *Library Bill of Rights* to oppose discrimination against library users by age, the *School Library Bill of Rights* became largely redundant. As increasing numbers of librarians pointed out, the school document simply repeated in different language the principles enunciated more forcefully in the *Library Bill of Rights*. This served to detract attention from and, hence, to weaken the impact of the Association's most basic document on intellectual freedom.

The problem was discussed extensively in both the Intellectual Freedom Committee and the AASL. At the 1976 Annual Conference in Chicago, the Board of Directors of the American Association of School Librarians withdrew the *School Library Bill of Rights* and endorsed the *Library Bill of Rights*.

Since 1976 and particularly in the 1980s, the challenge to materials in school libraries and media centers has increased in volume and intensity. The need became apparent for an Interpretation of the *Library Bill of Rights* that spoke directly to the unique role of school libraries and media centers in the educational process. A clear statement of the responsibility of school library media professionals for the selection process and of the centrality of intellectual freedom principles in this process was perceived as the central focus for this Interpretation.

In 1985–86, an Interpretation was drafted by the AASL with the cooperation of the IFC. At the 1986 Annual Conference in New York, "Access to Resources and Services in the School Library Media Program" was adopted by the ALA Council. It read as follows:

The school library media program plays a unique role in promoting intellectual freedom. It serves as a point of voluntary access to information and ideas and as a learning laboratory for students as they acquire critical thinking and problem solving skills needed in a pluralistic society. Although the educational level and program of the school necessarily shape the resources and services of a school library media program, the principles of the *Library Bill of Rights* apply equally to all libraries, including school library media programs.

School library media professionals assume a leadership role in promoting the principles of intellectual freedom within the school by providing resources and services that create and sustain an atmosphere of free inquiry. School library media professionals work closely with teachers to integrate instructional activities in classroom units designed to equip students to locate, evaluate, and use a broad range of ideas effectively. Through resources, programming, and educational processes, students and teachers experience the free and robust debate characteristic of a democratic society.

School library media professionals cooperate with other individuals in building collections of resources appropriate to the developmental and maturity levels of students. These collections provide resources which support the curriculum and are consistent with the philosophy, goals, and objectives of the school district. Resources in school library media collections represent diverse points of view and current as well as historic issues.

Members of the school community involved in the collection development process employ educational criteria to select resources unfettered by their personal, political, social, or religious views. Students and educators served by the school library media program have access to resources and services free of constraints resulting from personal, partisan, or doctrinal disapproval. School library media professionals resist efforts by individuals to define what is appropriate for all students or teachers to read, view, or hear.

Major barriers between students and resources include imposing age or grade level restrictions on the use of resources, limiting the use of interlibrary loan and access to electronic information, charging fees for information in specific formats, requiring permissions from parents or teachers, establishing restricted shelves or closed collections, and labeling. Policies, procedures, and rules related to the use of resources and services support free and open access to information.

The school board adopts policies that guarantee student access to a broad range of ideas. These include policies on collection development and procedures for the review of resources about which concerns have been raised. Such policies, developed by persons in the school community, provide for a timely and fair hearing and ensure that procedures are applied equitably to all expressions of concern. School library media professionals implement district policies and procedures in the school.

A revised Interpretation was circulated for comment in the fall of 1989. The sole substantive change was the addition of a paragraph stating that the school library media program should attempt to accommodate the needs of students for whom English is a second language. To ensure equality of access, librarians must provide resources reflecting the linguistic pluralism of the community that they serve.

At the 1990 Midwinter Meeting, comments received from the American Association of School Librarians, the Office for Library Personnel Resources (now known as Human Resources Development and Recruitment), the Standing Committee on Library Education, and the Professional Ethics Committee resulted in minor editorial changes. The revised policy was recommended to the Council and adopted on January 10, 1990.

As part of its review of all of the Interpretations in 1999–2000, the IFC proposed editorial changes in the Interpretation (the addition of "should" in some instances and the substitution of "that cross" for "across"). On July 12, 2000, the amended Interpretation was adopted by the ALA Council.

As a part of the 2004–5 review of intellectual freedom policies, the IFC received comments concerning this Interpretation. Several grammatical changes were made. In addition, there was consider-able discussion of the paragraph concerning collections. In order to clarify that the school library collection supports a wide range of needs in addition to the curriculum, the following additions (in bold) were proposed:

> School library media specialists cooperate with other individuals in building collections of resources appropri-ate to the **needs and to the** developmental and maturity levels of students. These collections provide resources that support the mission of the school district and are consistent with its philosophy, goals, and objectives. Resources in school library media collections **are an inte-gral component of the curriculum** and represent diverse points of view on both current and historical issues. **These resources include materials that support the intellectual growth, personal development, individual interests, and recreational needs of students**.

Finally, in response to a request from the AASL Board the term "school library media professional" was changed to "school library media specialists" throughout the document. The Council adopted the revised Interpretation on January 19, 2005.

NOTE

1. *School Libraries* 3, no. 1 (October 1953): 8.

2.5
Challenged Materials

An Interpretation of the
Library Bill of Rights

The American Library Association declares as a matter of firm principle that it is the responsibility of every library to have a clearly defined materials selection policy in written form which reflects the *Library Bill of Rights*, and which is approved by the appropriate governing authority.

Challenged materials that meet the criteria for selection in the materials selection policy of the library should not be removed under any legal or extra-legal pressure. The *Library Bill of Rights* states in Article I that "Materials should not be excluded because of the origin, background, or views of those contributing to their creation," and in Article II, that "Materials should not be proscribed or removed because of partisan or doctrinal disapproval." Freedom of expression is protected by the Constitution of the United States, but constitutionally protected expression is often separated from unprotected expression only by a dim and uncertain line. The Constitution requires a procedure designed to focus searchingly on challenged expression before it can be suppressed. An adversary hearing is a part of this procedure.

Therefore, any attempt, be it legal or extra-legal, to regulate or suppress materials in libraries must be closely scrutinized to the end that protected expression is not abridged.

Adopted June 25, 1971, by the ALA Council; amended July 1, 1981; January 10, 1990. http://www.ala.org/ala/oif/statementspols/ statementsif/interpretations/challengedmaterials.htm.

HISTORY

Challenged Materials

T he *Library Bill of Rights* states that library materials should not be "excluded because of the origin, background, or views" of their creators. The document states further, "Materials should not be proscribed or removed because of partisan or doctrinal disapproval." Nevertheless, libraries are still pressured by many groups and individuals to remove certain materials because they find their sexual, political, or religious content objectionable.

Particularly when sexually explicit materials are the object of censorship efforts, librarians and boards of trustees are often unaware of the legal procedures required to effect the removal of such items. Many attorneys, even when employed by state or local governing bodies, are not aware of the procedures to determine whether or not a work is obscene or otherwise illegal under the law. According to U.S. Supreme Court decisions, a work is not obscene until found to be so by a court of law and only after an adversary hearing to determine the question of obscenity. Until a work is specifically found to be unprotected by the First Amendment, the title remains a legal library acquisition and need not be removed.

In 1971, several attempts to ban publications from libraries involved charges that the works were obscene and therefore not legal or proper acquisitions for the library. In Groton, Connecticut, in a case involving *Evergreen Review*, the librarian and the board of trustees were threatened with prosecution under a state obscenity statute if they refused to remove the magazine from the library. The board, after several months of resisting efforts to remove the magazine, capitulated in the face of this threat to prosecute them as individuals.

The Groton, Connecticut, case prompted the Intellectual Freedom Committee, with the aid of legal counsel, to study U.S. Supreme Court and federal circuit court decisions concerning procedures whereby materials are determined to be obscene. Three cases in particular were reviewed: *Bantam Books, Inc. v. Sullivan*; *Marcus v. Search Warrants*; and *A Quantity of Copies of Books v. Kansas*.

Using the language of these three decisions as a basis, the Intellectual Freedom Committee developed the Resolution on Challenged Materials. The statement was submitted to the ALA Council during the 1971 Annual Conference in Dallas and was adopted as an ALA policy on June 25, 1971. It read as follows:

> WHEREAS, The *Library Bill of Rights* states that no library materials should be proscribed or removed because of partisan or doctrinal disapproval; and
>
> WHEREAS, Constitutionally protected expression is often separated from unprotected expression only by a dim and uncertain line; and
>
> WHEREAS, Any attempt, be it legal or extra-legal, to regulate or suppress material must be closely scrutinized to the end that protected expression is not abridged in the process; and
>
> WHEREAS, The Constitution requires a procedure designed to focus searchingly on the question before speech can be suppressed; and
>
> WHEREAS, The dissemination of a particular work which is alleged to be unprotected should be completely undisturbed until an independent determination has been made by a judicial officer, including an adversary hearing;
>
> THEREFORE, the premises considered, be it resolved, That the American Library Association declares as a matter of firm principle that no challenged library material should be removed from any library under any legal or extra-legal pressure, save after an independent determination

by a judicial officer in a court of competent jurisdiction
and only after an adversary hearing, in accordance with
well-established principles of law.

A decade later, legal standards for determining obscenity had
changed significantly. Nevertheless, the basic principle—that
expression is protected by the First Amendment until it has been
determined through an adversary procedure that such expression is
obscene, child pornography, libelous, or otherwise unprotected—
remained firmly established in U.S. constitutional law.

In reviewing the 1971 resolution in 1981, the IFC found that a
major revision still was necessary. The principal difficulties were
twofold. The first problem was format. Written as a formal resolution, with an implementary paragraph preceded by a series of
"whereas" clauses, the Resolution on Challenged Materials was
inconsistent in form with other Interpretations of the *Library Bill of
Rights* and lacked clarity and force as a document directed toward
the general public as well as library professionals.

The second problem was more substantive. The materials selection policies of most libraries correctly provide opportunities for
patron comments and citizen requests for reconsideration of library
materials. Yet the policy seemed to make a mockery of such procedures by declaring in advance that "no challenged library material
should be removed" unless the library were ordered to do so by a
court of law. Moreover, many librarians complained that such an
inflexible declaration served to tie the library's own hands in its
efforts to correct the inevitable mistakes that occur in any selection
process.

With these considerations in mind, the IFC presented the
Council with a new version of the document, written in a format
similar to the other Interpretations of the *Library Bill of Rights* and
more appropriate for a broader audience. The new version linked
the decision to remove or retain challenged materials to the maintenance of clear guidelines consistent with the *Library Bill of Rights*
and established by the library's materials selection policy. The revision designated the maintenance of a "clearly defined" selection
policy a "responsibility" of all libraries. The new version offered
libraries and patrons alike greater flexibility in the consideration of
challenges while at the same time reaffirming the principles of the

Library Bill of Rights, calling for the closest scrutiny of all efforts to remove materials, and maintaining due process in the reconsideration procedure. On July 1, 1981, the Council adopted the revised statement "Challenged Materials" as a policy of the American Library Association:

> The American Library Association declares as a matter of firm principle that it is the responsibility of every library to have a clearly defined materials selection policy in written form which reflects the *Library Bill of Rights*, and which is approved by the appropriate governing authority.
>
> Challenged materials which meet the materials selection policy of the library should not be removed under any legal or extra-legal pressure. The *Library Bill of Rights* states in Article I that "Materials should not be excluded because of the origin, background, or views of those contributing to their creation," and in Article II, that "Materials should not be proscribed or removed because of partisan or doctrinal disapproval." Freedom of expression is protected by the Constitution of the United States, but constitutionally protected expression is often separated from unprotected expression only by a dim and uncertain line. The Constitution requires a procedure designed to focus searchingly on challenged expression before it can be suppressed. An adversary hearing is a part of this procedure.
>
> Therefore, any attempt, be it legal or extra-legal, to regulate or suppress materials in libraries must be closely scrutinized to the end that protected expression is not abridged.

In 1986, in response to inquiries from librarians facing book or material challenges for the first time, the Intellectual Freedom Committee developed the following list of definitions to clarify terminology associated with challenges:

> *Expression of Concern*. An inquiry that has judgmental overtones.
>
> *Oral Complaint*. An oral challenge to the presence and/or appropriateness of the material in question.

Written Complaint. A formal, written complaint filed with the institution (library, school, etc.), challenging the presence and/or appropriateness of specific material.

Public Attack. A publicly disseminated statement challenging the value of the material, presented to the media and/or others outside the institutional organization in order to gain public support for further action.

Censorship. A change in the access status of material, based on the content of the work and made by a governing authority or its representatives. Such changes include exclusion, restriction, removal, or age/grade level changes.

As part of the Interpretation review process initiated in 1989, one minor change was made in this policy to state explicitly that materials must meet criteria stated in materials selection policies rather than simply the policy, per se. No substantive changes were recommended.

On January 10, at the 1990 Midwinter Meeting, the Council adopted the "Challenged Materials" Interpretation as amended.

In line with the ongoing practice of periodic review, the IFC reviewed "Challenged Materials" during 1999 and 2000, and did not recommend any changes.

In 2004, a grammatical change was made to this Interpretation as a part of a review of intellectual freedom policies. At the 2005 spring meeting in Chicago, the IFC discussed the 1986 definitions of terms related to challenges, particularly the definition of censorship related to age- and grade-level changes. Although most requests to change materials cataloged as juvenile to adult based on content are attempts to censor, there are some circumstances when such a change is appropriate. For example, many public libraries that formerly had only adult and juvenile collections have established young adult collections. When this occurs, some materials previously cataloged as juvenile titles are changed to young adult based on the intended audience of their content. The Committee decided that the definitions should be reviewed at a future meeting and any proposed changes circulated for comment.

2.6
Diversity in Collection Development

An Interpretation of the
Library Bill of Rights

Throughout history, the focus of censorship has fluctuated from generation to generation. Books and other materials have not been selected or have been removed from library collections for many reasons, among which are prejudicial language and ideas, political content, economic theory, social philosophies, religious beliefs, sexual forms of expression, and other potentially controversial topics.

Some examples of censorship may include removing or not selecting materials because they are considered by some as racist or sexist; not purchasing conservative religious materials; not selecting materials about or by minorities because it is thought these groups or interests are not represented in a community; or not providing information on or materials from non-mainstream political entities.

Librarians may seek to increase user awareness of materials on various social concerns by many means, including, but not limited to, issuing bibliographies and presenting exhibits and programs. Librarians have a professional responsibility to be inclusive, not exclusive, in collection development and in the provision of interlibrary loan. Access to all materials legally obtainable should be assured to the user, and policies should not unjustly exclude materials even if they are offensive to the librarian or the user. Collection development should reflect the philosophy inherent in Article II of the *Library Bill of Rights*: "Libraries should provide materials and information presenting all points of view on current and historical issues. Materials should not be proscribed or removed because of partisan or doctrinal disapproval." A balanced collection reflects a diversity of materials, not an equality of numbers. Collection development responsibilities include selecting materials in the languages in common use in the community the library serves. Collection development and the selection of materials should be done according to professional standards and established selection and review procedures.

There are many complex facets to any issue, and variations of context in which issues may be expressed, discussed, or interpreted. Librarians have a professional responsibility to be fair, just, and equitable and to give all library users equal protection in guarding against violation of the library patron's right to read, view, or listen to materials and resources protected by the First Amendment, no matter what the viewpoint of the author, creator, or selector. Librarians have an obligation to protect library collections from removal of materials based on personal bias or prejudice, and to select and support the access to materials on all subjects that meet, as closely as possible, the needs, interests, and abilities of all persons in the community the library serves. This includes materials that reflect political, economic, religious, social, minority, and sexual issues.

Intellectual freedom, the essence of equitable library services, provides for free access to all expressions of ideas through which any and all sides of a question, cause, or movement may be explored. Toleration is meaningless without tolerance for what some may consider detestable. Librarians cannot justly permit their own preferences to limit their degree of tolerance in collection development, because freedom is indivisible.

Adopted July 14, 1982, by the ALA Council; amended January 10, 1990.
http://www.ala.org/ala/oif/statementspols/statementsif/interpretations/
diversitycollection.htm.

HISTORY

Diversity in Collection Development

During the 1971 Midwinter Meeting in Los Angeles, the ALA Intellectual Freedom Committee met with representatives of the Executive Board of the International Conference of Police Associations. The meeting was to provide a forum for discussing police efforts to remove William Steig's *Sylvester and the Magic Pebble* from public and school libraries. During the meeting, the officers raised a provocative and embarrassing question for librarians. They asked why some librarians were quick to comply with requests to remove another children's book, *Little Black Sambo*, from their collections when blacks complained that its illustrations were degrading, yet now, when police officers found William Steig's pigs dressed as law enforcement officers to be degrading, librarians objected vociferously to taking the book out of their collections.

The evasive response from the IFC was generally to the effect that the Committee had difficulty impressing upon members of the library profession the importance of the principles of intellectual freedom. The inability to answer the officers' charge adequately acknowledged the accusation implicit in the question: some librarians do employ a double standard when it comes to their practice of intellectual freedom and their commitment to it. Many librarians express a strong commitment to the principles of intellectual freedom but fail to grasp that the concept of intellectual freedom, in its pure sense, promotes no causes, furthers no movements, and favors no viewpoints. *Little Black Sambo* and *Sylvester and the Magic Pebble* did not bring new issues before the library profession. These books only inherited the cloak of controversy that had already surrounded such diverse works as *The Adventures of Huckleberry Finn, Mother Goose Nursery Rhymes and Fairy Tales, Doctor Doolittle,* and *The Merchant of Venice.*

Until 1980, Article II of the *Library Bill of Rights* stated that "no library materials should be proscribed or removed from libraries because of partisan or doctrinal disapproval." The phrase "no library materials" did not appear by accident. Before June 1967, the sentence concluded, "books or other reading matter of sound factual authority should not be proscribed or removed from library shelves because of partisan or doctrinal disapproval." Article II was revised in 1967 because some librarians used an alleged lack of "sound factual authority" as a basis for removing library materials. To determine which materials lacked sound factual authority, many deferred to their personal conceptions of fact and authority. One of the most extreme examples, cited at the time of the revision, was of a Catholic librarian who excluded Protestant publications because they were not of "sound factual authority." Today, the even broader phrase "Materials should not be proscribed or removed" in the *Library Bill of Rights* leaves no room for interpretation. The revised statement reflects the philosophy that freedom is indivisible and that tolerance, if it is to be meaningful, must hold for all points of view.

At the 1972 Midwinter Meeting in Chicago, the Intellectual Freedom Committee reported its intention to prepare a statement making clear the meaning of the *Library Bill of Rights* as it pertains to attempts to censor library materials because of alleged racism, sexism, or any other isms. The Interpretation was approved by the IFC on June 25, 1972. It was subsequently submitted to the ALA Council at the 1973 Midwinter Meeting in Washington, D.C., and approved as an ALA policy on February 2, 1973. Entitled "Sexism, Racism, and Other -Isms in Library Materials," it read as follows:

> Traditional aims of censorship efforts have been to suppress political, sexual, or religious expressions. The same three subjects have also been the source of most complaints about materials in library collections. Another basis for complaints, however, has become more and more frequent. Due, perhaps, to increased awareness of the rights of minorities and increased efforts to secure

those rights, libraries are being asked to remove, restrict
or reconsider some materials which are allegedly deroga-
tory to specific minorities or which supposedly perpetu-
ate stereotypes and false images of minorities. Among the
several recurring "isms" used to describe the contents of
the materials objected to are "racism" and "sexism."

Complaints that library materials convey a deroga-
tory or false image of a minority strike the personal social
consciousness and sense of responsibility of some librarians who—accordingly—comply with the requests to
remove such materials. While such efforts to counteract
injustices are understandable, and perhaps even com-
mendable as reflections of deep personal commitments
to the ideal of equality for all people, they are—nonetheless—in conflict with the professional responsibility of
librarians to guard against encroachments upon intellectual freedom.

This responsibility has been espoused and reaffirmed
by the American Library Association in many of its basic
documents on intellectual freedom over the past thirty
years. The most concise statement of the Association's
position appears in Article II of the *Library Bill of Rights*,
which states that "Libraries should provide books and
materials presenting all points of view concerning the
problems and issues of our times; no library materials
should be proscribed or removed because of partisan or
doctrinal disapproval."

While the application of this philosophy may seem
simple when dealing with political, religious, or even
sexual expressions, its full implications become somewhat difficult when dealing with ideas, such as racism or
sexism, which many find abhorrent, repugnant, and
inhumane. But, as stated in "The Freedom to Read":

> It is inevitable in the give and take of the democratic
> process that the political, the moral, or the aesthetic
> concepts of an individual or group will occasionally
> collide with those of another individual or group. In
> a free society each individual is free to determine for
> himself what he wishes to read, and each group is
> free to determine what it will recommend to its

freely associated members. But no group has the
right to take the law into its own hands, and to
impose its own concept of politics or morality upon
other members of a democratic society. Freedom is
no freedom if it is accorded only to the accepted and
the inoffensive. . . . We realize that the application of
these propositions may mean the dissemination of
ideas and manners of expression that are repugnant
to many persons. We do not state these propositions
in the comfortable belief that what people read is
unimportant. We believe rather that what people
read is deeply important; that ideas can be dangerous; but that the suppression of ideas is fatal to a
democratic society. Freedom itself is a dangerous
way of life, but it is ours.

Some find this creed acceptable when dealing with
materials for adults but cannot extend its application to
materials for children. Such reluctance is generally based
on the belief that children are more susceptible to being
permanently influenced—even damaged—by objectionable materials than are adults. The *Library Bill of Rights*,
however, makes no distinction between materials and
services for children and adults. Its principles of free
access to all materials available apply to every person; as
stated in Article V, "The rights of an individual to the use
of a library should not be denied or abridged because of
his age, race, religion, national origins or social or political views."

Some librarians deal with the problem of objectionable materials by labeling them or listing them as "racist"
or "sexist." This kind of action, too, has long been opposed
by the American Library Association through its Statement on Labeling [renamed "Labels and Rating Systems:
An Interpretation of the *Library Bill of Rights*" in 2005]:

> If materials are labeled to pacify one group, there is
> no excuse for refusing to label any item in the
> library's collection. Because authoritarians tend to
> suppress ideas and attempt to coerce individuals to
> conform to a specific ideology, the American Library
> Association opposes such efforts which aim at clos-
> ing any path to knowledge.

Others deal with the problem of objectionable materials by instituting restrictive circulation or relegating materials to closed or restricted collections. This practice, too, is in violation of the *Library Bill of Rights* as explained in "Restricted Access to Library Materials":

> Too often only "controversial" materials are the subject of such segregation, leading to the conclusion that factors other than theft and mutilation were the true considerations. The distinction is extremely difficult to make, both for the librarian and the patron. Selection policies, carefully developed on the basis of principles of intellectual freedom and the *Library Bill of Rights*, should not be vitiated by administrative practices such as restricted access.

The American Library Association has made clear its position concerning the removal of library materials because of partisan or doctrinal disapproval, or because of pressures from interest groups, in the Resolution on Challenged Materials:

> The American Library Association declares as a matter of firm principle that no challenged material should be removed from any library under any legal or extra-legal pressure, save after an independent determination by a judicial officer in a court of competent jurisdiction and only after an adversary hearing, in accordance with well-established principles of law.

Intellectual freedom, in its purest sense, promotes no causes, furthers no movements, and favors no viewpoints. It only provides for free access to all ideas through which any and all sides of causes and movements may be expressed, discussed, and argued. The librarian cannot let his own preferences limit his degree of tolerance, for freedom is indivisible. Toleration is meaningless without toleration for the detestable.

It soon became apparent that this lengthy and somewhat unwieldy document had been formulated to address a specific situation arising in the late 1960s and early 1970s. During this time many people of a liberal or leftist political orientation, who in the past had stood in the forefront of the anticensorship battle, were falling, intentionally or not, into the very practice they had previously opposed when espoused by others. By the end of the 1970s, however, although the problem addressed by the policy continued, new instances of censorship had arisen in which other would-be censors also sought to justify their actions by support for broadly accepted social values. In reviewing the policy in the early 1980s, the IFC concluded that a broader statement covering the influence of conflicting values, philosophies, and points of view on library collections, and reaffirming the library's commitment to the inclusion of all, would be more appropriate.

At first, the Committee tried to expand the number of isms covered by the policy to include such phenomena as anti-Semitism, communism and anticommunism, homosexuality, and the like. It quickly became obvious, however, that this approach would not only be extremely awkward but also, like the original policy, would tie the document to the temporal particularities of the period in which it was written. The Committee, therefore, decided to formulate and present to the Council a new Interpretation, expanding more broadly on the call in the *Library Bill of Rights* for libraries "to provide materials and information presenting all points of view on current and historical issues."

The new policy was titled "Diversity in Collection Development." These words were not lightly chosen. Indeed, the IFC initially had preferred the title "Balanced Collections." In the early 1980s, however, several groups and individuals actively involved in increasing censorship pressures, largely from the right of center, also had raised the demand for balance in library holdings. Insofar as this was a call for libraries to be more inclusive in collection development, it was welcomed by ALA. Many, however, also saw in the demand for balance a dangerous, if hidden, threat of censorship.

The concept of balanced collections may be misunderstood to presuppose a bias toward moderation and to place limitations on the acquisition of materials thought to be extreme because they might skew the balance of the collection. The requirement that a library collection be balanced could be construed to imply, for instance, that leftist materials cannot be acquired if there is no equivalent material from the right, or vice versa. If balance is sought in this formal sense, librarians are placed in a position that requires them to act as validators of opinion by assigning values, or weights, to differing points of view across the spectrum of opinion. In other words, a misconceived if well-intentioned requirement for balance may also make of the librarian a kind of censor.

Recognizing this possible misapplication of the notion of balance, the Committee opted to emphasize instead the concept of diversity. Not only is the library obliged to include many differing views in its collection, but materials representing the broadest diversity of human thought and creativity should, in general, be actively sought, irrespective of the opinions, prejudices, values, and tastes of the librarian, and whether or not a given numerical or other balance of views can be achieved at a given moment.

The Committee completed work on the document at the 1982 Annual Conference in Philadelphia, and on July 14, 1982, the Council approved the new Interpretation of the *Library Bill of Rights,* noting that it replaced the former policy "Sexism, Racism, and Other -Isms in Library Materials," which was then rescinded. The new policy read as follows:

> Throughout history, the focus of censorship has vacillated from generation to generation. Books and other materials have not been selected or have been removed from library collections for many reasons, among which are prejudicial language and ideas, political content, economic theory, social philosophies, religious beliefs, and/or sexual forms of expression.
>
> Some examples of this may include removing or not selecting materials because they are considered by some as racist or sexist; not purchasing conservative religious materials; not selecting materials about or by minorities because it is thought these groups or interests are not represented in a community; or not providing information on or materials from nonmainstream political entities.
>
> Librarians may seek to increase user awareness of materials on various social concerns by many means, including, but not limited to, issuing bibliographies and presenting exhibits and programs.
>
> Librarians have a professional responsibility to be inclusive, not exclusive, in collection development and in the provision of interlibrary loan. Access to all materials

legally obtainable should be assured to the user, and policies should not unjustly exclude materials even if offensive to the librarian or the user. Collection development should reflect the philosophy inherent in Article II of the *Library Bill of Rights*: "Libraries should provide materials and information presenting all points of view on current and historical issues. Materials should not be proscribed or removed because of partisan or doctrinal disapproval." A balanced collection reflects a diversity of materials, not an equality of numbers. Collection development and the selection of materials should be done according to professional standards and established selection and review procedures.

There are many complex facets to any issue, and variations of context in which issues may be expressed, discussed, or interpreted. Librarians have a professional responsibility to be fair, just, and equitable and to give all library users equal protection in guarding against violation of the library patrons' liberty to read, view, or listen to materials and resources protected by the First Amendment, no matter what the viewpoint of the author, creator, or selector. Librarians have an obligation to protect library collections from removal of materials based on personal bias or prejudice, and to select and support the access to materials on all subjects that meet, as closely as possible, the needs and interests of all persons in the community which the library serves. This includes materials that reflect political, economic, religious, social, minority, and sexual issues.

Intellectual freedom, the essence of equitable library services, promotes no causes, furthers no movements, and favors no viewpoints. It only provides for free access to all expressions of ideas through which any and all sides of a question, cause, or movement may be explored. Toleration is meaningless without tolerance for what some may consider detestable. Librarians cannot justly permit their own preferences to limit their degree of tolerance in collection development, because freedom is indivisible.

Note: This policy replaces the policy "Sexism, Racism, and Other -Isms in Library Materials."

The Interpretation "Diversity in Collection Development" was revised in 1989 to acknowledge the responsibility of all librarians to be sensitive to the language(s) in common use in the community the library serves. Finally, the phrase claiming that intellectual freedom "promotes no causes, furthers no movements, and favors no viewpoints" was deleted from the text.

The newly revised Interpretation was adopted by the Council on January 10, 1990.

No changes in "Diversity in Collection Development" were recommended as part of the 1999–2000 periodic review of all Interpretations by the IFC. Minor edits for grammar and style were made by the IFC as a part of the 2004–5 review of Interpretations.

2.7
Economic Barriers to Information Access

An Interpretation of the
Library Bill of Rights

A democracy presupposes an informed citizenry. The First Amendment mandates the right of all persons to free expression, and the corollary right to receive the constitutionally protected expression of others. The publicly supported library provides free, equal, and equitable access to information for all people of the community the library serves. While the roles, goals and objectives of publicly supported libraries may differ, they share this common mission.

The library's essential mission must remain the first consideration for librarians and governing bodies faced with economic pressures and competition for funding. In support of this mission, the American Library Association has enumerated certain principles of library services in the *Library Bill of Rights*.

Principles Governing Fines, Fees, and User Charges

Article I of the *Library Bill of Rights* states:

> Books and other library resources should be provided for the interest, information, and enlightenment of all people of the community the library serves.

Article V of the *Library Bill of Rights* states:

> A person's right to use a library should not be denied
> or abridged because of origin, age, background, or
> views.

The American Library Association opposes the charging of user fees for the provision of information by all libraries and information services that receive their major support from public funds. All information resources that are provided directly or indirectly by the library, regardless of technology, format, or methods of delivery, should be readily, equally and equitably accessible to all library users.

Libraries that adhere to these principles systematically monitor their programs of service for potential barriers to access and strive to eliminate such barriers when they occur. All library policies and procedures, particularly those involving fines, fees, or other user charges, should be scrutinized for potential barriers to access. All services should be designed and implemented with care, so as not to infringe on or interfere with the provision or delivery of information and resources for all users. Services should be reevaluated regularly to ensure that the library's basic mission remains uncompromised.

Librarians and governing bodies should look for alternative models and methods of library administration that minimize distinctions among users based on their economic status or financial condition. They should resist the temptation to impose user fees to alleviate financial pressures, at long-term cost to institutional integrity and public confidence in libraries.

Library services that involve the provision of information, regardless of format, technology, or method of delivery, should be made available to all library users on an equal and equitable basis. Charging fees for the use of library collections, services, programs, or facilities that were purchased with public funds raises barriers to access. Such fees effectively abridge or deny access for some members of the community because they reinforce distinctions among users based on their ability and willingness to pay.

Principles Governing Conditions of Funding

Article II of the *Library Bill of Rights* states:

> Materials should not be proscribed or removed because of partisan or doctrinal disapproval.

Article III of the *Library Bill of Rights* states:

> Libraries should challenge censorship in the fulfillment of their responsibility to provide information and enlightenment.

Article IV of the *Library Bill of Rights* states:

> Libraries should cooperate with all persons and groups concerned with resisting abridgment of free expression and free access to ideas.

The American Library Association opposes any legislative or regulatory attempt to impose content restrictions on library resources, or to limit user access to information, as a condition of funding for publicly supported libraries and information services.

The First Amendment guarantee of freedom of expression is violated when the right to receive that expression is subject to arbitrary restrictions based on content.

Librarians and governing bodies should examine carefully any terms or conditions attached to library funding and should oppose attempts to limit through such conditions full and equal access to information because of content. This principle applies equally to private gifts or bequests and to public funds. In particular, librarians and governing bodies have an obligation to reject such restrictions when the effect of the restriction is to limit equal and equitable access to information.

Librarians and governing bodies should cooperate with all efforts to create a community consensus that publicly supported libraries require funding unfettered by restrictions. Such a consensus supports the library mission to provide the free and unrestricted exchange of information and ideas necessary to a functioning democracy.

The Association's historic position in this regard is stated clearly in a number of Association policies: 50.4 "Free Access to Information," 50.8 "Financing of Libraries," 51.2 "Equal Access to Library Service," 51.3 "Intellectual Freedom," 53 "Intellectual Freedom Policies," 59.1 "Policy Objectives," and 61 "Library Services for the Poor."

Adopted June 30, 1993, by the ALA Council. http://www.ala.org/ala/oif/statementspols/statementsif/interpretations/economicbarriers.htm.

HISTORY

Economic Barriers to Information Access

In 1989, the American Library Association's Minority Concerns Committee requested that the Council direct the Intellectual Freedom Committee to review the *Library Bill of Rights* to ensure that it included protection for intellectual freedom without regard to language or economic status. The ALA Council issued that directive, thereby launching a three-year process of review of all of the Interpretations of the *Library Bill of Rights*, of which all save one were amended to address the question of language. Throughout its discussions, the IFC discussed whether a separate or new Interpretation specifically dealing with questions relating to economic status was needed; it concluded that the prevalence of questions about fees for library services necessitated a new Interpretation.

The process of gathering information for what became "Economic Barriers to Information Access" began at the 1991 Annual Conference in Atlanta, where the IFC sponsored an open hearing on fees for library service to receive comments from librarians working in all areas of library service and types of libraries. A first draft of an Interpretation was developed at the 1992 Midwinter Meeting in San Antonio and widely circulated for comment prior to and during the 1992 Annual Conference in San Francisco. Continuing its process of receiving comments and suggestions on the draft, the Committee met at the 1993 Midwinter Meeting in Denver with representatives of the Library of Congress (LC), who themselves were contemplating charging fees for library services.

Since 1977, the American Library Association has had on the

books a policy (50.4) opposing fees for library services, specifically information services. But libraries have always felt pressure both from funding agencies and internally to recover the cost of providing certain types of services, particularly in times of economic hardship. In 1993, the atmosphere of fiscal restraint was being felt by all types of libraries all over the country and had reached to the Library of Congress itself.

Judith Farley, Daniel Molhollan, and Winston Tabb, representatives of the Library of Congress, met with the IFC at the 1993 Midwinter Meeting to discuss a bill then pending before Congress dealing with the LC's funding and fees. While expressing concerns about user charges, they were troubled by statements in the then-current draft Interpretation flatly opposing the charging of user fees. At that time, the LC was the subject of a funding bill in Congress defining three different types of library service: core, national, and specialized. Core services would be free, national services would have fees related to distribution costs only, and specialized services would be provided on a full-cost-recovery basis. The proposal generated intensive discussion at the Intellectual Freedom Committee meeting during that 1993 Midwinter Meeting. The net result of the discussion was to solidify the Committee's belief that an Interpretation of the *Library Bill of Rights* addressing economic barriers to information access must be concerning the provision of information by libraries and information services that receive their major support from public funds. In this society of information haves and have-nots, the provision of information based on the ability to pay must be avoided.

As IFC chair Candace Morgan explained in her report to Council for that Midwinter Meeting, the draft was revised to "address the Committee's growing concern over the creeping acceptance, by governing bodies and funding sources, of the idea that libraries should be required to recover some costs through user charges that have the potential to create barriers to access based on economic status."

Another issue that was raised during the discussion was potential restrictions and conditions imposed upon information access by donors. Libraries sometimes receive donations of money or materials that carry with them conditions imposing restrictions upon access that discriminate against some library users.

Finally, the pervasive atmosphere of fiscal restraint had generated pressures from local government upon libraries to charge fees for services. The Committee noted that much of that pressure reflected a lack of understanding of the unique mission of publicly supported libraries—no other agency serves as a public forum through which the ideals of the First Amendment may be realized. The Committee wanted to encourage libraries to educate their funding agencies about their unique role and to urge them to insist on being treated as unique by local governments. The introductory language in the revised draft Interpretation squarely placed libraries within the arena of First Amendment law—as public forums for access to information subject to First Amendment principles and responsible to their users to provide information access without charge.

Following consideration of testimony presented at the 1991 hearing, comments made on the draft, and the concerns of the representatives of the Library of Congress, a substantially revised version was circulated for comment to the ALA Executive Board; the ALA Council; ALA committees, divisions, and round tables; chairs of state intellectual freedom committees; and interested librarians prior to the 1993 Annual Conference. Additional written and oral comments continued to be received until and during the Conference, where the Committee again met with representatives of the Library of Congress. A final draft was offered to the Council for its adoption at that 1993 Annual Conference in New Orleans.

The final version takes a strong position against the charging of fees and urges libraries to examine their policies and practices to ensure that information access is not restricted by being based upon the ability to pay. Although the Interpretation was adopted by the Council at the 1993 Annual Conference, the discussion of the principles it states continues. During the discussion of the new Interpretation, the Intellectual Freedom Committee determined that the best description of the resources provided by publicly supported libraries that the Committee believed should be free of all user charges was "information resources and services." The document does not preclude the possibility of charging fees for non-information services, such as photocopying. The Interpretation sets forth an ideal toward which libraries are encouraged to aspire, and it encourages the continuous scrutiny of library policy, procedure, and operation for potential economic barriers in order to ensure that access to information is not restricted due to an inability to pay for it.

No changes in "Economic Barriers to Information Access" were recommended as part of the 1999–2000 periodic review of all Interpretations by the IFC. Grammatical edits were made during the 2004–5 review.

2.8

Evaluating Library Collections

An Interpretation of the *Library Bill of Rights*

The continuous review of library materials is necessary as a means of maintaining an active library collection of current interest to users. In the process, materials may be added and physically deteriorated or obsolete materials may be replaced or removed in accordance with the collection maintenance policy of a given library and the needs of the community it serves. Continued evaluation is closely related to the goals and responsibilities of all libraries and is a valuable tool of collection development. This procedure is not to be used as a convenient means to remove materials presumed to be controversial or disapproved of by segments of the community. Such abuse of the evaluation function violates the principles of intellectual freedom and is in opposition to the Preamble and Articles I and II of the *Library Bill of Rights*, which state:

> The American Library Association affirms that all libraries are forums for information and ideas, and that the following basic policies should guide their services.
>
> I. Books and other library resources should be provided for the interest, information, and enlightenment of all people of the community the library serves. Materials should not be excluded because of the origin, background, or views of those contributing to their creation.

II. Libraries should provide materials and information presenting all points of view on current and historical issues. Materials should not be proscribed or removed because of partisan or doctrinal disapproval.

The American Library Association opposes such "silent censorship" and strongly urges that libraries adopt guidelines setting forth the positive purposes and principles of evaluation of materials in library collections.

Adopted February 2, 1973, by the ALA Council; amended July 1, 1981. http://www.ala.org/ala/oif/statementspols/statementsif/interpretations/evaluatinglibrary.htm.

HISTORY

Evaluating Library Collections

I n both theory and practice, library collections undergo continual reevaluation to ensure that they fulfill and remain responsive to the goals of the institution and the needs of library patrons. The reevaluation process, however, can also be used to remove materials that are controversial or offensive to library staff or to members of the community. The use of collection evaluation for this purpose is manifestly inconsistent with Articles I and II of the *Library Bill of Rights*.

At the 1972 Midwinter Meeting in Chicago, the Intellectual Freedom Committee realized the necessity of an Interpretation of the *Library Bill of Rights* with regard to general issues involved in reevaluating library collections and announced its intent to prepare a statement on reevaluation. The document was approved by the Intellectual Freedom Committee at the 1972 Annual Conference in Chicago. It was submitted to the ALA Council at the 1973 Midwinter Meeting in Washington, D.C., and was adopted on February 2, 1973, under the title "Reevaluating Library Collections."

> The continuous review of library collections to remove physically deteriorated or obsolete materials is one means to maintain active library collections of current interest to users.* Continued reevaluation is closely related to the goals and responsibilities of libraries, and is

---

*The traditional term "weeding," implying "the removal of noxious growth," is purposely avoided due to the imprecise nature of the term.

a valuable tool of collection building. This procedure, however, is sometimes used as a convenient means to remove materials thought to be too controversial or disapproved of by segments of the community. Such abuse of the reevaluation function violates the principles of intellectual freedom and is in opposition to Articles I and II of the *Library Bill of Rights*, which state that:

> As a responsibility of library service, books and other library materials selected should be chosen for values of interest, information, and enlightenment of all the people of the community. In no case should library materials be excluded because of the race or nationality or the social, political, or religious views of the authors.
>
> Libraries should provide books and other materials presenting all points of view concerning the problems and issues of our times; no library materials should be proscribed or removed from libraries because of partisan or doctrinal disapproval.

The American Library Association opposes such "silent censorship," and recommends that libraries adopt guidelines setting forth the positive purposes and principles for reevaluation of materials in library collections.

In 1981, the policy was rewritten by the IFC to reflect the changes that had been made in the 1980 version of the *Library Bill of Rights*. In the process, a number of editorial changes were made in the text with the aim of increasing its forcefulness. The most significant amendment recommended by the IFC was a change in the title of the document from "Reevaluating Library Collections" to "Evaluating Library Collections." The change was suggested because the process of evaluating library materials for acquisition or retention is a single ongoing process and, in principle, is never completed and then redone. Moreover, the Intellectual Freedom Committee thought that it could be falsely inferred from the word "reevaluating" that initial evaluations of works had been incorrect. The revision was approved by the Council on July 1, 1981.

In line with the ongoing practice of periodic review, the IFC reviewed "Evaluating Library Collections" in 1999–2000 and did not recommend any changes. Grammatical edits were made during the 2004–5 review.

2.9
Exhibit Spaces and Bulletin Boards

An Interpretation of the
Library Bill of Rights

Libraries often provide exhibit spaces and bulletin boards. The uses made of these spaces should conform to the *Library Bill of Rights*: Article I states, "Materials should not be excluded because of the origin, background, or views of those contributing to their creation." Article II states, "Materials should not be proscribed or removed because of partisan or doctrinal disapproval." Article VI maintains that exhibit space should be made available "on an equitable basis, regardless of the beliefs or affiliations of individuals or groups requesting their use."

In developing library exhibits, staff members should endeavor to present a broad spectrum of opinion and a variety of viewpoints. Libraries should not shrink from developing exhibits because of controversial content or because of the beliefs or affiliations of those whose work is represented. Just as libraries do not endorse the viewpoints of those whose work is represented in their collections, libraries also do not endorse the beliefs or viewpoints of topics that may be the subject of library exhibits.

Exhibit areas often are made available for use by community groups. Libraries should formulate a written policy for the use of these exhibit areas to assure that space is provided on an equitable basis to all groups that request it.

Written policies for exhibit space use should be stated in inclusive rather than exclusive terms. For example, a policy that the library's exhibit space is open "to organizations engaged in educational, cultural, intellectual, or charitable activities" is an inclusive statement of the limited uses of the exhibit space. This defined limitation would permit religious groups to use the exhibit space because they engage in intellectual activities, but would exclude most commercial uses of the exhibit space.

A publicly supported library may designate use of exhibit space for strictly library-related activities, provided that this limitation is viewpoint neutral and clearly defined.

Libraries may include in this policy rules regarding the time, place, and manner of use of the exhibit space, so long as the rules are content neutral and are applied in the same manner to all groups wishing to use the space. A library may wish to limit access to exhibit space to groups within the community served by the library. This practice is acceptable provided that the same rules and regulations apply to everyone, and that exclusion is not made on the basis of the doctrinal, religious, or political beliefs of the potential users.

The library should not censor or remove an exhibit because some members of the community may disagree with its content. Those who object to the content of any exhibit held at the library should be able to submit their complaint and/or their own exhibit proposal to be judged according to the policies established by the library.

Libraries may wish to post a permanent notice near the exhibit area stating that the library does not advocate or endorse the viewpoints of exhibits or exhibitors.

Libraries that make bulletin boards available to public groups for posting notices of public interest should develop criteria for the use of these spaces based on the same considerations as those outlined above. Libraries may wish to develop criteria regarding the size of material to be displayed, the length of time materials may remain on the bulletin board, the frequency with which material may be posted for the same group, and the geographic area from which notices will be accepted.

Adopted July 2, 1991, by the ALA Council; amended June 30, 2004.
http://www.ala.org/Template.cfm?Section=interpretations&Template=/
ContentManagement/ContentDisplay.cfm&ContentID=72133.

HISTORY

Exhibit Spaces and
Bulletin Boards

Use of library exhibit spaces and meeting rooms became a subject of developing controversy in the 1970s. These years saw several publicized efforts to deny access to such facilities to controversial groups or exhibitors. In North Carolina, for example, an exhibit sponsored by the Ku Klux Klan at a public library sparked a violent confrontation with protesters. At the University of California library at Berkeley, Turkish students protested the one-sidedness of an exhibit on the early-twentieth-century massacre of Armenians by Turks, which had been placed in the library by students of Armenian ancestry. In several places, attempts were made to deny use of such facilities to certain groups on the grounds either that the groups themselves were advocates of violence or that the threat of violence associated with their meetings—including threats made against these meetings by the groups' opponents—posed a danger to library employees and patrons or to library property. At the same time, exhibits mounted by libraries themselves sometimes came under fire. In Virginia, for instance, an exhibit of books about homosexuality in a public library collection was accused of promoting this practice and of obscenity. All these efforts to censor library exhibits were in violation of Article VI of the *Library Bill of Rights*.

The 1970s were also marked by some confusion within ALA about the applicability of Article VI as it was formulated in the 1967 version of the *Library Bill of Rights*. In particular, academic and school libraries pointed out that the provision was written to apply in reality only to public libraries, and public librarians noted that it was not flexible enough to accommodate the varying situations of public libraries.

The 1980 revision of the *Library Bill of Rights* took account of these objections, and the revision of Article VI in that year successfully remedied its major defects. (See part 2, section 1, "*Library Bill of Rights*: History.") At the 1980 Annual Conference in New York, however, the IFC, with Frances C. Dean as chair, decided that, given both the increasing number of incidents and the admitted complexity of applying even the revised article in practice, a written policy interpreting the article would be desirable.

The Intellectual Freedom Committee agreed that the key to applying the article was the need to maintain flexibility while upholding a standard of fairness. On this basis a policy was prepared and, at the 1981 Midwinter Meeting in Washington, D.C., presented to the Council, which adopted it as an ALA policy on February 4, 1981. It read as follows:

> As part of their program of service, many libraries provide meeting rooms and exhibit spaces for individuals and groups. Article VI of the *Library Bill of Rights* states that such facilities should be made available to the public served by the given library "on an equitable basis, regardless of the beliefs or affiliations of individuals or groups requesting their use."
>
> In formulating this position, the American Library Association sought to accommodate the broad range of practices among public, academic, school and other libraries, while upholding a standard of fairness. Libraries maintaining exhibit and meeting room facilities for outside groups and individuals should develop and publish policy statements governing their use. These statements can properly define and restrict eligibility for use as long as the qualifications do not pertain to the content of a meeting or exhibit or to the beliefs or affiliations of the sponsors.
>
> It is appropriate for a library to limit access to meeting rooms or exhibit space to members of the specific community served by the library or to groups of a specific category. It is not proper to apply such limitations in

ways which favor points of view or organizations advocating certain viewpoints. For example, some libraries permit religious groups to use meeting facilities, while others do not. According to Article VI, both policies are acceptable as long as all religious groups are treated in the same way, irrespective of their doctrines.

Exhibits and meetings sponsored by the library itself should be organized in a manner consistent with the *Library Bill of Rights*, especially Article II which states that "libraries should provide materials and information presenting all points of view." However, in granting meeting or exhibit space to outside individuals and groups, the library should make no effort to censor or amend the content of the exhibit or meeting. Those who object to or disagree with the content of any exhibit or meeting held at the library should be entitled to submit their own exhibit or meeting proposals which should be judged according to the policies established by the library.

The library may properly limit the use of its meeting rooms to meetings which are open to the public, or it may make space available for both public and private sessions. Again, however, the same standard should be applicable to all.

In 1989, revisions were undertaken to reflect nondiscrimination on the basis of language or economic status. Discussion on appropriate changes in the Interpretation continued through June 26, 1990, at which time the Committee voted to rescind two sentences of the Interpretation as an interim measure:

> For example, some libraries permit religious groups to use meeting facilities, while others do not. According to Article VI, both policies are acceptable as long as all religious groups are treated in the same way, irrespective of their doctrines.

The sentences were rescinded in light of a recent court decision in favor of a religious organization that had been denied use of a library meeting room[1] (see part 4, section 1, "Public Libraries and the Public Forum Doctrine").

Following adoption of the interim language, continuing concerns about the meaning of viewpoint-neutral restrictions, the rules governing designated public forums, and commercial uses of library meeting rooms led to a consensus decision to rewrite the policy totally.

In January 1991, two separate Interpretations—"Meeting Rooms" and "Exhibit Spaces and Bulletin Boards"—were introduced. Recent court decisions supporting the right of religious groups to have access to public forums for their meetings raised questions that were best dealt with in a discrete meeting-room policy. After additional discussion about fees, commercial uses, and disclaimers to clarify the library's position as a neutral host and not an advocate of particular meetings or exhibits, the Committee voted to adopt the two Interpretations for circulation to all ALA units, the Council, and the Executive Board for comment.

The two policies were adopted as revised on July 2, 1991, at the Annual Conference. (For the policy "Meeting Rooms," see part 2, section 2.15.)

No changes in "Exhibit Spaces and Bulletin Boards" were recommended as part of the 1999–2000 periodic review of all Interpretations by the IFC.

As part of the 2004–5 review of Interpretations the IFC recommended revising one sentence for clarity. The sentence

> A publicly supported library may designate use of exhibit space for strictly library-related activities, provided that the limitation is clearly circumscribed and is viewpoint neutral.

was changed to:

> A publicly supported library may designate use of exhibit space for strictly library-related activities, provided that this limitation is viewpoint neutral and clearly defined.

Council approved the revised Interpretation on June 30, 2004.

NOTE

1. *Concerned Women for America, Inc. v. Lafayette County*, 883 F.2d 32, 34 (5th Cir. 1989).

2.10
Expurgation of Library Materials

An Interpretation of the
Library Bill of Rights

Expurgating library materials is a violation of the *Library Bill of Rights*. Expurgation as defined by this Interpretation includes any deletion, excision, alteration, editing, or obliteration of any part(s) of books or other library resources by the library, its agent, or its parent institution (if any). By such expurgation, the library is in effect denying access to the complete work and the entire spectrum of ideas that the work intended to express. Such action stands in violation of Articles I, II, and III of the *Library Bill of Rights*, which state that "Materials should not be excluded because of the origin, background, or views of those contributing to their creation," that "Materials should not be proscribed or removed because of partisan or doctrinal disapproval," and that "Libraries should challenge censorship in the fulfillment of their responsibility to provide information and enlightenment."

The act of expurgation has serious implications. It involves a determination that it is necessary to restrict access to the complete work. This is censorship. When a work is expurgated, under the assumption that certain portions of that work would be harmful to minors, the situation is no less serious.

Expurgation of any books or other library resources imposes a restriction, without regard to the rights and desires of all library users, by limiting access to ideas and information. (See also other Interpretations to the *Library Bill of Rights*, including Access to

Electronic Information, Services, and Networks and Free Access to Libraries for Minors.)

Further, expurgation without written permission from the holder of the copyright on the material may violate the copyright provisions of the United States Code.

Adopted February 2, 1973, by the ALA Council; amended July 1, 1981; January 10, 1990. The "see also" references to other policies were added by the Committee as a part of the 2004–5 review of Interpretations. http://www.ala.org/ala/oif/statementspols/statementsif/interpretations/expurgationlibrary.htm.

HISTORY

Expurgation of Library Materials

The December 1971 issue of *School Library Journal* (page 7) carried the following report submitted by one of its readers:

> Maurice Sendak might faint but a staff member of Caldwell Parish Library [Louisiana], knowing that the patrons of the community might object to the illustrations in *In the Night Kitchen*, solved the problem by diapering the little boys with white tempera paint. Other libraries might wish to do the same.

In response, Ursula Nordstrom, publisher of Harper Junior Books, sent a statement to more than 380 librarians, professors, publishers, authors, and artists throughout the United States:

> [The news item sent to *School Library Journal*] is representative of several such reports about Maurice Sendak's *In the Night Kitchen*, a book for children, that have come out of public and school libraries throughout the country.
>
> At first, the thought of librarians painting diapers or pants on the naked hero of Sendak's book might seem amusing, merely a harmless eccentricity on the part of some prim few. On reconsideration, however, this behavior should be recognized for what it is: an act of censorship by mutilation rather than by obvious suppression.

More than 425 persons signed the statement of protest circulated by Nordstrom. The expurgation of *In the Night Kitchen* was brought to the attention of the Intellectual Freedom Committee by the Children's Book Council in June 1972. During its meeting at the 1972 ALA Annual Conference in Chicago, the Committee decided that expurgation was covered by the Library Bill of Rights and that a statement should be issued specifically on that topic. During the 1973 Midwinter Meeting in Washington, D.C., the Committee approved a statement on expurgation of library materials and sent it to the ALA Council for approval. The document, which was adopted by the Council as an ALA policy on February 2, 1973, read as follows:

> Library materials are chosen for their value and interest to the community the library serves. If library materials were acquired for these reasons and in accordance with a written statement on materials selection, then to expurgate must be interpreted as a violation of the *Library Bill of Rights*. For purposes of this statement, expurgation includes deletion, excision, alteration or obliteration. By such expurgation, the library is in effect denying access to the complete work and the full ideas that the work was intended to express; such action stands in violation of Article II of the *Library Bill of Rights*, which states that "no library materials should be proscribed or removed from libraries because of partisan or doctrinal disapproval."
>
> The act of expurgation has serious implications. It involves a determination by an individual that it is necessary to restrict the availability of that material. It is, in fact, censorship.
>
> When a work is expurgated, under the assumption that certain sections of that work would be harmful to minors, the situation is no less serious. Expurgation of any library materials imposes a restriction, without regard to the rights and desires of all library users.

In 1981, during the review of all the Interpretations of the *Library Bill of Rights*, the IFC reviewed the policy on expurgation and made several changes designed to add clarity to and strengthen the document. Most important, the IFC recommended basing the argument of the Interpretation not only on Article II of the *Library Bill of Rights* but on Articles I and III as well. The revision was adopted by the Council on July 1, 1981, and read as follows:

Books and other library resources are selected for their value, interest, and importance to the people of the community the library serves. Since books and other library resources are acquired for these reasons and in accordance with a written statement on materials selection, then expurgating them must be interpreted as a violation of the *Library Bill of Rights*. Expurgation as defined by this Interpretation includes any deletion, excision, alteration, or obliteration of any part(s) of books or other library resources by the library. By such expurgation, the library is in effect denying access to the complete work and the entire spectrum of ideas that the work intended to express; such action stands in violation of Articles I, II, and III of the *Library Bill of Rights*, which state that "Materials should not be excluded because of the origin, background, or views of those contributing to their creation"; that "Materials should not be proscribed or removed because of partisan or doctrinal disapproval"; and that "Libraries should challenge censorship in the fulfillment of their responsibility to provide information and enlightenment."

The act of expurgation has serious implications. It involves a determination that it is necessary to restrict complete access to that material. This is censorship. When a work is expurgated, under the assumption that certain portions of that work would be harmful to minors, the situation is no less serious.

Expurgation of any books or other library resources imposes a restriction, without regard to the rights and desires of all library users, by limiting access to ideas and information.

At the 1989 ALA Annual Conference in Dallas, the Interpretation "Expurgation of Library Materials" was revised in accordance with the request of the Minority Concerns Committee for review of the *Library Bill of Rights* to ensure that discrimination on the basis of language and economic status would be addressed. The IFC adopted a revised version, which was subsequently circulated for comments. At the 1990 Midwinter Meeting, minor editorial changes were made, and the new draft was adopted and recommended to the Council. On January 10, 1990, the Interpretation became ALA policy.

In 1999–2000, "Expurgation of Library Materials" was carefully reviewed by the IFC and no changes were recommended. "See also" references to other policies were added during the 2004–5 review of Interpretations.

2.11
Free Access to Libraries for Minors

An Interpretation of the
Library Bill of Rights

Library policies and procedures that effectively deny minors equal and equitable access to all library resources available to other users violate the *Library Bill of Rights*. The American Library Association opposes all attempts to restrict access to library services, materials, and facilities based on the age of library users.

Article V of the *Library Bill of Rights* states, "A person's right to use a library should not be denied or abridged because of origin, age, background, or views." The "right to use a library" includes free access to, and unrestricted use of, all the services, materials, and facilities the library has to offer. Every restriction on access to, and use of, library resources, based solely on the chronological age, educational level, literacy skills, or legal emancipation of users violates Article V.

Libraries are charged with the mission of developing resources to meet the diverse information needs and interests of the communities they serve. Services, materials, and facilities that fulfill the needs and interests of library users at different stages in their personal development are a necessary part of library resources. The needs and interests of each library user, and resources appropriate to meet those needs and interests, must be determined on an individual basis. Librarians cannot predict what resources will best fulfill the needs and interests of any individual user based on a single criterion such as chronological age, educational level, literacy skills, or legal emancipation.

Libraries should not limit the selection and development of library resources simply because minors will have access to them. Institutional self-censorship diminishes the credibility of the library in the community, and restricts access for all library users.

Children and young adults unquestionably possess First Amendment rights, including the right to receive information in the library. Constitutionally protected speech cannot be suppressed solely to protect children or young adults from ideas or images a legislative body believes to be unsuitable for them.* Librarians and library governing bodies should not resort to age restrictions in an effort to avoid actual or anticipated objections, because only a court of law can determine whether material is not constitutionally protected.

The mission, goals, and objectives of libraries cannot authorize librarians or library governing bodies to assume, abrogate, or overrule the rights and responsibilities of parents. As "Libraries: An American Value" states, "We affirm the responsibility and the right of all parents and guardians to guide their own children's use of the library and its resources and services." Librarians and governing bodies should maintain that parents—and only parents—have the right and the responsibility to restrict the access of their children—and only their children—to library resources. Parents who do not want their children to have access to certain library services, materials, or facilities should so advise their children. Librarians and library governing bodies cannot assume the role of parents or the functions of parental authority in the private relationship between parent and child.

Lack of access to information can be harmful to minors. Librarians and library governing bodies have a public and professional obligation to ensure that all members of the community

---

* See *Erznoznik v. City of Jacksonville*, 422 U.S. 205 (1975), "Speech that is neither obscene as to youths nor subject to some other legitimate proscription cannot be suppressed solely to protect the young from ideas or images that a legislative body thinks unsuitable [422 U.S. 205, 214] for them. In most circumstances, the values protected by the First Amendment are no less applicable when government seeks to control the flow of information to minors." See *Tinker v. Des Moines School Dist., supra.* Cf. *West Virginia Bd. of Ed. v. Barnette*, 319 U.S. 624 (1943).

they serve have free, equal, and equitable access to the entire range of library resources regardless of content, approach, format, or amount of detail. This principle of library service applies equally to all users, minors as well as adults. Librarians and library governing bodies must uphold this principle in order to provide adequate and effective service to minors.

Adopted June 30, 1972, by the ALA Council; amended July 1, 1981; July 3, 1991; June 30, 2004. http://www.ala.org/ala/oif/statementspols/ statementsif/interpretations/freeaccesslibraries.htm.

HISTORY

Free Access to Libraries
for Minors

The question of whether or not intellectual freedom in libraries applies to children and young adults has been debated by librarians since the early years of the profession's involvement with intellectual freedom. The question was considered many times by the Intellectual Freedom Committee and led to the preconference institute titled Intellectual Freedom and the Teenager, held in San Francisco on June 23–25, 1967.

Sponsored jointly by the Intellectual Freedom Committee, the Young Adult Services Division, and the American Association of School Librarians, and attended by approximately four hundred librarians, the preconference featured a variety of speakers of national reputation, including author Kenneth Rexroth, attorneys Stanley Fleishman and Alex P. Allain, book review editor Robert Kirsh, and library young-adult consultant Esther Helfand. The most outspoken panelist was Edgar Z. Friedenberg, author of *Coming of Age in America*, who told participants:

> The library is just one more place where the kids are taught they are second-class citizens. They learn this not only from the books pressed upon them by the helpful librarian but even more so from the very atmosphere of the place.[1]

In his summary of the three-day meeting, Ervin Gaines, chair of the IFC, dwelled at length on Friedenberg's comments:

> He made the assumption that intellectual freedom was
> an inalienable right and that age is not a morally relevant
> factor and that adults have themselves no right to deter-
> mine for youth access to ideas. This assumption which
> came at the very beginning of this talk echoed and re-
> echoed throughout the conference. There was surprising
> unanimity of opinion on this particular point.[2]

As the preconference progressed, there was also surprising una-
nimity on the position that not only teenagers but all young people
were the focus of the discussions. This was reflected in one of the
major recommendations of the institute, "that free access to all
books in a library collection be granted to young people."[3]

Later, during the 1967 ALA Annual Conference, Gaines moved
that the Council adopt a revised version of the *Library Bill of Rights*.
He introduced his motion with the following remarks:

> At a meeting of the Intellectual Freedom Committee yes-
> terday two minor amendments were suggested to this
> text [the revised *Library Bill of Rights*]. In section 5 we sug-
> gest that the word "age" be inserted. . . . This suggestion
> comes as a result of recommendations from the precon-
> ference on Intellectual Freedom and the Teenager, which
> was held last week.

The change was approved by the Council, and the Association, well
in advance of society in general, took a significant stand, approving
free access for minors to all the materials in a library collection.

After 1967, the word "age" in the *Library Bill of Rights* was a constant source of confusion. Did it mean that children should be able
to take home any materials in a library collection, or were some
restrictions permissible? What about double card systems or multiple card systems restricting minors to the use of only part of the collection? These and other questions accrued until the IFC's 1972 midwinter meeting. Twenty hours of meetings were dominated by
discussions of minors and library access problems, all related to the
word "age" in the *Library Bill of Rights*.

After the meeting, the Committee announced plans to develop
a position statement concerning access to libraries for minors. A
draft was subsequently sent, in the spring of 1972, to the boards of

the Public Library Association, the American Association of School Librarians, the Children's Services Division, the Young Adult Services Division, and the American Library Trustee Association. At its annual meeting in June 1972, the IFC approved the statement and recommended it to the ALA Council, which adopted it on June 30, 1972, as an ALA policy titled "Free Access to Libraries for Minors." The statement read as follows:

> Some library procedures and practices effectively deny minors access to certain services and materials available to adults. Such procedures and practices are not in accord with the *Library Bill of Rights* and are opposed by the American Library Association.
>
> Restrictions take a variety of forms, including, among others, restricted reading rooms for adult use only, library cards limiting circulation of some materials to adults only, closed collections for adult use only, and interlibrary loan service for adult use only.
>
> All limitations in minors' access to library materials and services violate Article V of the *Library Bill of Rights*, which states, "The rights of an individual to the use of a library should not be denied or abridged because of age. . . ." Limiting access to some services and materials to only adults abridges the use of libraries for minors. "Use of the library" includes use of, and access to, all library materials and services.
>
> Restrictions are often initiated under the assumption that certain materials are "harmful" to minors, or in an effort to avoid controversy with parents who might think so. The librarian who would restrict the access of minors to materials and services because of actual or suspected parental objection should bear in mind that he is not in loco parentis in his position as librarian. Individual intellectual levels and family backgrounds are significant factors not accommodated by a uniform policy based upon age.
>
> In today's world, children are exposed to adult life much earlier than in the past. They read materials and view a variety of media on the adult level at home and elsewhere. Current emphasis upon early childhood

education has also increased opportunities for young people to learn and to have access to materials, and has decreased the validity of using chronological age as an index to the use of libraries. The period of time during which children are interested in reading materials specifically designed for them grows steadily shorter, and librarians must recognize and adjust to this change if they wish to maintain the patronage of young people.

The American Library Association holds that it is the parent—and only the parent—who may restrict his children—and only his children—from access to library materials and services. The parent who would rather his child did not have access to certain materials should so advise the child.

The word "age" was incorporated into Article V of the *Library Bill of Rights* as a direct result of a preconference titled Intellectual Freedom and the Teenager, held in San Francisco in June 1967. One recommendation of the preconference participants was "that free access to all books in a library collection be granted to young people." The preconference generally concluded that young people are entitled to the same access to libraries and to the materials in libraries as are adults and that materials selection should not be diluted on that account.

This does not mean, for instance, that issuing different types of borrowers' cards to minors and adults is, per se, contrary to the *Library Bill of Rights*. If such practices are used for purposes of gathering statistics, the various kinds of cards carry no implicit or explicit limitations on access to materials and services. Neither does it mean that maintaining separate children's collections is a violation of the *Library Bill of Rights*, provided that no patron is restricted to the use of only certain collections.

The Association's position does not preclude isolating certain materials for legitimate protection of irreplaceable or very costly works from careless use. Such "restricted-use" areas as rare book rooms are appropriate if the materials so classified are genuinely rare, and not merely controversial.

> Unrestrictive selection policies, developed with care
> for principles of intellectual freedom and the *Library Bill
> of Rights*, should not be vitiated by administrative prac-
> tices which restrict minors to the use of only part of a
> library's collections and services.

Following adoption of the 1980 revision of the *Library Bill of Rights*, the IFC reviewed the document anew. Working closely with the intellectual freedom committees of the Young Adult Services Division and the Association for Library Service to Children (previously the Children's Services Division) at the 1981 Midwinter Meeting and Annual Conference, the Committee made several changes aimed not only at eliminating sex-linked language but also at strengthening the impact of the Interpretation. Reference to the 1967 preconference was deleted as a historical detail irrelevant to a broad public statement of policy, and several key paragraphs were rewritten to communicate the Association's stand with greater force and clarity.

The Intellectual Freedom Committee also decided to delete from the document all references to specific administrative practices such as dual-card systems and restricted-use areas—which, although not always in violation of the principles of the *Library Bill of Rights*, have been employed at times in ways that unfairly limit minors' access to library resources. Limiting discussion of the intellectual freedom implications of such administrative practices to their effects on minors' access in itself tended to legitimize their misuse, and, the Committee concluded, the treatment in the document weakened its overall thrust by appearing to qualify the policy and limit its application. The Committee therefore decided to discuss such practices separately and in a more all-sided way by developing a new Interpretation to be titled "Administrative Policies and Procedures Affecting Access to Library Resources and Services." That Interpretation was adopted in 1982 but rescinded in 1992, when the Committee adopted Guidelines for the Development and Implementation of Policies, Regulations and Procedures Affecting Access to Library Materials, Services and Facilities (see part 3, section 4.1).

On July 1, 1981, the revision of "Free Access to Libraries for Minors" was adopted by the Council. It read as follows:

Some library procedures effectively deny minors access to certain services and materials available to adults. Such procedures and practices are not in accord with the *Library Bill of Rights* and are opposed by the American Library Association.

Restrictions take a variety of forms, including, among others, restricted reading rooms for adult use only, library cards limiting circulation of some materials to adults only, closed collections for adult use only, collections limited to teacher use, or restricted according to a student's grade level, and interlibrary loan service for adult use only.

Article V of the *Library Bill of Rights* states that, "A person's right to use a library should not be denied or abridged because of origin, age, background, or views." All limitations on minors' access to library materials and services violate that Article. The "right to use a library" includes use of, and access to, all library materials and services. Thus, practices which allow adults to use some services and materials which are denied to minors abridge the use of libraries based on age.

Materials selection decisions are often made and restrictions are often initiated under the assumption that certain materials may be "harmful" to minors, or in an effort to avoid controversy with parents. Libraries or library boards which would restrict the access of minors to materials and services because of actual or suspected parental objections should bear in mind that they do not serve in loco parentis. Varied levels of intellectual development among young people and differing family background and child-rearing philosophies are significant factors not accommodated by a uniform policy based upon age.

In today's world, children are exposed to adult life much earlier than in the past. They read materials and view a variety of media on the adult level at home and elsewhere. Current emphasis upon early childhood education has also increased opportunities for young people to learn and to have access to materials, and has decreased the validity of using chronological age as an index to the use of libraries. The period of time during which children are interested in reading materials specifically designed for them grows steadily shorter, and librarians must recognize and adjust to this change if they wish to serve young people effectively. Librarians have a responsibility to ensure that young people have access to a wide range of informational and recreational materials and services that reflects sufficient diversity to meet the young person's needs.

The American Library Association opposes libraries restricting access to library materials and services for minors and holds that it is the parents—and only parents—who may restrict their children—and only their children—from access to library materials and services. Parents who would rather their children did not have access to certain materials should so advise their children. The library and its staff are responsible for providing equal access to library materials and services for all library users.

The word "age" was incorporated into Article V of the *Library Bill of Rights* because young people are entitled to the same access to libraries and to the materials in libraries as are adults. Materials selection should not be diluted on that account.

Ten years later, at the 1991 Midwinter Meeting, a further revised "Free Access to Libraries for Minors" was adopted by the IFC. The Committee had extensively reworked the document to make the protections for minors' access more explicit and to outline with greater precision librarians' responsibilities toward minors and all library users. The new policy emphasized the role of librarians as information providers and placed the burden of guiding minors squarely on the shoulders of parents.

The definition of library usage was expanded to include use of facilities as well as materials and services. Library trustees were implicated in the new policy as being co-responsible with librarians for providing equal access to all library resources for all library users.

The Midwinter version also included a list of practices that librarians have used to restrict indirectly minors' access to expensive, controversial, or otherwise objectionable materials, including issuing limited-access cards; barring entry to stacks, reserve areas, or reading rooms; charging fees; and simply refusing to perform a service based solely on the age or educational level of the user. This list was intended to alert librarians to specific practices that inhibited minors' access to library materials, services, and facilities, and to discourage these all-too-common practices.

At the 1991 Annual Conference, the Council deleted the list of examples from the final Interpretation before approving it as ALA policy. Many councilors believed that ALA's official position would be more effective and adaptable to changing societal circumstances if the Interpretation were written in broad terms, without a list of potential violations of the principle.

The list of examples that follows is not comprehensive but is suggestive of some of the most commonly used practices that violate the *Library Bill of Rights*. Copies are available upon request from the Office for Intellectual Freedom.

Examples of Age-Based Access Limitations

Some specific examples of denial of equal access include, but are not limited to, the following:

> restricting access to reading or reference rooms, or to otherwise open stack areas, on the basis of the age or school grade level of the user;

> issuing limited-access library cards, or otherwise restricting the circulation of materials, on the basis of the age or school grade level of the user;

> assigning materials to special collections, such as parenting, teacher-professional, and historical-genealogical, and restricting access to these collections, on the basis of the age or school grade level of the user;

> using manual or computerized registration or circulation systems to restrict access to materials, on the basis of the age or school grade level of the user;

> sequestering or otherwise restricting access to material because of its content, on the basis of the age or school grade level of the user;

requiring or soliciting written permission from a parent or guardian to gain or restrict access to materials because of their content, on the basis of the age or school grade level of the user;

restricting access to interlibrary loan, fax, electronic reference services, or electronic information, on the basis of the age or school grade level of the user;

restricting access to materials because of their format or their cost—such as computer software, compact discs, periodicals, microfilm-fiche, and videocassettes, on the basis of the age or school grade level of the user;

charging fees or requiring deposits to gain access to services, materials, or facilities, on the basis of the age or school grade level of the user;

refusing to process interlibrary loans, reserves, or reference requests for materials classified as juvenile;

assigning professional-nonprofessional staff to reference searches, on the basis of the age or school grade level of the user;

restricting access to library-sponsored programs or events otherwise designed for general audiences, on the basis of the age or school grade level of the user;

restricting access to public facilities, such as meeting rooms, display cases, and notice boards, on the basis of the age or school grade level of the user.

In 1999–2000, in line with their ongoing practice of periodic review of all Interpretations, the IFC carefully reviewed "Free Access to Libraries for Minors," especially in regard to its applicability to the Internet. The Committee did not recommend any changes.

Much of the Committee's discussion of this Interpretation during the 2004–5 review of intellectual freedom policies focused on the rising tide of legislative assaults on the First Amendment rights of minors. At this writing, twenty-one states have adopted Internet filtering laws that apply to public schools or libraries. The majority of these states require school boards or public libraries to adopt Internet use policies to prevent minors from gaining access to sexually explicit, obscene, or harmful materials. Some states also require publicly funded institutions to install filtering software on library public access terminals or school computers.[4] There is a widespread denial of the fact that minors have First Amendment rights. Librarians are frequently called upon to defend those rights, sometimes in a very hostile environment. In light of this situation the IFC proposed a revision of "Free Access to Libraries for Minors" to clarify, strengthen, and support the message concerning minors' rights based on judicial opinions interpreting the First Amendment, with the following changes from the previous policy:

- "Literacy skills" was added to the list of access restrictions that violate Article V of the *Library Bill of Rights* in paragraph 2. This potentially restrictive criterion also was added to paragraph 3.
- Paragraph 5 of the old policy stated:

    Librarians and governing bodies should not resort to age restrictions on access to library resources in an effort to avoid actual or anticipated objections from parents or anyone else. The mission, goals, and objectives of libraries do not authorize librarians or governing bodies to assume, abrogate, or overrule the rights and responsibilities of parents or legal guardians. Librarians and governing bodies should maintain that parents—and only parents—have the right and the responsibility to restrict the access of their children—and only their children—to library resources. Parents or legal guardians who do not want their children to have access to certain library services, materials or facilities, should so advise their children. Librarians and governing bodies cannot assume the role of parents or the functions of parental authority in the private relationship between parent and child. Librarians and governing bodies have a public and professional obligation to provide equal access to all library resources for all library users.

    The messages of this paragraph were divided into two paragraphs meant to clarify the First Amendment rights of children and the rights and responsibilities of parents and guardians. A footnote with reference to judicial decisions confirming these rights was added.

- The sentence "Lack of access to information can be harmful to minors" was added to the final paragraph. There was much discussion of the addition. The Committee pointed out that the same statement had earlier been added to the Interpretation "Access for Children and Young Adults to Nonprint Materials." (See the history of that Interpretation in part 2, section 2.1.) Examples were given, including that AIDS is not only a medical problem but also a problem associated with a lack of access to information. Furthermore, the statement is relevant because many children and young adults are negatively affected by the digital divide.

Council approved the revised Interpretation on June 30, 2004.

NOTES

1. *San Francisco Examiner and Chronicle*, June 25, 1967.
2. *Newsletter on Intellectual Freedom* 16 (September 1967): 54.
3. Ibid., 55.
4. National Council of State Legislatures, "Children and the Internet: Laws Relating to Filtering, Blocking and Usage Policies in Schools and Libraries," http://www.ncsl.org/programs/lis/CIP/filterlaws.htm.

2.12

Intellectual Freedom Principles
for Academic Libraries

An Interpretation of the
Library Bill of Rights

A strong intellectual freedom perspective is critical to the development of academic library collections and services that dispassionately meet the education and research needs of a college or university community. The purpose of this statement is to outline how and where intellectual freedom principles fit into an academic library setting, thereby raising consciousness of the intellectual freedom context within which academic librarians work. The following principles should be reflected in all relevant library policy documents.

1. The general principles set forth in the *Library Bill of Rights* form an indispensable framework for building collections, services, and policies that serve the entire academic community.

2. The privacy of library users is and must be inviolable. Policies should be in place that maintain confidentiality of library borrowing records and of other information relating to personal use of library information and services.

3. The development of library collections in support of an institution's instruction and research programs should transcend the personal values of the selector. In the interests of research and learning, it is essential that collections contain materials repre-

senting a variety of perspectives on subjects that may be considered controversial.

4. Preservation and replacement efforts should ensure that balance in library materials is maintained and that controversial materials are not removed from the collections through theft, loss, mutilation, or normal wear and tear. There should be alertness to efforts by special interest groups to bias a collection through systematic theft or mutilation.

5. Licensing agreements should be consistent with the *Library Bill of Rights*, and should maximize access.

6. Open and unfiltered access to the Internet should be conveniently available to the academic community in a college or university library. Content filtering devices and content-based restrictions are a contradiction of the academic library mission to further research and learning through exposure to the broadest possible range of ideas and information. Such restrictions are a fundamental violation of intellectual freedom in academic libraries.

7. Freedom of information and of creative expression should be reflected in library exhibits and in all relevant library policy documents.

8. Library meeting rooms, research carrels, exhibit spaces, and other facilities should be available to the academic community regardless of research being pursued or subject being discussed. Any restrictions made necessary because of limited availability of space should be based on need, as reflected in library policy, rather than on content of research or discussion.

9. Whenever possible, library services should be available without charge in order to encourage inquiry. Where charges are necessary, a free or low-cost alternative (e.g., downloading to disc rather than printing) should be available when possible.

10. A service philosophy should be promoted that affords equal access to information for all in the

academic community with no discrimination on the basis of race, values, gender, sexual orientation, cultural or ethnic background, physical or learning disability, economic status, religious beliefs, or views.

11. A procedure ensuring due process should be in place to deal with requests by those within and outside the academic community for removal or addition of library resources, exhibits, or services.

12. It is recommended that this statement of principles be endorsed by appropriate institutional governing bodies, including the faculty senate or similar instrument of faculty governance.

Approved June 29, 1999, by the ACRL Board of Directors; adopted July 12, 2000, by the ALA Council; endorsed November 11, 2000, by the American Association of University Professors. http://www.ala.org/ala/oif/statementspols/statementsif/interpretations/intellectual.htm.

HISTORY

Intellectual Freedom Principles
for Academic Libraries

The Association of College and Research Libraries' Intellectual Freedom Committee began work on "Intellectual Freedom Principles for Academic Libraries" during the fall of 1998. By the 1999 ALA Midwinter Meeting in Philadelphia, the document had gone through two drafts. At the Midwinter Meeting, the Committee endorsed a third draft, which was published in the June issue of *C&RL News*. Accompanying the draft was notice of an open hearing scheduled for June 28 at the 1999 ALA Annual Conference in New Orleans. At the same time, response was solicited from readers of the third draft. Deliberations by ALA's Intellectual Freedom Committee before and after the 1999 Annual Conference hearing provided the basis for the fourth draft, which was submitted to the ACRL Board of Directors for approval. The ACRL Board unanimously approved the document on June 29, 1999. Subsequently, on January 16, 2000, the statement was endorsed by ALA's Intellectual Freedom Committee. The ALA Council adopted the document as an Interpretation on July 12, 2000.

On November 11, 2000, the American Association of University Professors endorsed the document, stating their concern that college and university librarians are designated the same rights afforded to other faculty in regard to intellectual freedom and requesting that their endorsement be prefaced with the following language from the Joint Statement on Faculty Status of College and University Librarians, as contained in *AAUP: Policy Documents and Reports*, 1995 edition:

College and university librarians share the professional concerns of faculty members. Academic freedom, for example, is indispensable to librarians, because they are trustees of knowledge with responsibility of ensuring the availability of information and ideas, no matter how controversial, so that teachers may freely teach and students may freely learn. Moreover, as members of the academic community, librarians should have latitude in the exercise of their professional judgment within the library, a share in shaping policy within the institution, and adequate opportunities for professional development and appropriate reward.

No changes were made in this Interpretation during the 2004–5 review of all Interpretations.

2.13
Labels and Rating Systems

An Interpretation of the
Library Bill of Rights

Libraries do not advocate the ideas found in their collections or in resources accessible through the library. The presence of books and other resources in a library does not indicate endorsement of their contents by the library. Likewise, the ability for library users to access electronic information using library computers does not indicate endorsement or approval of that information by the library.

Labels

Labels on library materials may be viewpoint-neutral directional aids that save the time of users, or they may be attempts to prejudice or discourage users or restrict their access to materials. When labeling is an attempt to prejudice attitudes, it is a censor's tool. The American Library Association opposes labeling as a means of predisposing people's attitudes toward library materials.

Prejudicial labels are designed to restrict access, based on a value judgment that the content, language or themes of the material, or the background or views of the creator(s) of the material, render it inappropriate or offensive for all or certain groups of users. The prejudicial label is used to warn, discourage or prohibit users or certain groups of users from accessing the material. Such labels may be used to remove materials from open shelves to restricted locations where access depends on staff intervention.

Viewpoint-neutral directional aids facilitate access by making it easier for users to locate materials. The materials are housed on open shelves and are equally accessible to all users, who may choose to consult or ignore the directional aids at their own discretion.

Directional aids can have the effect of prejudicial labels when their implementation becomes proscriptive rather than descriptive. When directional aids are used to forbid access or to suggest moral or doctrinal endorsement, the effect is the same as prejudicial labeling.

Rating Systems

A variety of organizations promulgate rating systems as a means of advising either their members or the general public concerning their opinions of the contents and suitability or appropriate age for use of certain books, films, recordings, Web sites, or other materials. The adoption, enforcement, or endorsement of any of these rating systems by the library violates the *Library Bill of Rights*. Adopting such systems into law may be unconstitutional. If such legislation is passed, the library should seek legal advice regarding the law's applicability to library operations.

Publishers, industry groups, and distributors sometimes add ratings to material or include them as part of their packaging. Librarians should not endorse such practices. However, removing or destroying such ratings—if placed there by, or with permission of, the copyright holder—could constitute expurgation (see "Expurgation of Library Materials: An Interpretation of the *Library Bill of Rights*").

Some find it easy and even proper, according to their ethics, to establish criteria for judging materials as objectionable. However, injustice and ignorance, rather than justice and enlightenment, result from such practices. The American Library Association opposes any efforts that result in closing any path to knowledge.

Adopted July 13, 1951, by the ALA Council; amended June 25, 1971; July 1, 1981; June 26, 1990; January 19, 2005. http://www.ala.org/ala/oif/statementspols/statementsif/interpretations/statementlabeling.htm.

HISTORY

Labels and Rating Systems

In late 1950, the Intellectual Freedom Committee received a report that the Montclair, New Jersey, chapter of the Sons of the American Revolution (SAR) was exerting pressure on New Jersey libraries to put a prominent label or inscription on "publications which advocate or favor communism, or which are issued or distributed by any communist organization or any other organization formally designated by any authorized government official or agency as communistic or subversive." The SAR said further that such publications "should not be freely available in libraries to readers or in schools to pupils, but should be obtainable only by signing suitable applications."[1]

Rutherford D. Rogers, then chair of the IFC, reported the matter to the ALA Council on July 13, 1951, and said groups other than the SAR have tried to use such labeling as a means of limiting the freedom to read. He cited religious groups that sometimes asked libraries to label publications "objectionable," and he mentioned that other self-described patriotic organizations were moving toward similar proposals. Rogers also reported that in April 1951 the Association received a letter from the Montclair chapter of the SAR requesting ALA to adopt a policy advocating that communistic and subversive materials not only be labeled but also be segregated from other materials in the library collection and given out only upon written and signed application.

The Intellectual Freedom Committee believed that such practices violated the principles of intellectual freedom and that the labeling of books according to points of view should not be undertaken by any library. The Committee also noted that it was not clear who would do such labeling, who would decide what is communistic or subversive, or by what criteria such decisions would be made. In addition, the process was envisioned as expensive and time-consuming, involving examination of all materials in a library collection. The impracticality and financial problems of such a project, however, were not deemed relevant to the Association's policy concerning the practice. As Rogers pointed out, policy was to be based on the principle involved.

The IFC's study of the SAR proposal resulted in a six-point statement. Before presenting the statement to the Council for adoption as an ALA policy, the Committee conducted an informal survey of twenty-four libraries around the country. Twenty responded, all agreeing that labeling violated basic principles of intellectual freedom and should not be practiced by libraries. The IFC's six-point Statement on Labeling was approved by the Council as an ALA policy on July 13, 1951:

1. Although totalitarian states find it easy and even proper, according to their ethics, to establish criteria for judging publications as "subversive," injustice and ignorance rather than justice and enlightenment result from such practices, and the American Library Association has a responsibility to take a stand against the establishment of such criteria in a democratic state.

2. Libraries do not advocate the ideas found in their collections. The presence of a magazine or book in a library does not indicate an endorsement of its contents by the library.

3. No one person should take the responsibility of labeling publications. No sizeable group of persons would be likely to agree on the types of materials which should be labeled or the sources of information which should be regarded with suspicion. As a practical consideration, a librarian who labeled a book or magazine procommunist might be sued for libel.

4. Labeling is an attempt to prejudice the reader, and as such, it is a censor's tool.

5. Labeling violates the spirit of the *Library Bill of Rights*.
6. Although we are all agreed that communism is a threat to the free world, if materials are labeled to pacify one group, there is no excuse for refusing to label any item in the library's collection. Because communism, fascism, or other authoritarianisms tend to suppress ideas and attempt to coerce individuals to conform to a specific ideology, American librarians must be opposed to such "isms." We are, then, anti-communist, but we are also opposed to any other group which aims at closing any path to knowledge.

The 1951 Statement on Labeling was adopted as policy by many libraries and, over the years, was a useful tool in combating this brand of censorship. One incident involving an attempt to label library materials occurred at the St. Charles County Library, St. Charles, Missouri, in 1968 and concluded with a unique twist. The case began when Nina S. Ladof, the librarian, was presented with a petition requesting the removal of *Ramparts* magazine. The library dismissed the petition, explaining that *Ramparts* was purchased in accordance with the library's book selection policy, which included the *Library Bill of Rights* and The Freedom to Read.

After the initial attempt to remove *Ramparts*, several months passed. Eventually, though, the original complainant presented the librarian with a sheaf of petitions from the Veterans of Foreign Wars, the American Legion, the Lions Club, and a church. With variations, the petitions read as follows:

> We, the undersigned, do hereby petition the Library Board of the County of St. Charles, requesting that any book or publication on file in the St. Charles County Library System authored, published, or edited by any individual or group of individuals having been cited by any official Federal or State Un-American Activities Committee or Fact-Finding Committee as subversive or un-American in nature or belonging to any organization having been cited as subversive or un-American, be so explicitly labeled in a conspicuous manner for the information of the patrons of the St. Charles County Libraries.

Ladof pointed out that Dr. Benjamin Spock, author of *The Common Sense of Baby Care*, was sentenced on charges of aiding young men to avoid military service. Would this book require a label? Pursuing this example further, Ladof wrote to Spock's publishers to ask what action they would take if she did, in fact, affix a label to his works. Two replied that they would consider it possible grounds for legal action against the library. Dr. Spock's own attorney concurred.

Both the American Civil Liberties Union and the Freedom of Information Center at the University of Missouri provided Nina Ladof with the legal opinion that labeling a work, as requested in the petition, would be grounds for a libel action by the author whose works were involved because of the injury to the sale of his works that might result. Even if the label were factual, such as "so-and-so was a member of the Communist Party in 1941," he would have grounds to prove such injury. In fact, injury need not actually occur; it need only be a possibility for a court to award substantial damages to a plaintiff in such a case. And, since library boards of trustees cannot be sued as a body, each member would be liable for the damages awarded.

Armed with this information, and with the board's unanimous belief that labels are forms of censorship—and, as such, are completely opposed to basic library policies—the library issued a firm statement rejecting the proposed labeling. The statement included information from legal sources and paraphrased and expanded the six points of the ALA Statement on Labeling. All persons interested in the matter were sent copies with an explanatory letter. *Ramparts* and other literature written by so-called subversives continued to circulate unlabeled.

The 1951 Statement on Labeling stood without revision until 1971. At that time, study of the policy confirmed that some sections were framed in language that reflected the Association's response to a specific threat—the labeling as "subversive" or "communist" of specific materials. The Intellectual Freedom Committee concluded that, although these sections once met a particular need, they limited the document's usefulness.

To make the Statement on Labeling applicable to a broader range of labeling problems, even encompassing "harmful matter," the Intellectual Freedom Committee recommended a revised version to the Council. The 1971 revision was designated an Interpretation of the *Library Bill of Rights* to emphasize the relationship between Articles I, II, and III of that document and the Statement on Labeling. The revision was adopted by the Council on June 25, 1971:

> Because labeling violates the spirit of the Library Bill of Rights, the American Library Association opposes the technique of labeling as a means of predisposing readers against library materials for the following reasons:
>
> 1. Labeling[*] is an attempt to prejudice the reader, and as such it is a censor's tool.
> 2. Although some find it easy and even proper, according to their ethics, to establish criteria for judging publications as objectionable, injustice and ignorance rather than justice and enlightenment result from such practices, and the American Library Association must oppose the establishment of such criteria.
> 3. Libraries do not advocate the ideas found in their collections. The presence of a magazine or book in a library does not indicate an endorsement of its contents by the library.
> 4. No one person should take the responsibility of labeling publications. No sizeable group of persons would be likely to agree either on the types of material which should be labeled or the sources of information which should be regarded with suspicion. As a practical consideration, a librarian who labels a book or magazine might be sued for libel.
> 5. If materials are labeled to pacify one group, there is no excuse for refusing to label any item in the library's collection. Because authoritarians tend to suppress ideas and attempt to coerce individuals to conform to a specific ideology, the American Library Association opposes such efforts which aim at closing any path to knowledge.

---

* "Labeling," as it is referred to in the "Statement on Labeling," is the practice of describing or designating certain library materials, by affixing a prejudicial label to them or segregating them by a prejudicial system, so as to predispose readers against the materials.

Following the 1980 revision of the *Library Bill of Rights*, the IFC again reviewed the statement, recommending three major changes. First, the Committee noted that relegating definition of the labeling practice to a footnote detracted from the policy's unity and effectiveness and suggested incorporating the definition into the opening paragraph. Second, the Committee recommended that points 4 and 5 be dropped, because these were not considerations of principle but, rather, "practical" objections to labeling.

Although librarians should certainly be aware that the labeling of library materials could provoke legal action, and although it is certainly true that adoption of labels at the instigation of one group might open a veritable Pandora's box of labeling demands by others, neither of these considerations lies at the basis of the Association's opposition to labeling. The American Library Association opposes labeling of library materials not because this is impractical or legally dangerous but because this practice flagrantly violates both the spirit and the letter of the *Library Bill of Rights* and stands in fundamental opposition to the most basic principles of intellectual freedom.

In addition, the Committee recommended adding a sentence to the statement indicating that the Association's objections to labeling should not be construed as opposition to legitimate organizational schemes designed to facilitate access. The second revision of the "Statement on Labeling" was adopted by the Council on July 1, 1981. It read as follows:

> Labeling is the practice of describing or designating certain library materials by affixing a prejudicial label to them or segregating them by a prejudicial system. The American Library Association opposes this as a means of predisposing people's attitudes towards library materials for the following reasons:
>
> 1. Labeling is an attempt to prejudice attitudes and as such, it is a censor's tool.
> 2. Some find it easy and even proper, according to their ethics, to establish criteria for judging publications as objectionable. However, injustice and ignorance rather than justice and enlightenment result from such practices, and the American Library Association opposes the establishment of such criteria.

3. Libraries do not advocate the ideas found in their collections. The presence of books and other resources in a library does not indicate endorsement of their contents by the library.

The American Library Association opposes efforts which aim at closing any path to knowledge. This statement does not, however, exclude the adoption of organizational schemes designed as directional aids or to facilitate access to materials.

In keeping with the review of *Library Bill of Rights* Interpretations undertaken in response to the 1988 Minority Concerns Committee resolution, the "Statement on Labeling" was the first to be revised by the Intellectual Freedom Committee at the 1989 ALA Annual Conference. The importance of this policy increased significantly in light of attempts, in 1990, to pass legislation in Congress requiring warning labels for musical recordings with allegedly obscene lyrics or lyrics deemed offensive or unsuitable for minors.

Policy revisions made clear ALA's opposition to labeling and emphasized librarians' responsibility to prevent the imposition of private or voluntary labeling schemes on library materials while leaving permanently affixed labels intact to avoid expurgation of copyrighted material. The new Interpretation also encouraged librarians to become familiar with local laws and regulations on the issue.

Following adoption by the IFC in June 1989, the revised "Statement on Labeling" was circulated to other ALA units. At the 1990 Midwinter Meeting, the revision was reconsidered in light of comments received from the other units. The final version of this Interpretation was accepted by the Committee and then adopted by the Council on June 26, 1990.

In 1999–2000, as part of its ongoing practice of periodic review of all Interpretations, the IFC reviewed this policy. No changes were recommended.

The "Statement on Labeling" was reviewed again as a part of the 2004–5 cyclical review process. The Committee received a number of comments when a revised draft was circulated to all ALA units. As a result, several significant changes were made, beginning with a change in the title to "Labels and Rating Systems," which more accurately describes the coverage of the Interpretation and also clarifies that it is a policy, not a statement.

Comments were received on the sentence added in 1981 concerning directional aids:

> This statement, however, does not exclude the adoption of organizational schemes designed as directional aids or to facilitate access to materials.

The Committee learned that some public libraries have established a fiction genre for Christian literature and label the materials with a cross or other religious symbol. In response to this and similar practices, the wording was revised to distinguish between prejudicial and viewpoint-neutral directional aids, clarifying that when directional aids "suggest moral or doctrinal endorsement, the effect is the same as prejudicial labeling."

The Committee discussed several comments received concerning the paragraph dealing with private rating systems:

> A variety of private organizations promulgate rating systems and/or review materials as a means of advising either their members or the general public concerning their opinions of the contents and suitability or appropriate age for use of certain books, films, recordings, or other materials. For the library to adopt or enforce any of these private systems, to attach such ratings to library materials, to include them in bibliographic records, library catalogs, or other finding aids, or otherwise to endorse them would violate the *Library Bill of Rights*.

Some questioned whether this statement applies to online catalogs that bundle bibliographic records with databases and other electronic informational resources, including book reviews, book covers, and other evaluative materials. Others pointed out that libraries often provide library users with lists of ALA award-winning, notable, and recommended books as finding aids. How does this differ, they asked, from finding aids produced by other private organizations? The IFC concluded that the Interpretation should provide broad policy guidance and that the Committee would prepare questions and answers concerning specific applications of the Interpretation. Questions and Answers on Labels and Rating Systems is available at http://www.ala.org/ala/oif/state mentspols/statementsif/interpretations/qandalabelsratingsys tems.htm.

NOTE

1. *ALA Bulletin* 45 (July–August 1951): 241.

2.14
Library-Initiated Programs as a Resource

An Interpretation of the *Library Bill of Rights*

Library-initiated programs support the mission of the library by providing users with additional opportunities for information, education, and recreation. Article I of the *Library Bill of Rights* states: "Books and other library resources should be provided for the interest, information, and enlightenment of all people of the community the library serves."

Library-initiated programs take advantage of library staff expertise, collections, services and facilities to increase access to information and information resources. Library-initiated programs introduce users and potential users to the resources of the library and to the library's primary function as a facilitator of information access. The library may participate in cooperative or joint programs with other agencies, organizations, institutions, or individuals as part of its own effort to address information needs and to facilitate information access in the community the library serves.

Library-initiated programs on site and in other locations include, but are not limited to, speeches, community forums, discussion groups, demonstrations, displays, and live or media presentations.

Libraries serving multilingual or multicultural communities should make efforts to accommodate the information needs of those for whom English is a second language. Library-initiated programs that cross language and cultural barriers introduce otherwise underserved populations to the resources of the library and provide access to information.

Library-initiated programs "should not be proscribed or removed [or canceled] because of partisan or doctrinal disapproval" of the contents of the program or the views expressed by the participants, as stated in Article II of the *Library Bill of Rights*. Library sponsorship of a program does not constitute an endorsement of the content of the program or the views expressed by the participants, any more than the purchase of material for the library collection constitutes an endorsement of the contents of the material or the views of its creator.

Library-initiated programs are a library resource and, as such, are developed in accordance with written guidelines, as approved and adopted by the library's policy-making body. These guidelines should include an endorsement of the *Library Bill of Rights* and set forth the library's commitment to free and open access to information and ideas for all users.

Library staff select topics, speakers and resource materials for library-initiated programs based on the interests and information needs of the community. Topics, speakers and resource materials are not excluded from library-initiated programs because of possible controversy. Concerns, questions or complaints about library-initiated programs are handled according to the same written policy and procedures that govern reconsiderations of other library resources.

Library-initiated programs are offered free of charge and are open to all. Article V of the *Library Bill of Rights* states: "A person's right to use a library should not be denied or abridged because of origin, age, background, or views."

The "right to use a library" encompasses all the resources the library offers, including the right to attend library-initiated programs. Libraries do not deny or abridge access to library resources, including library-initiated programs, based on an individual's economic background or ability to pay.

Adopted January 27, 1982, by the ALA Council; amended June 26, 1990; July 12, 2000. http://www.ala.org/ala/oif/statementspols/statementsif/interpretations/libraryinitiated.htm.

HISTORY

Library-Initiated Programs as a Resource

A s libraries have sought in recent years to broaden their appeal and to strengthen their ties with the communities they serve, library-initiated programs such as invited public speeches, film showings, reading clubs, family literacy programs, and teen and children's game groups have become an increasingly important and visible part of library service. Such programming, however, also has increasingly become a target for would-be censors. In the 1970s, many communities witnessed efforts to ban controversial speakers from appearing in libraries. Elsewhere, showings of R-rated or allegedly explicit films were attacked. In New Rochelle, New York, an Italian-American group objected to a library showing of *The Godfather*, and in North Carolina, a French comedy about a homosexual couple, *La Cage aux Folles*, was successfully banned from a public library.

In the early 1980s, some parents' groups objected to several library-sponsored theme programs for children, especially those emphasizing magic or the occult. In a few communities, citizens concerned about the alleged spread of occultism and witchcraft sought to terminate the use of library facilities for organized playing of the popular game Dungeons and Dragons.

In response to incidents of this sort and a growing number of inquiries from librarians and library users about the applicability of the *Library Bill of Rights* to such programs, in 1981, at the urging of the intellectual freedom committees of the Young Adult Services Division and the Association for Library Service to Children, the

IFC, with J. Dennis Day as chair, decided to develop a policy statement. At the 1982 ALA Midwinter Meeting in Denver, the Committee approved the statement and recommended it to the Council, which adopted it on January 27, 1982, as an Interpretation of the *Library Bill of Rights* entitled "Library-Initiated Programs as a Resource." It read as follows:

> Library-initiated programming is a library resource that provides information, education, and recreation to library users. Library-initiated programming utilizes library staff, books, library and community resources, resource people, displays, and media presentations. The library often incorporates cooperative programming with other agencies, organizations, and educational institutions, as well as other resources, to communicate with library users. Library-initiated programs should provide "for the interest, information, and enlightenment of all the people of the community the library serves," as stated in Article I of the *Library Bill of Rights*.
>
> The American Library Association believes that library-sponsored programs, as well as library resources, "should not be proscribed or removed (or canceled) because of partisan or doctrinal disapproval" (Article II of the *Library Bill of Rights*).
>
> A person's right to attend a library-initiated program should not be denied or abridged because of origin, age, background, or views (Article V of the *Library Bill of Rights*).
>
> A written policy on library-initiated programming, approved by the library's policy-making body, should reflect the library's philosophy regarding free access to information and ideas. Similarly, concerns expressed regarding library-initiated programs should be handled as they are for library resources.
>
> Selection of library program topics, speakers, courses, classes, and resource materials should be made by library staff on the basis of the interests and needs of library users and the community. Library programming should not exclude topics, books, speakers, media, and other resources because they might be controversial.

Review of the Interpretation "Library-Initiated Programs as a Resource" began in January 1989. A draft of a revised document was circulated in the spring of 1990. Comments received on the proposed draft raised questions of fees, access for handicapped and deaf patrons, and the practical problems of abolishing age-based restrictions on program attendance.

As a result of these comments, the Interpretation was expanded to include library programs held on- and off-site and those produced in cooperation with other groups. Provisions were included to encourage librarians to formulate written policies on programming that conform to the intellectual freedom standards set by the *Library Bill of Rights*.

In addition, librarians were exhorted to consider the multicultural or multilingual composition of their communities in planning library events and not to shrink from addressing controversial topics. A special provision was added to emphasize the librarian's duty to ensure equal access to all patrons, explicitly stating that economic background and ability to pay cannot be used to restrict access to library-sponsored events. The new Interpretation was adopted by the Council on June 26, 1990.

As part of the ongoing review of the Interpretations in 1999–2000, the IFC proposed some grammatical corrections. On July 12, 2000, the Council adopted the Interpretation as amended. Grammatical edits were made during the 2004–5 review of intellectual freedom policies.

2.15
Meeting Rooms

An Interpretation of the
Library Bill of Rights

Many libraries provide meeting rooms for individuals and groups as part of a program of service. Article VI of the *Library Bill of Rights* states that such facilities should be made available to the public served by the given library "on an equitable basis, regardless of the beliefs or affiliations of individuals or groups requesting their use."

Libraries maintaining meeting room facilities should develop and publish policy statements governing use. These statements can properly define time, place, or manner of use; such qualifications should not pertain to the content of a meeting or to the beliefs or affiliations of the sponsors. These statements should be made available in any commonly used language within the community served.

If meeting rooms in libraries supported by public funds are made available to the general public for non-library sponsored events, the library may not exclude any group based on the subject matter to be discussed or based on the ideas that the group advocates. For example, if a library allows charities and sports clubs to discuss their activities in library meeting rooms, then the library should not exclude partisan political or religious groups from discussing their activities in the same facilities. If a library opens its meeting rooms to a wide variety of civic organizations, then the library may not deny access to a religious organization. Libraries may wish to post a permanent notice near the meeting room stating that the library does not advocate or endorse the viewpoints of meetings or meeting room users.

Written policies for meeting room use should be stated in inclusive rather than exclusive terms. For example, a policy that the library's facilities are open "to organizations engaged in educational, cultural, intellectual, or charitable activities" is an inclusive statement of the limited uses to which the facilities may be put. This defined limitation would permit religious groups to use the facilities because they engage in intellectual activities, but would exclude most commercial uses of the facility.

A publicly supported library may limit use of its meeting rooms to strictly "library-related" activities, provided that the limitation is clearly circumscribed and is viewpoint neutral.

Written policies may include limitations on frequency of use, and whether or not meetings held in library meeting rooms must be open to the public. If state and local laws permit private as well as public sessions of meetings in libraries, libraries may choose to offer both options. The same standard should be applicable to all.

If meetings are open to the public, libraries should include in their meeting room policy statement a section that addresses admission fees. If admission fees are permitted, libraries shall seek to make it possible that these fees do not limit access to individuals who may be unable to pay, but who wish to attend the meeting. Article V of the *Library Bill of Rights* states that "a person's right to use a library should not be denied or abridged because of origin, age, background, or views." It is inconsistent with Article V to restrict indirectly access to library meeting rooms based on an individual's or group's ability to pay for that access.

Adopted July 2, 1991, by the ALA Council. http://www.ala.org/ala/oif/statementspols/statementsif/interpretations/meetingrooms.htm.

HISTORY

Meeting Rooms

The Interpretation "Meeting Rooms" was developed concurrently with the Interpretation "Exhibit Spaces and Bulletin Boards." See part 2, section 2.9, for that history.

"Meeting Rooms" was reviewed as part of the 1999–2000 and the 2004–5 reviews of all Interpretations by the IFC. No changes were recommended.

2.16
Privacy

An Interpretation of the
Library Bill of Rights

Introduction

Privacy is essential to the exercise of free speech, free thought, and free association. The courts have established a First Amendment right to receive information in a publicly funded library.* Further, the courts have upheld the right to privacy based on the Bill of Rights of the U.S. Constitution.† Many states provide guar-

---

* Court opinions establishing a right to receive information in a public library include *Board of Education. v. Pico*, 457 U.S. 853 (1982); *Kreimer v. Bureau of Police for the Town of Morristown*, 958 F.2d 1242 (3d Cir. 1992); and *Reno v. American Civil Liberties Union*, 521 U.S. 844 (1997).

† See in particular the Fourth Amendment's guarantee of "[t]he right of the people to be secure in their persons, houses, papers, and effects, against unreasonable searches and seizures," the Fifth Amendment's guarantee against self-incrimination, and the Ninth Amendment's guarantee that "[t]he enumeration in the Constitution, of certain rights, shall not be construed to deny or disparage others retained by the people." This right is explicit in Article Twelve of the Universal Declaration of Human Rights: "No one shall be subjected to arbitrary interference with his privacy, family, home or correspondence, nor to attacks upon his honour and reputation. Everyone has the right to the protection of the law against such interference or attacks." See: http://www.un.org/Overview/rights.html. This right has further been explicitly codified as Article Seventeen of the "International Covenant on Civil and Political Rights," a legally binding international human rights agreement ratified by the United States on June 8, 1992. See: http://www.unhchr.ch/html/menu3/b/a_ccpr.htm.

antees of privacy in their constitutions and statute law.[*] Numerous decisions in case law have defined and extended rights to privacy.[†]

In a library (physical or virtual), the right to privacy is the right to open inquiry without having the subject of one's interest examined or scrutinized by others. Confidentiality exists when a library is in possession of personally identifiable information about users and keeps that information private on their behalf.[‡]

Protecting user privacy and confidentiality has long been an integral part of the mission of libraries. The ALA has affirmed a

---

[*] Ten state constitutions guarantee a right of privacy or bar unreasonable intrusions into citizens' privacy. Forty-eight states protect the confidentiality of library users' records by law, and the attorneys general in the remaining two states have issued opinions recognizing the privacy of users' library records. See: State Privacy Laws [http://www.ala.org/oif/stateprivacylaws/].

[†] Cases recognizing a right to privacy include: *NAACP v. Alabama*, 357 U.S. 449 (1958); *Griswold v. Connecticut* 381 U.S. 479 (1965); *Katz v. United States*, 389 U.S. 347 (1967); and *Stanley v. Georgia*, 394 U.S. 557 (1969). Congress recognized the right to privacy in the Privacy Act of 1974 and Amendments (5 USC Sec. 552a), which addresses the potential for government's violation of privacy through its collection of personal information. The Privacy Act's "Congressional Findings and Statement of Purpose" state in part: "the right to privacy is a personal and fundamental right protected by the Constitution of the United States." See: http://caselaw.lp.findlaw.com/scripts/ts_ search.pl?title=5&sec=552a.

[‡] The phrase "Personally identifiable information" was established in ALA policy in 1991. See: "Policy concerning Confidentiality of Personally Identifiable Information about Library Users." Personally identifiable information can include many types of library records, for instance: information that the library requires an individual to provide in order to be eligible to use library services or borrow materials, information that identifies an individual as having requested or obtained specific materials or materials on a particular subject, and information that is provided by an individual to assist a library staff member to answer a specific question or provide information on a particular subject. Personally identifiable information does not include information that does not identify any individual and that is retained only for the purpose of studying or evaluating the use of a library and its materials and services. Personally identifiable information does include any data that can link choices of taste, interest, or research with a specific individual.

right to privacy since 1939.* Existing ALA policies affirm that confidentiality is crucial to freedom of inquiry.† Rights to privacy and
confidentiality also are implicit in the *Library Bill of Rights*' guarantee of free access to library resources for all users.‡

Rights of Library Users

The *Library Bill of Rights* affirms the ethical imperative to provide
unrestricted access to information and to guard against impedi-
ments to open inquiry. Article IV states: "Libraries should cooperate with all persons and groups concerned with resisting
abridgement of free expression and free access to ideas." When
users recognize or fear that their privacy or confidentiality is
compromised, true freedom of inquiry no longer exists.

In all areas of librarianship, best practice leaves the user in
control of as many choices as possible. These include decisions
about the selection of, access to, and use of information. Lack of

---

* Article Eleven of the Code of Ethics for Librarians (1939) asserted that
"It is the librarian's obligation to treat as confidential any private information obtained through contact with library patrons." See: Code of Ethics for
Librarians (1939). Article Three of the current Code (1995) states: "We protect each library user's right to privacy and confidentiality with respect to
information sought or received and resources consulted, borrowed, acquired, or transmitted." See: http://www.ala.org/alaorg/oif/ethics.html.

† See these ALA Policies: "Access for Children and Young People
to Videotapes and Other Nonprint Formats"; "Free Access to Libraries
for Minors"; "Freedom to Read" (http://www.ala.org/ala/oif/
statementspols/ftrstatement/freedomreadstatement.htm); "Libraries: An
American Value"; the newly revised "Library Principles for a Networked
World"; "Policy concerning Confidentiality of Personally Identifiable
Information about Library Users"; "Policy on Confidentiality of Library
Records"; "Suggested Procedures for Implementing Policy on the
Confidentiality of Library Records."

‡ Adopted June 18, 1948; amended February 2, 1961, and
January 23, 1980; inclusion of "age" reaffirmed January 23, 1996, by
the ALA Council. See: http://www.ala.org/ala/oif/statementspols/
statementsif/librarybillrights.htm.

privacy and confidentiality has a chilling effect on users' choices. All users have a right to be free from any unreasonable intrusion into or surveillance of their lawful library use.

Users have the right to be informed what policies and procedures govern the amount and retention of personally identifiable information, why that information is necessary for the library, and what the user can do to maintain his or her privacy. Library users expect and in many places have a legal right to have their information protected and kept private and confidential by anyone with direct or indirect access to that information. In addition, Article V of the *Library Bill of Rights* states: "A person's right to use a library should not be denied or abridged because of origin, age, background, or views." This article precludes the use of profiling as a basis for any breach of privacy rights. Users have the right to use a library without any abridgement of privacy that may result from equating the subject of their inquiry with behavior.*

Responsibilities in Libraries

The library profession has a long-standing commitment to an ethic of facilitating, not monitoring, access to information. This commitment is implemented locally through development, adoption, and adherence to privacy policies that are consistent with applicable federal, state, and local law. Everyone (paid or unpaid) who provides governance, administration, or service in libraries has a responsibility to maintain an environment respectful and protective of the privacy of all users. Users have the responsibility to respect each other's privacy.

For administrative purposes, librarians may establish appropriate time, place, and manner restrictions on the use of library

---

* Existing ALA Policy asserts, in part, that: "The government's interest in library use reflects a dangerous and fallacious equation of what a person reads with what that person believes or how that person is likely to behave. Such a presumption can and does threaten the freedom of access to information." "Policy concerning Confidentiality of Personally Identifiable Information about Library Users."

resources.* In keeping with this principle, the collection of personally identifiable information should only be a matter of routine or policy when necessary for the fulfillment of the mission of the library. Regardless of the technology used, everyone who collects or accesses personally identifiable information in any format has a legal and ethical obligation to protect confidentiality.

Conclusion

The American Library Association affirms that rights of privacy are necessary for intellectual freedom and are fundamental to the ethics and practice of librarianship.

---

* See: "Guidelines for the Development and Implementation of Policies, Regulations and Procedures Affecting Access to Library Materials, Services and Facilities."

Adopted June 19, 2002, by the ALA Council. http://www.ala.org/ala/oif/statementspols/statementsif/interpretations/privacy.htm.

HISTORY

Privacy

In 1999, ALA Council resolved that the Library and Information Technology Association be asked to examine the impact of new technologies on patron privacy and the confidentiality of electronic records. The Task Force on Privacy and Confidentiality in the Electronic Environment was formed at the 1999 ALA Midwinter Conference with broad participation from across ALA.

In July 2000, ALA Council approved the Final Report of the Task Force on Privacy and Confidentiality in the Electronic Environment (Council Document #62) and referred it to the Intellectual Freedom Committee for review. The recommendations contained therein were

> that ALA revise its policy statements related to Confidentiality of Library Records (rev. 1986), and Concerning Confidentiality of Personally Identifiable Information about Library Users (1991), in order to specifically and appropriately incorporate Internet privacy;
>
> that ALA develop model privacy policies, instructional materials, and privacy "best practices" documents for libraries; and
>
> that ALA urge that all libraries adopt a privacy statement on web pages and post privacy policies in the library which cover the issues of privacy in Internet use as accessed through the library's services.

In its own end-of-conference report to Council, the IFC responded to this referral by saying, "The Intellectual Freedom Committee gladly accepts Council's charge to review the recommendations. IFC has been reviewing and will continue to monitor the appropriateness of all ALA policies regarding privacy and confidentiality and will address all three recommendations in our Midwinter Meeting report to Council."

At the 2001 ALA Midwinter Meeting, the IFC established a standing Privacy Subcommittee, which is charged to monitor ongoing privacy developments in technology, politics, and legislation and to identify needs and resources for librarians and library users (cf. 2000–2001 CD#19.1).

At its 2001 spring meeting, the Committee returned to Council's original request to consider developing an Interpretation of the *Library Bill of Rights* on privacy. Initial work began on a draft Interpretation at that time and continued through the 2001 Annual Conference and the Committee's 2001 fall meeting. In its deliberations, the Committee thought carefully about the implications of September 11 on privacy issues. They sought to develop the Interpretation for lasting impact, knowing that this issue was of importance to libraries prior to those events and that it has enduring importance for those who rely on ALA in their libraries (cf. 2002–2003 CD#19).

ALA Council adopted "Privacy: An Interpretation of the *Library Bill of Rights*" on June 19, 2002, at the ALA Annual Conference in Atlanta, Georgia.

See also Questions and Answers on Privacy and Confidentiality, http://www.ala.org/ala/oif/statementspols/statementsif/interpretations/questionsanswers.htm.

2.17

Restricted Access to Library Materials

An Interpretation of the
Library Bill of Rights

Libraries are a traditional forum for the open exchange of information. Attempts to restrict access to library materials violate the basic tenets of the *Library Bill of Rights*.

Some libraries place materials in a "closed shelf," "locked case," "adults only," "restricted shelf," or "high-demand" collection. Some libraries have applied filtering software to their Internet stations to prevent users from finding targeted categories of information, much of which is constitutionally protected. Some libraries block access to certain materials by placing other barriers between the user and those materials.

Because restricted materials often deal with controversial, unusual, or sensitive subjects, having to ask a librarian or circulation clerk for access to them may be embarrassing or inhibiting for patrons desiring the materials. Requiring a user to ask for materials may create a service barrier or pose a language-skills barrier. Even when a title is listed in the catalog with a reference to its restricted status, a barrier is placed between the patron and the publication. (See also "Labels and Rating Systems.") Because restricted materials often feature information that some people consider objectionable, potential library users may be predisposed to think of the materials as objectionable and, therefore, be reluctant to ask for access to them.

Limiting access by relegating materials into physically or virtually restricted or segregated collections or restricting materials by creating age-related, linguistic, economic, psychological, or other barriers violates the *Library Bill of Rights*. However, some libraries have established restrictive policies to protect their materials from theft or mutilation, or because of statutory authority or institutional mandate. Such policies must be carefully formulated and administered to ensure they do not violate established principles of intellectual freedom. This caution is reflected in ALA policies, such as "Evaluating Library Collections," "Free Access to Libraries for Minors," "Preservation Policy," and the ACRL "Code of Ethics for Special Collections Librarians."

In keeping with the "Joint Statement on Access" of the American Library Association and Society of American Archivists, libraries should avoid accepting donor agreements or entering into contracts that impose permanent restrictions on special collections. As stated in the "Joint Statement," it is the responsibility of libraries with such collections "to make available original research materials in its possession on equal terms of access."

All proposals for restricted access collections should be carefully scrutinized to ensure that the purpose is not to suppress a viewpoint or to place a barrier between certain patrons and particular content. A primary goal of the library profession is to facilitate access to all points of view on current and historical issues.

Adopted February 2, 1973, by the ALA Council; amended July 1, 1981; July 3, 1991; July 12, 2000; June 30, 2004. http://www.ala.org/ala/oif/statementspols/statementsif/interpretations/restrictedaccess.htm.

HISTORY

Restricted Access
to Library Materials

On January 11, 1971, the City Council of San Jose, California, received a formal request from T. J. Owens, president of the San Jose branch of the National Association for the Advancement of Colored People (NAACP), that the book *Epaminondas and His Auntie* be removed from general circulation in the San Jose libraries. Owens charged that the book depicts a black child in a manner that makes him look "completely idiotic and stupid."[1]

Subsequent to a discussion of the book with Owens, Homer L. Fletcher, city librarian, recommended to the city council that *Epaminondas and His Auntie* be retained on open shelf in all the city's libraries and that the option remain for children's librarians to reorder the book should they choose to do so. Fletcher's recommendation was based on his view that any other action would be inconsistent with the *Library Bill of Rights*, which stated that "no library materials should be proscribed or removed from libraries because of partisan or doctrinal disapproval." Despite the recommendation of the city librarian, the San Jose City Council voted to remove the book from general circulation in city libraries and to put the book on reserve, thereby necessitating that each individual who wished to use it make a special request to the librarian. On March 29, 1971, however, the city council reconsidered its action and, upon recommendation of the Library Commission, adopted the *Library Bill of Rights* as city policy and removed the restrictions on the book.

An advisory statement concerning restricted circulation of library materials, drafted in response to the problem in San Jose, was approved by the Intellectual Freedom Committee during the 1971 ALA Annual Conference in Dallas. This statement, in slightly amended form, was submitted to the Council at the 1973 Midwinter Meeting in Washington, D.C., and approved as an ALA policy on February 2, 1973:

> Restricting access of certain titles and certain classes of library materials is a practice common to many libraries in the United States. Collections of these materials are referred to by a variety of names such as "closed shelf," "locked case," "adults only," or "restricted shelf" collections.
>
> Three reasons generally advanced to justify restricted access are:
>
> 1. It provides a refuge for materials that belong in the collection but which may be considered "objectionable" by some library patrons.
> 2. It provides a means for controlling distribution of materials which allegedly should not be read by those who are not "prepared" for such materials by experience, education, or age.
> 3. It provides a means to protect certain materials from theft and mutilation.
>
> Though widely used—and often practical—restricted access to library materials is frequently in opposition to the principles of intellectual freedom. While the limitation differs from direct censorship activities, such as removal of library materials or refusal to purchase certain publications, it nonetheless constitutes censorship, albeit in a subtle form. As a form of censorship, restricted access violates the spirit of the *Library Bill of Rights* in the following ways:
>
> 1. It violates that portion of Article II which states that "no library materials should be proscribed . . . because of partisan or doctrinal disapproval."
>
>> The word "proscribed," as used in Article II, means "suppressed." Restricted access achieves de facto suppression of certain materials.
>> Even when a title is listed in the card catalog with a reference to its restricted shelf status, a barrier is

placed between the patron and the publication. Because a majority of materials placed in restricted collections deal with controversial, unusual, or "sensitive" subjects, asking a librarian or circulation clerk for them is an embarrassment for patrons desiring the materials. Because restricted collections are often composed of materials which some library patrons consider "objectionable," the potential user is predisposed to thinking of the materials as "objectionable," and is accordingly inhibited from asking for them. Although the barrier between the materials and the patron is psychological, it is nonetheless a tangible limitation on his access to information.

2. It violates Article V, which states that "the rights of an individual to the use of a library should not be denied or abridged because of his age . . ."

Limiting access of certain materials to adults only abridges the use of the library for minors. "Use of the library" includes use of, and access to, library materials. Such restrictions are generally instituted under the assumption that certain materials are "harmful" to minors, or in an effort to avoid controversy with parents who might think so.

The librarian who would restrict the availability of materials to minors because of actual or suspected parental objection should bear in mind that he is not in loco parentis in his position as librarian. The American Library Association holds that it is the parent—and only the parent—who may restrict his children—and only his children—in reading matter. The parent who would rather his child did not read certain materials or certain kinds of materials should so advise the child.

When restricted access is implemented to protect materials from theft or mutilation, the use of the practice may be legitimate. However, segregation of materials to protect them must be administered with extreme attention to the rationale for restricting access. Too often only "controversial" materials are the subject of such segregation, leading to the conclusion that factors other than theft and mutilation were the true considerations. The distinction is extremely difficult to make, for both the librarian and the patron.

> Selection policies, carefully developed on the basis of principles of intellectual freedom and the *Library Bill of Rights*, should not be vitiated by administrative practices such as restricted access.

As part of the overall review of all Interpretations of the *Library Bill of Rights* following that document's revision in 1980, the IFC recommended several relatively minor changes in the policy on restricted access, mainly aimed at removing sex-linked pronoun usage and strengthening the arguments against restricting access for minors. The recommendations were presented to the Council, which adopted the revised policy on July 1, 1981. It read as follows:

> Restricting access of certain titles and classes of library materials is a practice common to many libraries in the United States. Collections of these materials are referred to by a variety of names such as "closed shelf," "locked case," "adults only," or "restricted shelf."
>
> Three reasons generally advanced to justify restricted access are:
>
> 1. It provides a refuge for materials that belong in the collection but which may be considered "objectionable" by some library patrons;
> 2. It provides a means for controlling distribution of materials, to those who are allegedly not "prepared" for such materials or who have been labeled less responsible, because of experience, education, or age;
> 3. It provides a means to protect certain materials from theft and mutilation.
>
> Restricted access to library materials is frequently in opposition to the principles of intellectual freedom. While the limitation differs from direct censorship activities, such as removal of library materials or refusal to purchase certain publications, it nonetheless constitutes censorship, albeit in a subtle form. Restricted access often violates the spirit of the *Library Bill of Rights* in the following ways:
>
> 1. It violates that portion of Article II which states that "No library materials should be proscribed . . . because of partisan or doctrinal disapproval."

"Materials . . . proscribed" as used in Article II includes "suppressed" materials. Restricted access achieves de facto suppression of certain materials.

Even when a title is listed in the catalog with a reference to its restricted status, a barrier is placed between the patron and the publication. Because a majority of materials placed in restricted collections deal with controversial, unusual, or "sensitive" subjects, asking a librarian or circulation clerk for them may be embarrassing for patrons desiring the materials. Because restricted collections are often composed of materials which some library patrons consider "objectionable" the potential user is predisposed to thinking of the materials as "objectionable," and may be reluctant to ask for them. Although the barrier between the materials and the patron is psychological, it is nonetheless a limitation on access to information.

2. It violates Article V, which states that, "A person's right to use a library should not be denied or abridged because of . . . age."

Limiting access of certain materials only to adults abridges the use of the library for minors. Access to library materials is an integral part of the right to use a library. Such restrictions are generally instituted under the assumption that certain materials are "harmful" to minors, or in an effort to avoid controversy with adults who might think so.

Libraries and library boards who would restrict the availability of materials to minors because of actual or anticipated parental objection should bear in mind that they do not serve in loco parentis. The American Library Association holds that it is parents—and only parents—who may restrict their children—and only their children—from access to library materials and services. Parents who would rather their children not have access to certain materials should so advise their children.

When restricted access is implemented solely to protect materials from theft or mutilation, the practice may be legitimate. However, segregation of materials to protect them must be administered with extreme attention to the reason for restricting access. Too often, only "controversial" materials are the subject of such segregation, indicating that factors other than theft and mutilation—including content—were the true considerations. When loss rates

of items popular with young people are high, this
cannot justify the labeling of all minors as irresponsi-
ble and the adoption of prejudiced restrictions on the
right of minors to use library services and materials.

Selection policies, carefully developed to include
principles of intellectual freedom and the *Library
Bill of Rights*, should not be vitiated by administrative practices such as restricted access.

Note: See also "Free Access to Libraries for Minors,"
adopted June 30, 1972; amended July 1, 1981, by ALA
Council.

In 1990, "Restricted Access to Library Materials" was substantially revised. Barriers between materials and patrons that were
deemed psychological, linguistic, or related to other patron characteristics were addressed. New language relating to preservation of
library materials was added that also referenced related Interpretations of the *Library Bill of Rights*, including "Evaluating Library
Collections" and "Free Access to Libraries for Minors" as well as
ALA's Preservation Policy. Also added was an explanation of how
the *Library Bill of Rights* applies to restrictions resulting from agreements made with donors of materials or contracts for special collections materials. The new version of "Restricted Access to Library
Materials" was adopted by the Council on July 3, 1991.

As part of the ongoing review of the Interpretations in
1999–2000, the IFC proposed some grammatical corrections and the
addition of the following sentence: "More recently, some libraries
have applied filtering software to their Internet stations that prevent
users from finding targeted categories of information, much of
which is constitutionally protected." On July 12, 2000, the Council
adopted the amended Interpretation.

In 2004 "Restricted Access to Library Materials" was revised
again. Most of the changes were for clarity and readability. The
sentence "Some libraries block access to certain materials by placing
other barriers between the user and the materials" was added at the
end of the first paragraph to clarify that the Interpretation applies to
other types of inappropriate restrictions that are not specifically
listed. A direct quotation was added from the Joint Statement on
Access of the ALA and the Society of American Archivists. Finally,

a concluding paragraph was added strengthening the message of the Interpretation by firmly anchoring it to intellectual freedom principles.

NOTE

1. *San Jose News*, March 2, 1971.

2.18

The Universal Right to Free Expression

An Interpretation of the Library Bill of Rights

Freedom of expression is an inalienable human right and the foundation for self-government. Freedom of expression encompasses the freedoms of speech, press, religion, assembly, and association, and the corollary right to receive information.

The American Library Association endorses this principle, which is also set forth in the Universal Declaration of Human Rights, adopted by the United Nations General Assembly. The Preamble of this document states that ". . . recognition of the inherent dignity and of the equal and inalienable rights of all members of the human family is the foundation of freedom, justice, and peace in the world . . ." and ". . . the advent of a world in which human beings shall enjoy freedom of speech and belief and freedom from fear and want has been proclaimed as the highest aspiration of the common people. . . ."

Article 18 of this document states:

> Everyone has the right to freedom of thought, conscience and religion; this right includes freedom to change his religion or belief, and freedom, either alone or in community with others and in public or private, to manifest his religion or belief in teaching, practice, worship and observance.

Article 19 states:

Everyone has the right to freedom of opinion and expression; this right includes freedom to hold opinions without interference and to seek, receive and impart information and ideas through any media regardless of frontiers.

Article 20 states:

1. Everyone has the right to freedom of peaceful assembly and association.
2. No one may be compelled to belong to an association.

We affirm our belief that these are inalienable rights of every person, regardless of origin, age, background, or views. We embody our professional commitment to these principles in the *Library Bill of Rights* and *Code of Ethics*, as adopted by the American Library Association.

We maintain that these are universal principles and should be applied by libraries and librarians throughout the world. The American Library Association's policy on International Relations reflects these objectives: ". . . to encourage the exchange, dissemination, and access to information and the unrestricted flow of library materials in all formats throughout the world."

We know that censorship, ignorance, and limitations on the free flow of information are the tools of tyranny and oppression. We believe that ideas and information topple the walls of hate and fear and build bridges of cooperation and understanding far more effectively than weapons and armies.

The American Library Association is unswerving in its commitment to human rights and intellectual freedom; the two are inseparably linked and inextricably entwined. Freedom of opinion and expression is not derived from or dependent on any form of government or political power. This right is inherent in every individual. It cannot be surrendered, nor can it be denied. True justice comes from the exercise of this right.

We recognize the power of information and ideas to inspire justice, to restore freedom and dignity to the oppressed, and to change the hearts and minds of the oppressors.

Courageous men and women, in difficult and dangerous circumstances throughout human history, have demonstrated that freedom lives in the human heart and cries out for justice even in the face of threats, enslavement, imprisonment, torture, exile, and death. We draw inspiration from their example. They challenge us to remain steadfast in our most basic professional responsibility to promote and defend the right of free expression.

There is no good censorship. Any effort to restrict free expression and the free flow of information aids the oppressor. Fighting oppression with censorship is self-defeating.

Threats to the freedom of expression of any person anywhere are threats to the freedom of all people everywhere. Violations of human rights and the right of free expression have been recorded in virtually every country and society across the globe.

In response to these violations, we affirm these principles:

> The American Library Association opposes any use of governmental prerogative that leads to the intimidation of individuals that prevents them from exercising their rights to hold opinions without interference, and to seek, receive, and impart information and ideas. We urge libraries and librarians everywhere to resist such abuse of governmental power, and to support those against whom such governmental power has been employed.

> The American Library Association condemns any governmental effort to involve libraries and librarians in restrictions on the right of any individual to hold opinions without interference, and to seek, receive, and impart information and ideas. Such restrictions pervert the function of the library and violate the professional responsibilities of librarians.

> The American Library Association rejects censorship in any form. Any action that denies the inalienable human rights of individuals only damages the will to resist oppression, strengthens the hand of the oppressor, and undermines the cause of justice.

The American Library Association will not abrogate these principles. We believe that censorship corrupts the cause of justice, and contributes to the demise of freedom.

Adopted January 16, 1991, by the ALA Council. http://www.ala.org/ala/oif/statementspols/statementsif/interpretations/universalright.htm.

HISTORY

The Universal Right to Free Expression

Out of a long and emotional debate about support for sanctions—including books and informational materials—against South Africa, a new Interpretation of the *Library Bill of Rights* was created. Modeled after Article 19 of the United Nations Universal Declaration of Human Rights, the "Universal Right to Free Expression" advocates the free flow of information within all countries and across national boundaries.

In 1989, ALA was asked to support the Association of American Publishers (AAP) in its efforts to end the book boycott against South Africa. The ALA Council asked the Intellectual Freedom Committee for its recommendation. Concurrently, the Social Responsibilities Round Table had proposed a set of guidelines for librarians interacting with South Africa that was opposed by the IFC. The debate within ALA over South African policy was emotional, vigorous, and sometimes vituperative. It became clear that no extant ALA policy provided an adequate framework from which to respond fully to the complicated questions about international intellectual freedom and human rights raised during the course of the debate.

To address this glaring need, in 1990 the IFC began work on a policy on the international free flow of information. The new policy was to provide a secure foundation from which to respond to the AAP's request and from which to address other issues of international intellectual freedom. The drafters used Articles 18, 19, and 20 of the Universal Declaration of Human Rights as models for the new policy.

In January 1991, the IFC considered comments on the "Free Flow of Information" draft. The title of the Interpretation was changed to "The Universal Right to Free Expression," and the IFC voted to seek endorsements of other ALA units and to present the Interpretation to the Council.

On January 16, 1991, the Council voted to adopt the policy as the most recent addition to the *Library Bill of Rights* and its Interpretations.

"The Universal Right to Free Expression" was reviewed in 1999–2000 by the IFC as part of its ongoing periodic review of all Interpretations. No changes were recommended. Grammatical edits were made to the Interpretation during the 2004–5 policy review.

PART III

Protecting the Freedom to Read

1

The Freedom to Read

The freedom to read is essential to our democracy. It is continuously under attack. Private groups and public authorities in various parts of the country are working to remove or limit access to reading materials, to censor content in schools, to label "controversial" views, to distribute lists of "objectionable" books or authors, and to purge libraries. These actions apparently rise from a view that our national tradition of free expression is no longer valid; that censorship and suppression are needed to counter threats to safety or national security, as well as to avoid the subversion of politics and the corruption of morals. We, as individuals devoted to reading and as librarians and publishers responsible for disseminating ideas, wish to assert the public interest in the preservation of the freedom to read.

Most attempts at suppression rest on a denial of the fundamental premise of democracy: that the ordinary individual, by exercising critical judgment, will select the good and reject the bad. We trust Americans to recognize propaganda and misinformation, and to make their own decisions about what they read and believe. We do not believe they are prepared to sacrifice their heritage of a free press in order to be "protected" against what others think may be bad for them. We believe they still favor free enterprise in ideas and expression.

These efforts at suppression are related to a larger pattern of pressures being brought against education, the press, art and images, films, broadcast media, and the Internet. The problem is not only one of actual censorship. The shadow of fear cast by these pressures leads, we suspect, to an even larger voluntary curtailment of expression by those who seek to avoid controversy or unwelcome scrutiny by government officials.

Such pressure toward conformity is perhaps natural to a time of accelerated change. And yet suppression is never more dangerous than in such a time of social tension. Freedom has given the United States the elasticity to endure strain. Freedom keeps open the path of novel and creative solutions, and enables change to come by choice. Every silencing of a heresy, every enforcement of an orthodoxy, diminishes the toughness and resilience of our society and leaves it the less able to deal with controversy and difference.

Now as always in our history, reading is among our greatest freedoms. The freedom to read and write is almost the only means for making generally available ideas or manners of expression that can initially command only a small audience. The written word is the natural medium for the new idea and the untried voice from which come the original contributions to social growth. It is essential to the extended discussion that serious thought requires, and to the accumulation of knowledge and ideas into organized collections.

We believe that free communication is essential to the preservation of a free society and a creative culture. We believe that these pressures toward conformity present the danger of limiting the range and variety of inquiry and expression on which our democracy and our culture depend. We believe that every American community must jealously guard the freedom to publish and to circulate, in order to preserve its own freedom to read. We believe that publishers and librarians have a profound responsibility to give validity to that freedom to read by making it possible for the readers to choose freely from a variety of offerings.

The freedom to read is guaranteed by the Constitution. Those with faith in free people will stand firm on these constitutional guarantees of essential rights and will exercise the responsibilities that accompany these rights.

We therefore affirm these propositions:

1. *It is in the public interest for publishers and librarians to make available the widest diversity of views and expressions, including those that are unorthodox, unpopular, or considered dangerous by the majority.*

   Creative thought is by definition new, and what is new is different. The bearer of every new thought is a rebel until that idea is refined and tested. Totalitarian systems attempt to maintain themselves in power by the ruthless suppression of any concept that challenges the established orthodoxy. The power of a democratic system to adapt to change is vastly strengthened by the freedom of its citizens to choose widely from among conflicting opinions offered freely to them. To stifle every nonconformist idea at birth would mark the end of the democratic process. Furthermore, only through the constant activity of weighing and selecting can the democratic mind attain the strength demanded by times like these. We need to know not only what we believe but why we believe it.

2. *Publishers, librarians, and booksellers do not need to endorse every idea or presentation they make available. It would conflict with the public interest for them to establish their own political, moral, or aesthetic views as a standard for determining what should be published or circulated.*

   Publishers and librarians serve the educational process by helping to make available knowledge and ideas required for the growth of the mind and the increase of learning. They do not foster education by imposing as mentors the patterns of their own thought. The people should have the freedom to read and consider a broader range of ideas than those that may be held by any single librarian or publisher or government or church. It is wrong that what one can read should be confined to what another thinks proper.

3. *It is contrary to the public interest for publishers or librarians to bar access to writings on the basis of the personal history or political affiliations of the author.*

No art or literature can flourish if it is to be measured by the political views or private lives of its creators. No society of free people can flourish that draws up lists of writers to whom it will not listen, whatever they may have to say.

4. *There is no place in our society for efforts to coerce the taste of others, to confine adults to the reading matter deemed suitable for adolescents, or to inhibit the efforts of writers to achieve artistic expression.*

To some, much of modern expression is shocking. But is not much of life itself shocking? We cut off literature at the source if we prevent writers from dealing with the stuff of life. Parents and teachers have a responsibility to prepare the young to meet the diversity of experiences in life to which they will be exposed, as they have a responsibility to help them learn to think critically for themselves. These are affirmative responsibilities, not to be discharged simply by preventing them from reading works for which they are not yet prepared. In these matters values differ, and values cannot be legislated; nor can machinery be devised that will suit the demands of one group without limiting the freedom of others.

5. *It is not in the public interest to force a reader to accept the prejudgment of a label characterizing any expression or its author as subversive or dangerous.*

The ideal of labeling presupposes the existence of individuals or groups with wisdom to determine by authority what is good or bad for others. It presupposes that individuals must be directed in making up their minds about the ideas they examine. But Americans do not need others to do their thinking for them.

6. *It is the responsibility of publishers and librarians, as guardians of the people's freedom to read, to contest encroachments upon that freedom by individuals or groups seeking to impose their own standards or tastes upon the community at large; and by the government whenever it seeks to reduce or deny public access to public information.*

It is inevitable in the give and take of the democratic process that the political, the moral, or the aesthetic concepts of an individual or group will occasionally collide with those of another individual or group. In a free society individuals are free to determine for themselves what they wish to read, and each group is free to determine what it will recommend to its freely associated members. But no group has the right to take the law into its own hands, and to impose its own concept of politics or morality upon other members of a democratic society. Freedom is no freedom if it is accorded only to the accepted and the inoffensive. Further, democratic societies are more safe, free, and creative when the free flow of public information is not restricted by governmental prerogative or self-censorship.

7. *It is the responsibility of publishers and librarians to give full meaning to the freedom to read by providing books that enrich the quality and diversity of thought and expression. By the exercise of this affirmative responsibility, they can demonstrate that the answer to a "bad" book is a good one, the answer to a "bad" idea is a good one.*

The freedom to read is of little consequence when the reader cannot obtain matter fit for that reader's purpose. What is needed is not only the absence of restraint, but the positive provision of opportunity for the people to read the best that has been thought and said. Books are the major channel by which the intellectual inheritance is handed down, and the principal means of its testing and growth. The defense of the freedom to read requires of all publishers and librarians the utmost of their faculties, and deserves of all Americans the fullest of their support.

We state these propositions neither lightly nor as easy generalizations. We here stake out a lofty claim for the value of the written word. We do so because we believe that it is possessed of enormous variety and usefulness, worthy of cherishing and keeping free. We realize that the application of these propositions may mean the dissemination of ideas and manners of expression that are repugnant to many persons. We do not state these propositions in the comfortable belief that what people read is unimportant. We believe rather that what people read is deeply important;

that ideas can be dangerous; but that the suppression of ideas is fatal to a democratic society. Freedom itself is a dangerous way of life, but it is ours.

This statement was originally issued in May of 1953 by the Westchester Conference of the American Library Association and the American Book Publishers Council, which in 1970 consolidated with the American Educational Publishers Institute to become the Association of American Publishers.

Adopted June 25, 1953, by the ALA Council and the AAP Freedom to Read Committee; revised January 28, 1972; January 16, 1991; July 12, 2000; June 30, 2004. http://www.ala.org/ala/oif/statementspols/ftrstatement/freedomreadstatement.htm.

A Joint Statement by:
American Library Association
Association of American Publishers

Subsequently endorsed by:
American Booksellers Foundation for Free Expression
The Association of American University Presses, Inc.
The Children's Book Council
Freedom to Read Foundation
National Association of College Stores
National Coalition Against Censorship
National Council of Teachers of English
The Thomas Jefferson Center for the Protection of Free Expression

HISTORY

The Freedom to Read

T he Freedom to Read, the best known of the American Library
Association's documents supporting the principles of intellectual freedom as embodied in the *Library Bill of Rights*, had its begin-
nings during the Intellectual Freedom Committee's 1953 midwinter
meeting in Chicago.[1] At that meeting, Chair William S. Dix suggested the Committee "discuss the current wave of censorship and
attacks on books and libraries" and "help clarify the stand which
libraries might take and point to ways in which our own position
might be strengthened in the minds of the public." The Committee
directed Dix to consider a small, off-the-record conference with in-
depth discussion of the matter.

Dix's efforts resulted in a conference on the freedom to read,
sponsored jointly by the American Library Association and the
American Book Publishers Council (ABPC), held at the Westchester
Country Club, in Rye, New York, on May 2–3, 1953. The object of the
meeting was to bring together nationally known figures representing librarians, publishers, and the public interest. Spokesmen for
the public interest, viewed as vitally important to the success of the
conference, included representatives of business, foundations, law,
and education. Luther Evans, former Librarian of Congress—and
head of the United Nations Educational, Scientific and Cultural
Organization—served as chair of the conference.

In their invitation to potential participants, the joint sponsors
said:

Recent months have seen the emergence in our country of a pattern of pressures whose effect must be to limit the range and variety of expression. This pattern has affected in one way or another all the media of communications and indeed the entire area of free inquiry. Books are the last of the communications media to be affected by these pressures toward conformity. They remain preeminently the medium for the free expression of facts, ideas, and human experience in all its varieties. Librarians and publishers feel a deep responsibility for doing their part to see that this continues to be so, and they share with thoughtful men in every profession a conviction that freedom of communication is indispensable to a creative culture and a free society.

The objectives of the conference were:

1. To define the rights and responsibilities of publishers and librarians in maintaining the freedom of Americans to read what they choose;
2. To assay recent developments tending to restrict this freedom;
3. To consider where lines should be drawn between permissible expression and impermissible expression, and who is to draw the lines; and
4. To ascertain the public interest in this area and, if the group agrees, consider ways of asserting it.

Debate at the conference focused on the specific problem areas of obscenity and pornography and disloyalty and subversive materials. The participants considered a number of questions: What is the function of publishers and librarians in circulating ideas? Should they be responsible guides or simply caterers to public taste? Do they have a special responsibility to make available nonconforming expression and unpopular views? Do citizens have a right to read everything not expressly prohibited by law? Should a book be judged only by its content, and should the political and personal background of the author be ignored? Is the role of the public library entirely neutral? Can books be subversive?

The conference resulted in substantial agreement on principles. A Continuations Committee was appointed to draft a statement based on the proceedings and to consider action and research projects designed to publicize and explore further the matters discussed. The Continuations Committee consisted of Arthur A. Houghton, Jr., president of Steuben Glass; Harold D. Lasswell, professor of law and political science at Yale Law School; Bernard Berelson, director of the Behavioral Sciences Division at the Ford Foundation; William S. Dix, librarian at Princeton University; and Dan Lacy, managing director of the American Book Publishers Council.

By the end of May, the Continuations Committee, with the assistance of other individuals, produced a final version of "The Freedom to Read" for the approval of the Westchester conference participants. On June 18, 1953, the following statement was endorsed by the Board of Directors of the American Book Publishers Council and on June 25, 1953, by the Council of the American Library Association:

> The freedom to read is essential to our democracy. It is under attack. Private groups and public authorities in various parts of the country are working to remove books from sale, to censor textbooks, to label "controversial" books, to distribute lists of "objectionable" books or authors, and to purge libraries. These actions apparently rise from a view that our national tradition of free expression is no longer valid; that censorship and suppression are needed to avoid the subversion of politics and the corruption of morals. We, as citizens devoted to the use of books and as librarians and publishers responsible for disseminating them, wish to assert the public interest in the preservation of the freedom to read.
>
> We are deeply concerned about these attempts at suppression. Most such attempts rest on a denial of the fundamental premise of democracy: that the ordinary citizen, by exercising his critical judgment, will accept the good and reject the bad. The censors, public and private, assume that they should determine what is good and what is bad for their fellow-citizens.
>
> We trust Americans to recognize propaganda, and to reject obscenity. We do not believe they need the help of censors to assist them in this task. We do not believe they are prepared to sacrifice their heritage of a free press in order to be "protected" against what others think may be

bad for them. We believe they still favor free enterprise in ideas and expression.

We are aware, of course, that books are not alone in being subjected to efforts at suppression. We are aware that these efforts are related to a larger pattern of pressures being brought against education, the press, films, radio, and television. The problem is not only one of actual censorship. The shadow of fear cast by these pressures leads, we suspect, to an even larger voluntary curtailment of expression by those who seek to avoid controversy.

Such pressure toward conformity is perhaps natural to a time of uneasy change and pervading fear. Especially when so many of our apprehensions are directed against an ideology, the expression of a dissident idea becomes a thing feared in itself, and we tend to move against it as against a hostile deed, with suppression.

And yet suppression is never more dangerous than in such a time of social tension. Freedom has given the United States the elasticity to endure strain. Freedom keeps open the path of novel and creative solutions, and enables change to come by choice. Every silencing of a heresy, every enforcement of an orthodoxy, diminishes the toughness and resilience of our society and leaves it the less able to deal with stress.

Now as always in our history, books are among our greatest instruments of freedom. They are almost the only means for making generally available ideas or manners of expression that can initially command only a small audience. They are the natural medium for the new idea and the untried voice from which come the original contributions to social growth. They are essential to the extended discussion which serious thought requires and to the accumulation of knowledge and ideas into organized collections.

We believe that free communication is essential to the preservation of a free society and a creative culture. We believe that these pressures towards conformity present the danger of limiting the range and variety of inquiry and expression on which our democracy and our culture depend. We believe that every American community must jealously guard the freedom to publish and to circulate, in order to preserve its own freedom to read. We believe that publishers and librarians have a profound responsibility to give validity to that freedom to read by making it possible for the reader to choose freely from a variety of offerings.

The freedom to read is guaranteed by the Constitution. Those with faith in free men will stand firm on these constitutional guarantees of essential rights and will exercise the responsibilities that accompany these rights.

We therefore affirm these propositions:

1. *It is in the public interest for publishers and librarians to make available the widest diversity of views and expressions, including those which are unorthodox or unpopular with the majority.*

   Creative thought is by definition new, and what is new is different. The bearer of every new thought is a rebel until that idea is refined and tested. Totalitarian systems attempt to maintain themselves in power by the ruthless suppression of any concept which challenges the established orthodoxy. The power of a democratic system to adapt to change is vastly strengthened by the freedom of its citizens to choose widely from among conflicting opinions offered freely to them. To stifle every nonconformist idea at birth would mark the end of the democratic process. Furthermore, only through the constant activity of weighing and selecting can the democratic mind attain the strength demanded by times like these. We need to know not only what we believe but why we believe it.

2. *Publishers and librarians do not need to endorse every idea or presentation contained in the books they make available. It would conflict with the public interest for them to establish their own political, moral, or aesthetic views as the sole standard for determining what books should be published or circulated.*

Publishers and librarians serve the educational process by helping to make available knowledge and ideas required for the growth of the mind and the increase of learning. They do not foster education by imposing as mentors the patterns of their own thought. The people should have the freedom to read and consider a broader range of ideas than those that may be held by any single librarian or publisher or government or church. It is wrong that what one man can read should be confined to what another thinks proper.

3. *It is contrary to the public interest for publishers or librarians to determine the acceptability of a book solely on the basis of the personal history or political affiliations of the author.*

A book should be judged as a book. No art or literature can flourish if it is to be measured by the political views or private lives of its creators. No society of free men can flourish which draws up lists of writers to whom it will not listen, whatever they may have to say.

4. *The present laws dealing with obscenity should be vigorously enforced. Beyond that, there is no place in our society for extralegal efforts to coerce the taste of others, to confine adults to the reading matter deemed suitable for adolescents, or to inhibit the efforts of writers to achieve artistic expression.*

To some, much of modern literature is shocking. But is not much of life itself shocking? We cut off literature at the source if we prevent serious artists from dealing with the stuff of life. Parents and teachers have a responsibility to prepare the young to meet the diversity of experiences in life to which they will be exposed, as they have a responsibility to help them learn to think critically for themselves. These are affirmative responsibilities, not to be discharged simply by preventing them from reading works for which they are not yet prepared. In these matters taste differs, and taste cannot be legislated; nor can machinery be devised which will suit the demands of one group without limiting the freedom of others. We deplore the catering to the immature, the retarded, or the maladjusted taste. But those concerned with freedom have the responsibility of seeing to it that each individual book or publication, whatever its contents, price or method of distribution, is dealt with in accordance with due process of law.

5. *It is not in the public interest to force a reader to accept with any book the prejudgment of a label characterizing the book or author as subversive or dangerous.*

The idea of labeling presupposes the existence of individuals or groups with wisdom to determine by authority what is good or bad for the citizen. It presupposes that each individual must be directed in making up his mind about the ideas he examines. But Americans do not need others to do their thinking for them.

6. *It is the responsibility of publishers and librarians, as guardians of the people's freedom to read, to contest encroachments upon that freedom by individuals or groups seeking to impose their own standards or tastes upon the community at large.*

It is inevitable in the give and take of the democratic process that the political, the moral, or the aesthetic concepts of an individual or group will occasionally collide with those of another individual or group. In a free society each individual is free to determine for himself what he wishes to read, and each group is free to determine what it will recommend to its freely associated members. But no group has the right to take the law into its own hands, and to impose its own concept of politics or morality upon other members of a democratic society. Freedom is no freedom if it is accorded only to the accepted and the inoffensive.

7. *It is the responsibility of publishers and librarians to give full meaning to the freedom to read by providing books that enrich the quality of thought and expression. By the exercise of this affirmative responsibility, bookmen can demonstrate*

*that the answer to a bad book is a good one, the answer to a
bad idea is a good one.*

The freedom to read is of little consequence when expended on the trivial; it is frustrated when the reader
cannot obtain matter fit for his purpose. What is
needed is not only the absence of restraint, but the
positive provision of opportunity for the people to
read the best that has been thought and said. Books are
the major channel by which the intellectual inheritance
is handed down, and the principal means of its testing
and growth. The defense of their freedom and
integrity, and the enlargement of their service to society,
requires of all bookmen the utmost of their faculties,
and deserves of all citizens the fullest of their support.

From a deceptively comfortable position in the middle of the
1960s, most librarians looked forward to the 1970s with optimism,
hoping for a favorable climate for intellectual freedom. The U.S.
Supreme Court extended constitutional support and protection in
many areas of human and civil rights. Very encouraging to librarians was the expansion of freedom of expression and other First
Amendment rights to allow publications that could not have been
found fifteen years earlier. An unfettered climate in which all ideas
could be freely exchanged seemed imminent.

But the sense of optimism was soon undercut as increased
American involvement in the Vietnam War prompted rancorous
divisions among citizens and members of the government. And
then came 1968: on April 4, Dr. Martin Luther King Jr. was assassi-
nated in Memphis, and the riots provoked in Washington, D.C., and
elsewhere led President Lyndon B. Johnson to call out troops to
restore order. By April 14, violence had erupted in twenty-nine
states. On June 6, Robert F. Kennedy died in Los Angeles, also a vic-
tim of an assassin's bullet. From August 25 to 29, the Democratic
National Convention in Chicago became the scene of violent clashes
between the police and National Guard troops on one side and
more than ten thousand antiwar demonstrators on the other. This
period of violent dissent, countered by equally violent reactions,
continued into 1970 with the Kent State and Jackson, Mississippi,
incidents and battles between the Black Panther Party and police,
and between the radical Weather Underground and police.

It became increasingly clear that such incidents of violent dissent and violent reactions were gradually eroding prospects for the open society many had envisioned. The "permissive" atmosphere collided with demands for law and order. One effect of the collision was that, little by little, the supports for intellectual freedom in the society at large were weakened.

In the form of subpoenas, pressure was brought against news reporters, photographers, and television broadcasting corporations to divulge sources of information and to produce unpublished materials deleted from final reports. Vice President Spiro Agnew gave a series of speeches condemning the news media for biased reporting and calling on citizens to protest such reporting. President Richard M. Nixon promised to appoint conservatives to the Supreme Court.

Recognizing the increasing conservatism of the nation, and mindful that "The Freedom to Read" might be tied too closely to the McCarthy era, the IFC began, in the fall of 1968, to consider the need for and desirability of a new statement to serve the 1970s. A careful review of the document resulted in the following points:

1. Article 4, urging the vigorous enforcement of "the present laws dealing with obscenity," should be revised or deleted entirely.
2. The basic sentiments expressed in "The Freedom to Read" remain valid and should not be distorted.
3. The document has historical significance.
4. A new statement is needed dealing specifically with the pressures on today's society and those foreseen arising during the next decade.

Believing a new statement should at least be attempted, the IFC asked the National Book Committee (NBC) and the American Book Publishers Council, the cosponsor of "The Freedom to Read," whether they were interested in joining the undertaking. Both replied affirmatively. Theodore Waller and Peter Jennison met with the IFC during the 1969 Midwinter Meeting in Washington, D.C., and formed a subcommittee composed of representatives from the ABPC, ALA, and NBC, charged with determining content and preparing a draft document.

Meeting during the 1969 ALA Annual Conference in Atlantic City, the subcommittee—composed of Edwin Castagna, Peter Jennison, Judith F. Krug, Dan Lacy, and Theodore Waller—discussed the two major items: (1) Should "The Freedom to Read" be revised, or should a new document be produced? and (2) What kind of ammunition is needed to meet the challenge of the 1970s? Like the IFC, the subcommittee decided to design a new statement that would meet the challenges of the 1970s. The subcommittee also considered such questions as: Can freedom to read be separated from intellectual freedom? Is a broader concept of intellectual freedom, embracing the First Amendment together with other aspects of the Bill of Rights, such as the invasion of privacy, needed? Should all media, not just books, be considered? Should complete intellectual freedom be called for, or must one retreat in the end to the principle of the freedom to read?

The subcommittee next met in August of that year, with a membership augmented by the presence of William DeJohn, Freeman Lewis, Harriet Pilpel, and Richard Sullivan. They drafted several statements and asked Jennison to assemble them into one cohesive document. Five drafts were subsequently produced, and the IFC, in a ten-to-one mail vote, approved the fifth draft. By the time of the 1970 Midwinter Meeting, however, a sixth draft had been prepared.

The ABPC Board of Directors received the draft and approved it by acclamation on January 28. The sixth draft was resubmitted to the IFC, which approved it in a ten-to-one vote.

Following the 1970 Midwinter Meeting, the staff of the Office for Intellectual Freedom carefully reviewed the sixth draft of the document, tentatively entitled "The Promise of the First Freedom: A Statement of Free Men." The staff could not join with the IFC in endorsing this document and recommended to the IFC that "The Freedom to Read" be revised, as opposed to rewritten, to meet contemporary needs. This decision was based on several factors:

1. The major part of "The Freedom to Read" remained valid.
2. Among those parts that needed change were the specific references to books, for libraries were concerned with all types of materials.
3. Although "The Freedom to Read" had historical significance, subsequent policy statements, as well as actions, of the Association were in opposition to a few parts, primarily Article 4.
4. The few parts in opposition were believed to be serious matters and should not be permitted to stand.

The revision was undertaken by the Office for Intellectual Freedom and W. Lester Smith of the Association of American Publishers (AAP), the organization resulting from the consolidation of the ABPC and the American Educational Publishers Institute. The new document differed from the 1953 version on only a few significant points: the earlier call for "vigorous enforcement of present obscenity laws" was omitted, as was the reference to "the immature, the retarded, and the maladjusted taste."

The revised Freedom to Read statement was approved by the ALA Council at the 1972 Midwinter Meeting and by the AAP as follows:

> The freedom to read is essential to our democracy. It is continuously under attack. Private groups and public authorities in various parts of the country are working to remove books from sale, to censor textbooks, to label "controversial" books, to distribute lists of "objectionable" books or authors, and to purge libraries. These actions apparently rise from a view that our national tradition of free expression is no longer valid; that censorship and suppression are needed to avoid the subversion of politics and the corruption of morals. We, as citizens devoted to the use of books and as librarians and publishers responsible for disseminating them, wish to assert the public interest in the preservation of the freedom to read.
>
> We are deeply concerned about these attempts at suppression. Most such attempts rest on a denial of the fundamental premise of democracy: that the ordinary citizen, by exercising his critical judgment, will accept the good and reject the bad. The censors, public and private, assume that they should determine what is good and what is bad for their fellow-citizens.
>
> We trust Americans to recognize propaganda and to reject it. We do not believe they need the help of censors to assist them in this task. We do not believe they are prepared to sacrifice their heritage of a free press in order to be "protected" against what others think may be bad for them. We believe they still favor free enterprise in ideas and expression.

We are aware, of course, that books are not alone in being subjected to efforts at suppression. We are aware that these efforts are related to a larger pattern of pressures being brought against education, the press, films, radio, and television. The problem is not only one of actual censorship. The shadow of fear cast by these pressures leads, we suspect, to an even larger voluntary curtailment of expression by those who seek to avoid controversy.

Such pressure toward conformity is perhaps natural to a time of uneasy change and pervading fear. Especially when so many of our apprehensions are directed against an ideology, the expression of a dissident idea becomes a thing feared in itself, and we tend to move against it as against a hostile deed, with suppression.

And yet suppression is never more dangerous than in such a time of social tension. Freedom has given the United States the elasticity to endure strain. Freedom keeps open the path of novel and creative solutions, and enables change to come by choice. Every silencing of a heresy, every enforcement of an orthodoxy, diminishes the toughness and resilience of our society and leaves it the less able to deal with stress.

Now as always in our history, books are among our greatest instruments of freedom. They are almost the only means for making generally available ideas or manners of expression that can initially command only a small audience. They are the natural medium for the new idea and the untried voice from which come the original contributions to social growth. They are essential to the extended discussion which serious thought requires, and to the accumulation of knowledge and ideas into organized collections.

We believe that free communication is essential to the preservation of a free society and a creative culture. We believe that these pressures towards conformity present the danger of limiting the range and variety of inquiry and expression on which our democracy and our culture depend. We believe that every American community must jealously guard the freedom to publish and to circulate, in order to preserve its own freedom to read. We believe that publishers and librarians have a profound responsibility to give validity to that freedom to read by making it possible for the readers to choose freely from a variety of offerings.

The freedom to read is guaranteed by the Constitution. Those with faith in free people will stand firm on these constitutional guarantees of essential rights and will exercise the responsibilities that accompany these rights.

We therefore affirm these propositions:

1. *It is in the public interest for publishers and librarians to make available the widest diversity of views and expressions, including those which are unorthodox or unpopular with the majority.*

   Creative thought is by definition new, and what is new is different. The bearer of every new thought is a rebel until that idea is refined and tested. Totalitarian systems attempt to maintain themselves in power by the ruthless suppression of any concept which challenges the established orthodoxy. The power of a democratic system to adapt to change is vastly strengthened by the freedom of its citizens to choose widely from among conflicting opinions offered freely to them. To stifle every nonconformist idea at birth would mark the end of the democratic process. Furthermore, only through the constant activity of weighing and selecting can the democratic mind attain the strength demanded by times like these. We need to know not only what we believe but why we believe it.

2. *Publishers, librarians, and booksellers do not need to endorse every idea or presentation contained in the books they make available. It would conflict with the public interest for them to establish their own political, moral, or aesthetic views as a standard for determining what books should be published or circulated.*

Publishers and librarians serve the educational process by helping to make available knowledge and ideas required for the growth of the mind and the increase of learning. They do not foster education by imposing as mentors the patterns of their own thought. The people should have the freedom to read and consider a broader range of ideas than those that may be held by any single librarian or publisher or government or church. It is wrong that what one can read should be confined to what another thinks proper.

3. *It is contrary to the public interest for publishers or librarians to determine the acceptability of a book on the basis of the personal history or political affiliations of the author.*

A book should be judged as a book. No art or literature can flourish if it is to be measured by the political views or private lives of its creators. No society of free men can flourish which draws up lists of writers to whom it will not listen, whatever they may have to say.

4. *There is no place in our society for efforts to coerce the taste of others, to confine adults to the reading matter deemed suitable for adolescents, or to inhibit the efforts of writers to achieve artistic expression.*

To some, much of modern literature is shocking. But is not much of life itself shocking? We cut off literature at the source if we prevent writers from dealing with the stuff of life. Parents and teachers have a responsibility to prepare the young to meet the diversity of experiences in life to which they will be exposed, as they have a responsibility to help them learn to think critically for themselves. These are affirmative responsibilities, not to be discharged simply by preventing them from reading works for which they are not yet prepared. In these matters taste differs, and taste cannot be legislated; nor can machinery be devised which will suit the demands of one group without limiting the freedom of others.

5. *It is not in the public interest to force a reader to accept with any book the prejudgment of a label characterizing the book or author as subversive or dangerous.*

The idea of labeling presupposes the existence of individuals or groups with wisdom to determine by authority what is good or bad for the citizen. It presupposes that each individual must be directed in making up his mind about the ideas he examines. But Americans do not need others to do their thinking for them.

6. *It is the responsibility of publishers and librarians, as guardians of the people's freedom to read, to contest encroachments upon that freedom by individuals or groups seeking to impose their own standards or tastes upon the community at large.*

It is inevitable in the give and take of the democratic process that the political, the moral, or the aesthetic concepts of an individual or group will occasionally collide with those of another individual or group. In a free society each individual is free to determine for himself what he wishes to read, and each group is free to determine what it will recommend to its freely associated members. But no group has the right to take the law into its own hands, and to impose its own concept of politics or morality upon other members of a democratic society. Freedom is no freedom if it is accorded only to the accepted and the inoffensive.

7. *It is the responsibility of publishers and librarians to give full meaning to the freedom to read by providing books that enrich the quality and diversity of thought and expression. By the exercise of this affirmative responsibility, bookmen can demonstrate that the answer to a bad book is a good one, the answer to a bad idea is a good one.*

The freedom to read is of little consequence when expended on the trivial; it is frustrated when the reader cannot obtain matter fit for his purpose. What is needed is not only the absence of restraint, but the positive provision of opportunity for the people to read the best that has been thought and said. Books are the major channel by which the intellectual inheritance is handed down, and the principal means of its testing and growth. The defense of their freedom and integrity; and the enlargement of their service to society, requires of all bookmen the utmost of their faculties, and deserves of all citizens the fullest of their support.

We state these propositions neither lightly nor as easy generalizations. We here stake out a lofty claim for the value of books. We do so because we believe that they are good, possessed of enormous variety and usefulness, worthy of cherishing and keeping free. We realize that the application of these propositions may mean the dissemination of ideas and manners of expression that are repugnant to many persons. We do not state these propositions in the comfortable belief that what people read is unimportant. We believe rather that what people read is deeply important; that ideas can be dangerous; but that the suppression of ideas is fatal to a democratic society. Freedom itself is a dangerous way of life, but it is ours.

The document was subsequently endorsed by many other organizations: American Booksellers Association; American Civil Liberties Union; American Federation of Teachers, AFL-CIO; Anti-Defamation League of B'nai B'rith; Association of American University Presses; Bureau of Independent Publishers and Distributors; Children's Book Council; Freedom of Information Center; Freedom to Read Foundation; Magazine Publishers Association; Motion Picture Association of America; National Association of College Stores; National Board of the Young Women's Christian Association of the U.S.A.; National Book Committee; National Council of Negro Women; National Council of Teachers of English; National Library Week Program; P.E.N.–American Center; Periodical and Book Association of America; Sex Information and Education Council of the U.S.; and Women's National Book Association.

By 1990, both the IFC and the AAP Freedom to Read Committee were in agreement that "The Freedom to Read" needed minor revisions. In addition, it recently had gone out of print. At the Annual Conference in June, Richard Kleeman of the Association of American Publishers recommended minor changes, including removal of gender-specific language. It also was suggested that the new draft incorporate international concerns about the freedom to read.

A major question in regard to a revised statement was whether it should be more explicitly inclusive of the arts and music—targets of many then-recent censorship battles. Again the view was strongly expressed that the statement had stood the test of time and would only be diminished by extensive revisions. The IFC agreed to proceed with a review and report back at the 1991 Midwinter Meeting. Richard Kleeman said the AAP Freedom to Read Committee would follow the same timetable.

In January 1991, the IFC considered two new drafts: one without gender-specific language and the other with a new international focus. Ultimately, the Committee decided to adopt only the first version and to address international and other concerns in separate documents. On January 16, 1991, the Committee adopted "The Freedom to Read" as revised and so informed the Council. Given the editorial nature of the changes, no action by the Council was required. On the same date, at its regular monthly meeting, the AAP Freedom to Read Committee adopted the same revision.

In line with the ongoing practice of periodic review, the IFC carefully reviewed all statements, including "The Freedom to Read," in 1999–2000, especially in regard to their applicability to the Internet. At the 2000 Midwinter Meeting, IFC member Carolyn Caywood, who had been assigned the task of reviewing "The Freedom to Read," presented a revision that she said did not tamper with the spirit of the statement but only updated certain phrases and terminologies. After discussion by the IFC, Caywood, along with IFC members Vivian Wynn and Paul Vermouth, drafted further refinements that they felt broadened the statement beyond print material. The revised document was adopted by the ALA Council and the AAP Freedom to Read Committee on July 12, 2000, and read as follows.

> The freedom to read is essential to our democracy. It is continuously under attack. Private groups and public authorities in various parts of the country are working to remove or limit access to reading materials, to censor

content in schools, to label "controversial" views, to distribute lists of "objectionable" books or authors, and to purge libraries. These actions apparently rise from a view that our national tradition of free expression is no longer valid; that censorship and suppression are needed to avoid the subversion of politics and the corruption of morals. We, as citizens devoted to reading and as librarians and publishers responsible for disseminating ideas, wish to assert the public interest in the preservation of the freedom to read.

Most attempts at suppression rest on a denial of the fundamental premise of democracy: that the ordinary citizen, by exercising critical judgment, will accept the good and reject the bad. The censors, public and private, assume that they should determine what is good and what is bad for their fellow citizens.

We trust Americans to recognize propaganda and misinformation, and to make their own decisions about what they read and believe. We do not believe they need the help of censors to assist them in this task. We do not believe they are prepared to sacrifice their heritage of a free press in order to be "protected" against what others think may be bad for them. We believe they still favor free enterprise in ideas and expression.

These efforts at suppression are related to a larger pattern of pressures being brought against education, the press, art and images, films, broadcast media, and the Internet. The problem is not only one of actual censorship. The shadow of fear cast by these pressures leads, we suspect, to an even larger voluntary curtailment of expression by those who seek to avoid controversy.

Such pressure toward conformity is perhaps natural to a time of accelerated change. And yet suppression is never more dangerous than in such a time of social tension. Freedom has given the United States the elasticity to endure strain. Freedom keeps open the path of novel and creative solutions, and enables change to come by choice. Every silencing of a heresy, every enforcement of an orthodoxy, diminishes the toughness and resilience of our society and leaves it the less able to deal with controversy and difference.

Now as always in our history, reading is among our greatest freedoms. The freedom to read and write is almost the only means for making generally available ideas or manners of expression that can initially command only a small audience. The written word is the natural medium for the new idea and the untried voice from which come the original contributions to social growth. It is essential to the extended discussion that serious thought requires, and to the accumulation of knowledge and ideas into organized collections.

We believe that free communication is essential to the preservation of a free society and a creative culture. We believe that these pressures toward conformity present the danger of limiting the range and variety of inquiry and expression on which our democracy and our culture depend. We believe that every American community must jealously guard the freedom to publish and to circulate, in order to preserve its own freedom to read. We believe that publishers and librarians have a profound responsibility to give validity to that freedom to read by making it possible for the readers to choose freely from a variety of offerings. The freedom to read is guaranteed by the Constitution. Those with faith in free people will stand firm on these constitutional guarantees of essential rights and will exercise the responsibilities that accompany these rights.

We therefore affirm these propositions:

1. *It is in the public interest for publishers and librarians to make available the widest diversity of views and expressions, including those that are unorthodox or unpopular with the majority.*

   Creative thought is by definition new, and what is new is different. The bearer of every new thought is a rebel until that idea is refined and tested. Totalitarian systems attempt to maintain themselves in power by the ruthless suppression of any concept that challenges the established orthodoxy. The power of a democratic system to adapt to change is vastly strengthened by the freedom of its citizens to choose widely from among conflicting opinions offered freely to them. To stifle every nonconformist idea at birth would mark the end of the democratic process. Furthermore, only through the constant activity of weighing and selecting can the democratic mind attain the strength demanded by times like these. We need to know not only what we believe but why we believe it.

2. *Publishers, librarians, and booksellers do not need to endorse every idea or presentation they make available. It would conflict with the public interest for them to establish their own political, moral, or aesthetic views as a standard for determining what should be published or circulated.*

Publishers and librarians serve the educational process by helping to make available knowledge and ideas required for the growth of the mind and the increase of learning. They do not foster education by imposing as mentors the patterns of their own thought. The people should have the freedom to read and consider a broader range of ideas than those that may be held by any single librarian or publisher or government or church. It is wrong that what one can read should be confined to what another thinks proper.

3. *It is contrary to the public interest for publishers or librarians to bar access to writings on the basis of the personal history or political affiliations of the author.*

No art or literature can flourish if it is to be measured by the political views or private lives of its creators. No society of free people can flourish that draws up lists of writers to whom it will not listen, whatever they may have to say.

4. *There is no place in our society for efforts to coerce the taste of others, to confine adults to the reading matter deemed*

suitable for adolescents, or to inhibit the efforts of writers to achieve artistic expression.

To some, much of modern expression is shocking. But is not much of life itself shocking? We cut off literature at the source if we prevent writers from dealing with the stuff of life. Parents and teachers have a responsibility to prepare the young to meet the diversity of experiences in life to which they will be exposed, as they have a responsibility to help them learn to think critically for themselves. These are affirmative responsibilities, not to be discharged simply by preventing them from reading works for which they are not yet prepared. In these matters values differ, and values cannot be legislated; nor can machinery be devised that will suit the demands of one group without limiting the freedom of others.

5. *It is not in the public interest to force a reader to accept with any expression the prejudgment of a label characterizing it or its author as subversive or dangerous.*

The idea of labeling presupposes the existence of individuals or groups with wisdom to determine by authority what is good or bad for the citizen. It presupposes that individuals must be directed in making up their minds about the ideas they examine. But Americans do not need others to do their thinking for them.

6. *It is the responsibility of publishers and librarians, as guardians of the people's freedom to read, to contest encroachments upon that freedom by individuals or groups seeking to impose their own standards or tastes upon the community at large.*

It is inevitable in the give and take of the democratic process that the political, the moral, or the aesthetic concepts of an individual or group will occasionally collide with those of another individual or group. In a free society, individuals are free to determine for themselves what they wish to read, and each group is free to determine what it will recommend to its freely associated members. But no group has the right to take the law into its own hands, and to impose its own concept of politics or morality upon other members of a democratic society. Freedom is no freedom if it is accorded only to the accepted and the inoffensive.

7. *It is the responsibility of publishers and librarians to give full meaning to the freedom to read by providing books that enrich the quality and diversity of thought and expression. By the exercise of this affirmative responsibility, they can demonstrate that the answer to a "bad" book is a good one, the answer to a "bad" idea is a good one.*

The freedom to read is of little consequence when the reader cannot obtain matter fit for that reader's purpose. What is needed is not only the absence of restraint, but the positive provision of opportunity for the people to read the best that has been thought and said. Books are the major channel by which the intellectual inheritance is handed down, and the principal means of its testing and growth. The defense of the freedom to read requires of all publishers and librarians the utmost of their faculties, and deserves of all citizens the fullest of their support.

We state these propositions neither lightly nor as easy generalizations. We here stake out a lofty claim for the value of the written word. We do so because we believe that it is possessed of enormous variety and usefulness, worthy of cherishing and keeping free. We realize that the application of these propositions may mean the dissemination of ideas and manners of expression that are repugnant to many persons. We do not state these propositions in the comfortable belief that what people read is unimportant. We believe rather that what people read is deeply important; that ideas can be dangerous; but that the suppression of ideas is fatal to a democratic society. Freedom itself is a dangerous way of life, but it is ours.

The Freedom to Read statement was reconsidered by the IFC during the 2004–5 review of intellectual freedom policies. The Committee decided to recommend a few changes in light of the political environment since September 11, 2001. Judith Platt represented the AAP Freedom to Read Committee during the discussions.

The changes made fell into three categories:

1. During this review, all uses of the word "censor" were reviewed to ensure they are not gratuitous. As a result, the two statements about censors in the second and third paragraphs were determined to be unnecessary for the strength of the message and were removed.
2. References to "citizens" were examined to ensure that the use was not unnecessarily limiting. With one exception ("The power of a democratic system to adapt to change is vastly strengthened by the freedom of its citizens to choose widely from among conflicting opinions offered freely to them"), the Committee changed "citizens" to "others," "individuals," and "Americans."
3. Phrases were added in appropriate places throughout the statement to address threats to the freedom to read and the free flow of information resulting from government surveillance, censorship, and secrecy.

The revised Freedom to Read statement was adopted by the ALA Council and the AAP Freedom to Read Committee on June 30, 2004.

NOTE

1. For full details of national and international events surrounding the development of The Freedom to Read, see Everett T. Moore, "Intellectual Freedom," in *Research Librarianship: Essays in Honor of Robert B. Downs*, ed. Jerrold Orne (New York: Bowker, 1971).

2
Code of Ethics of the American Library Association

As members of the American Library Association, we recognize the importance of codifying and making known to the profession and to the general public the ethical principles that guide the work of librarians, other professionals providing information services, library trustees and library staffs.

Ethical dilemmas occur when values are in conflict. The American Library Association Code of Ethics states the values to which we are committed, and embodies the ethical responsibilities of the profession in this changing information environment.

We significantly influence or control the selection, organization, preservation, and dissemination of information. In a political system grounded in an informed citizenry, we are members of a profession explicitly committed to intellectual freedom and the freedom of access to information. We have a special obligation to ensure the free flow of information and ideas to present and future generations.

The principles of this Code are expressed in broad statements to guide ethical decision making. These statements provide a framework; they cannot and do not dictate conduct to cover particular situations.

I. We provide the highest level of service to all library users through appropriate and usefully organized resources; equitable service policies; equitable access; and accurate, unbiased, and courteous responses to all requests.

II. We uphold the principles of intellectual freedom and resist all efforts to censor library resources.

III. We protect each library user's right to privacy and confidentiality with respect to information sought or received and resources consulted, borrowed, acquired or transmitted.

IV. We recognize and respect intellectual property rights.

V. We treat co-workers and other colleagues with respect, fairness and good faith, and advocate conditions of employment that safeguard the rights and welfare of all employees of our institutions.

VI. We do not advance private interests at the expense of library users, colleagues, or our employing institutions.

VII. We distinguish between our personal convictions and professional duties and do not allow our personal beliefs to interfere with fair representation of the aims of our institutions or the provision of access to their information resources.

VIII. We strive for excellence in the profession by maintaining and enhancing our own knowledge and skills, by encouraging the professional development of co-workers, and by fostering the aspirations of potential members of the profession.

Adopted June 28, 1995, by the ALA Council. http://www.ala.org/oif/policies/codeofethics/.

HISTORY

Code of Ethics

The *Intellectual Freedom Manual* focuses on the areas of responsibility of the Intellectual Freedom Committee. ALA's Code of Ethics is the responsibility of the Committee on Professional Ethics (COPE). The Code of Ethics has been included because it is the document that translates the values of intellectual freedom that define the profession of librarianship into broad principles that may be used by individual members of that profession as well as by others employed in a library as a framework for dealing with situations involving ethical conflicts.

The Code of Ethics has a long history. As noted by John A. Moorman in 1995:

> Since its formation, the American Library Association has worked on a Code of Ethics for its membership. In 1903, 1929, 1938, 1975, 1981 and since 1992, special attention has been given to either formulating, revising or revisiting the American Library Association Code of Ethics. The Association's Code of Ethics Committee was first noted in 1928 and was established as an ALA Council standing committee in 1975.[1]

ALA adopted its first code of ethics in 1939. The code was revised in 1981 and again in 1995. Space limitations in this manual make it impossible to include a detailed history of the Code of Ethics. However, review of the drafts that preceded the 1939 and 1981 codes, along with the adopted codes themselves, sheds considerable light on the evolution of this document.

The March 30, 1930, *American Library Association Bulletin* published a Suggested Code of Ethics.[2] The committee that developed the code was chaired by Josephine Adams Rathbone, who served as ALA president from 1931 to 1932. This document covered specific ethical principles related to the governance and operation of a library. Although this early code bears very little resemblance to later codes of ethics, it includes concepts that remain in the current code. For example, a paragraph in part B, section 2, "Librarian and Constituency," states:

> The librarian, representing the governing body, should see that the library serves impartially all individuals, groups, and elements that make up its constituency. In the case of the public library as a non-partisan institution the books purchased should represent all phases of opinion and interest rather than the personal tastes of the librarian or board members. In an official capacity, the librarian and members of the staff should not express personal opinions on controversial questions, as political, religious, or economic issues; especially those of a local nature.

The full Suggested Code of Ethics read as follows:

> The library as an institution exists for the benefit of a given constituency. This may be the nation, a state, a county, a municipality, a school or college, a special field of research, industry or commerce, or some more limited group.
>
> Libraries differ so widely in size, type of constituents, support and character of work that a code of ethics would have to be excessively detailed to apply to all situations, but certain fundamental principles may be laid down that are generally applicable.
>
> The library's obligations relate to such collection, organization and administration of printed material or other records as will give the best possible service to its constituents. The human factors in this service are:
>
> > The trustees or other governing body or agency;
> > The librarian;

The staff;

The people whom the library serves.

A. Governing Bodies

These may be the Board of Trustees or city officials (on whom the responsibility rests) of public or semi-public libraries; the library board or committee of college or university trustees or faculty; Board of Education or a committee thereof for school libraries or for public libraries organized under school law; officer or committee or department of a business corporation.

1. Functions.

The functions of a governing body are usually prescribed by law but generally include:

> The representation of the constituency for which the library exists;
>
> The determination of the policies of the library in its service and relation to its constituency;
>
> The exercise or delegation of the appointing and removing power;
>
> Responsibility for bringing the needs of the library before the authorities who control the appropriation of funds and for using all proper influence to get such increases as are necessary for the growth and development of the work;
>
> The administration of the funds for the support of the library;
>
> Responsibility for the economic, social and physical well-being of the staff, including a retirement system which is needed for the good of the service as well as of the individual.

Trustees of tax-supported public libraries remembering that they are representatives of the whole community, should be careful not to ask special privileges for themselves or their families. The Board of Trustees should recognize that the librarian, as its executive, should attend the meetings of the board in order to be fully informed as to its desires and purposes and to aid in the formulation of its policies.

2. Appointments.

The appointing power in any institution should be definitely vested in some one board, committee or person. The appointee should not consider an appointment final unless made by the agency or person in whom that authority is lodged.

Appointments should be made for fitness only; no merely personal consideration should enter into the selection of the personnel of any library; conversely, no librarian should accept an appointment, however attractive, unless he believes that he has the ability, the training and the experience needed for ultimate success in that position, and no one should continue to hold a position unless he finds himself qualified to meet all its requirements.

3. Tenure.

Having accepted a position in a library the appointee incurs certain definite obligations:

> To remain long enough to repay the library for the expenditure of time and money incident to the period of adjustment; this length of time differs in different positions, but is seldom less than a year;

> To remain long enough to accomplish definite results in work undertaken;

> Unless a larger opportunity offers, it is best to remain in a position as long as one is able to do creative or effective work or to get satisfaction from the work; otherwise it is probable that one's usefulness in that position is at an end.

4. Resignations.

Resignations should be made in writing to the authority from which the appointment came with due notification to the immediate supervisor. Adequate time should be given before the resignation takes effect for the work to be put into shape; for the appointment and, when practicable, the initiation of a successor.

5. Dismissals.

Dismissals should be made whenever the good of the service demands. The employee's length of service, need of the position and personal worthiness may be considered, but these elements should never outweigh a clear case of incompetence or incompatibility. It should be remembered that an employee who is unsatisfactory in one position may often prove effective in another department or position. Such adjustment may be attempted where practicable before dismissal. Dismissal should be made by the highest executive officer.

6. Recommendations.

Trustees and librarians are sometimes dependent for information about candidates on recommendation from trustees, librarians, library schools, and other employment agencies. Recommendations should present a fair statement of the strong and weak points of the candidate.

B. Librarian (Or chief administrative officer)

The librarian is the executive officer for the governing body of the library. The position of librarian involves a threefold relation: 1. To the trustees or governing body; 2. To the constituents of the library; 3. To the staff.

1. In relation to the Board of Trustees the librarian:

Should make a loyal effort to carry out its policies;

Should make regular and systematic reports upon the work accomplished;

Should initiate plans for improvement of the service of the library;

Should act as liaison officer between the trustees
and staff, interpreting each to the other and
establishing, where possible, friendly relations
between them.

2. Librarian and constituency.

The librarian represents the library—book power and
book service—and should so represent it as to win recognition for the institution rather than credit for the individual.

The librarian has a further obligation to the community or constituency which the library serves and should, as representative of the library (with due respect for other duties), take part in the life and activities of the community or constituency.

As representative of the library, the librarian and the staff should feel an obligation to maintain in personal conduct the dignity of the position and take care not to offend against the standards of decorum that prevail in that community or constituency.

The librarian, representing the governing body, should see that the library serves impartially all individuals, groups, and elements that make up its constituency. In the case of the public library as a non-partisan institution the books purchased should represent all phases of opinion and interest rather than the personal tastes of the librarian or board members. In an official capacity, the librarian and members of the staff should not express personal opinions on controversial questions, as political, religious, or economic issues; especially those of a local nature.

3. Librarian and staff.

The relations of the librarian to the staff within the library should be impersonal, and absolutely impartial. The librarian owes to the members of the staff:

Stimulus to growth, to the exercise of the creative
impulse, to the development of initiative and of
a professional spirit;

Constructive criticism;

Freedom to achieve results and credit for such achievement;

Respect for the authority delegated to the staff;

Friendliness of attitude;

Justice in decision;

Opportunity for professional and economic advancement within that institution or some other;

Encouragement of reasonable suggestions and criticisms for the improvement of the service.

C. The Staff

1. Loyalty.

Loyalty to the institution is the primary duty of all members of the staff.

Loyalty involves, in part, submergence of the individual to the institution. Such manifestations of egoism as criticism of the library or librarian outside, or the claiming of individual credit for work done as a staff member when credit should belong to the institution, are examples of disloyalty. Constructive criticism offered to the proper authority should not be considered disloyalty and should be encouraged.

Good health is a pre-requisite of good service and involves the right use of free time so that a proper balance is maintained between work, recreation and rest.

The atmosphere of the library is disturbed unless the workers preserve harmony and a spirit of cooperation among themselves; hence the staff relations, while impersonal within the building, should be friendly. Envy, jealousy, or gossip should have no place in a library staff. The staff should refrain from discussion of personal affairs in the library or from attention to personal business in library time.

2. Relations to the public.

The members of the staff are the interpreters of the library to the public, and its service may be materially helped or harmed by their individual contacts.

The staff owes impartial, courteous service to all persons using the library. Among the patrons entitled to use the library no distinctions of race, color, creed or condition should influence the attitude of the staff, and no favoritism should be tolerated. On the other hand, a cold officialism is to be avoided and a cordial attitude which welcomes approach should be manifested by those in direct contact with the public.

3. Department heads.

Heads of departments should consider their departments in relation to the institution as a whole and never magnify unduly the importance of their own part.

Understanding and cooperation between departments is essential to the efficiency of the library's service to the community.

The heads of departments bear much the same relation to those under them that the librarian does to the library staff as a whole, and have on a smaller scale the same duties and responsibilities.

4. Assistants.

Assistants are an integral part of the institution as a whole, and their suggestions for the improvement of the service should be encouraged. These suggestions should be made to the immediate superior. If differences of opinion concerning the work arise between assistants in a department, the matter in question should be taken to the head of the department for adjustment. If an assistant is critical of the policy of the department or feels that he has been unfairly dealt with, he should first discuss the matter with the head. If unable to obtain satisfaction, he may then appeal to the next higher authority. Constructive criticism or correction by responsible heads is necessary to the efficiency of any service and should be accepted by assistants without personal resentment.

The advancement of assistants should come as the result of the recommendation of heads of departments or of the librarian. Assistants should never use outside relationships to obtain a position or promotion.

The relation of staff members to the non-professional group of workers, as janitors and pages, should be strictly impersonal. Personal favors should never be asked. Their work should be directed by those assigned to the duty, and never interfered with by other staff members.

D. Library Profession

All libraries and all librarians have a duty not only to their constituents but to the profession as a whole; or to some division of it, because cooperation between libraries and librarians makes for better service to the constituents of every library. This duty involves membership and activities in one or more professional organizations, subscription to and the reading of professional literature, interchange of ideas and, as far as possible, of material.

While these principles may not cover every case that may arise, we believe that if applied intelligently they would make for harmony in staff relations and for the general good of the service.

In November 1938, the Code of Ethics Committee distributed a revised code that was adopted at the 1939 Midwinter Meeting.[3] The new code was more succinct, and the focus shifted somewhat from governing bodies to librarians, which it defined as "any person who is employed by a library to do the work that is recognized to be professional in character according to standards established by the American Library Association."

The code put forth twenty-eight principles of ethical behavior for professional librarians. Then, as now, the principles were not intended to be "a declaration of prerogatives nor a statement of recommended practices in specific situations" (principle 3). The eleventh principle is noteworthy as it stated that "It is the librarian's obligation to treat as confidential any private information obtained through contact with library patrons." The 1939 Code of Ethics read as follows:

Preamble

1. The library as an institution exists for the benefit of a given constituency, whether it be the citizens of a community, members of an educational institution, or some larger or more specialized group. Those who enter the library profession assume an obligation to maintain ethical standards of behavior in relation to the governing authority under which they work, to the library constituency, to the library as an institution and to fellow workers on the staff, to other members of the library profession, and to society in general.

2. The term librarian in this code applies to any person who is employed by a library to do work that is recognized to be professional in character according to standards established by the American Library Association.

3. This code sets forth principles of ethical behavior for the professional librarian. It is not a declaration of prerogatives nor a statement of recommended practices in specific situations.

I. Relation of the Librarian to the Governing Authority

4. The librarian should perform his duties with realization of the fact that final jurisdiction over the administration of the library rests in the officially constituted governing authority. This authority may be vested in a designated individual, or in a group such as a committee or board.

5. The chief librarian should keep the governing authority informed on professional standards and progressive action. Each librarian should be responsible for carrying out the policies of the governing authority

and its appointed executives with a spirit of loyalty to the library.

6. The chief librarian should interpret decisions of the governing authority to the staff, and should act as liaison officer in maintaining friendly relations between staff members and those in authority.

7. Recommendations to the governing authority for the appointment of a staff member should be made by the chief librarian solely upon the basis of the candidate's professional and personal qualifications for the position. Continuance in service and promotion should depend upon the quality of performance, following a definite and known policy. Whenever the good of the service requires a change in personnel, timely warning should be given. If desirable adjustment cannot be made, unsatisfactory service should be terminated in accordance with the policy of the library and the rules of tenure.

8. Resolutions, petitions, and requests of a staff organization or group should be submitted through a duly appointed representative to the chief librarian. If a mutually satisfactory solution cannot be reached, the chief librarian, on request of the staff, should transmit the matter to the governing authority. The staff may further request that they be allowed to send a representative to the governing authority, in order to present their opinions in person.

II. Relation of the Librarian to His Constituency

9. The chief librarian, aided by staff members in touch with the constituency, should study the present and future needs of the library, and should acquire materials on the basis of those needs. Provision should be made for as wide a range of publications and as varied a representation of viewpoints as is consistent with the policies of the library and with the funds available.

10. It is the librarian's responsibility to make the resources and services of the library known to its potential users. Impartial service should be rendered to all who are entitled to use the library.
11. It is the librarian's obligation to treat as confidential any private information obtained through contact with library patrons.
12. The librarian should try to protect library property and to inculcate in users a sense of their responsibility for its preservation.

III. Relations of the Librarian within His Library

13. The chief librarian should delegate authority, encourage a sense of responsibility and initiative on the part of staff members, provide for their professional development, and appreciate good work. Staff members should be informed of the duties of their positions and the policies and problems of the library.
14. Loyalty to fellow workers and a spirit of courteous cooperation, whether between individuals or between departments, are essential to effective library service.
15. Criticism of library policies, service, and personnel should be offered only to the proper authority for the sole purpose of improvement of the library.
16. Acceptance of a position in a library incurs an obligation to remain long enough to repay the library for the expense incident to adjustment. A contract signed or agreement made should be adhered to faithfully until it expires or is dissolved by mutual consent.
17. Resignations should be made long enough before they are to take effect to allow adequate time for the work to be put in shape and a successor appointed.
18. A librarian should never enter into a business dealing on behalf of the library which will result in personal profit.
19. A librarian should never turn the library's resources to personal use, to the detriment of services which the library renders to its patrons.

IV. Relation of the Librarian to His Profession

20. Librarians should recognize librarianship as an educational profession and realize that the growing effectiveness of their service is dependent upon their own development.
21. In view of the importance of ability and personality traits in library work, a librarian should encourage only those persons with suitable aptitudes to enter the library profession and should discourage the continuance in service of the unfit.
22. Recommendations should be confidential and should be fair to the candidate and the prospective employer by presenting an unbiased statement of strong and weak points.
23. Librarians should have a sincere belief and a critical interest in the library profession. They should endeavor to achieve and maintain adequate salaries and proper working conditions.
24. Formal appraisal of the policies or practices of another library should be given only upon the invitation of that library's governing authority or chief librarian.
25. Librarians, in recognizing the essential unity of their profession, should have membership in library organizations and should be ready to attend and participate in library meetings and conferences.

V. Relation of the Librarian to Society

26. Librarians should encourage a general realization of the value of library service and be informed concerning movements, organizations, and institutions whose aims are compatible with those of the library.
27. Librarians should participate in public and community affairs and so represent the library that it will take its place among educational, social, and cultural agencies.
28. A librarian's conduct should be such as to maintain public esteem for the library and for library work.

Members of the Code of Ethics Committee submitting the foregoing report are John S. Cleavinger, Coit Coolidge, Edwin Sue Goree, Helen L. Purdum, Alfred Rawlinson, Rena Reese, Frank K. Walter, Ruth Worden, and Flora B. Ludington, chairman.

---

http://www.ala.org/ala/oif/statementspols/codeofethics/coehistory/1939codeethics.htm.

More than four decades passed before ALA adopted a revised code of ethics. During that time the organization adopted the Freedom to Read statement in 1953 and the *Library Bill of Rights* in 1948. These two policies embodied for ALA the professional values that would serve as the framework for a new code of ethics reflecting the significant changes in the economic, social, and political environment in the United States since 1939.

A 1975 draft of a new code and a 1979 revised draft were published in the November 1979 issue of *American Libraries*.[4] They were as follows:

Statement on Professional Ethics, 1975 Draft

Introduction

The American Library Association has a special concern for the free flow of information and ideas. Its views have been set forth in such policy statements as the *Library Bill of Rights* and the Freedom to Read Statement where it has said clearly that in addition to the generally accepted legal and ethical principles and the respect for intellectual freedom which should guide the action of every citizen, membership in the library profession carries with it special obligations and responsibilities.

Every citizen has the right as an individual to take part in public debate or to engage in social and political activity. The only restrictions on these activities are those imposed by specific and well-publicized laws and regulations which are generally applicable. However, since personal views and activities may be interpreted as representative of the institution in which a librarian is employed, proper precaution should be taken to distinguish between private actions and those one is authorized to take in the name of an institution.

The statement which follows sets forth certain ethical norms which, while not exclusive to, are basic to librarianship. It will be augmented by explanatory interpretations and additional statements as they may be needed.

The Statement

A Librarian

- Has a special responsibility to maintain the principles of the *Library Bill of Rights*.

- Should learn and faithfully execute the policies of the institution of which one is a part and should endeavor to change those which conflict with the spirit of the *Library Bill of Rights*.

- Must protect the essential confidential relationship which exists between a library user and the library.

- Must avoid any possibility of personal financial gain at the expense of the employing institution.

- Has an obligation to insure equality of opportunity and fair judgment of competence in actions dealing with staff appointments, retentions, and promotions.

- Has an obligation when making appraisals of the qualifications of any individual to report the facts clearly, accurately, and without prejudice, according to generally accepted guidelines concerning the disclosing of personal information.

Statement on Professional Ethics, Revised Draft, August 26, 1979

Librarians have a special concern for the free flow of information and ideas. The American Library Association has set forth its views in such policy statements as the *Library Bill of Rights* and the Freedom to Read Statement where it is clearly stated that in addition to the generally accepted legal and ethical principles and the respect for intellectual freedom which should guide the action of every citizen, membership in the library profession carries with it special obligations and responsibilities. The statement which follows sets forth certain ethical norms which are basic to librarianship.

The Statement

A Librarian

- Has a special responsibility to maintain the principles of the *Library Bill of Rights*.

- Should know and execute the policies of the organization of which the librarian is a part and should endeavor to change any policy which conflicts with the spirit of the *Library Bill of Rights*.

- Should provide competent and complete professional service both to the individual user and to the clientele as a whole.

- Should recognize and protect the user's right to privacy with respect to information sought or received and materials consulted or borrowed.

- Should recognize and avoid situations in which the librarian's personal interests are served or financial benefits are gained at the expense of the employing institution.

- Has an obligation to insure equality of opportunity in actions dealing with staff appointments, retentions, and promotions.

---

http://www.ala.org/ala/oif/statementspols/codeofethics/coehistory/19751979drafts.htm.

The Committee on Professional Ethics revised the document based on comments received on the two drafts. The resulting revision of the Code of Ethics was adopted by ALA Membership and Council on June 30, 1981. It read as follows:

Statement on Professional Ethics, 1981

Introduction

Since 1939, the American Library Association has recognized the importance of codifying and making known to the public and the profession the principles which guide librarians in action. This latest revision of the Code of Ethics reflects changes in the nature of the profession and in its social and institutional environment. It should be revised and augmented as necessary.

Librarians significantly influence or control the selection, organization, preservation, and dissemination of information. In a political system grounded in an informed citizenry, librarians are members of a profession explicitly committed to intellectual freedom and the freedom of access to information. We have a special obligation to ensure the free flow of information and ideas to present and future generations.

Librarians are dependent upon one another for the bibliographical resources that enable us to provide information services, and have obligations for maintaining the highest level of personal integrity and competence.

Code of Ethics

I. Librarians must provide the highest level of service through appropriate and usefully organized collections, free and equitable circulation and service policies, and skillful, accurate, unbiased, and courteous responses to all requests for assistance.

II. Librarians must resist all efforts by groups or individuals to censor library materials.

III. Librarians must protect each user's right to privacy with respect to information sought or received, and materials consulted, borrowed, or acquired.

IV. Librarians must adhere to the principles of due process and equality of opportunity in peer relationships and personnel actions.

V. Librarians must distinguish clearly in their actions and statements between their personal philosophies

and attitudes and those of an institution or professional body.

VI. Librarians must avoid situations in which personal
interests might be served or financial benefits gained
at the expense of library users, colleagues, or the
employing institution.

Adopted June 30, 1981, by ALA Membership and ALA
Council. http://www.ala.org/ala/oif/statementspols/
codeofethics/coehistory/1981statement.htm.

The Committee on Professional Ethics began working on a revision of the Code of Ethics in 1991. Over a four-year period, the committee solicited comments from ALA units and members. When the
document was submitted to Council at the 1995 Annual Meeting,
Jeanne Isacco, chair, reported that during this process, the Committee received numerous comments, many of which were incorporated into the revision. In addition, the Committee encouraged
members in individual libraries to use the code, discuss the implications of each statement, and adopt it as part of their institution's
practices.[5]

The most striking difference between the 1995 Code of Ethics
and those that preceded it is the voice in which it is expressed.
Previous codes were in the impersonal third person, "librarians
should" in the 1939 code and "librarians must" in the 1981 code.
The 1995 code represented the voice of ALA's members. Furthermore, the principles were expressed as facts (e.g., "We provide the
highest level of service") rather than as the obligations based on
"should" or the commands based on "must" of previous codes. The
1995 code also included two new principles related to copyright
(IV) and excellence in the profession (VIII).

Finally, the 1995 code included a statement concerning its use.
This concept was included in the 1939 code but was absent from the
1981 version. The 1939 code stated:

> This code sets forth principles of ethical behavior for the
> professional librarian. It is not a declaration of preroga-
> tives nor a statement of recommended practices in spe-
> cific situations.

The 1995 code addressed this issue by stating:

> The principles of this Code are expressed in broad state-
> ments to guide ethical decision making. These statements
> provide a framework; they cannot and do not dictate
> conduct to cover particular situations.

Throughout the history of the Code of Ethics there have been debates about whether there should be a means for enforcing it. The inevitable conclusion to these discussions has been that ALA has neither the resources nor the legal authority to do so. When the 1995 code was presented to Council, COPE expressed the opinion that the most effective way to make the code a meaningful part of the library profession would be for it to be discussed and considered for adoption as policy by local and state libraries.

In 2000, the Committee began work on the first explanatory statement of the Code of Ethics, Questions and Answers on Librarian Speech in the Workplace. The previous year, Council had considered and referred to the Committee a resolution on an amendment to the *Library Bill of Rights* that addressed the free speech rights of library personnel. After careful consideration, the Committee concluded the existing tenets of the Code of Ethics addressed the issue, but that further clarification and explanation would be beneficial to the profession. Because workplace speech is a complicated matter affected by employment law and First Amendment rights in addition to professional ethics, the Committee developed a question-and-answer document addressing the legal and ethical complexities of workplace speech. In July 2001, the Committee adopted Questions and Answers on Librarian Speech in the Workplace: An Explanatory Statement of the ALA Code of Ethics (http://www.ala.org/ala/oif/ifgroups/cope/copeinaction/explanatory/questionsanswers.htm).

ALA Council revisited the topic over the next few years and adopted CD#38.1, Resolution on Workplace Speech (http://www.ala.org/ourassociation/governanceb/council/councilagendas/annual2005a/CD38_1.doc) at the 2005 Annual Conference in Chicago. The resolution states that "Libraries should encourage discussion among library workers, including library administrators, of non-confidential, professional and policy matters about the operation of the library and matters of public concern within the framework of applicable laws."

Also at the 2005 Annual Conference, the Committee on Professional Ethics began a series of programs and open forums to discuss the code and its role in the Association and the profession. The Committee will consider the feedback it receives at these programs to determine if the Code of Ethics needs revision.

NOTES

1. John A. Moorman, "Knowledge of the American Library Association's Code of Ethics among Illinois Public Library Directors: A Study," *Illinois Libraries* 77, no. 3 (1995): 140–47.
2. "Suggested Code of Ethics," *American Library Association Bulletin* 24, no. 3 (1930): 58–62.
3. American Library Association, "Midwinter Council Minutes," *American Library Association Bulletin* 33, no. 2 (1939): 128–29.
4. *American Libraries* 10, no. 11 (November 1979): 666.
5. American Library Association, 1995 Annual Conference, Report of the Committee on Professional Ethics (CD#36-36.1).

3
Libraries
An American Value

L ibraries in America are cornerstones of the communities they serve. Free access to the books, ideas, resources, and information in America's libraries is imperative for education, employment, enjoyment, and self-government.

Libraries are a legacy to each generation, offering the heritage of the past and the promise of the future. To ensure that libraries flourish and have the freedom to promote and protect the public good in the 21st century, we believe certain principles must be guaranteed.

To that end, we affirm this contract with the people we serve:

- We defend the constitutional rights of all individuals, including children and teenagers, to use the library's resources and services;
- We value our nation's diversity and strive to reflect that diversity by providing a full spectrum of resources and services to the communities we serve;
- We affirm the responsibility and the right of all parents and guardians to guide their own children's use of the library and its resources and services;
- We connect people and ideas by helping each person select from and effectively use the library's resources;
- We protect each individual's privacy and confidentiality in the use of library resources and services;

- We protect the rights of individuals to express their opinions about library resources and services;
- We celebrate and preserve our democratic society by making available the widest possible range of viewpoints, opinions and ideas, so that all individuals have the opportunity to become lifelong learners—informed, literate, educated, and culturally enriched.

Change is constant, but these principles transcend change and endure in a dynamic technological, social, and political environment.

By embracing these principles, libraries in the United States can contribute to a future that values and protects freedom of speech in a world that celebrates both our similarities and our differences, respects individuals and their beliefs, and holds all persons truly equal and free.

Adopted February 3, 1999, by the Council of the American Library Association. http://www.ala.org/ala/oif/statementspols/americanvalue/librariesamerican.htm.

HISTORY

Libraries: An American Value

L ibraries: An American Value is intended to inform the public
about a library's role in the community, particularly in the face
of accelerating change and uncertainty. It was the first major intellectual freedom policy adopted by ALA in nearly twenty years, and
it was the first one available for distribution and discussion via the
Internet and e-mail.

In 1997, ALA president-elect Ann K. Symons asked her organizing committee to explore writing a new basic policy for ALA.
The first step was to determine the purpose of the policy and its
relation to existing policies, such as the Library Bill of Rights, the
Freedom to Read statement, and the Code of Ethics. The committee,
chaired by June Pinnell-Stephens, met with ALA members at the
1998 Midwinter Meeting, where discussion centered on the need to
reaffirm intellectual freedom principles and the democratic mandates on which they are based in the face of the changing legal, technical, and political environment. The participants agreed that a new
document should contain the library's implicit contract with the
community and that the primary difference between Libraries: An
American Value and the Library Bill of Rights should be the targeted
audience: the first, directed to the public, explaining the role of the
library in a democracy and the second, directed to both libraries and
the public, addressing the library's obligations to the individual.
The other documents clearly differed from the proposed new policy,
with the Freedom to Read statement describing the underlying

value of reading to the individual and society, and the Code of Ethics addressing appropriate professional behavior.

A drafting committee met in Chicago in February 1998 to write the first draft of the policy. This was circulated to ALA members for comment and was the subject of a hearing at the 1998 Annual Conference in Washington, D.C. In September 1998, a final draft was released. Between e-mail messages and speakers at the hearing, the committee received more than two hundred comments and suggestions, ranging from complete agreement to total rewrites. By the time the document came to the ALA Council for adoption, every ALA division and fifty-six state chapters and school media associations had endorsed it. It was adopted by Council on February 3, 1999.

At the 2004 Annual Conference in Orlando, Florida, the Committee on Diversity placed a resolution on the Council agenda (CD#32.1) to amend Libraries: An American Value by adding a statement concerning the recruiting of library workers. With the addition, the second statement in the policy would read (additions are in caps): "We value our nation's diversity and strive to reflect that diversity BY RECRUITING LIBRARY WORKERS OF DIVERSE BACKGROUNDS, AND by providing a full spectrum of resources and services to the communities we serve" to ensure the imperative inclusion of library workforce diversity in any and all statements or reports related to the Association's core values. Council referred the resolution to the IFC.

As a part of the 2004–5 review of intellectual freedom policies, the IFC reconsidered Libraries: An American Value, including the referred resolution. The Committee recommended no changes in the policy. In his report to Council at the 2005 Midwinter Meeting (CD#19), IFC chair Kenton L. Oliver stated:

> As directed by Council, the IFC reviewed Libraries: An American Value and reaffirmed the policy is a contract between the public and the profession. The Committee conveyed its decision to the Committee on Diversity at this Midwinter, and both committees are in agreement that the suggested revision to Libraries: An American Value would be unsuitable.
>
> During its discussions, the IFC found a reference in the *ALA Policy Manual* which addresses the goal of this

association to promote the recruitment of a racially and ethnically diverse group of high caliber persons to librarianship (*ALA Policy Manual*, 1.3.E.8.). In light of this ALA policy, and being appreciative of the Committee on Diversity's concerns, the IFC will address diversity recruitment in other policies, as appropriate.

4
Policies and Statements Related to Access to Information and Library Services

4.1

Guidelines for the Development and Implementation of Policies, Regulations and Procedures Affecting Access to Library Materials, Services and Facilities

The American Library Association has adopted the *Library Bill of Rights* and Interpretations of the *Library Bill of Rights* to provide library governing authorities, librarians and other library staff and library users with guidelines on how constitutional principles apply to libraries in the United States of America.

Publicly supported libraries exist within the context of a body of law derived from the United States Constitution and appropriate state constitutions, defined by statute, and implemented by regulations, policies and procedures established by their governing bodies and administrations. These regulations, policies and procedures establish the mission of the library, define its functions, services and operations and ascertain the rights and responsibilities of the individuals served by the library.

Publicly supported library service is based upon the First Amendment right of free expression. The publicly supported library is a governmental entity that provides free, equal, and equitable access to information for all people of the community it serves. When this purpose is confirmed in policies and practices, the library is a designated limited public forum for access to information. When library policies or practices make meeting rooms, exhibit spaces, and/or bulletin boards available for public use, these spaces are designated as limited public forums for the exchange of information.

Since the *Library Bill of Rights* "affirms that all libraries are forums for information and ideas," libraries that are not publicly supported are encouraged to observe these guidelines as they develop policies, regulations and procedures.

Libraries adopt administrative policies and procedures regulating the organization and use of library materials, services and facilities. These policies and procedures affect access and may have the effect of restricting, denying or creating barriers to access to the library as a public forum, including the library's resources, facilities and services. Library policies and procedures that impinge upon First Amendment rights are subject to a higher standard of review than may be required in the policies of other public services and facilities.

Policies, procedures or regulations that may result in denying, restricting or creating physical or economic barriers to access to the library's public forum must be based on a compelling government interest. However, library governing authorities may place reasonable and narrowly drawn restrictions on the time, place or manner of access to library resources, services or facilities, provided that such restrictions are not based upon arbitrary distinctions between individuals or classes of individuals.

Guidelines

The American Library Association's Intellectual Freedom Committee recommends that publicly supported libraries use the following guidelines, based on constitutional principles, to develop policies, regulations, and procedures.

All library policies, regulations, and procedures should be carefully examined to determine if they may result in denying, restricting or creating barriers to access. If they may result in such restrictions, they:

1. should be developed and implemented within the legal framework that applies to the library. This includes: the United States Constitution, including the First and Fourteenth Amendments, due process and equal and equitable

treatment under the law; the applicable state constitution; federal and state civil rights legislation; all other applicable federal, state and local legislation; and applicable case law;

2. should cite statutes or ordinances upon which the authority to make that policy is based, when appropriate;

3. should be developed and implemented within the framework of the *Library Bill of Rights* and its Interpretations;

4. should be based upon the library's mission and objectives;

5. should only impose restrictions on the access to, or use of library resources, services or facilities when those restrictions are necessary to achieve the library's mission and objectives;

6. should narrowly tailor prohibitions or restrictions, in the rare instances when they are required, so they are not more restrictive than needed to serve their objectives;

7. should attempt to balance competing interests and avoid favoring the majority at the expense of individual rights, or allowing individual users' rights to interfere materially with the majority's rights to free, equal, and equitable access to library resources, services and facilities;

8. should avoid arbitrary distinctions between individuals or classes of users, and should not have the effect of denying or abridging a person's right to use library resources, services or facilities based upon arbitrary distinctions such as origin, age, background or views;

In the *Library Bill of Rights* and all of its Interpretations, it is intended that: "origin" encompasses all the characteristics of individuals that are inherent in the circumstances of their birth; "age" encompasses all the characteristics of individuals that are inherent in their levels of development and maturity; "background" encompasses all the characteristics of individuals that are a result of their life experiences; and "views" encompasses all the opinions and beliefs held and expressed by individuals;

9. should not target specific users or groups of users based upon an assumption or expectation that such users might engage in behavior that will materially interfere with the achievement of substantial library objectives;

10. must be clearly stated so that a reasonably intelligent person will have fair warning of what is expected;

11. must provide a means of appeal;

12. must be reviewed regularly by the library's governing authority and by its legal counsel.

13. must be communicated clearly and made available in an effective manner to all library users;

14. must be enforced evenhandedly, and not in a manner intended to benefit or disfavor any person or group in an arbitrary or capricious manner;

Libraries should develop an ongoing staff training program designed to foster the understanding of the legal framework and principles underlying library policies and to assist staff in gaining the skill and ability to respond to potentially difficult circumstances in a timely, direct and open manner. This program should include training to develop empathy and understanding of the social and economic problems of some library users;

15. should, if reasonably possible, provide adequate alternative means of access to information for those whose behavior results in the denial or restriction of access to any library resource, service or facility.

See the glossary for definitions of terms used in these guidelines.

Adopted June 28, 1994, by the ALA Intellectual Freedom Committee; revised January 19, 2005.

HISTORY

Guidelines for the Development and Implementation of Policies, Regulations and Procedures Affecting Access to Library Materials, Services and Facilities

As part of the review of all of the Interpretations of the *Library Bill of Rights*, begun in 1989 in response to a request by the Minority Concerns Committee that the policy reflect equity of access without regard to language or economic status, the Intellectual Freedom Committee took up the Interpretation entitled "Administrative Policies and Procedures Affecting Access to Library Resources and Services." In 1991, that Interpretation was revised substantially and retitled "Regulations, Policies, and Procedures Affecting Access to Library Resources and Services." The newly revised Interpretation responded to issues raised in two 1991 court cases which had important implications for libraries. The policy also addressed intellectual freedom concerns raised by challenges to materials that were inappropriately handled where the challenges had originated within libraries by librarians, library administration, or library staff.

The two court cases referenced in the Interpretation were *Rust v. Sullivan* and *Kreimer v. Morristown*.[1] In *Rust v. Sullivan*, the U.S. Supreme Court upheld Department of Health and Human Services regulations prohibiting the recipients of Title X funds (primarily, family planning clinics) from providing information about abortion or any abortion counseling whatsoever to their clients. In a close 5-to-4 decision, the Court held that the prohibition was a permissible government choice, favoring some activities over others. In a stinging dissent, Justice Harry A. Blackmun pointed out that, for the first time, the Court had sanctioned outright viewpoint-based discrimination in a federally funded program. In other words, the Supreme

Court had said that it was permissible for the federal government to selectively fund speech promoting one point of view while prohibiting the mention of the opposing position.

The decision was significant for libraries because, although libraries take no position on the underlying issue, they do provide materials and information from all points of view on topics of current and historical interest, including abortion. Librarians realized that, if medical professionals working in facilities supported by federal funds could be "gagged," so could libraries that received public money. The *Rust* decision was issued in an atmosphere of severe fiscal conservancy, when many public libraries already had experienced massive funding cuts. The potential of those cuts to be linked to ideological, viewpoint-based restrictions on library collections was clear.

The other significant court decision addressed in the 1991 revision of the Interpretation was *Kreimer v. Morristown*, a case that came from the U.S. District Court in New Jersey. Richard Kreimer, a homeless man, challenged rules and regulations of the Morristown, New Jersey, Public Library, on the grounds that they, on their face, discriminated against homeless and economically disadvantaged patrons.[2] Library officials, in turn, contended that Kreimer had annoyed other patrons, exuded a body odor so offensive as to interfere with other patrons' use of the library, stared at people, and followed children around the stacks. According to the court's decision, the library admitted that some of the regulations had specifically been designed to bar Kreimer from the institution.

The district court found that the library's regulations prohibiting patrons from staring or annoying other patrons were overbroad and vague and, therefore, unconstitutional. The court recognized and firmly supported the right and the responsibility of public libraries to make rules governing their use and governing patron behavior, but the court also firmly upheld the First Amendment right to receive information in publicly funded libraries. The court held that, in the interest of all patrons, library rules should be specific, necessary, and neutral, and not susceptible of discriminatory application. In addition, they must not be so vague that their application is subject to the whims of individual library staff members.

The *Morristown* decision firmly upheld First Amendment rights to receive information in libraries and provided a powerful argument supporting libraries' resistance to censorship. At the same time, the judge recognized the necessity of specific, necessary, and neutral rules governing patron behavior to ensure equal access for all.

The Morristown Library appealed the district court's decision to the U.S. Court of Appeals for the Third Circuit. That court reversed the lower court's decision, finding that the Morristown Library's rules were constitutional on their face. However, the court also found that rules that could result in the expulsion of a person from a public library do implicate First Amendment rights and must be analyzed under First Amendment principles. In addition, the court held that public libraries are limited public forums for access to information. This is a highly significant holding, placing public libraries squarely within the First Amendment realm and recognizing, for the first time by any court, that libraries have a unique position in the fulfillment of the First Amendment right to receive information.

The Intellectual Freedom Committee believed it would be beneficial to produce a policy statement of the American Library Association that placed ALA's intellectual freedom policy within the framework of First Amendment law. Such placement would counter accusations by opposition pressure groups that the American Library Association's policies were simply ALA's opinion and not in any way binding in effect. Whereas it is true that no library is compelled to adopt ALA's policies, publicly supported libraries are subject to First Amendment legal principles. The newly revised Interpretation made this explicit by quoting language from both the *Rust* and *Morristown* decisions.

The document adopted by the Council at the 1991 Annual Conference included quotes from the district court's opinion in the *Morristown* case, which was subsequently reversed by the Third Circuit, necessitating a review for possible revision. The process of revising the Interpretation began at the Annual Conference in 1993. At the 1994 Midwinter Meeting in Los Angeles, it became apparent that the Interpretation attempted to address very broad areas of library operation that could conceivably be addressed in many different library policies; revision was proving difficult.

Given the difficulty the IFC had had in attempting revision, the Committee concluded that it might be more appropriate and successful to revise the Interpretation into a set of guidelines. A draft of Guidelines for the Development of Policies, Regulations and

Procedures Affecting Access to Library Materials, Services and Facilities was produced at the Midwinter Meeting and circulated to ALA units for comment following that meeting. At the 1994 Annual Conference in Miami Beach, the Committee revised and renamed the document, and formally adopted it. Guidelines for the Development and Implementation of Policies, Regulations and Procedures Affecting Access to Library Materials, Services and Facilities was presented to the Council for its information, together with a recommendation that the Interpretation of the *Library Bill of Rights* entitled "Regulations, Policies, and Procedures Affecting Access to Library Resources and Services" be rescinded. The Council acted on the IFC's recommendation, rescinding the Interpretation.

The guidelines were intended to provide signposts for libraries as they develop policies, procedures, and regulations governing many areas of library operation, encouraging libraries to consider at the outset the First Amendment implications of their policies, as well as the potential applicability of state constitutional principles and federal, state, and local law. In addition, the guidelines suggest that policies address considerations such as due process and equity of access, and that they ensure nondiscrimination between classes of library patrons.

In line with the ongoing practice of periodic review, the IFC carefully reviewed all statements in 1999–2000, especially in regard to their applicability to the Internet. No changes were recommended in these guidelines.

The guidelines were revised for clarity and readability as a result of the 2004–5 review of intellectual freedom documents. Changes were made in the order of the paragraphs, a sentence encouraging libraries that are not publicly funded to follow the guidelines was added, and the phrase "equal access" was expanded to "equal and equitable access" whenever it was appropriate to do so.

NOTES

1. *Rust v. Sullivan*, 500 US 173 (1991); *Richard R. Kreimer v. Bureau of Police for the Town of Morristown*, et al., 765 F.Supp 181 (D.N.J. 1991), rev'd and remanded, 958 F.2d 1242 (3rd Cir. 1992).

2. For more on the *Morristown* case, see part 4, section 1, "Public Libraries and the Public Forum Doctrine."

4.2

Guidelines for the Development of Policies and Procedures regarding User Behavior and Library Usage

ibraries are faced with problems of user behavior that must be addressed to ensure the effective delivery of service and full access to facilities. Library governing bodies should approach the regulation of user behavior within the framework of the ALA Code of Ethics, the *Library Bill of Rights* and the law, including local and state statutes, constitutional standards under the First and Fourteenth Amendments, due process and equal and equitable treatment under the law.

Publicly supported library service is based upon the First Amendment right of free expression. Publicly supported libraries are recognized as limited public forums for access to information. Courts have recognized a First Amendment right to receive information in a public library. Library policies and procedures that could impinge upon such rights are subject to a higher standard of review than may be required in the policies of other public services and facilities.

There is a significant government interest in maintaining a library environment that is conducive to all users' exercise of their constitutionally protected right to receive information. This significant interest authorizes publicly supported libraries to maintain a safe and healthy environment in which library users and staff can be free from harassment, intimidation, and threats to their safety and well-being. Libraries should provide appropriate safeguards against such behavior and enforce policies and procedures addressing that behavior when it occurs.

In order to protect all library users' right of access to library facilities, to ensure the safety of users and staff, and to protect library resources and facilities from damage, the library's governing authority may impose reasonable restrictions on the time, place, or manner of library access.

Guidelines

The American Library Association's Intellectual Freedom Committee recommends that publicly supported libraries use the following guidelines, based upon constitutional principles, to develop policies and procedures governing the use of library facilities:

1. Libraries are advised to rely upon existing legislation and law enforcement mechanisms as the primary means of controlling behavior that involves public safety, criminal behavior, or other issues covered by existing local, state, or federal statutes. In many instances, this legal framework may be sufficient to provide the library with the necessary tools to maintain order.

2. If the library's governing body chooses to write its own policies and procedures regarding user behavior or access to library facilities, services, and resources, the policies should cite statutes or ordinances upon which the authority to make those policies is based.

3. Library policies and procedures governing the use of library facilities should be carefully examined to ensure that they embody the principles expressed in the *Library Bill of Rights*.

4. Reasonable and narrowly drawn policies and procedures designed to prohibit interference with use of the facilities and services by others, or to prohibit activities inconsistent with achievement of the library's mission statement and objectives, are acceptable.

5. Such policies and the attendant implementing procedures should be reviewed frequently and updated as needed by the library's legal counsel for compliance with federal and state constitutional requirements, federal and state civil rights legislation, all other applicable federal and state legislation, and applicable case law.

6. Every effort should be made to respond to potentially difficult circumstances of user behavior in a timely, direct, and open manner. Common sense, reason and sensitivity should be used to resolve issues in a constructive and positive manner without escalation.

7. Libraries should develop an ongoing staff training program based upon their user behavior policy. This program should include training to develop empathy and understanding of the social and economic problems of some library users.

8. Policies and regulations that impose restrictions on library access:

   a. should apply only to those activities that materially interfere with the public's right of access to library facilities, the safety of users and staff, and the protection of library resources and facilities;

   b. should narrowly tailor prohibitions or restrictions so that they are not more restrictive than needed to serve their objectives;

   c. should attempt to balance competing interests and avoid favoring the majority at expense of individual rights, or allowing individual users' rights to supersede those of the majority of library users;

   d. should be based solely upon actual behavior and not upon arbitrary distinctions between individuals or classes of individuals. Policies should not target specific users or groups of users based upon an assumption or expectation that such users might engage in behaviors that could disrupt library service;

   e. should not restrict access to the library by persons who merely inspire the anger or annoyance of others. Policies based upon appearance or behavior that is merely annoying or that merely generates negative subjective reactions from others, do not meet the necessary standard. Such policies should employ a reasonable, objective standard based on the behavior itself;

f. must provide a clear description of the behavior that is prohibited and the various enforcement measures in place so that a reasonably intelligent person will have both due process and fair warning; this description must be continuously and clearly communicated in an effective manner to all library users;

g. to the extent possible, should not leave those affected without adequate alternative means of access to information in the library;

h. must be enforced evenhandedly, and not in a manner intended to benefit or disfavor any person or group in an arbitrary or capricious manner.

The user behaviors addressed in these Guidelines are the result of a wide variety of individual and societal conditions. Libraries should take advantage of the expertise of local social service agencies, advocacy groups, mental health professionals, law enforcement officials, and other community resources to develop community strategies for addressing the needs of a diverse population.

See the glossary for definitions of terms used in these guidelines.

Adopted January 24, 1993, by the Intellectual Freedom Committee; revised November 17, 2000; January 19, 2005. http://www.ala.org/ala/oif/ statementspols/otherpolicies/guidelinesdevelopment.htm.

HISTORY

Guidelines for the Development of Policies and Procedures regarding User Behavior and Library Usage

In the wake of the 1991 district court decision in *Kreimer v. Morristown*, a case involving a challenge to regulations implemented by the Morristown, New Jersey, Public Library, the Intellectual Freedom Committee recognized a need for guidance in the development of library policies governing patron behavior.[1] At the 1991 ALA Annual Conference in Atlanta, the Committee established a task force to draft guidelines. The task force was charged with seeking expert legal advice in developing suggestions to assist local libraries in reviewing or drafting policies to deal with problem patrons that would meet constitutional standards. From the very beginning, the Intellectual Freedom Committee recognized that it would be impossible to present a set of model regulations, because the legal considerations governing actual behavior in differing jurisdictions vary. Instead, the Committee took the approach of providing a constitutional framework and encouraging libraries to consider carefully local statutory law that might apply to particular patron-behavior situations.

The task force, chaired by then Public Library Association IFC chair Candace Morgan, presented a draft at the 1992 Midwinter Meeting in San Antonio. In presenting the draft to the Committee, Morgan explained that it was based almost entirely on advice obtained from the ALA and Freedom to Read Foundation legal counsel firm Jenner & Block. The Committee also sponsored an open hearing at that Midwinter Meeting to receive additional comment on the draft from librarians. Despite explanations of why it would be unwise and probably impossible to provide a model set of rules, many librarians who testified and offered comments requested more specificity. Following the hearing, the task force met and agreed that, although it would be difficult to promulgate specific regulations within the context of widely varying local and state law, the task force could address the need for specificity by highlighting the necessity to refer to that local law.

The task force also decided to address, in a similar, general way, health and safety regulations, equal access concerns, civil rights and due process, and so forth. Reference to staff training was also added. Another open forum was held at the 1992 Annual Conference in San Francisco to receive additional comment on a revised draft addressing these issues.

Throughout the development of the guidelines, the library community continued to discuss the *Kreimer v. Morristown* case. The Intellectual Freedom Committee and the task force to develop the guidelines took great pains to inform the library community that the guidelines were not meant as a specific response to the *Morristown* case. The subject of the task force's hearings was not the *Morristown* case but the draft guidelines, which went far beyond the specifics of that dispute. The task force stressed that it was attempting to provide a constitutional framework in which libraries could proceed in the development of their own regulations regarding user behavior of all types, not just the conduct addressed by the rules of the Morristown Library that were challenged in the litigation.

However, because questions and misunderstandings persisted about the legal issues involved, Judge H. Lee Sarokin, the federal district court judge who rendered the original opinion in the *Kreimer v. Morristown* case, appeared at the 1992 Annual Conference in San Francisco to speak generally about those legal issues. The reception he received from some librarians in the audience, many of whom had not read his opinion and did not understand the legal status of the case, could only be described as openly hostile. Librarians from New Jersey continued to focus on the alleged behavior of one library patron, Richard Kreimer, rather than the broader legal issues the judge addressed.

Following Judge Sarokin's appearance, the task force once again revised the draft guidelines. The intent was to make the guidelines as broad and general as possible so that local libraries would have a framework in which to formulate their own rules with reference to both local law and constitutional principles. The task force stressed that the guidelines did not, and were not intended to, constitute an ALA response to the *Morristown* decision. The IFC voted to approve the revised draft and to circulate it once again for additional comment.

After final editorial revisions in light of additional comments, the IFC adopted the final version of Guidelines for the Development of Policies and Procedures regarding User Behavior and Library Usage and presented it for information to the ALA Council at the 1993 Midwinter Meeting in Denver.

In line with the ongoing practice of periodic review, the IFC carefully reviewed all statements in 1999–2000, especially in regard to their applicability to the Internet. The IFC recommended only slight editorial changes to this policy, with one exception. Under point 8, paragraph f, the IFC included the phrase "and the various enforcement measures in place," so that it is clearer that not only should a fair warning measure be in place, but also a means for due process.

During the periodic review of 2004–5 the term "equitable" was added to the phrase "equal treatment under the law" in the first paragraph.

NOTE

1. *Richard R. Kreimer v. Bureau of Police for the Town of Morristown, et al.,* 765 F.Supp. 181 (D.N.J. 1991); rev'd in part and remanded, 958 F.2d 1242 (3rd Cir. 1992). For more on the *Morristown* case, see part 4, section 1, "Public Libraries and the Public Forum Doctrine."

4.3

Resolution on Access to the Use of Libraries and Information by Individuals with Physical or Mental Impairment

WHEREAS, The Intellectual Freedom Committee is concerned with freedom of access; and

WHEREAS, The *Library Bill of Rights* states that "books and other library resources should be provided for the interest, information, and enlightenment of all people of the community the library serves" and "a person's right to use a library should not be denied or abridged . . ."; and

WHEREAS, Federal and state constitutional and statutory laws forbid public institutions from discriminating against handicapped individuals, i.e., persons who have a physical or mental impairment; and

WHEREAS, Court opinions have clearly interpreted said laws as proscribing discrimination against persons who have acquired immune deficiency syndrome ("AIDS"), AIDS-related complex ("ARC"), or who test positive for the human immunodeficiency virus ("HIV"); and

WHEREAS, The American Medical Association and the United States Department of Health and Human Services have opined that while the human immunodeficiency virus that causes AIDS is a contagious disease, it cannot be transmitted by casual contact;

NOW THEREFORE BE IT RESOLVED, That the *Library Bill of Rights* of the American Library Association which insures access to library facilities, materials and services by all people of the community, includes individuals with physical or mental impairments; and

BE IT FURTHER RESOLVED, That the American Library Association deplores discrimination against and denial or abridgment of library and information access to persons of all ages who have acquired immune deficiency syndrome ("AIDS"), AIDS-related complex ("ARC"), or who test positive for the human immunodeficiency virus ("HIV").

Adopted January 13, 1988, by the ALA Council. http://www.ala.org/ala/oif/statementspols/ifresolutions/resolutionaccess.htm.

HISTORY

Resolution on Access to the Use of Libraries and Information by Individuals with Physical or Mental Impairment

I mmediately before the 1988 Midwinter Meeting in San Antonio, the Intellectual Freedom Committee received a request for a statement of ALA's position concerning access to libraries and information by those with physical and mental impairments, particularly persons with the AIDS virus.

The occasion for this request was the barring of a child in Lake City, Tennessee, from attendance at the public school because the child had AIDS. Public librarians in the area perceived a need for their boards to adopt a clear policy about the access rights of persons with AIDS. In the search for existing policy statements, the Intellectual Freedom Committee was contacted, but no such statements were found.

Recognizing the need for definitive language affirming the access rights of all physically and mentally impaired persons and in light of a rising hysteria over AIDS, the IFC took to the ALA Council the Resolution on Access to the Use of Libraries and Information by Individuals with Physical or Mental Impairment. It was adopted by the Council on January 13, 1988.

In line with the practice of periodic review, the IFC reviewed Resolution on Access to the Use of Libraries and Information by Individuals with Physical or Mental Impairment in 1999–2000 and 2004–5 and recommended no changes.

4.4
Related Policies and Statements

Selected other ALA documents related to access to information and library services are listed below. Links to new or revised documents will be posted to "Intellectual Freedom Statements and Policies" under the heading "Access" at http://www.ala .org/ala/oif/statementspols/statementspolicies.htm#access.

- Destruction of Libraries (ALA Policy 53.7, 1971)
  http://www.ala.org/ala/oif/statementspols/
  otherpolicies/destructionlibraries.htm

- The Glasgow Declaration on Libraries, Information
  Services and Intellectual Freedom (CD#19.3,
  Annual Conference 2003)
  http://www.ifla.org/faife/policy/iflastat/
  gldeclar-e.html

- Library Services for the Poor (ALA Policy 61,
  Annual Conference 1990)
  http://www.ala.org/ala/ourassociation/
  governingdocs/policymanual/servicespoor.htm

- Resolution on Access to and Ownership of
  Government Information (CD#20.8, Annual
  Conference 2004)
  http://www.ala.org/ala/ourassociation/
  governanceb/council/councilactions/
  2004acas.htm

- Resolution on Security and Access to Government Information (2003) http://www.ala.org/ala/oif/ifissues/ issuesrelatedlinks/securityresolution.htm
- Resolution for Guidelines on Sensitive Information (CD#20.6, Annual Conference 2004) http://www.ala.org/ala/ourassociation/ governanceb/council/councilactions/ 2004acas.htm

5
Policies and Statements Related to Confidentiality, Privacy, and Governmental Intimidation

5.1
Policy on Confidentiality of Library Records

The Council of the American Library Association strongly recommends that the responsible officers of each library, cooperative system, and consortium in the United States:

1. Formally adopt a policy that specifically recognizes its circulation records and other records identifying the names of library users to be confidential. (See also ALA Code of Ethics, Article III, "We protect each library user's right to privacy and confidentiality with respect to information sought or received, and resources consulted, borrowed, acquired or transmitted" and "Privacy: An Interpretation of the *Library Bill of Rights*.")

2. Advise all librarians and library employees that such records shall not be made available to any agency of state, federal, or local government except pursuant to such process, order or subpoena as may be authorized under the authority of, and pursuant to, federal, state, or local law relating to civil, criminal, or administrative discovery procedures or legislative investigative power.

3. Resist the issuance of enforcement of any such process, order, or subpoena until such time as a proper showing of good cause has been made in a court of competent jurisdiction.[*]

---

[*] Point 3, above, means that upon receipt of such process, order, or subpoena, the library's officers will consult with their legal counsel to determine if such process, order, or subpoena is in proper form and if there is a showing of good cause for its issuance; if the process, order, or subpoena is not in proper form or if good cause has not been shown, they will insist that such defects be cured.

Adopted January 20, 1971, by the ALA Council; revised July 4, 1975, July 2, 1986. http://www.ala.org/ala/oif/statementspols/otherpolicies/policyconfidentiality.htm.

HISTORY

Policy on Confidentiality
of Library Records

During the spring of 1970, the Milwaukee Public Library was visited by agents of the U.S. Treasury Department, who were requesting permission to examine the circulation records of books and materials on explosives. Initially rebuffed by the assistant librarian, the agents later returned with an opinion from the city attorney's office that circulation records were public records and that the agents should be allowed access to the files. The library complied. At about the same time, the ALA Office for Intellectual Freedom received reports of similar visits from Treasury agents at public libraries in Cleveland, Ohio, and Richmond, California. On July 1 of that year, a report was received from Atlanta, Georgia, stating that in the Atlanta area, twenty-seven libraries and branches were visited.

On July 21, the ALA Executive Board issued an emergency advisory statement urging all libraries to make circulation records confidential as a matter of policy. The advisory statement read:

> The American Library Association has been advised that the Internal Revenue Service of the Treasury Department has requested access to the circulation records of public libraries in Atlanta, Georgia, and Milwaukee, Wisconsin, for the purpose of determining the identity of persons reading matter pertaining to the construction of explosive devices. The Association is further advised that such requests were not based on any process, order, or sub-

poena authorized by federal, civil, criminal, or administrative discovery procedures.

The Executive Board of the ALA believes that the efforts of the federal government to convert library circulation records into "suspect lists" constitute an unconscionable and unconstitutional invasion of the right of privacy of library patrons and, if permitted to continue, will do irreparable damage to the educational and social value of the libraries of this country.

Accordingly, the Executive Board of the American Library Association strongly recommends that the responsible officers in each U.S. library:

1. Formally adopt a policy which specifically recognizes its circulation records to be confidential in nature.
2. Advise all librarians and library employees that such records shall not be made available to any agency of state, federal, or local government except pursuant to such process, order, or subpoena as may be authorized under the authority of, and pursuant to, federal, state, or local law relating to civil, criminal, or administrative discovery procedures or legislative investigatory power.
3. Resist the issuance or enforcement of any such process, order, or subpoena until such time as a proper showing of good cause has been made in a court of competent jurisdiction.

David H. Clift, ALA executive director, and staff members met with Randolph W. Thrower, commissioner of the Internal Revenue Service (IRS), on August 5, 1970, to discuss their mutual concern over the inquiries. Little was agreed upon at the meeting except that "efforts would begin, in a spirit of cooperation, to develop guidelines acceptable to the American Library Association and the Internal Revenue Service." That afternoon, Clift received a copy of a letter sent to Senator Sam J. Ervin, Jr., chair of the Senate Subcommittee on Constitutional Rights, by Secretary of the Treasury David M. Kennedy in response to Senator Ervin's earlier expressed concern about the IRS inquiries. Secretary Kennedy's letter stated that the visits had been conducted to "determine the advisability of the use of library records as an investigative technique to assist in quelling bombings. That survey . . . has terminated and will not be repeated." But the door was not being closed on future surveys. The secretary added that "it is our judgment that checking such records in certain limited circumstances is an appropriate investigative technique" and that the Alcohol, Tobacco, and Firearms Division of the Treasury Department has the authority, under federal statute, to conduct limited investigations in specific cases.[1]

ALA indicated its awareness of the Internal Revenue Service's responsibility to enforce the statutes, but noted that the Association's primary concern was not the enforcement itself but, rather, the means by which this enforcement was undertaken regarding libraries. While not intending to hinder effective enforcement of federal statutes, the Association made it clear that circulation records were "not to be made available to any agency of state, federal, or local government except pursuant to such process, order, or subpoena as may be authorized under the authority of, and pursuant to, federal, state, or local law relating to civil, criminal, or administrative discovery procedures or legislative investigatory power."

In anticipation of presenting the matter to the ALA Council at the 1971 Midwinter Meeting in Los Angeles, Intellectual Freedom Committee members were polled by telegram in October 1970, concerning a proposed draft of a policy statement. Suggestions for modification of the July statement were made by the IFC and the Executive Board at the latter's 1970 fall meeting. The Board suggested that the original introductory paragraph be shortened, that the phrase "and other records identifying the names of library users with specific materials" be added to Article 1, and that Article 3 be clarified.

The Policy on Confidentiality of Library Records was formally adopted by the IFC at a special meeting in December 1970. It was submitted to the ALA Council at the 1971 Midwinter Meeting in Los Angeles, and was approved on January 20, 1971. On that date, in his progress report to Council, IFC chair David K. Berninghausen stated the following:

> When the time comes in any society that government
> officials seek information as to what people are reading,

it must be presumed that they expect to use these records as evidence of dangerous thinking. And when a government takes action to control what its citizens are thinking, it is a tell-tale sign that all is not well in that society.

We recognize that the U.S. Treasury agents probably did not realize that their investigations would be viewed as an invasion of privacy of readers or as an infringement on the freedom of thought guaranteed by the U.S. Constitution and Bill of Rights. But it is such small, beginning steps that lead a nation down the road to tyranny. We are pleased to note that these programs of inquiry have been stopped. We are proud of ALA's prompt action which helped to bring the investigations to an end.[2]

At the 1975 Annual Conference in San Francisco, a new problem of confidentiality was considered by the IFC. Earlier, the Intellectual Freedom Committee of the Washington Library Association had called ALA's attention to the fact that in the Policy on Confidentiality of Library Records "identifying the names of library users with specific materials" had been used to justify the release of other kinds of library records on patrons to police officers.

After reviewing this issue, the IFC voted to recommend to the Council that the phrase "with specific materials" be deleted from the policy, thus making it applicable to all patron records. The IFC's recommendation was accepted by the Council at its meeting on July 4, 1975.

During the 1980–82 revision of the ALA's intellectual freedom policies, the IFC considered several suggested revisions of the Policy on Confidentiality of Library Records. After considerable discussion and consultation with ALA counsel, however, the Committee decided not to recommend any changes in the policy. At the 1983 Midwinter Meeting in San Antonio, however, it was voted to append to the document a note referring to Article III of the ALA Code of Ethics protecting the library user's right to privacy. At San Antonio, the IFC also adopted a series of suggested procedures for implementing the confidentiality policy (part 3, section 5.2).

In line with the ongoing practice of periodic review, in 1999–2000 the IFC reviewed the Policy on Confidentiality of Library

Records and recommended no changes. As a result of the 2004–5 review, an explanatory note was added relative to point 3.

NOTES

1. David M. Kennedy, letter to Senator Sam J. Ervin Jr., July 29, 1970 (copy in ALA files).
2. American Library Association, Minutes of Council Meetings 14 (1971–72): 76.

5.2
Suggested Procedures for Implementing "Policy on Confidentiality of Library Records"

When drafting local policies, libraries should consult with their legal counsel to ensure these policies are based upon and consistent with applicable federal, state, and local law concerning the confidentiality of library records, the disclosure of public records, and the protection of individual privacy. (See Interpretations to the *Library Bill of Rights*, including Access to Electronic Information, Services, and Networks and Privacy.)

Suggested procedures include the following:*

1. The library staff member receiving the request to examine or obtain information relating to circulation or other records identifying the names of library users must immediately refer the person making the request to the responsible officer of the institution, who shall explain the confidentiality policy.

2. The director, upon receipt of such process, order, or subpoena, shall consult with the appropriate legal officer assigned to the institution to determine if such process, order, or subpoena is in good form and if there is a showing of good cause for its issuance.

---

* See also "Confidentiality and Coping with Law Enforcement Inquiries: Guidelines for the Library and Its Staff." Adopted July 2, 1991, by the ALA Council; amended June 30, 2004.

3. If the process, order, or subpoena is not in proper form or if good cause has not been shown, the library should insist that such defects be cured before any records are released.

4. The legal process requiring the production of circulation or other library records is ordinarily in the form of a subpoena duces tecum (bring your records) requiring the responsible library officer to attend court or to provide testimony at his or her deposition. It also may require him or her to bring along certain designated circulation or other specified records.

5. Staff should be trained and required to report any threats or unauthorized demands (e.g., those not supported by a process, order, or subpoena) concerning circulation and other records to the appropriate officer of the institution.

6. Any problems relating to the privacy of circulation and other records identifying the names of library users that are not provided for above shall be referred to the responsible officer.

Adopted January 9, 1983, by the ALA Intellectual Freedom Committee; revised January 11, 1988; March 18, 2005. http://www.ala.org/ala/oif/statementspols/otherpolicies/suggestedprocedures.htm.

HISTORY

Suggested Procedures for Implementing "Policy on Confidentiality of Library Records"

In the early 1980s, the IFC began the practice, when appropriate, of developing procedures and guidelines to provide more specific information concerning the implementation of intellectual freedom policies. Since these procedures and guidelines were not policies, they did not require Council approval. As a result, these documents have become a convenient and efficient vehicle for providing up-to-date guidance in rapidly changing areas.

At the 1988 Midwinter Meeting in San Antonio, the IFC revised the suggested procedures for implementing the confidentiality policy. Changes were made to bring the language in this document into conformance with the language in the policy, to stress the need for a court order before any records are released, and to emphasize the need for libraries to consult applicable federal, state, and local law when drafting such a policy for local use. Later in 1988, responding to concerns about whether the language in the Policy on Confidentiality of Library Records was sufficient to cover all records, rather than just registration or circulation records, the IFC reviewed both the policy and the procedures for implementing it. The Committee decided that the language of the policy was sufficient but that the language in the procedures was not uniformly inclusive and should be revised. The Committee chair noted that the procedures should include a direction to librarians to ascertain the status of their state law on confidentiality of library records. In addition, the chair suggested that all state IFCs be encouraged to review their state statutes to determine the inclusivity of the records covered.

A new draft of the procedure incorporating the above-mentioned concerns was adopted by the Intellectual Freedom Committee on January 11, 1988. The procedures were revised again in March 2005 as a part of the IFC's periodic review of intellectual freedom documents.

5.3
Confidentiality and Coping with Law Enforcement Inquiries

Guidelines for the Library and Its Staff

Increased visits to libraries by law enforcement agents, including FBI agents and officers of state, county, and municipal police departments, are raising considerable concern among the public and the library community. These visits are not only a result of the increased surveillance and investigation prompted by the events of September 11, 2001, and the subsequent passage of the USA PATRIOT Act (http://www.ala.org/oif/ifissues/usapatriotact/), but also as a result of law enforcement officers investigating computer crimes, including e-mail threats and possible violations of the laws addressing online obscenity and child pornography.

These guidelines, developed to assist libraries and library staff in dealing with law enforcement inquiries, rely upon the ALA's policies and guidelines:

- Privacy: An Interpretation of the *Library Bill of Rights*
  http://www.ala.org/oif/policies/interpretations/privacy/

- Questions and Answers on Privacy and Confidentiality
  http://www.ala.org/oif/policies/interpretations/privacyqanda/

- Policy on Confidentiality of Library Records
  http://www.ala.org/ala/oif/statementspols/otherpolicies/Default2544.htm

- Suggested Procedures for Implementing Policy
  on Confidentiality of Library Records
  http://www.ala.org/oif/iftoolkits/privacy/
  guidelines/

- Policy concerning Confidentiality of Personally
  Identifiable Information about Library Users
  http://www.ala.org/ala/oif/statementspols/
  otherpolicies/Default2544.htm

- American Library Association Code of Ethics
  http://www.ala.org/oif/policies/codeofethics/

[See also State Laws on the Confidentiality of Library Records
(http://www.ala.org/oif/stateprivacylaws/), ALA's Privacy
Tool Kit (http://www.ala.org/oif/iftoolkits/privacy/), and two
pages on the OIF website: Privacy and Confidentiality (http://
www.ala.org/oif/ifissues/privacy/) and Intellectual Freedom
Issues (http://www.ala.org/oif/ifissues/).]

Fundamental Principles

Librarians' professional ethics require that personally identifiable
information about library users be kept confidential. This principle is reflected in Article III of the Code of Ethics, which states
that "[librarians] protect each library user's right to privacy and
confidentiality with respect to information sought or received,
and resources consulted, borrowed, acquired, or transmitted."
Privacy: An Interpretation of the *Library Bill of Rights*, notes that
"[p]rotecting user privacy and confidentiality has long been an
integral part of the mission of libraries."

Currently, 48 states and the District of Columbia have laws
protecting the confidentiality of library records, and the attorneys
general of the remaining two states, Hawaii and Kentucky, have
ruled that library records are confidential and may not be disclosed under the laws governing open records. Confidential
library records should not be released or made available in any
format to a federal agent, law enforcement officer, or other person

unless a court order in proper form has been entered by a court of competent jurisdiction after a showing of good cause by the law enforcement agency or person seeking the records.

General Guidelines

Confidentiality of library records is a basic principle of librarianship. As a matter of policy or procedure, the library administrator should ensure that:

- The library staff and governing board are familiar with the ALA Policy on Confidentiality of Library Records, the Policy concerning Confidentiality of Personally Identifiable Information about Library Users, and other ALA documents on users' privacy and confidentiality.

- The library staff and governing board are familiar with their state's library confidentiality statute or attorney general's opinion.

- The library adopts a policy on users' privacy and confidentiality. Such policies should inform users about their expectation of privacy and how the library handles their confidential information.

- The library adopts staff policies that inform the staff and board about the procedures to follow if the library is served with judicial process (search warrants or subpoenas) seeking library records or if law enforcement agents conduct inquiries in the library.

- The library staff is familiar with the library's policy on confidentiality and its procedures for handling court orders and law enforcement inquiries.

Library Procedures Affect Confidentiality

Law enforcement visits aside, be aware that library operating procedures have an impact on confidentiality. The following recommendations are suggestions to bring library procedures into compliance with most state confidentiality statutes, ALA policies on confidentiality and its Code of Ethics:

- Avoid creating unnecessary records. Only record a user's personally identifiable information when necessary for the efficient operation of the library.

- Avoid retaining records that are not needed for efficient operation of the library. Check with your local governing body to learn if there are laws or policies addressing record retention and in conformity with these laws or policies, develop policies on the length of time necessary to retain a record. Ensure that all kinds and types of records are covered by the policy, including data-related logs, digital records, and system backups.

- Once record retention policies are in place, ensure that records are destroyed or archived on schedule. A library cannot destroy records after it receives notice from law enforcement agents that the records may be subject to judicial process.

- Be aware of library practices and procedures that place information on public view. Some examples are the use of postcards for overdue notices or requested materials; staff terminals placed so that the screens can be read by the public; sign-in sheets to use computers or other devices; and the provision of titles of reserve requests or interlibrary loans provided over the telephone to users' family members or answering machines.

- Remember that there is no affirmative duty to collect or retain information about library patrons on behalf of law enforcement.

Recommended Procedures for Law Enforcement Visits

Before any visit:

- Designate the person or persons who will be responsible for handling law enforcement requests. In most circumstances, it should be the library director, and, if available, the library's legal counsel.

- Review the library's confidentiality policy and state confidentiality law with library counsel. Communicate those policies and the requirements of the law to both staff and volunteer workers in the library.

- Train all library staff, including volunteers, on the library's procedure for handling law enforcement requests. They should understand that it is lawful to refer the agent or officer to an administrator in charge of the library, and that they do not need to respond immediately to any request.

- A court order may require the removal of a computer workstation or other computer storage device from the library. Have plans in place to address service interruptions and any necessary backups for equipment and software.

During the visit:

- Staff should immediately ask for identification if they are approached by an agent or law enforcement officer, and then record the information. If possible, verify the information with the local FBI office or the police department. The agent or officer should then immediately be referred to the library director or the designated supervisor.

- The director or supervisor should meet with the agent with another colleague in attendance. If possible, one person should take notes in the event a record of the encounter is needed in the future.

- If the agent or officer does not have a court order compelling the production of records, the library director should explain the library's confidentiality policy and the state's confidentiality law, and inform the agent or officer that users' records are not available except when a proper court order in good form has been presented to the library.

- Without a court order, neither the FBI nor local law enforcement has authority to compel cooperation with an investigation or require answers to questions, other than the name and address of the person speaking to the agent or officer. If the agent or officer persists, or makes an appeal to patriotism, the library director should explain that, as good citizens, the library staff will not respond to informal requests for confidential information, in conformity with professional ethics, First Amendment freedoms, and state law.

- If the agent or officer presents a search warrant or other judicial process, the library director should immediately call the library's counsel and ask for assistance.

If the judicial process is in the form of a subpoena:

- Remember that a subpoena does not require an immediate response from the library. Thank the officer serving the subpoena and inform him or her that the library will respond to the subpoena within the time allotted and in conformity with the law. Immediately refer the subpoena to the library's legal counsel.

- Counsel should examine the subpoena for any legal defect, including the manner in which it was served on the library, the breadth of its request, its form, or an insufficient showing of good cause made to a court. If a defect exists, counsel will advise on the best method to resist the subpoena.

- Through legal counsel, insist that any defect be cured before records are released and that the subpoena is strictly limited to require release of specifically identified records or documents. If there does not appear to be good cause for the subpoena, or if it seems too broad or intrusive, ask your attorney to file a motion to quash the subpoena in its entirety.

- Require that the agent, officer, or party requesting the information submit a new subpoena in good form and without defects.

- If you decide to comply with the subpoena after consulting with the library's legal counsel, review the information that may be produced in response to the subpoena before releasing the information. Follow the subpoena strictly and do not provide any information that is not specifically requested in it.

- If disclosure is required, ask the court to enter a protective order (drafted by the library's counsel) keeping the information confidential and limiting its use to the particular case. Ask that access be restricted to those persons working directly on the case.

If the court order is in the form of a search warrant:

- Unlike a subpoena, a search warrant may be executed immediately. The agent or officer may begin a search of library records as soon as the library is served with the court's order.

- Ask to have library counsel present before the search begins in order to allow counsel an opportunity to examine the search warrant and to ensure that the search conforms to the terms of the search warrant.

- If the officer refuses to delay the search, examine the warrant. Ensure that the warrant has been issued by a local or federal court in your state and is current and not expired. If you question the validity of the warrant, call the issuing court to confirm the validity of the warrant.

- The warrant will include information that identifies the premises to be searched and the items or records to be produced under the warrant. Ask that the officer observe the boundaries set by the search warrant.

- Cooperate with the search to ensure that only the records identified in the warrant are produced and that no other users' records are viewed or scanned. Staff should be trained not to discuss the warrant with the officer, identify any documents, or to volunteer information without first consulting with the library's counsel.

- Record and keep an inventory of the records or items seized from the library. If possible, keep the originals and provide the agent with copies (or make copies for the library's reference).

- While most law enforcement officers will cooperate with a library's request to allow counsel to examine the warrant, it is possible that an officer will refuse to delay his or her search. Train staff to step aside and not to interfere with the officer in those cases. They should continue their attempt to notify the library director and library counsel, and make every effort to keep a record of the incident.

If the court order is a search warrant issued under the Foreign Intelligence Surveillance Act (FISA) (USA PATRIOT Act amendment):

- The recommendations for a regular search warrant still apply. However, a search warrant issued by a FISA court also contains a "gag order." That means that no person or institution served with the warrant can disclose that it has been served or that records have been produced pursuant to the warrant.

- The library and its staff must comply with this order. No information can be disclosed to any other party, including the patron whose records are the subject of the search warrant. Note that the FISA gag order permits the person receiving the FISA warrant to inform the library director and those members of the staff who are needed to produce the records.

- The gag order does not change a library's right to legal representation during the search. The library can still seek legal advice concerning the warrant and request that the library's legal counsel be present during the actual search and execution of the warrant.

- If the library does not have legal counsel and wishes legal advice, the library can still obtain legal assistance through the Freedom to Read Foundation's legal counsel. Simply call the Office for Intellectual Freedom (800-545-2433, ext. 4223) and inform the staff that you need legal advice. OIF staff will ensure that an attorney returns your call. You do not have to and should not inform OIF staff of the existence of the warrant.

After the visit:

- Review the subpoena or search warrant with library counsel to ensure that the library complies with any remaining requirements, including restrictions on sharing information with others.

- Review library policies and staff response and make any necessary revisions in light of experience.

- Be prepared to communicate with the news media. Designate one person who will be responsible for communicating with the media. Develop a public information statement detailing the principles upholding library confidentiality that includes an explanation of the chilling effect on First Amendment rights caused by public access to users' personally identifiable information, and share it with your staff, so they are able to communicate the library's message to their acquaintances and neighbors in the community.

- If possible, notify the ALA about your experience by calling the Office for Intellectual Freedom at 800-545-2433, extension 4223.

See also:

- Sample National Security Letters
  http://www.ala.org/ala/oif/ifissues/
  nationalsecurityletter.pdf
- Sample FISA (section 215) Order for Business Records
  http://www.ala.org/ala/oif/ifissues/215formorder.pdf
- Sample Federal Search Warrants and Subpoenas
  http://www.ala.org/ala/oif/ifissues/sample
  warrants.pdf

American Library Association
Office for Intellectual Freedom
April 2005
http://www.ala.org/oif/ifissues/lawenforcementinquiries/

5.4
Policy concerning Confidentiality of Personally Identifiable Information and Library Users

"In a library (physical or virtual), the right to privacy is the right to open inquiry without having the subject of one's interest examined or scrutinized by others. Confidentiality exists when a library is in possession of personally identifiable information about users and keeps that information private on their behalf" (Privacy: An Interpretation of the *Library Bill of Rights*).

The ethical responsibilities of librarians, as well as statutes in most states and the District of Columbia, protect the privacy of library users. Confidentiality extends to "information sought or received and resources consulted, borrowed, acquired or transmitted" (ALA Code of Ethics), and includes, but is not limited to, database search records, reference interviews, circulation records, interlibrary loan records and other personally identifiable uses of library materials, facilities, or services.

The First Amendment's guarantee of freedom of speech and of the press requires that the corresponding rights to hear what is spoken and read what is written be preserved, free from fear of government intrusion, intimidation, or reprisal. The American Library Association reaffirms its opposition to "any use of governmental prerogatives that lead to the intimidation of individuals or groups and discourages them from exercising the right of free expression as guaranteed by the First Amendment to the U.S. Constitution" and "encourages resistance to such abuse of governmental power . . ." (ALA Policy 53.4). In seeking access or in the pursuit of information, confidentiality is the primary means of providing the privacy that will free the individual from fear of intimidation or retaliation.

The American Library Association regularly receives reports of visits by agents of federal, state, and local law enforcement agencies to libraries, asking for personally identifiable information about library users. These visits, whether under the rubric of simply informing libraries of agency concerns or for some other reason, reflect insensitivity to the legal and ethical bases for confidentiality, and the role it plays in the preservation of First Amendment rights, rights also extended to foreign nationals while in the United States. The government's interest in library use reflects a dangerous and fallacious equation of what a person reads with what that person believes or how that person is likely to behave. Such a presumption can and does threaten the freedom of access to information. It also is a threat to a crucial aspect of First Amendment rights: that freedom of speech and of the press include the freedom to hold, disseminate and receive unpopular, minority, extreme, or even dangerous ideas.

The American Library Association recognizes that law enforcement agencies and officers may occasionally believe that library records contain information that would be helpful to the investigation of criminal activity. The American judicial system provides the mechanism for seeking release of such confidential records: a court order, following a showing of good cause based on specific facts, by a court of competent jurisdiction.[*]

The American Library Association also recognizes that, under limited circumstances, access to certain information might be restricted due to a legitimate national security concern. However, there has been no showing of a plausible probability that national security will be compromised by any use made of unclassified information available in libraries. Access to this unclassified information should be handled no differently than access to any other information. Therefore, libraries and librarians have a legal

---

[*] See "Confidentiality and Coping with Law Enforcement Inquiries: Guidelines for the Library and Its Staff." Adopted July 2, 1991; amended June 30, 2004, by the ALA Council.

and ethical responsibility to protect the confidentiality of all library users, including foreign nationals.

Libraries are one of the great bulwarks of democracy. They are living embodiments of the First Amendment because their collections include voices of dissent as well as assent. Libraries are impartial resources providing information on all points of view, available to all persons regardless of origin, age, background, or views. The role of libraries as such a resource must not be compromised by an erosion of the privacy rights of library users.

---

http://www.ala.org/ala/oif/statementspols/otherpolicies/policyconcerning.htm.

HISTORY

Policy concerning Confidentiality of Personally Identifiable Information and Library Users

In 1989, the Intellectual Freedom Committee prepared a statement sent to then-FBI director William Sessions, outlining the ALA's concerns about the FBI Library Awareness Program. (For more on the FBI Library Awareness Program, see part 1, section 2, "ALA and Intellectual Freedom: A Historical Overview.") Although the FBI had indicated it would exchange a similar statement of its own about the program, none was ever received by the ALA. Inquiries to the Office for Intellectual Freedom from librarians seeking assistance in handling law enforcement requests for confidential information about library users continued.

In response to the increasing number of inquiries, the lack of cooperation from the FBI, and concern about law enforcement requests for personally identifiable information about patrons whether found in library records per se or not, the ALA Council requested that a policy addressing the FBI and law enforcement issues be drafted.

The IFC revised and reformatted the statement prepared for the FBI in 1989 to explain library concerns about confidentiality to produce the Policy concerning Confidentiality of Personally Identifiable Information about Library Users.

In 1991, the first draft was further revised to broaden the language concerning what constitutes personally identifiable information about library users. This was done in response to a case in Oregon, where law enforcement officials took fingerprints from library materials as part of a criminal investigation. Members questioned whether fingerprints could be considered personally identifiable information according to the policy.

The new draft also included a statement expressing the ALA's contention that the use of unclassified materials in libraries cannot reasonably be deemed a national security threat, as alleged by the FBI in an attempt to justify the Library Awareness Program. The final version of the new policy was adopted by the Council on July 2, 1991.

In line with the ongoing review of all policies in 1999–2000, the IFC reviewed this policy and made no changes.

This policy was revised as a part of the 2004–5 review of policies. A new first paragraph was added consisting of the definitions of privacy and confidentiality from "Privacy: An Interpretation of the *Library Bill of Rights*." The remaining paragraphs were reordered for strength and clarity.

5.5
Guidelines for Developing a Library Privacy Policy
Privacy Tool Kit

PREPARED BY
THE ALA INTELLECTUAL FREEDOM COMMITTEE

I. Introduction

Privacy is essential to the exercise of free speech, free thought, and free association. In libraries, the right to privacy is the right to open inquiry without having the subject of one's interest examined or scrutinized by others. Confidentiality exists when a library is in possession of personally identifiable information (PII) about users and keeps that information private on their behalf.

With technology changes, increased incidence of identity theft, and new laws, as well as increased law enforcement surveillance, librarians must act now to develop and/or revise their privacy policies and procedures in order to ensure that confidential information in all formats is protected from abuse. They must also protect their organizations from liability and public relations problems. When developing and revising policies, librarians need to ensure that they:

- Limit the degree to which personally identifiable information is monitored, collected, disclosed, and distributed.
- Avoid creating unnecessary records.

Edited to remove links and model policies. For the complete document see http://www.ala.org/oif/iftoolkits/privacy/guidelines/.

- Avoid retaining records that are not needed for efficient operation of the library, including data-related logs, digital records, vendor-collected data, and system backups.
- Avoid library practices and procedures that place personally identifiable information on public view.

A privacy policy communicates the library's commitment to protecting users' personally identifiable information. A well-defined privacy policy tells library users how their information is utilized and explains the circumstances under which personally identifiable information might be disclosed. When preparing a privacy policy, librarians need to consult an attorney in order to ensure that the library's statement harmonizes with the many state and federal laws governing the collection and sharing of personally identifiable information.

Libraries need to post privacy policies publicly. Privacy: An Interpretation of the *Library Bill of Rights* states that, "Users have the right to be informed what policies and procedures govern the amount and retention of personally identifiable information, why that information is necessary for the library, and what the user can do to maintain his or her privacy."

PII: Personally Identifiable Information

One of the key concepts to understand when developing policies and procedures is that defined as: "Personally identifiable information" (PII). PII has become the generally accepted language; ALA began using this term in 1991 when it adopted the Policy concerning Confidentiality of Personally Identifiable Information about Library Users. PII connects individuals to what they bought with their credit cards, what they checked out with their library cards, and what Web sites they visited where they picked up cookies. More than simple identification, PII can build up a picture of tastes and interests—a dossier of sorts, though crude and often inaccurate. While targeted advertising is the obvious use for PII, some people would use this information to assess an individual's character, decide if they were a security risk, or embarrass them for opposing a particular position. Because of the chilling effect that such scrutiny can have on open inquiry and freedom of expression, libraries and bookstores have long resisted requests to release information that connects individual persons with specific books.

Privacy Policies and the Law

Library privacy and confidentiality policies must be in compliance with applicable federal, state, and local laws. The courts have upheld the right to privacy based on the Bill of Rights of the U.S. Constitution. Many states provide guarantees of privacy in their constitutions and statute law. Numerous decisions in case law have defined and extended rights to privacy.

Privacy Policies and ALA

A number of ALA policies and recommendations have been passed in recent years on privacy and confidentiality issues. But recognition of the importance of this issue dates back as far as the 1930's in ALA policy. Article Eleven of the Code of Ethics for Librarians (1939) asserted that "It is the librarian's obligation to treat as confidential any private information obtained through contact with library patrons." Article Three of the current Code (1995) states: "We protect each library user's right to privacy and confidentiality with respect to information sought or received and resources consulted, borrowed, acquired, or transmitted."

Your Library's Policy Should Incorporate Standard Privacy Principles

In addition to ALA policies, there are many very good frameworks for establishing privacy policies. The privacy policy guidelines outlined here are based in part on what are known as the five "Fair Information Practice Principles." These five principles outline the rights of Notice, Choice, Access, Security, and Enforcement. Another widely accepted European legal framework establishing rights of data privacy and confidentiality calls for ensuring Collection limitation, Data quality, Purpose specification, Use limitation, Security safeguards, Openness, Individual participation, and Accountability. These frameworks provide the basis for recommendations from other consumer and privacy advocacy groups, whose checklists are well worth reviewing.

II. How to Draft a Library Privacy Policy

All types of libraries are urged to draft and/or revise privacy and confidentiality policies. This document offers guidance for public, academic, research, school, and special libraries, as well as library systems. Special considerations are raised in Section III for school and academic libraries and for public library services to minors because each are affected by laws and practices unique to those particular situations. Other considerations may also apply. When drafting a policy, library administrators should check with their parent institutions to ensure they are complying with appropriate norms and policies. Some elements of this guidance may not pertain to all libraries.

1. Notice and Openness

Policies should provide notice to users of their rights to privacy and confidentiality and of the policies of the library that govern these issues. Such notice should dictate the types of information gathered and the purposes for and limitations on its use. It is critical that library privacy policies be made widely available to users through multiple means. This is because safeguarding personal privacy requires that individuals know what personally identifiable information (PII) is gathered about them, where and how it is stored (and for how long), who has access to it and under what conditions, and how that PII is used.

2. Choice and Consent

Choice means giving users options as to how any personal information collected from them may be used. Provision of many library services requires the collection and retention of personally identifiable information. Whether this is required (e.g. in order to circulate library material), automatic (e.g. as in some Web-based library services), or voluntary (e.g. when engaging in e-mail-based reference), this information should be retained only as long as is necessary to fulfill the function for which it was initially acquired. Two commonly used schemes for choice/consent are "opt-in," where the default is not to include the information and affirmative steps are required for inclusion, or "opt-out" where the default is to include the information and affirmative steps are required for exclusion.

3. Access by Users

Users have the right of access to their own personally identifiable information (PII). The right to this access should be mentioned in the privacy policy. Verifying the accuracy and status of PII helps ensure that library services that rely on personally identifiable information can function properly. The right of access covers all types of information gathered about a library user or about his or her use of the library, including mailing addresses, circulation records, computer use logs, etc. Access to personal information should be made available onsite or through online access with security parameters in effect to verify the existence of individual users.

Right to access should also address instances in which age may be a factor. The *Children's Online Privacy Protection Act of 1998* (COPPA) provides for "a parent's ability to review, make changes to, or have deleted the child's personal information." For more on COPPA, see the section called "School Libraries and COPPA" below under part III.

4. Data Integrity and Security

Data Integrity: The library needs to assure data integrity. Whenever personally identifiable information (PII) is collected, the library must take reasonable steps to ensure integrity, including using only reputable sources of data, providing library users access to their personal data, updating information regularly, destroying untimely data or converting it to anonymous form, and stripping PII from aggregated, summary data. It is the responsibility of library staff to destroy information in confidential or privacy-protected records in order to ensure unauthorized disclosure. Information that should be regularly purged or shredded includes PII on library resource use, material circulation history, security/surveillance tapes and use logs, both paper and electronic.

Shared Data: If patron records are supplied by or shared with a parent institution such as a college registrar or a library consortium, the library needs to adopt measures to ensure timely corrections and deletions of data. Likewise, when the library exchanges data with other departments such as bursars and tax collectors, vendors, or any other organizations, it must ensure that records are accurate and up to date. Libraries issuing passwords should avoid choosing passwords or PIN's that can reveal a user's identity, including social security numbers.

Security: Security involves both managerial and technical measures to protect against loss and the unauthorized access, destruction, use, or disclosure of the data. Security measures should be integrated into the design, implementation and day-to-day practices of the library's entire operating environment as part of its continuing commitment to risk management. These measures are intended to prevent corruption of data, block unknown or unauthorized access to library systems and information, and provide reasonable protection of private information in a library's custody, even if stored offsite on servers or back up tapes.

Administrative Measures: The library needs to implement internal organizational measures that limit access to data while ensuring that those individuals with access do not utilize the data for unauthorized purposes. The library must also prevent unauthorized access through such technical security measures as including encryption in the transmission and storage of data; limits on access through use of passwords; and the storage of data on secure servers or computers that are inaccessible by modem or network connection. If libraries store PII on servers or back up tapes that are offsite, they must ensure that comparable measures to limit access to data are followed. Libraries should develop routine schedules for shredding PII collected on paper.

Electronic Tracking: Neither local nor external electronic systems used by the library should collect PII by logging or tracking e-mail, chat room use, Web browsing, cookies, middleware, or other usage. Nevertheless, users should be advised of the limits to library privacy protection when using remote sites. If the library enables cookies (small files sent to a browser by a Web site to enable customization of individual visits), it should alert users how to refuse, disable, or remove cookies from their hard drives. In addition, the library should not maintain cookies after users terminate their sessions nor share them with external third parties. Libraries should regularly remove cookies, Web history, cached files, or other computer and Internet use records and other software code that is placed on their networks. Those libraries that authenticate patrons for use of external databases by middleware systems and/or proxy servers should simply verify the attributes of valid users and not release PII.

Data Retention: It is the responsibility of library staff to destroy information in confidential or privacy-protected records in order to safeguard data from unauthorized disclosure. Information that should be regularly purged or shredded includes PII on library resource use, material circulation history, and security/surveillance tapes and logs. If this data is maintained off site, library administrators must ensure that appropriate data retention policies and procedures are employed. Libraries that use surveillance cameras should have written policies stating that the cameras are not to be used for any other purpose. If the cameras create any records, the library must recognize its responsibility to protect their confidentiality like any other library record. This is best accomplished by purging the records as soon as their purpose is served.

Encryption: Data encryption can be used to enhance privacy protection. Encrypted data requires others to use a pre-defined electronic "key" to decipher the contents of a message, file, or transaction. Libraries should negotiate with vendors to encourage the use of such technology in library systems (e.g., in the document delivery, saved searches, and e-mail features now offered by many OPAC vendors). Whenever possible, libraries should consider making encryption tools available to library users who are engaging in personalized online transactions or communications.

5. *Enforcement and Redress*

Libraries that develop privacy policies need to establish and maintain an effective mechanism to enforce them. They should conduct regular privacy audits in order to ensure that all library programs and services are enforcing this privacy policy. Redress must be available for library users who feel their privacy and confidentiality rights are violated. Libraries should provide a means to investigate complaints and re-audit policy and procedures in cases of potential violation of library privacy and confidentiality. Library educational efforts should include informing users how to protect their own privacy and confidentiality, both in and outside of the library setting.

Libraries must ensure they have well-established procedures to enforce their policies by informing users about the legal conditions under which they might be required to release personally identifiable information (PII). Libraries should only consider a law enforcement request for any library record if it is issued by a court of competent jurisdiction that shows good cause and is in proper form. Only library administrators after conferring with legal counsel should be authorized to accept or comply with subpoenas, warrants, court orders or other investigatory documents directed to the library or pertaining to library property. All library staff, however, should be trained and required to contact a designated Library Privacy Officer or previously designated administrator immediately should a law enforcement officer appear and request the library comply with a request to release PII.

Libraries should develop and implement procedures for dealing with law enforcement requests before, during, and after a visit.

III. Special Privacy Policy Considerations: Academic Libraries, School Libraries, and Public Library Services to Minors

Academic Libraries

The heart of the mission of academic institutions is the freedom to research unfamiliar and controversial topics. Academic libraries

serve those needs well. Often, they offer their personal, professional, and educational information services to a wide variety of
users. If academic libraries provide different levels of service or
access to different categories of borrowers (e.g., faculty, graduate
students, undergraduate students, or community members), they
must ensure that their services and access are offered equitably
within a borrower type. Such restrictions should not impede
intellectual freedom.

Academic Libraries and Students: Students in academic institutions are adults and must be accorded the same privacy safeguards as adults in other types of libraries. The mere fact that students are enrolled in courses should not jeopardize their privacy
rights. Thus, student circulation records for course-required and
reserve reading should be protected from inquiry with the same
rigor as their circulation records for personal reading. Librarians
assisting in investigations of plagiarism should take care to protect the usage records of individual students. Librarians can assist
faculty in the development of classroom instruction and procedures that meet educational goals without compromising student
rights to privacy.

Academic Libraries and FERPA and SEVIS: The Family Educational Rights and Privacy Act (FERPA) was passed to protect the
privacy of student education records and to define who can
access these records. FERPA grants parents the rights until the
child turns 18 years old or attends a school beyond the high
school level. The Student and Exchange Visitors Information
System (SEVIS) maintains updated information on approximately one million non-immigrant foreign students and
exchange visitors during the course of their stay in the United
States each year. Colleges and universities are now required to
report a foreign student's failure to enroll or if students drop out
of their programs. Colleges and university librarians need to
identify how their institutions implement these laws and whether
they have any impact on the collection and retention of library
user records.

Academic Libraries and Faculty: Academic institutions often
rely on principles of academic freedom to protect the intellectual
freedom of faculty. While the principles of academic freedom are

intended to protect faculty from professional consequences of researching in unpopular or controversial areas, they do not necessarily protect the privacy of faculty. Academic libraries should also have in place appropriate policies based on First Amendment and Fourth Amendment rights to protect the privacy of faculty members' library records.

Academic Libraries and Computer Systems: The computer networks of academic libraries are often part of institutional networks, under the ultimate control of units outside the library. Academic libraries should work with campus computer departments to ensure that student and faculty information-seeking activity is kept confidential and well protected throughout the institution. In addition, library personnel should review library procedures and arrangements with outside vendors to ensure the highest level of protection for such records as online digital reference logs, proxy server and other authentication devices, e-mail reference transactions, personalized searching, and SDI profiles.

School Libraries

School library media specialists have an ethical obligation to protect and promote student privacy. Although the educational level and program of the school necessarily shapes the resources and services of a school library, the principles of the *Library Bill of Rights* apply equally to all librarians, including school library media specialists.

School Libraries and FERPA: School records are governed by the Family Educational Rights and Privacy Act (FERPA) that grants parents the rights to access student educational records until the child turns 18 years old. School library media specialists need to identify how their institutions implement this law and its impact on collection and retention of library user records.

Students as Library Users: Students who use school libraries need to learn about the concepts of privacy and confidentiality. They may not know the dangers of sharing personally identifiable information with others. School library media specialists may face the situation of an adult asking for information pertaining to students' library use. These situations must be handled in accordance with all school and library policies. In an ideal situation, that information would not be released. Teachers should not be able to "check" on students to see if they have borrowed assigned readings or used specific resources. School library media specialists are best served when they assist teachers in developing classroom procedures and policies that preserve user privacy and meet educational goals.

School Library Procedures: School library media specialists have a responsibility to "assume a leadership role in promoting the principles of intellectual freedom within the school by providing resources and services that create and sustain an atmosphere of free inquiry." This includes safeguarding student and teacher privacy. School library personnel must strive to: educate all members of the school community about the value of privacy to school library media center users; develop board approved policies that provide the highest level of protection for all records; and, teach all members of the educational community about the policies and procedures that govern privacy. School libraries operate as part of larger educational structures. In some cases, school systems may create policies and procedures that infringe on students' rights to privacy. School library personnel are encouraged to educate all policy makers about the dangers of abridging students' privacy rights.

School Libraries and COPPA: The Children's Online Privacy Protection Act (COPPA) directly affects commercial Web sites targeted to children, as well as those sites that know they are collecting personally identifiable information from children 12 and under. Such sites have a legal obligation to comply with the law. Prosecution is one of the penalties for non-compliance. Noncommercial Web sites, such as library, nonprofit, community groups, and government agencies are not covered by COPPA. A library collecting personal information from children in order to e-mail them summer reading lists or reference assistance is not required to seek parental consent. Although libraries are not directly impacted by COPPA, children using the Internet in a library may need help understanding the law and getting consent from their parents. In some instances, children will find that COPPA may restrict their ability to participate in some activities on Web sites while they await parental approval. It is the librarians' role to guide children through the process or help them find alternative activities online. Parents may need assistance in understanding the law and the significance of the requests they receive from Web sites. Librarians and libraries should play a key role in helping all library users understand and comply with COPPA. (Note: The extent to which schools can or do assume parental responsibilities for students will depend in large part on decisions made by the local school board or superintendent. It also will depend on the nature of the resources being used in the classroom and whether those resources require students to divulge personally identifiable information. Some schools may decide to act on behalf of the child, others may decide to seek consent through an Acceptable Use Policy signed by students and parents at the beginning of the year, while others may take no responsibility at all and leave it up to parents. However the school implements the law, it must take care not to allow COPPA to interfere with curricular decisions.)

Public Library Services to Minors

The rights of minors vary from state to state. Libraries may wish to consult the legal counsel of their governing authorities to ensure that policy and practice are in accord with applicable law. In addition, the legal responsibilities and standing of library staff in regard to minors differ substantially in school and public libraries. In all instances, best practice is to extend to minors the maximum allowable confidentiality and privacy protections.

The *Children's Online Privacy Protection Act* (COPPA) requires commercial Web sites that collect personally identifiable information from children 12 and under to obtain consent from their parents or guardians in advance. COPPA was written with three parties in mind: parents, children, and commercial Web sites. Although COPPA does not place any special obligations on public libraries, there are two impacts to consider:

1. When children use Internet access in libraries, library staff need to be able to explain COPPA's effects to children and their parents.

2. When a library designs Web pages and services for children, it may wish to provide the same privacy protections as the protections mandated for commercial Web sites.

Parents are responsible not only for the choices their minor children make concerning the selection of materials and the use of library facilities and resources, but also for communicating with their minor children about those choices. Librarians should not breach a minor's confidentiality by giving out information readily available to the parent from the minor directly. Libraries should take great care to limit the extenuating circumstances in which they release such information.

Parental responsibility is key to a minor's use of the library. Notifying parents about the library's privacy and confidentiality policies should be a part of the process of issuing library cards to minors. In some public libraries, the privacy rights of minors may differ slightly from those of adults, often in proportion to the age of the minor. The legitimate concerns for the safety of children in a public place can be addressed without unnecessary invasion of minors' privacy while using the library.

The rights of minors to privacy regarding their choice of library materials should be respected and protected.

IV. Questions to Ask When Drafting Privacy and Confidentiality Policies and Procedures

Policy drafts should be reviewed against existing local policies, state and local legislation, and ALA recommendations and guidelines. It may also help policy drafting teams and trainers to ask themselves and their staff questions from the checklists below, considering how and whether policies and procedures under consideration provide appropriate guidance. Common privacy- or confidentiality-violating scenarios are also available for use in training or policy review.

SOURCES

Carolyn Caywood, "Questions and Answers about Privacy in Libraries," presented at the Virginia Library Association 2002 Conference, October 17, 2002.

"Confidentiality Inventory," in *Confidentiality in Libraries: An Intellectual Freedom Modular Education Program Trainer's Manual* (Chicago: ALA, 1993), p. 30.

Barbara Jones, "Intellectual Freedom Policies for Privacy," in *Libraries, Access, and Intellectual Freedom: Developing Policies for Public and Academic Libraries* (Chicago: ALA, 1999), p. 147–68.

Confidentiality in Libraries: An Intellectual Freedom Modular Education Program Trainer's Manual (Chicago: ALA, 1993).

HISTORY

Guidelines for Developing a Library Privacy Policy
Privacy Tool Kit

At the 2001 Midwinter Meeting, the Intellectual Freedom Committee (IFC) established a standing Privacy Subcommittee, which was charged to monitor ongoing privacy developments in technology, politics, and legislation and to identify needs and resources for librarians and library users. The IFC began work on the "Privacy" Interpretation of the *Library Bill of Rights* at its spring 2001 meeting. Drafts of the Interpretation were distributed to all ALA units. From discussions at the 2001 Annual Conference, the 2002 Midwinter Meeting, state and regional conferences, and on the IFC electronic discussion list, as well as via e-mail and regular mail, the Committee received numerous questions about how the proposed Interpretation would apply to specific situations in libraries. Since many of the questions were repetitive, the Committee decided to develop and circulate a series of questions and answers.

After Council adoption of the Interpretation at the 2002 Annual Conference, the Privacy Subcommittee continued work on the questions and answers. It soon became apparent that libraries and librarians were in need of additional resources. By the 2003 Midwinter Meeting, work had begun on a Privacy Tool Kit. Topics to be covered were ALA privacy policies, guidelines for developing a library privacy policy, privacy procedures, privacy communications, and a privacy bibliography. All parts of the tool kit were completed prior to the 2005 Annual Conference. They will continue to be updated as necessary.

5.6
Policy on Governmental Intimidation

The American Library Association opposes any use of governmental prerogatives that lead to the intimidation of individuals or groups and discourages them from exercising the right of free expression as guaranteed by the First Amendment to the U.S. Constitution. ALA encourages resistance to such abuse of governmental power and supports those against whom such governmental power has been employed.

Adopted February 2, 1973, by the ALA Council; amended July 1, 1981; June 30, 2004, http://www.ala.org/ala/oif/statementspols/otherpolicies/policygovernmental.htm.

HISTORY

Policy on Governmental Intimidation

The issue of the federal government's abuse of authority was brought before the ALA membership at the Association's 1971 Annual Conference in Dallas. At the general membership meeting on June 23, Zoia Horn and Patricia Rom (then librarians at Bucknell University in Lewisburg, Pennsylvania) introduced a resolution on governmental intimidation. Approved by the membership and two days later amended and approved by the ALA Council, the original statement on governmental intimidation read as follows:

> WHEREAS, ALA is concerned with the preservation of intellectual freedom; and
>
> WHEREAS, The freedom to think, to communicate, and discuss alternatives are essential elements of intellectual freedom; and
>
> WHEREAS, These freedoms have been threatened by actions of the federal government through the use of informers, electronic surveillance, grand juries, and indictments under the Conspiracy Act of 1968 as demonstrated in the case of the Harrisburg 6;
>
> NOW THEREFORE BE IT RESOLVED,
>
> 1. That the ALA Membership Meeting at Dallas recognizes the danger to intellectual freedom presented by the use of spying in libraries by government agencies;

2. That ALA go on record against the use of the grand
   jury procedure to intimidate anti–Vietnam War
   activists and people seeking justice for minority communities;

3. That ALA deplore and go on record against the use of
   the Conspiracy Act of 1968 as a weapon against the
   citizens of this country who are being indicted for
   such overt acts as meeting, telephoning, discussing
   alternative methods of bringing about change, and
   writing letters;

4. That the ALA Membership at Dallas assert the confidentiality of the professional relationships of librarians to the people they serve, that these relationships
   be respected in the same manner as medical doctors to
   their patients, lawyers to their clients, priests to the
   people they serve; and

5. That ALA assert that no librarian would lend himself
   to a role as informant, whether of voluntarily revealing circulation records or identifying patrons and
   their reading habits.

In March 1972, the Social Responsibilities Round Table asked
the Executive Board to give the Association's moral support and
financial aid to a librarian who had been called to testify in a federal
court and, after refusing, had been jailed for civil contempt. The
Social Responsibilities Round Table held that the Dallas Resolution
on Governmental Intimidation committed the ALA to supporting
this librarian. The Executive Board directed the IFC to review the
resolution and "develop a statement which would interpret the resolution in terms of guidance for possible action."

At the 1972 Annual Conference in Chicago, the IFC spent a
great portion of its scheduled meetings trying to fulfill this charge.
The Committee felt that it was unable to develop an interpretive
statement because, in the Committee's words, the 1971 statement
was "good in intent, but inoperable . . . due to its narrowness of
focus." Because the 1971 statement was tied to a specific piece of
legislation and a specific incident, the Intellectual Freedom
Committee felt the document was difficult to apply. Rather than
develop an interpretive statement, the Committee promised to

develop a new resolution, expressing similar concerns, for presentation to the ALA Council at the Association's 1973 Midwinter Meeting. The IFC turned its full attention to preparing a new statement at the 1973 Midwinter Meeting. The new document was presented to the Council on February 2, 1973.

The Committee originally moved that the resolution be adopted and substituted in its entirety for the 1971 Dallas statement. However, the Council felt that the new resolution omitted one important concern: an affirmation of the confidential nature of the librarian-patron relationship, covered by Articles 4 and 5 of the Dallas resolution. To ensure that this point would be retained as part of official ALA policy, the Council rescinded all of the Dallas resolution except for Articles 4 and 5. In addition, the Council amended the IFC's resolution, confirming the ALA's support of all those against whom governmental power has been employed. The Resolution on Governmental Intimidation, approved by the ALA Council on February 2, 1973, read as follows:

> WHEREAS, The principle of intellectual freedom protects the rights of free expression of ideas, even those which are in opposition to the policies and actions of government itself; and
>
> WHEREAS, The support of that principle is guaranteed by the First Amendment, thus insuring constitutional protection of individual or collective dissent; and
>
> WHEREAS, Government, at whatever level, national, state, or local, must remain ever vigilant to the protection of that principle; and
>
> WHEREAS, Government, although properly empowered to promulgate, administer, or adjudicate law, has no right to use illicitly its legally constituted powers to coerce, intimidate, or harass the individual or the citizenry from enunciating dissent; and
>
> WHEREAS, The illegitimate uses of legitimate governmental powers have become increasingly a matter of public record, among them being the misuse of the Grand Jury and other investigative Governmental intimidation

procedures, the threat to deny licenses to telecommunications media, the indictment of citizens on charges not relevant to their presumed offenses, and the repressive classification, and hence denial, of documentary material to the very public taxed for its accumulation; and

WHEREAS, These illicit uses not only constitute an abrogation of the right to exercise the principle of freedom of expression but also, and perhaps more dangerously, prefigure a society no longer hospitable to dissent;

NOW THEREFORE BE IT RESOLVED, That the American Library Association, cognizant that in the scales of justice the strength of individual liberty may outweigh the force of power, express its unswerving opposition to any use of governmental prerogative which leads to the intimidation of the individual or the citizenry from the exercise of the constitutionally protected right of free expression; and

BE IT FURTHER RESOLVED, That the American Library Association encourage its members to resist such improper uses of governmental power; and

FURTHER, That the American Library Association support those against whom such governmental power has been employed.

During the review of the ALA intellectual freedom policies and statements that followed Council's adoption in 1980 of the revision of the *Library Bill of Rights,* the Intellectual Freedom Committee determined that two problems existed with the Resolution on Governmental Intimidation. The first was the matter of format. It was a resolution and included a series of "whereas" clauses, which were helpful in explaining the policy section but were not theoretically a part of the policy. The second problem related to the policy section itself, which the Committee believed should stand alone without the necessity of explanatory phrases. As in all cases when examples are used, these tend to date the policy to the period in which it was originally created. They also tend to dilute the clarity and force of the policy statement.

The Committee agreed that any policy on governmental intimidation should strongly oppose this activity and that, in addition, the policy should indicate ALA support of those who resist governmental intimidation. In presenting the amended policy to the ALA Council, the Intellectual Freedom Committee decided that the 1973 version would be maintained in full in the historical file and that it would be made available as necessary. The amended Policy on Governmental Intimidation was adopted by the ALA Council on July 1, 1981.

In 1999–2000, as part of the periodic review of all policies, the IFC reviewed the Policy on Governmental Intimidation and did not recommend any changes.

During the 2004–5 review of policies, the IFC examined references to "citizens" in all intellectual policies to ensure that the use of this term was not unnecessarily limiting. As a result of this review the Committee recommended that "governmental prerogatives which lead to the intimidation of the individual or the citizenry from the exercise of free expression" be revised to read "governmental prerogatives that lead to the intimidation of individuals or groups and discourages them from exercising the right of free expression as guaranteed by the First Amendment to the U.S. Constitution. The revised policy was approved by Council on June 30, 2004.

5.7
Related Policies and Statements

Selected other ALA documents related to confidentiality and privacy are listed below. Links to new or revised documents will be posted to "Information Freedom Statements and Policies" under the heading "Privacy" on the OIF website, http://www.ala.org/ala/oif/statementspols/statementspolicies.htm#privacy.

- ALA Privacy Audit Templates
  http://www.ala.org/ala/oif/statementspols/otherpolicies/privacyaudit.htm
- Guidelines for Librarians on the USA PATRIOT Act: What to do before, during, and after a "knock at the door"? (2002)
  http://ala.org/ala/washoff/WOissues/civilliberties/theusapatriotact/patstep.pdf
- Principles for the Networked World (2002)
  http://www.ala.org/ala/washoff/washpubs/principles .pdf
- Questions and Answers on Privacy and Confidentiality
  http://www.ala.org/oif/policies/interpretations/privacyqanda/

- Privacy Tool Kit
  http://www.ala.org/ala/oif/iftoolkits/toolkitsprivacy/
  privacy.htm

  Introduction
  http://www.ala.org/ala/oif/iftoolkits/
  toolkitsprivacy/introduction/introduction.htm

  Privacy Policy
  http://www.ala.org/ala/oif/iftoolkits/
  toolkitsprivacy/privacypolicy/
  privacypolicy.htm

  Guidelines for Developing a Library Privacy Policy
  http://www.ala.org/oif/iftoolkits/privacy/
  guidelines/

  Privacy Procedures
  http://www.ala.org/ala/oif/iftoolkits/
  toolkitsprivacy/privacyprocedures/
  procedures.htm

  Crisis Communication
  http://www.ala.org/ala/oif/iftoolkits/
  toolkitsprivacy/crisiscommunication/
  crisiscommunication.htm

  Select Bibliography
  http://www.ala.org/ala/oif/iftoolkits/
  toolkitsprivacy/selectbibliography/
  selectbibliography.htm

- Resolution on Radio Frequency Identification (RFID)
  Technology and Privacy Principles (2005)
  http://www.ala.org/ala/oif/statementspols/
  ifresolutions/rfidresolution.htm
- RFID: Radio Frequency Identification Chips and
  Systems
  http://www.ala.org/ala/oif/ifissues/rfid.htm
- Resolution on the USA PATRIOT Act and Related
  Measures That Infringe on the Rights of Library
  Users (2003)
  http://www.ala.org/ala/oif/statementspols/
  ifresolutions/resolutionusa.htm

- Resolution Reaffirming the Principles of Intellectual Freedom in the Aftermath of the Terrorist Attacks (2002)
  http://www.ala.org/ala/oif/statementspols/
  ifresolutions/resolutionreaffirming.htm
- Resolution on the Terrorism Information Awareness Program (2003)
  http://www.ala.org/ala/oif/ifissues/
  issuesrelatedlinks/tiaresolution.htm

6

Guidelines, Resolutions, and Statements Related to the Internet

6.1
Guidelines and Considerations for Developing a Public Library Internet Use Policy
Introduction and Background

L ibraries are a major information source in our society for access to the world of human expression. By providing information across the spectrum of human interests, and making it available and accessible to anyone who wants it, libraries make it possible for individuals to exercise their First Amendment right to seek and receive all types of expression, from all points of view. For some, libraries are the only available access point.

Materials in any given library cover the spectrum of human experience and thought, even those that some people may consider false, offensive, or dangerous. The First Amendment protects each person's right to access these materials, whether the materials appear in print or appear electronically on the Internet. In a unanimous decision, the U.S. Supreme Court held that the Internet, a critical tool for libraries to provide that spectrum, enjoys the highest level of First Amendment protection, equal to that of newspapers and books.[*]

The development of a public library Internet use policy is a very complex process. This document provides a legal overview, a discussion of filters and specific recommendations for developing an Internet use policy. Other information is available to help with this process including "Access to Electronic Information, Services, and Networks: An Interpretation of the *Library Bill of*

---

[*] *Reno v. ACLU,* 521 U.S. 844 (1997).

Rights." (http://www.ala.org/work/freedom/lbr.html, page #); "Questions and Answers: Access to Electronic Information, Services, and Networks: An Interpretation of the *Library Bill of Rights*" (http://www.ala.org/alaorg/oif/oif_q&a.html) and "Libraries and the Internet Tool Kit" (http://www.ala.org/oif/iftoolkits/internet/). The tool kit contains, among other things, a checklist for creating the use policy, best practices under "What you can do" and "Educate! Inform! Promote!" and information on CIPA and the use of filters. Also included is a section of answers to tough questions, as well as many links to additional helpful sources.

Legal Framework

I. Public Forum and the First Amendment

Courts have held that the public library is a "limited public forum."[*] "Limited" means it is a place for access to free and open communication, subject to reasonable restrictions as to the time, place, and manner for doing so. As with any public forum the government has opened for people to use for communication, the First Amendment protects people's right to use the forum without the government interfering with what is communicated there. This is the very essence of the Constitution's guarantee of freedom of speech.

In a public forum, the government is prohibited from exercising discrimination with respect to the *content* of communication, unless the government demonstrates first that the restriction is necessary to achieve a "compelling" government interest and second, there is no less restrictive alternative for achieving that interest. An example of discrimination with respect to content would be a public library excluding resources about abortion or any other subject based upon a moral objection or fear of community reprisal. Resources can be selected on the basis of content-neutral criteria such as the quality of the writing, their position on best-

---

[*] *Kreimer v. Bureau of Police for the Town of Morristown*, 958 F.2d 1242 (3d Cir. 1992).

seller lists, the presence or absence of other materials in the collection related to certain time periods or historical figures, and the like; they can be deselected on the basis of wear and tear, the availability of more current materials, and similar criteria. Libraries that deliberately suppress the record of human thought on a particular subject or topic are in violation of the *Library Bill of Rights* and may be violating their users' First Amendment rights.

2. Definitions of "Obscenity," "Child Pornography" and "Harmful to Minors"

In the millions of Web sites available on the Internet, there are some—often loosely called "pornography"—that parents, or adults generally, do not want children to see. Although sexually explicit, the vast majority of these sites are protected by the First Amendment, as they have not been judged to be obscenity or child pornography by a court with appropriate jurisdiction.

Obscenity and child pornography are illegal, but only a court of law can make that determination. In order to determine whether or not material is protected by the First Amendment, courts must use the tests mandated by the U.S. Supreme Court.

Obscenity must be determined using a three-part test. To be obscene, (1) the average person, applying contemporary community standards, must find that the work, taken as a whole, appeals to prurient interests; (2) the work must depict or describe, in a patently offensive way, sexual conduct as specified in the applicable statutes; and (3) the work, taken as a whole, must lack serious literary, artistic, political, or scientific value.[*]

Child pornography may be determined using a slightly less rigorous test. To be child pornography, the work must involve depictions of sexual conduct specified in the applicable statutes and use images of actual children below a specified age.[†]

---

[*] *Miller v. California*, 413 U.S. 15 (1973).

[†] *Ashcroft v. Free Speech Coalition*, 535 U.S. 234 (2002); 18 USC. 2251 et seq.

Many states and some localities have *"harmful to minors"* laws. These laws regulate free speech with respect to minors, typically forbidding the display or dissemination of certain sexually explicit materials to children, as further specified in state laws.

Materials "harmful to minors" may include descriptions or representations of nudity, sexual conduct, or sexual excitement that appeal to the prurient, shameful, or morbid interest of minors; are patently offensive to prevailing standards in the adult community as a whole with respect to what is suitable material for minors; and lack serious literary, artistic, political, or scientific value for minors.

Libraries should be cautioned that laws differ from state to state, and they should seek advice on laws applicable in their jurisdiction from legal counsel well-versed in First Amendment law. In particular, they should determine whether any "harmful to minors" law applies to materials available at the library, either through Internet access or otherwise. States frequently exempt libraries from coverage under their "harmful to minors" laws, and libraries should specifically inquire whether their state provides such an exemption.

Moreover, libraries should be aware that the legal framework and context of regulation is rapidly changing; in addition to existing federal law, state and local governments may have begun to legislate specifically in the area of library Internet use. As always, libraries should be vigilant about new regulations controlling access to Constitutionally-protected speech.

3. Authority to Enforce Obscenity Laws

It is difficult to know what materials are actually obscene or "harmful to minors," as is knowing when minors are actually involved in the production of sexually explicit materials. The applicable statutes and laws, together with the written decisions of courts that have applied them in actual cases, are the only official guides. Libraries and librarians are *not* in a position to make those decisions for library users or for citizens generally. Only courts have the constitutional authority to determine, in accordance with due process, what materials are obscenity, child pornography, or "harmful to minors."

Filters

Internet filters are mechanisms designed to discriminate with respect to the *content*, but, because of the nature of the Internet and the technical limitations of computer software, they are incapable of blocking sites containing the targeted content without also blocking sites that were never intended to be excluded. As a result, filters both over-block and under-block, excluding a wide range of information and ideas protected under the Constitution while permitting "objectionable" materials to be viewed. For example, filters may block sex education or health facts, political and historical information, or other protected materials. This over-inclusive blocking violates the First Amendment rights of youth and children (see Minors' Rights to Receive Information under the First Amendment at http://www.ala.org/ala/ourassociation/othergroups/ftrf/ftrfinaction/jennerblockmemo/minorsrightreceive.htm), as well as adults' right to access constitutionally protected materials.

The rapid expansion of Web sites on the Internet and the sheer impossibility of keeping up with this growth are factors that limit the reliability of filtering devices. Neither humans nor machines are capable of processing and reviewing everything available, with the result that filters will block some materials while other equivalent materials will remain unblocked.

Although filters have been demonstrated to block access to constitutionally protected resources, federal, state or local governing bodies may require libraries to use them, either to receive funding or for other reasons. The U.S. Supreme Court has held that use of filters does not violate the First Amendment rights of users so long as adults can readily obtain unfiltered access upon request.[*] Minors also retain their First Amendment rights, and even though the library may not be able to completely disable the

---

[*] *U.S. v. American Library Association*, 539 U.S. 194 (2003).

filter, it should be prepared to unblock a site that was filtered erroneously for a minor.

Libraries that use filters should set them to the least restrictive level possible and should train their staffs to respond quickly and effectively to requests for access, especially if adults are not allowed to disable the filters themselves. Libraries also must inform users that they have a right to obtain constitutionally protected resources and instruct them how to gain access to those resources. The U.S. Supreme Court has held that adults' reading cannot be reduced to the level of what is fit for children and the public library, therefore, cannot restrict them to Internet-access computers with filtering software that cannot be disabled.[*]

Librarians and the strength of their commitment to professional standards and values assure that, at least through the public library, the least restrictive means available to achieve the government's interest in protecting children must be implemented.

Specific Guidelines
for Internet Use Policies

The position of the American Library Association is set forth in several documents adopted by the Council, its governing body. The Interpretation of the *Library Bill of Rights* entitled "Access to Electronic Information, Services, and Networks" calls for free and unfettered access to the Internet for any library user, regardless of age. The "Resolution on the Use of Filtering Software in Libraries" and the "Statement on Library Use of Filtering Software" reiterate the U.S. Supreme Court's declaration in *Reno v. American Civil Liberties Union* that the Internet is a forum of free expression deserving full constitutional protection.

Consistent with these policies, which collectively embody the library profession's understanding of First Amendment constraints on library Internet use, the Intellectual Freedom Committee offers guidelines to public libraries, as follows:

---

[*] *Reno v. ACLU*, 521 US 844 (1997).

Adopt a comprehensive, written Internet use policy that is approved by the governing body and includes, but is not limited to the following:

- protect the confidentiality of the library's users;
- set forth reasonable time, place, and manner restrictions;
- set Internet filters to the least restrictive level;
- provide mechanism for allowing both adults and children access to constitutionally protected resources;
- provide information to users on how to exercise these rights;
- prohibit any use of library equipment that violates federal, state, or local laws; and
- provide for the privacy of users with respect to public terminals.

The library also should:

- protect the confidentiality of records, electronic or otherwise, that identify individual users and link them to search strategies, sites accessed, or other specific data about the information they retrieved or sought to retrieve;
- communicate the relevant policies for use of Internet-access computers to all library users;
- review retention policies to ensure confidentiality issues are addressed;
- destroy all unnecessary Internet use records;
- post notices at all Internet-access computers that use of library equipment to access the illegal materials specified in the Internet use policy is prohibited;
- offer a variety of programs, at convenient times, to educate library users, including parents and children, on the use of the Internet and publicize them widely; and

- offer library users recommended Internet sites. For youth and children, especially, offer them, according to age group, direct links to sites with educational and other types of material best suited to their typical needs and interests.

Issued June 1998; revised November 2000; March 2005.
http://www.ala.org/oif/policies/other/internetusepolicy/.

HISTORY

Guidelines and Considerations for Developing a Public Library Internet Use Policy

To guide librarians in developing Internet use policies, American Library Trustee Association (ALTA), Association for Library Service to Children (ALSC), and Public Library Association (PLA) published "Children and the Internet: Guidelines for Developing Public Library Policy." To complement this and other materials to help librarians develop such policies, the Intellectual Freedom Committee requested that OIF write Guidelines and Considerations for Developing a Public Library Internet Use Policy, which was designed to answer specific policy questions from an intellectual freedom perspective. The guidelines are not legal advice but were written to reinforce the principle that libraries, because they link individuals with knowledge, information, literature, and other resources, are the information source in our society and that it is never libraries' role to keep individuals from learning what other people have to say. Written in 1998, the guidelines were discussed by the IFC at their June 1998 meeting and then presented to the ALA Council as part of the Intellectual Freedom Committee's report on July 1, 1998.

In line with the ongoing practice of periodic review, the IFC carefully reviewed these guidelines in 1999–2000, especially in regard to their applicability to the Internet. The IFC revised the Guidelines and Considerations for Developing a Public Library Internet Use Policy for clarity and removed outdated filtering examples but emphasized that filters either are underinclusive or overinclusive. The concepts of privacy and confidentiality were included as important points in any Internet use policy. In addition, the committee included URLs to related OIF and FTRF websites.

As a part of the 2004–5 review of intellectual freedom documents the IFC revised the guidelines to bring them up-to-date in light of the U.S. Supreme Court's decision on the Children's Internet Protection Act (CIPA).

6.2
Related Policies and Statements

Selected other ALA documents related to the Internet are listed below. Links to new or revised documents will be posted to "Information Freedom Statements and Policies" under the heading "Internet" on the OIF website, http://www.ala.org/ala/oif/statementspols/statementspolicies.htm#internet.

- Libraries and the Internet Tool Kit: Tips and Guidance for Managing and Communicating about the Internet
  http://www.ala.org/oif/iftoolkits/internet/
- Questions and Answers: Access to Electronic Information, Services, and Networks
  http://www.ala.org/ala/oif/statementspols/statementsif/interpretations/qandaaccesselectronic.htm
- Resolution on the Use of Filtering Software in Libraries (1997)
  http://www.ala.org/ala/oif/statementspols/ifresolutions/resolutionuse.htm
- ALA Intellectual Freedom Committee Statement on Library Use of Filtering Software (2000)
  http://www.ala.org/ala/oif/statementspols/ifresolutions/statementlibrary.htm
- Especially for Children and Their Parents
  http://www.ala.org/oif/youngpeople/children/

- Lester Ashcim in Cyberspace: A Tribute to Sound Reasoning (2002)
  http://www.ala.org/ala/oif/ifissues/
  issuesrelatedlinks/lesterasheim.htm

7
Statements and Documents Related to Library Resources

7.1
Dealing with Concerns about Library Resources

As with any public service, libraries receive complaints and expressions of concern. One of the librarian's responsibilities is to handle these complaints in a respectful and fair manner. The complaints that librarians often worry about most are those dealing with library resources or free access policies. The key to successfully handling these complaints is to be sure the library staff and the governing authorities are all knowledgeable about the complaint procedures and their implementation. As normal operating procedure each library should:

1. Maintain a materials selection policy. It should be in written form and approved by the appropriate governing authority. It should apply to all library materials equally.

2. Maintain a library service policy. This should cover registration policies, programming and services in the library that involve access issues.

3. Maintain a clearly defined method for handling complaints. The complaint must be filed in writing and the complainant must be properly identified before action is taken. A decision should be deferred until fully considered by appropriate administrative authority. (A sample form appears immediately after this statement.) The process should be followed, whether the complaint originates internally or externally.

4. Maintain in-service training. Conduct periodic in-service training to acquaint staff, administration, and the governing authority with the materials selection policy and library service policy and procedures for handling complaints.

5. Maintain lines of communication with civic, religious, educational, and political bodies of the community. Library board and staff participation in local civic organizations and presentations to these organizations should emphasize the library's selection process and intellectual freedom principles.

6. Maintain a vigorous public information program on behalf of intellectual freedom. Newspapers, radio, and television should be informed of policies governing resource selection and use, and of any special activities pertaining to intellectual freedom.

7. Maintain familiarity with any local municipal and state legislation pertaining to intellectual freedom and First Amendment rights.

Following these practices will not preclude receiving complaints from pressure groups or individuals but should provide a base from which to operate when these concerns are expressed. When a complaint is made, follow one or more of the steps listed below:

a. Listen calmly and courteously to the complaint. Remember the person has a right to express a concern. Use of good communication skills helps many people understand the need for diversity in library collections and the use of library resources. In the event the person is not satisfied, advise the complainant of the library policy and procedures for handling library resource statements of concern. If a person does fill out a form about their concern, make sure a prompt written reply related to the concern is sent.

b. It is essential to notify the administration and/or the governing authority (library board, etc.) of the complaint and assure them that the library's procedures are being followed. Present full, written information giving the nature of the complaint and identifying the source.

c. When appropriate, seek the support of the local media. Freedom to read and freedom of the press go hand in hand.

d. When appropriate, inform local civic organizations of the facts and enlist their support. Meet negative pressure with positive pressure.

e. Assert the principles of the *Library Bill of Rights* as a professional responsibility. Laws governing obscenity, subversive material and other questionable matter are subject to interpretation by courts. Library resources found to meet the standards set in the materials selection or collection development policy should not be removed or restricted from public access until after an adversary hearing resulting in a final judicial determination.

f. Contact the ALA Office for Intellectual Freedom and your state intellectual freedom committee to inform them of the complaint and to enlist their support and the assistance of other agencies.

The principles and procedures discussed above apply to all kinds of resource related complaints or attempts to censor and are supported by groups such as the National Education Association, the American Civil Liberties Union and the National Council of Teachers of English, as well as the American Library Association. While the practices provide positive means for preparing for and meeting pressure group complaints, they serve the more general purpose of supporting the *Library Bill of Rights*, particularly Article 3 which states that "Libraries should challenge censorship in the fulfillment of the responsibility to provide information and enlightenment."

Revised by the Intellectual Freedom Committee, January 12, 1983; November 17, 2000.

Request for Reconsideration of Library Resources

[This is where you identify who in your own structure has authorized use of this form—Director, Board of Trustees, Board of Education, etc.—and to whom to return the form.]

EXAMPLE: The school board of Mainstream County, U.S.A., has delegated the responsibility for selection and evaluation of library/educational resources to the school library media specialist/curriculum committee and has established reconsideration procedures to address concerns about those resources. Completion of this form is the first step in those procedures. If you wish to request reconsideration of school or library resources, please return the completed form to the Coordinator of Library Media Resources, Mainstream School Dist., 1 Mainstream Plaza, Anytown, U.S.A.

Name _____ Date _____

Address _____ City _____

State _____ Zip _____

Phone _____

Do you represent self? ____ Organization? ____

1. Resource on which you are commenting:

_____

___Book ___Textbook ___Video ___Display ___Magazine
___Library Program ___Audio Recording ___Newspaper
___Electronic information/network (please specify):

_____

___Other: _____

Title: _____

Author/producer: _____

2. What brought this resource to your attention?

_____

3. Have you examined the entire resource?

_____

4. What concerns you about the resource? (use other side or additional pages if necessary)

_____

5. Are there resource(s) you suggest to provide additional information and/or other viewpoints on this topic?

_____

Revised June 27, 1995, by the American Library Association Intellectual Freedom Committee. http://www.ala.org/ala/oif/challengesupport/dealing/dealingconcerns.htm.

HISTORY

Dealing with Concerns
about Library Resources

The *Library Bill of Rights* and its Interpretations are all broad statements of policy. Their purpose is to clarify application of the
basic principles of intellectual freedom to libraries. As statements of
policy, they offer general guidance for the resolution of practical
problems, but they are not in and of themselves practical or procedural documents. Yet in the course of applying the principles of the
Library Bill of Rights, librarians frequently encounter pressures and
concerns from those who, consciously or not, may seek to distort the
library into an instrument of their own beliefs. "Dealing with
Concerns about Library Resources" outlines basic procedural and
practical measures for responding to such pressure.

"Dealing with Concerns about Library Resources" is a procedural document. Its goal is to assist librarians in implementing
ALA's intellectual freedom policies; it is not itself a policy statement. Its roots, however, lie in a previous document titled "How
Libraries and Schools Can Resist Censorship," first adopted in 1962
but rescinded by the ALA Council at the request of the IFC in 1981.

The early 1960s saw increased censorship attacks on libraries
and strenuous assaults on the freedom to read; "witch hunts" in
Georgia, censorship of some best sellers, and heated controversy
over Henry Miller's *Tropic of Cancer* were prominent during the
period. In response to this situation, a group of librarians and publishers met in Washington, D.C., on January 5, 1962, to draft a statement on censorship. The committee was composed of David H.
Clift, executive director of the American Library Association; Dan

Lacy, managing director of the American Book Publishers Council; Margaret Dudley, executive secretary of the National Book Committee; Emerson Greenaway, chair of the ALA Legislative Committee; and Archie McNeal, chair of the ALA Intellectual Freedom Committee. The statement this group wrote, titled "How Libraries and Schools Can Resist Censorship," gave support and step-by-step guidelines whereby a library can thwart the censor.

In introducing the statement to the ALA Council, McNeal urged its support, especially in light of the countrywide attempts at censorship. "How Libraries and Schools Can Resist Censorship" was approved unanimously by the ALA Council on February 1, 1962. The statement was endorsed by the Adult Education Association Executive Committee, the American Book Publishers Council, the American Civil Liberties Union, the National Book Committee, the National Council of Teachers of English, the National Education Association Commission on Professional Rights and Responsibilities, and the National Education Association Department of Class Room Teachers.

At the 1972 midwinter meeting of the Intellectual Freedom Committee, the original statement on resisting censorship was altered to include all types of libraries, not just school and public libraries; and "library materials" was substituted for "books." The new document, "How Libraries Can Resist Censorship," was adopted by the ALA Council on January 28, 1972:

> Libraries of all sizes and types continue to be targets of pressure from groups and individuals who wish to use the library as an instrument of their own tastes and views. The problem differs somewhat between the public library, with a responsibility to present as wide a spectrum of materials as its budget can afford, and the school or academic library, whose collection is designed to support the educational objectives of the institution. Both, however, involve the freedom of the library to meet its professional responsibilities to the whole community.
>
> To combat censorship efforts from groups and individuals, every library should take certain measures to clarify policies and establish community relations. While these steps should be taken regardless of any attack or

prospect of attack, they will provide a firm and clearly defined position if selection policies are challenged. As normal operating procedure, each library should:

1. Maintain a definite materials selection policy. It should be in written form and approved by the appropriate regents or other governing authority. It should apply to all library materials equally.

2. Maintain a clearly defined method for handling complaints. Basic requirements should be that the complaint be filed in writing and the complainant be properly identified before his request is considered. Action should be deferred until full consideration by appropriate administrative authority.

3. Maintain lines of communication with civic, religious, educational, and political bodies of the community. Participation in local civic organizations and in community affairs is desirable. Because the library and the school are key centers of the community, the librarian should be known publicly as a community leader.

4. Maintain a vigorous public relations program on behalf of intellectual freedom. Newspapers, radio, and television should be informed of policies governing materials selection and use, and of any special activities pertaining to intellectual freedom.

Adherence to the practices listed above will not preclude confrontations with pressure groups or individuals but may provide a base from which to counter efforts to place restraints on the library. If a confrontation does occur, librarians should remember the following:

1. Remain calm. Don't confuse noise with substance. Require the deliberate handling of the complaint under previously established rules. Treat the group or individual who complains with dignity, courtesy, and good humor. Given the facts, most citizens will support the responsible exercise of professional freedom by teachers and librarians, and will insist on protecting their own freedom to read.

2. Take immediate steps to assure that the full facts surrounding a complaint are known to the administration and the governing authority. The school librarian–media specialist should go through the principal
to the superintendent and the school board; the public librarian, to the board of trustees or to the appropriate governing authority of the community; the college or university librarian, to the president and
through him to the board of trustees. Present full,
written information giving the nature of the complaint and identifying the source.

3. Seek the support of the local press when appropriate.
The freedom to read and freedom of the press go hand
in hand.

4. Inform local civic organizations of the facts and enlist
their support when appropriate. Meet negative pressure with positive pressure.

5. In most cases, defend the principle of the freedom to
read and the professional responsibility of teachers
and librarians. Only rarely is it necessary to defend
the individual item. Laws governing obscenity, subversive material, and other questionable matter are
subject to interpretation by courts. Responsibility for
removal of any library materials from public access
rests with this established process.

6. Inform the ALA Office for Intellectual Freedom and
other appropriate national and state organizations
concerned with intellectual freedom of the nature of
the problem. Even though censorship must be fought
at the local level, there is value in the support and
assistance of agencies outside the area which have no
personal involvement. They can often cite parallel
cases and suggest methods of meeting an attack.

The foregoing principles and procedures apply to all kinds of
censorship attacks and are supported by groups such as the
National Education Association, the American Civil Liberties
Union, and the National Council of Teachers of English, as well as
the American Library Association. Whereas the practices provide

positive means for preparing for and meeting pressure group complaints, they serve the more general purpose of supporting the *Library Bill of Rights,* particularly Article III, which states that "censorship should be challenged by libraries in the maintenance of their responsibility to provide public information and enlightenment." Adherence to this principle is especially necessary when the library is under pressure.

In 1980–81, following the 1980 revision of the *Library Bill of Rights,* the Intellectual Freedom Committee reviewed "How Libraries Can Resist Censorship" and found that the bulk of the document was simply a procedural elaboration and repetitive of other policies. Stripped to its essentials, its main utility was as a concise statement of practical measures libraries can and should take in preparing for and responding to potentially censorious complaints and pressures. At the 1981 Annual Conference, the IFC voted to request ALA Council to rescind the document, which the Council did. Later that year "Dealing with Complaints about Resources," based in part on the former document and on discussions by the IFC, was published as a procedural statement. At the 1983 Midwinter Meeting in San Antonio, the statement was again revised by the Committee and retitled "Dealing with Concerns about Library Resources." This document is the basis for part 5 of this manual, "Preparing to Preserve and Protect Intellectual Freedom."

In line with the ongoing practice of periodic review, the IFC carefully reviewed all statements in 1999–2000, especially in regard to their applicability to the Internet. The IFC recommended only slight editorial changes to this policy. Under point 7, paragraph e, the IFC substituted the word "resources" for "materials," included both materials selection "or collection development," and emphasized that library resources must be neither removed nor "restricted." No changes were recommended in the 2004–5 review of intellectual freedom policies.

7.2
Related Policies and Statements

Selected other ALA documents related to library resources are listed below. Links to new or revised documents will be posted to "Information Freedom Statements and Policies" under the heading "Library Resources" on the OIF website, http://www.ala.org/ala/oif/statementspols/statementspolicies.htm#libresources.

- Coping with Challenges: Strategies and Tips for Dealing with Challenges to Library Materials http://www.ala.org/ala/oif/challengesupport/dealing/copingchallengesstrategies.htm

- Coping with Challenges: Kids and Libraries http://www.ala.org/ala/oif/challengesupport/dealing/copingchallenges.htm

- Workbook for Selection Policy Writing http://www.ala.org/ala/oif/challengesupport/dealing/workbookselection.htm

PART IV

Intellectual Freedom
and the Law

I

Public Libraries and the Public Forum Doctrine

THERESA CHMARA

When we think about the exercise of First Amendment rights we usually think of the person giving a speech, the group passing out pamphlets, or the organization carrying picket signs or banners. In the public library context, however, we need to think about the patron not as speech giver or sign holder but as a person entitled under the First Amendment to receive information or access. An analysis of access to information in the public library context requires an evaluation of four aspects of the library: (1) access to the library itself and patron-behavior rules, (2) access to material in the library and book removal issues, (3) access to the Internet and filtering issues, and (4) access to meeting rooms and display cases. An understanding of what rights are applicable under the First Amendment in each of these areas necessitates an evaluation of general First Amendment principles and public forum doctrine.

General First Amendment Principles

It is well established that the right to receive information is a corollary to the right to speak. In *Board of Education v. Pico*,[1] the Supreme Court considered whether a local school board violated the Constitution by removing books from a school library and in doing so held unequivocally that "the right to receive ideas is a necessary predicate to the *recipient's* meaningful exercise of his own rights of speech, press, and political freedom."[2] More recently, the Supreme Court held in *Reno v. American Civil Liberties Union*,[3] that "the CDA [Communications Decency Act] lacks the precision that the First Amendment requires when a statute regulates the content of speech" because "[i]n order to deny minors access to potentially harmful speech, the CDA effectively suppresses a large amount of speech that adults have a constitutional *right to receive* and to address to one another" [emphasis added].[4] The analysis of what the right to receive information means must begin with an exploration of the library as public forum.

Public Forum Doctrine

There are three types of forums: (1) public forums, (2) designated or limited public forums, and (3) nonpublic forums. Traditional public forums are locations such as streets, parks, or sidewalks that "have immemorially been held in trust for the use of the public and, time out of mind, have been used for purposes of assembly, communicating thoughts between citizens, and discussing public questions."[5] If the government creates restrictions that are *content-based* in a traditional public forum, its actions will be reviewed for constitutionality by a *strict scrutiny* standard. Under strict scrutiny, the restriction will be deemed unconstitutional unless the government can demonstrate that the restriction is necessary to achieve a "compelling" government interest and the restriction is narrowly tailored to achieve that interest.[6] Of course, governments may impose valid time, place, and manner restrictions even in a traditional public forum provided that the regulations are content-neutral, narrowly tailored to serve a significant government interest, and leave open ample channels of communication.[7]

A designated public forum is "property that the State has opened for expressive activity by part or all of the public."[8] Courts have held that "[t]he government does not create a [designated] public forum by inaction or by permitting limited discourse, but only by intentionally opening a nontraditional public forum for public discourse."[9] In determining whether a nontraditional public forum has become a "designated public forum," courts will look to the "policy and practice of the government to ascertain whether it intended to designate a place not traditionally open to assembly and debate as a public forum."[10] Once a court determines that a government entity has created a designated or limited public forum, any content-based restrictions will be evaluated to determine if the government has a compelling interest for the restriction and whether the restriction is narrowly tailored to achieve that interest.[11]

A nonpublic forum is government property that has been reserved for its intended purposes even if used for communication. For example, a public library might utilize a meeting room in its facility for its own purposes without allowing any use of the room by the public. Thus, the room would be used for staff meetings, library reading group meetings, children's story hours conducted by staff, or meetings of the Friends of the Library. Although the meeting room is used for communication purposes by the library, it remains a nonpublic forum. The Supreme Court has held that "[c]ontrol over access to a non-public forum can be based on subject matter and speaker identity so long as the distinctions drawn are reasonable in light of the purpose served by the forum and are viewpoint neutral."[12]

Generally, courts will look to the policy of the entity, the practice of use of the forum, and "its compatibility with expressive activity."[13] Courts will evaluate specific factors in determining what type of forum has been created by the government, such as (1) whether there is a written policy, (2) whether it is applied consistently, (3) whether the policy is based on subjective or overly general criteria, (4) the selectivity of the criteria used to determine access, and (5) consistency with the principal function of the forum.[14]

Court precedents demonstrate that both a public library's policies and its practices will determine the type of forum it has created. Specific application of these principles demonstrates further that different considerations apply in the context of the distinct services provided to patrons by public libraries.

Access to the Library: Patron-Behavior Rules

Courts have held that the public library is a designated public forum for the receipt of information. Restrictions on access to the library itself must, therefore, be evaluated with First Amendment principles in mind. This critical issue was first considered in the case of *Kreimer v. Bureau of Police*.[15] Richard Kreimer, a homeless man, was banned from the Morristown, New Jersey, library for disrupting patrons and because his personal hygiene was offensive to other patrons. The Third Circuit held unequivocally that the First Amendment protects the right to *receive* information and "includes the right to some level of access to a public library, the quintessential locus of the receipt of information."[16]

The appellate court emphasized, however, that public libraries are quintessential public forums for *access to information*, but *not*, unless specifically authorized by the library, for engaging in other types of expressive activities (such as making speeches, distributing pamphlets, and the like). The court found that Morristown Library had "intentionally opened the Library to the public" for "specified purposes: reading, studying, using the Library materials."[17] The court thus held that the library has the right to establish reasonable rules governing library use and that the library's power to regulate patron behavior is *not* limited to cases of "actual disruption." The Third Circuit held specifically that libraries may regulate nonexpressive activity designed to promote safety or efficient access to materials, such as rules requiring patrons to be engaged in library-associated activities, rules prohibiting harassment, and a rule that permitted librarians to remove patrons with offensive bodily hygiene that constitutes a nuisance to others. Importantly, the *Kreimer* case settled before the court had an opportunity to apply these general principles to the particular facts of the case and determine whether the Morristown rules were applied in a constitutional manner to Richard Kreimer.[18]

The principles established by the *Kreimer* case have been applied and expanded by numerous courts. Critically, however, a restriction upheld as constitutional in one library setting may not necessarily be upheld in another. In each case, the courts will evaluate whether the particular library had a compelling need for the restriction. The cases demonstrate the types of issues raised by restrictions on access. For example, in *Brinkmeier v. City of Freeport*,[19] a library patron was served with a notice prohibiting him from entering the library on the ground that he had harassed a library employee in a location removed from the library premises. Relying on *Kreimer*, the district court held that library patrons have a First

Amendment right to access the public library but that the right has some limits. The court held that Freeport's policy against harassment was unreasonable for the following reasons: (1) it was unwritten and broadly stated, (2) there was no definition of terms such as "harassing" and "intimidation," (3) the expulsion was not tied to use of the library by other patrons or employees, (4) the policy did not have geographical limitations in that it seemed to apply to conduct occurring outside the library, and (5) there was no formal or informal procedure for challenging denial of access to the library.[20] Of course, the library employee would have recourse to other remedies, such as applying for a stay-away order through the courts that would prevent the person harassing her from approaching her anywhere, including at her place of employment.

Similarly, in *Armstrong v. District of Columbia Public Library*,[21] a patron's exclusion from the library on the ground that his appearance was objectionable was deemed unconstitutional. The district court held that the standard was unconstitutionally vague and overbroad: "It threatens to compromise access to information and ideas found within the Library's limited public forum by directly precluding, or otherwise discouraging, use of the D.C. Public Library system by persons that Library staff, in their discretion, find objectionable."[22] The court also held that the appearance rule violated the patron's due process rights: "Not only does the vague appearance regulation increase the risk of discriminatory decisions regarding library access, its arbitrary nature and application prevents the type of uniform decision-making required to provide fair notice of what hygiene conditions will be prohibited."[23]

By contrast, the court will uphold exclusions where the rules are objective and precisely defined and the library offers some process, formal or informal, for appeal. For example, in *Neinast v. Board of Trustees*,[24] a court upheld the constitutionality of evicting a barefoot patron from library premises. The district court held that the library was a limited public forum but that the shoe requirement was constitutional. The court held that "[t]he shoe requirement is a valid, content-neutral regulation that promotes communication of the written word in a safe and sanitary condition" because "[a]s evidenced by various incident reports, the Library's floor sometimes contains feces, semen, blood, and broken glass, all of which pose a significant danger to barefoot individuals."[25] The Sixth Circuit appellate court affirmed the trial court's decision, concluding that the shoe requirement was narrowly drawn to achieve the goal of protecting barefoot patrons from harm that might come to them from materials found on the library floors and to protect the library itself from the potential of lawsuits and litigation costs if sued by a patron for injuries sustained while barefoot.[26]

Thus, when crafting policies on use of the public library and its various services, library officials must ensure that the policies are (1) written, (2) objective, (3) consistently enforced, (4) reasonable and related to library use, and (5) accompanied by an appeal mechanism, even if that mechanism is informal.

Access to Library Materials: Book or Video Removals

In addition to gaining access to the physical facility of the library itself, patrons have concerns about the type of information that can be accessed in the library. Book removal issues arise in both the school library and the public library. Decisions to remove materials from either a school library or a public library raise serious constitutional concerns.

In *Board of Education v. Pico*, as mentioned earlier, the Court considered whether a local school board violated the Constitution by removing books from a school library. The Court acknowledged that local school boards have broad discretion to manage school affairs and make decisions regarding curriculum issues but held that the school board's broad discretion over matters of curriculum is "misplaced where, as here, they attempt to extend their claim of absolute discretion beyond the compulsory environment of the classroom, into the school library and the regime of voluntary inquiry that there holds sway."[27] The Court held that "[i]f petitioners *intended* by their removal decision to deny respondents access to ideas with which petitioners disagreed, and if this intent was the decisive factor in petitioner's decision, then petitioners have exercised their discretion in violation of the Constitution."[28]

The principles established by *Pico* have been applied and expanded by numerous courts. In *Case v. Unified School District* No. 233,[29] a federal district court held that a high school in Olathe,

Kansas, violated the First Amendment by removing *Annie on My Mind* from the school library. Although the book had been in the general collection of the library since the early 1980s, the school board argued that the book was educationally unsuitable. Applying *Pico,* the district court held that the school board's action was unconstitutional because the "substantial motivation" in their removal decision was "their own disagreement with the ideas expressed in the book."[30] The court's holding of improper motivation was based on several factors: (1) during the trial, many school board members stated expressly that they voted to remove the book because it "glorified homosexuality" and they believed that homosexuality was "unhealthy" or "sinful"; (2) the school board failed to consider other, less restrictive alternatives to complete removal; and (3) the school board disregarded its own established review procedures.[31]

Book-removal issues also arise in the public library context. In *Sund v. City of Wichita Falls,*[32] the book-removal issue was raised in the context of a public library. In response to a petition signed by three hundred library card holders, the city council passed a resolution that allowed books to be removed from the children's section of the public library and placed in the sections designated for adult books. This mechanism was used to remove two books dealing with homosexuality: *Daddy's Roommate* and *Heather Has Two Mommies.* The court held that the library is a limited public forum (conceded by both parties) and that the books could not be constitutionally removed from the children's room based on the petitioners' disagreement with the content and views expressed in those books. The court held that the First Amendment was violated despite the fact that the books were not removed entirely from the library premises because "the burdens on Plaintiffs' First Amendment rights imposed by the Resolution are nonetheless constitutionally objectionable."[33] The court held that the removal placed significant burdens on the ability of children and their parents to find the books while browsing in the children's section of the library.

As demonstrated by *Sund,* courts have held that the First Amendment is violated even where a governmental entity has stopped short of complete removal of a book. That principle was demonstrated as well in *Counts v. Cedarville School District,*[34] when the Cedarville School District removed Harry Potter books from general circulation in the school library and permitted student access only with parental permission. Parents in the school district sued the school board, alleging that their child's rights were violated by the removal of the book from the open shelves of the library. The district court agreed, holding that the minor's rights were violated by the removal of the books from the open shelves because the books were "stigmatized."[35] The court held, moreover, that having to request the books from a librarian placed a burden on the minor's exercise of her First Amendment rights. The court also held that it was irrelevant that the minor plaintiff had the books at home or otherwise had access to the books because it violated her rights to remove them from her school library. Finally, the court held that the school board did not allege a sufficient justification for the removal of the books in that there was no evidence to support the claim that the books would promote disobedience, disrespect for authority, or disruption in the school.

Cases such as *Case* and *Counts* also demonstrate the importance of public libraries' following their policies and procedures for reviewing book challenges. The *Counts* case began when a parent of two children in the Cedarville School District filed a complaint arguing that *Harry Potter and the Sorcerer's Stone* should be removed from the library. Following procedures for resolving challenges to library materials, the book was reviewed by the Library Committee, a committee of fifteen reviewers that concluded unanimously that the book should remain in the library. The Cedarville School Board—including several members who had not even read the book—then ignored that decision and ordered that all of the books in the Harry Potter series be removed from the library shelves, held in the offices of the librarian, and allowed only to children with parental permission to read the books. In *Case*, the court specifically relied on the failure to follow procedures as an indication of improper motivation.

Access to the Internet: Filtering Issues

The provision of Internet access in the library raises a multitude of First Amendment issues surrounding the use of filtering or blocking software. The Supreme Court established several important constitutional principles related to this critical information source in *United States v. American Library Association*,[36] a challenge to the Children's

Internet Protection Act (CIPA). The act provides that schools and libraries applying for certain funds for Internet access available pursuant to the Communications Act of 1934, amended 1996 (e-rate discounts), or the Museum and Library Services Act (LSTA grants) may not receive such funds unless they certify that they have in place a policy of Internet safety that includes the use of technology protection measures, such as filtering or blocking software, that protects against access to certain visual depictions available on the Internet. Specifically, the school or library seeking funds must certify that it has filtering or blocking software in place that will block access for *minors* to visual depictions that are obscene, child pornography, or harmful to minors. The school or library also must certify that it has filtering or blocking software in place that will block access for *adults* to visual depictions that are obscene or child pornography. The technology protection measure must be placed on *all* computers, including those used by staff. An administrator, supervisor, or other authorized person may disable the filtering software for adults, but only to enable access for "bona fide research or other lawful purposes."[37]

In June 2003, the Supreme Court held in a plurality opinion that CIPA was constitutional. The basis for that holding was that six of the nine justices accepted the solicitor general's assurance during oral argument that adults could ask that filtering be disabled without specifying any reason for the request. Thus, in the plurality opinion, Chief Justice Rehnquist concluded that the statute was not unconstitutional because "[t]he Solicitor General confirmed that a 'librarian can, in response to a request from a patron, unblock the filtering mechanism altogether' . . . and further explained that a patron would not 'have to explain . . . why he was asking a site to be unblocked or the filtering to be disabled.'"[38] The Court's plurality opinion contemplated that "[w]hen a patron encounters a blocked site, he need only ask a librarian to unblock it or (at least in the case of adults) disable the filter."[39] Thus, while it would appear to be impermissible for librarians to entirely disable a filter for minors, librarians may unblock particular sites for them. And, in fact, given that minors have explicit First Amendment rights, it would raise serious constitutional questions if a librarian refused to unblock a site that did not constitute obscenity, child pornography, or material harmful to minors.

Several of the justices in the CIPA case suggested that the public forum doctrine was inapplicable in the context of Internet services in the public library. The plurality opinion suggested that public forum analysis was inapplicable to any selections of material in the library, including materials purchased for the physical collection of the library as well as the provision of Internet service. Thus, the plurality would apply a lower standard of review to the question of whether use of filtering is constitutional—and not strict scrutiny as required by the public forum doctrine. Nonetheless, the question of how the public forum doctrine applies in the public library was not resolved in CIPA because a majority of the justices did not join the plurality opinion.

At bottom, public libraries must remain cautious about using filtering. Ultimately, the CIPA scheme was upheld because it was tied to funding and the government conceded that an adult's request for disabling of the filter could never be denied and did not have to be justified. The Supreme Court also left no doubt that in a case challenging the *application* of filtering, a library would be liable if it did not disable a filter to provide access to constitutionally protected material.

Access to Meeting Rooms and Display Cases

The use of meeting rooms and display cases raises an additional array of issues for public libraries. Similar issues have arisen with respect to use of meeting rooms or display cases at public schools and universities. As an initial matter, courts have held unequivocally that governments need not make their meeting room facilities available to the public.[40] In *Lehman v. City of Shaker Heights*,[41] the Supreme Court concluded that the denial of access to advertising space on a city's rapid transit vehicles to a political candidate did not violate the First Amendment. The Court held that "[n]o First Amendment forum is here to be found," because the city did not intend to open the forum and had restricted it to commercial advertising.[42] The Court held that "[w]ere we to hold to the contrary, display cases in public hospitals, libraries, office buildings, military compounds, and other public facilities immediately would become Hyde Parks open to every would-be pamphleteer and politician" and "[t]his the Constitution does not require."[43]

Once a meeting room or display case is open to the public, however, restrictions on use will be upheld only if the state has a compelling interest and the restrictions are narrowly tailored to achieve that interest. As part of that analysis, the Court will evaluate whether the restriction is objective and narrowly defined. Thus, "[c]ourts have been reluctant to accept policies based on subjective or overly general criteria."[44]

Once a facility is opened for public use, then the exclusion of an entire category of speech on the basis of its content cannot be justified under the First Amendment. Courts have, for example, rejected the theory that public libraries must exclude religious groups from facilities on the ground that permitting access to religious groups violates the Establishment Clause of the First Amendment. The mere fact that a group is religious is insufficient to exclude the group and constitutes exclusion on the basis of content. In *Lamb's Chapel v. Center Moriches School District*,[45] a church group was denied access to a school facility on the ground that it was planning to show a film with a religious theme. The Court concluded the exclusion was unconstitutional because "[t]he challenged governmental action has a secular purpose, does not have the principal or primary effect of advancing or inhibiting religion, and does not foster an excessive entanglement with religion."[46]

An open question remains as to whether a government entity may permit religious groups to *use* a facility but deny access to groups intending to conduct a religious *service*. In *Good News Club v. Milford Central School*,[47] the Court held that it was unconstitutional to exclude a private children's Christian organization from a school facility and reiterated that excluding a group from a limited public forum on the basis that it is a religious organization constitutes viewpoint discrimination.[48] The Court alluded to, but failed to resolve, whether there is a distinction between a religious group's use of a facility to hold a meeting and a religious group's use of a facility to hold a religious service.[49] There has been disagreement on this issue among the lower courts.

There is no question, however, that a library may impose restrictions on use of its facilities, provided that the restrictions are content-neutral and pertain to time, place, and manner. For example, in *Concerned Women for America, Inc. v. Lafayette County*,[50] the Court held unconstitutional a public library's refusal of access to an auditorium by a prayer group, holding that "[t]here is no evidence that CWA's meeting would disrupt or interfere with the general use of the library" and that "[s]hould the contrary prove to be true, library officials may respond by imposing reasonable time, place or manner restrictions on access to the auditorium, provided any regulations are justified without reference to the content of the regulated speech."[51]

In order to advance their avowed mission of serving the community, many public libraries prefer to open their facilities for use by nonlibrary groups but are interested in preventing use of public facilities for business ventures. While that would appear to be consistent with the mission of public libraries, drafters of library policies must be cautious to use narrow, precise definitions in drafting such restrictions. For example, in *Board of Trustees of State University of New York v. Fox*,[52] a university regulation that prohibited use of dormitories for a "commercial purpose" was challenged. While remanding the case for further proceedings, the Supreme Court cautioned that "government restrictions upon commercial speech may be no more broad than is necessary to serve its substantial interests"[53] and that restrictions must not "burden substantially more speech than is necessary to further the government's legitimate interests."[54]

In recent years, public libraries have sought to offer meeting rooms or display cases to the public but also to craft restrictions to exclude groups that might cause a controversy or whose use would result in public disapproval. Courts unequivocally have rejected such attempts. See, for example, the Supreme Court decision in *Cornelius*,[55] holding that "avoidance of controversy is not a valid ground for restricting speech in a public forum" but that "[t]he First Amendment does not forbid a viewpoint-neutral exclusion of speakers who would disrupt a non-public forum and hinder its effectiveness for its intended purpose."[56]

Conclusion

In sum, public forum analysis is applicable to various aspects of the public library. Once open to the public, restrictions on use will be permitted only if the government can demonstrate a compelling interest and if the restrictions are narrowly tailored to achieve that interest. Time, place, and manner restrictions that leave open ample access to constitutionally protected speech may address such issues as hours of operation, disruptions in the library, music playing, costs for copying, Internet sign-up times, removal of damaged books, capacity for use of meeting rooms, and limits on number of days a display may be mounted. Such restrictions will be upheld if they are content-neutral, objectively defined, and consistently applied.

NOTES

1. 457 U.S. 853 (1982).
2. *Id.* at 867.
3. 521 U.S. 844 (1997).
4. *Id.* at 876.
5. *Perry Education Association v. Perry Local Educators' Association*, 460 U.S. 37, 45 (1983) (quoting *Hague v. CIO*, 307 U.S. 496, 515 (1939)).
6. *Perry*, 460 U.S. at 45; *Widmar v. Vincent*, 454 U.S. 263, 269–70 (1981).
7. *Perry*, 460 U.S. at 45.
8. *International Soc. for Krishna Consciousness, Inc. v. Lee*, 505 U.S. 672, 678 (1992).
9. *Cornelius v. NAACP Legal Defense & Ed. Fund, Inc.*, 473 U.S. 788, 802 (1985); see also *Arkansas Educ. Television Com'n v. Forbes*, 523 U.S. 666, 677 (1998) (holding that designated public forums are created by "purposeful government action").
10. *Cornelius*, 473 U.S. at 802.
11. *Arkansas Educ. Television Com'n v. Forbes*, 523 U.S. 666, 677 (1998).
12. *Cornelius*, 473 U.S. at 806.
13. *Id.* at 802.
14. *Hopper v. City of Pasco*, 241 F.3d 1067 (9th Cir.) cert. denied, 534 U.S. 951 (2001) (holding that the city violated the First Amendment when it denied artists access to a city hall display area); see also *Planned Parenthood/Chicago Area v. Chicago Transit Authority*, 767 F.2d 1225 (7th Cir. 1985) (concluding that the city violated the First Amendment when it denied a non-profit group access to advertising space on transit authority vehicles).
15. 958 F.2d 1242 (3d Cir. 1992).
16. *Id.* at 1255.
17. *Id.* at 1259–60.
18. In examining constitutional challenges, a court must determine if a restriction is facially unconstitutional or unconstitutional as applied. A statute will be deemed facially unconstitutional if it could never be applied in a constitutional manner. If a statute is facially constitutional,

then a court examines whether it has been applied in an unconstitutional manner to the complaining party.

19. (Case No. 93C 20039), 1993 U.S. Dist. Lexis 9255 (N.D. Ill. July 2, 1993).

20. See also *Wayfield v. Town of Tisbury*, 925 F. Supp. 880, 884–85 (D. Mass. 1996), holding that a library card was a type of license giving its holder access to the library, deprivation of which infringed upon a liberty or property right requiring library to provide due process before imposing restrictions on the right to enter the library.

21. 154 F. Supp. 2d 67, 75 (D.D.C. 2001).

22. *Id*. at 79.

23. *Id*. at 81.

24. 190 F. Supp. 2d 1040 (S.D. Ohio 2002), aff'd, 346 F.3d 585 (6th Cir. 2003), cert. denied, 124 S.Ct. 2040 (2004).

25. *Id*. at 1044.

26. See also *People v. Taylor*, 630 N.Y.S.2d 625, 164 Misc. 2d 868 (Sup.Ct. 1995), in which the court upheld the conviction for trespass of a patron who violated a ban against playing cards and board games in the library after being unsuccessful in his attempt to have the library lift its ban and despite being requested by the director of the library and three police officers to abide by the library rules.

27. *Pico*, 457 U.S. at 869.

28. *Id*. at 871; see also *Campbell v. St. Tammany Parish School Board*, 64 F.3d 184, 190 (5th Cir. 1995) (holding that in determination of whether a school board unconstitutionally removed *Voodoo and Hoodoo*, a history of Louisiana customs related to voodoo, "the key inquiry . . . is the school official's substantial motivation in arriving at the removal decision").

29. 908 F. Supp. 864 (D. Kan. 1995).

30. *Id*. at 875.

31. *Id*. at 874.

32. 121 F. Supp. 2d 530 (N.D. Tex. 2000).

33. *Id*. at 549.

34. 295 F. Supp. 2 996 (W.D. Ark. 2003).

35. *Id*. at 999.

36. 539 U.S. 194 (2003).

37. The provisions of CIPA are codified at 20 U.S.C. § 9134(f)(3) and 47 U.S.C. § 254(h)(6)(D).

38. *American Library Association*, 539 U.S. at 209.

39. *Id*.

40. *Lamb's Chapel v. Center Moriches Union Free School District*, 508 U.S. 384 (1993).

41. 418 U.S. 298 (1974).

42. *Id.* at 304.

43. *Id.*; see also *Widmar*, 454 U.S. at 267–68: "[t]he Constitution forbids a State to enforce certain exclusions from a forum generally open to the public, even if it was not required to create the forum in the first place."

44. *Hopper*, 241 F.3d at 1077; see also *DeBoer v. Village of Oak Park*, 267 F.3d 558, 573 (7th Cir. 2001) (holding that "[a]ny regulations governing a speaker's access to a forum must contain 'narrow, objective, and definite standards' to guide a governmental authority, so that such regulations do not operate as a prior restraint that may result in censorship").

45. *Lamb's Chapel*, 508 U.S. 384.

46. *Id.* at 395.

47. 533 U.S. 98 (2001).

48. *Id.* at 120.

49. *Id.* at 133–34 (Stevens, J., dissenting).

50. 883 F.2d 32, 35 (5th Cir. 1989).

51. *Id.*

52. 492 U.S. 469 (1989).

53. *Id.* at 476.

54. *Id.* at 478 (quoting *Ward v. Rock against Racism*, 491 U.S. 781 (1989)).

55. *Cornelius*, 473 U.S. at 811.

56. See also *Pfeifer v. City of West Allis*, 91 F. Supp. 2d 1253, 1267 (E.D. Wis. 2000), holding that "the avoidance of controversy is not a valid ground for restricting speech in a public forum"; *Hopper*, 241 F.3d at 1079, holding that "[a] ban on 'controversial art' may all too easily lend itself to viewpoint discrimination, a practice forbidden even in limited public fora"; and *Planned Parenthood*, 767 F.2d at 1230, "question[ing] whether a regulation of speech that has as its touchstone a government official's subjective view that the speech is 'controversial' could ever pass constitutional muster.

2
Minors' First Amendment Rights to Access Information

THERESA CHMARA

The Supreme Court has long recognized that minors enjoy some degree of First Amendment protection. It was well established in the landmark case *Tinker v. Des Moines Independent Community School District* that students do not "shed their constitutional rights to freedom of speech or expression at the schoolhouse gate."[1] In that case, the U.S. Supreme Court ordered a public school to allow students to wear black armbands in protest of the Vietnam War, explaining that "[i]n our system, students may not be regarded as closed-circuit recipients of only that which the State chooses to communicate."[2] More recently, in *American Amusement Machine Association v. Kendrick*,[3] an appellate court considering the constitutionality of an ordinance restricting minors' access to certain video arcade games echoed the Supreme Court's admonition in *Tinker* that minors must have a broad range of information for intellectual growth, holding that "[p]eople are unlikely to become well-functioning, independent-minded adults and responsible citizens if they are raised in an intellectual bubble."[4] Building on the recognition that access to information is fundamentally necessary, courts have held that minors' First Amendment liberties include the right to receive information and plainly extend beyond schools.

In *Board of Education v. Pico*,[5] a school board had attempted to remove from a school library controversial titles such as *Slaughterhouse Five* and *Soul on Ice*. The school board's action did not restrict minors' own expression, as the ban on armbands in *Tinker* had, but the Supreme Court rejected the action because the board was restricting what minors could read. The Court stated that "the right to receive ideas is a necessary predicate to the recipient's meaningful exercise of his own rights of speech, press, and political freedom"[6] and made clear that "students too are beneficiaries of this principle."[7]

The Supreme Court has limited minors' right to receive information in two instances in which adults' constitutional rights remain broader. First, the Court has given public schools significant latitude to restrict minors' receipt of information if the school's judgment is based objectively on the fact that information is "educationally unsuitable" rather than on an official's subjective disagreement with or disapproval of the content of the information. The *Pico* plurality held unconstitutional the removal of books from school libraries where the removal was based on the ideas the books expressed, but it permitted removal of books if officials were motivated by concerns that the books were "educationally unsuitable" or "pervasively vulgar."[8] The plurality also recognized that schools must have substantial discretion in designing curricula.[9]

The second restriction on minors' right to receive information is that states may deem certain materials "obscene" for minors even if the materials are protected for adults. In *Ginsberg v. New York*,[10] the Court upheld the conviction of a magazine vendor for selling an adult magazine to a sixteen-year-old. The Court explained that although the magazine clearly was not "obscene" for adults, the state had acted within First Amendment bounds in adopting a distinct, broader definition of "obscenity" for minors. Because obscene speech enjoys no First Amendment protection, under *Ginsberg* states may completely bar minors from receiving material deemed obscene for them but not for adults. Accordingly, most states have enacted "harmful to minors" obscenity statutes. In *FCC v. Pacifica Foundation*,[11] the Supreme Court restricted the broadcast of speech that was merely "indecent," not "obscene as to minors" under *Ginsberg*, largely because children might hear the indecent speech.[12] The Court, however, has declined to extend *Pacifica* to other media, including telephone communications[13] and, most notably, the Internet.[14]

Moreover, courts have recognized limits on the *Ginsberg* principle. First, the Supreme Court has made clear that states may not simply ban minors' exposure to a full category of speech, such as nudity, when only a subset of that category can plausibly be deemed obscene for them.[15] Second, courts have held that states must determine *Ginsberg* "obscenity" by reference to the entire population of minors—including the oldest minors. One of the grounds on which the Supreme Court distinguished *Reno* from *Ginsberg* was that the "harmful to minors" statute at issue in *Ginsberg* did not apply to seventeen-year-olds, whereas the Communications Decency Act at issue in *Reno* did.[16] The Court went on to stress "that the strength of the Government's interest in protecting minors is not equally strong throughout the [age] coverage of this broad statute."[17] Likewise, some lower courts have upheld restrictions on displays of adult magazines only if the restrictions did not prohibit the display of materials that would be appropriate for older minors.[18]

Minors in School and in the School Library

Although minors do not shed their First Amendment rights at the schoolhouse gate, the Supreme Court has held that students' speech rights are not "automatically coextensive with the rights of adults in other settings"[19] and has generally applied those rights "in light of the special characteristics of the school environment."[20] In *Pico*, for example, although the Court's plurality opinion prohibited school officials from removing school library books based on the officials' disagreement with the ideas expressed in the books, it noted that removal decisions motivated by concerns that a book was "educationally unsuitable" or "pervasively vulgar" would be constitutional.[21]

Likewise, the Court in *Hazelwood School District v. Kuhlmeier*[22] permitted a high school principal to order the removal of certain articles from a school newspaper. The student journalism class that wrote and edited the newspaper had planned to run several controversial stories about student pregnancy and the impact of divorce on the school's students. The principal justified the removal decision on the grounds that the articles were inappropriate for the maturity level of the intended readers, that the privacy interests of the articles' subjects were not adequately protected, and that the danger that the controversial views would be attributed to the school.[23] The Supreme Court rejected the students' First Amendment claims, finding that a lower standard of review should apply when there is a danger that student expression will be perceived as "bear[ing] the imprimatur of the school."[24]

Similarly, in *Bethel School District*, the Court held that a student could be disciplined for having delivered a speech that was sexually explicit, but not legally obscene, at an official school assembly.[25] In upholding the school's disciplinary action, the Court found it "perfectly appropriate for the school to disassociate itself to make the point to the pupils that vulgar speech and lewd conduct is wholly inconsistent with the 'fundamental values' of public school education."[26]

Hazelwood and *Bethel School District* are significant decisions but are of limited application to disputes involving students' speech rights in public school libraries. School officials certainly cannot rely on those decisions to restrict students' speech at will, especially when that speech cannot reasonably be perceived as bearing the imprimatur of the school. Moreover, while courts plainly have given school officials a greater degree of control over decisions related to the school curriculum,[27] these decisions do not directly implicate school libraries, which provide students with both curricular and extracurricular materials.[28]

Numerous lower court decisions have recognized the distinction in *Hazelwood* between curricular and noncurricular speech restrictions. In applying the *Hazelwood* case to other situations, lower courts have applied greater deference to school officials attempting to control curricular speech restrictions. For example, in *Virgil v. School Bd. of Columbia County*, the court of appeals affirmed a school board's decision to remove selected portions of *The Miller's Tale* and *Lysistrata* from a humanities course curriculum, stating that "[i]n matters pertaining to the curriculum, educators have been accorded greater control over expression than they may enjoy in other spheres of activity."[29] In upholding the removal, the court emphasized that the disputed materials remained in the school library,[30] which, unlike a course curriculum, was a "repository for 'voluntary inquiry.'"[31]

Students' First Amendment rights in the school library context, therefore, are broader than those in a class, a school-sponsored assembly, or other curriculum-based activities. In the context of book removals from libraries, courts must make the determination whether the removal is based on educational suitability or is an attempt to impose viewpoint or content discrimination.

Minors in the Library

Recent decisions of lower federal courts have echoed the reasoning and the result of *Pico* and further clarified the rights of minors. For example, in *Campbell v. St. Tammany Parish School Board*,[32] the court of appeals confirmed that "the key inquiry in a book removal case is the school officials' substantial motivation in arriving at the removal decision."[33] Considering the plaintiffs' constitutional challenge to a school board's decision to remove a book on voodoo from the town's school libraries, the court held that a determination of the board's motivation could not be made without a trial. The court observed that "in light of the special role of the school library as a place where students may freely and voluntarily explore diverse topics, the School Board's non-curricular decision to remove a book well after it had been placed in the public school libraries evokes the question whether that action might not be an unconstitutional attempt to 'strangle the free mind at its source.'"[34]

Similarly, the district court in *Case v. Unified School District No. 233*[35] found a school board's removal of *Annie on My Mind* unconstitutional where a "substantial motivation" behind the library removal was the officials' disagreement with the views expressed in the book. The defendants had claimed that the book was "educationally unsuitable," a removal criterion deemed permissible by the Supreme Court's plurality decision in *Pico*.[36] Nonetheless, the court refused to credit the defendant's assertions, explaining that "[t]here is no basis in the record to believe that these Board members meant by 'educational suitability' anything other than their own disagreement with the ideas expressed in the book."[37]

In a case that predates *Pico*, the court in *Minarcini v. Strongsville City School District*[38] held that the First Amendment prohibited school officials from removing *Catch-22* and *Cat's Cradle* from the school library solely because the books conflicted with "the social or political tastes of the school board members."[39] Noting that "[a] library is a mighty resource in the free marketplace of ideas . . . specially dedicated to broad dissemination of ideas,"[40] the court distinguished the removal action from a decision not to approve or purchase certain texts, which the court found to be within the sound discretion of the school board.

More recently, a federal district court in Arkansas addressed a dispute over whether books from the Harry Potter series should be removed from a school library. A parent of two children in the Cedarville School District filed a complaint arguing that *Harry Potter and the Sorcerer's Stone* should be removed from the library. Following procedures for resolving challenges to library materials, the book was reviewed by the Library Committee. That committee of fifteen reviewers concluded unanimously that the book should remain in the library. The Cedarville School Board then ignored that decision and ordered that all of the books in the Harry Potter series be removed from the library shelves and held in the offices of the librarian, available only to children with parental permission to read the books.[41]

Parents in the school district sued the school board, alleging that their child's rights were violated by the removal of the book from the open shelves of the library. The district court agreed. The court held that the minor's rights were violated even by the removal of the books from the open shelves because the books were "stigmatized."[42] The court held, moreover, that having to request the books from a librarian placed a burden on the minor's exercise of her First Amendment rights. The court also held that it was irrelevant that the minor plaintiff had the books at home, had parental permission, or otherwise had access to the books because the books' removal from the open shelves of her school library violated her rights—absent a showing that the books were educationally unsuitable or pervasively vulgar. Finally, the court held that the school board did not allege a sufficient justification for the removal of the books in that there was no evidence to support the claim that the books would promote disobedience, disrespect for authority, or disruption in the school.

Overall, courts carefully scrutinize any decision to remove a book from a school library, imposing stricter constitutional standards than those applicable to curricular decisions. Certainly, the case law forbids any removal action motivated by the school officials' disagreement with the views or ideas expressed in the book. Even purportedly viewpoint-neutral justifications—such as "educational suitability"—likely will be subjected to skeptical, exacting judicial review.

Minors and the Internet

In *United States v. American Library Association*, a recent case considering a challenge to the Children's Internet Protection Act, the Supreme Court plainly upheld the constitutionality of a filtering software system applicable to minors.[43] Importantly, however, the Court recognized that the filtering must be disabled at the request of an adult and that minors also had a right to request unblocking of material constitutionally protected as to them.

The Children's Internet Protection Act provides that schools and libraries applying for certain funds for Internet access available pursuant to the Communications Act of 1996 (e-rate discounts) or the Museum and Library Services Act (LSTA grants) may not receive such funds unless they certify that they have in place a policy of Internet safety that includes the use of technology protection measures, such as filtering or blocking software, that protect against access to certain visual depictions available on the Internet. Specifically, the school or library seeking funds must certify that it has filtering or blocking software in place that will block access for *minors* to visual depictions that are obscene, child pornography, or harmful to minors. The school or library must also certify that it has filtering or blocking software in place that will block access for *adults* to visual depictions that are obscene or child pornography. The technology protection measure must be placed on *all* computers, including those computers used by staff. An administrator, supervisor, or other authorized person may disable the filtering software for adults, but only to enable access for "bona fide research or other lawful purposes."[44]

The Children's Internet Protection Act was challenged in two lawsuits filed in the Eastern District of Pennsylvania. Both lawsuits alleged that application of CIPA in the context of the public library violated the First Amendment. On May 31, 2002, a three-judge panel held unanimously that the statute was unconstitutional. The court's holding was premised on the finding that "[b]ecause of the inherent limitations in filtering technology, public libraries can never comply with CIPA without blocking access to a substantial amount of speech that is both constitutionally protected and fails to meet even the filtering companies' own blocking criteria."[45] The court also concluded that the disabling provision did not cure the unconstitutionality of the statute because requiring a patron to request access to constitutionally protected speech was stigmatizing and significantly burdened the patron's First Amendment rights.

In June 2003, the Supreme Court reversed the holding of the court below in a plurality opinion. The reversal was premised on the fact that six of the nine justices of the Supreme Court accepted the solicitor general's assurance during oral argument that adults could ask that filtering be disabled without specifying any reason for the request. Thus, in the plurality opinion, Chief Justice Rehnquist (joined by Justices O'Connor, Scalia, and Thomas) concluded that the statute was not unconstitutional because "[t]he Solicitor General confirmed that a 'librarian can, in response to a request from a patron, unblock the filtering mechanism altogether' . . . and further explained that a patron would not 'have to explain . . . why he was asking a site to be unblocked or the filtering to be disabled.'"[46]

The Court's plurality opinion contemplated that "[w]hen a patron encounters a blocked site, he need only ask a librarian to unblock it or (at least in the case of adults) disable the filter."[47] Thus, while it would appear to be impermissible for librarians to entirely disable a filter for minors, librarians may unblock particular sites for them. And, in fact, given that minors have explicit First Amendment rights, it would raise serious constitutional questions if a librarian refused to unblock a site that did not constitute obscenity, child pornography, or material harmful to minors.

Conclusion

It is well established that minors have First Amendment rights and that those rights include the right to receive information. Although school officials retain substantial discretion in designing school curricula, attempts to censor access to materials in the school library and public library will not be permitted absent a demonstration that the restricted materials are educationally unsuitable or pervasively vulgar. Although in CIPA the Supreme Court has permitted the federal government to require the use of filtering systems on public library terminals, the Court nonetheless recognized that both adults and minors have the right to access material that is constitutionally protected.

NOTES

1. 393 U.S. 503, 506 (1969).

2. *Id.* at 511.

3. 244 F3d 572, 577 (7th Cir. 2001).

4. *Id.* at 577.

5. *Board of Education v. Pico*, 457 U.S. 853 (1982) (plurality opinion).

6. *Id.* at 867.

7. *Id.* at 868. Other cases in which the Supreme Court emphasized minors' right to receive information include *Erznoznik v. City of Jacksonville*, 422 U.S. 205, 213–14 (1975), (holding that "[s]peech . . . cannot be suppressed solely to protect the young from ideas or images that a legislative body thinks unsuitable for them") and *Bolger v. Youngs Drug Products Corp.*, 463 U.S. 60, 75 n.30 (1983) (criticizing a federal ban on mailing unsolicited contraceptive advertisements because it ignored adolescents' "pressing need for information about contraception").

8. *Pico*, 457 U.S. at 871.

9. *Id.* at 864.

10. 390 U.S. 629 (1968).

11. 438 U.S. 726 (1978).

12. *Id.* at 749–50.

13. *Sable Communications of California v. FCC*, 492 U.S. 115, 127–28 (1989).

14. *Reno v. ACLU*, 524 U.S. 844, 864–65 (1997).

15. *Erznoznik*, 422 U.S. at 212–14 (1975).

16. See *Reno*, 524 U.S. at 864–65.

17. *Id.* at 878.

18. *American Booksellers Association v. Webb*, 919 F.2d 1493, 1504-05 (11th Cir. 1990); *American Booksellers Association v. Virginia*, 882 F.2d 125, 127 (4th Cir. 1989).

19. *Bethel School District No. 403 v. Fraser*, 478 U.S. 675, 682 (1986).

20. *Pico*, 457 U.S. at 868, quoting *Tinker*, 393 U.S. at 506.

21. *Id.* at 871.

22. 484 U.S. 267 (1988).

23. *Id.* at 274.

24. *Id.* at 271, 273 (holding that curriculum decisions are permissible if they are "reasonably related to legitimate pedagogical concerns").

25. *Bethel School District*, 478 U.S. at 685–86.

26. *Id.*

27. See, e.g., *Pico*, 457 U.S. at 864.

28. See *id.* at 860.

29. 862 F.2d 1517, 1520 (11th Cir. 1989); see also n. 3 at 1521 (citing cases rejecting First Amendment claims that challenged various curricular decisions).

30. *Id.* at 1523, n. 8.

31. *Id.* at 1525, quoting *Pico,* 457 U.S. at 869; but see *Pratt v. Independent School District No. 831,* 670 F.2d 771, 779 (8th Cir. 1982) (refusing to allow a school board to strike a short story, "The Lottery," from the school curriculum merely because the story remained available in the school library).

32. 64 F.3d 184 (5th Cir. 1995).

33. *Id.* at 190.

34. *Id.*

35. 908 F. Supp. 864 (D. Kan. 1995).

36. *Pico,* 457 U.S. at 871

37. *Case,* 908 F. Supp. at 875.

38. 541 F.2d 577 (6th Cir. 1976).

39. *Id.* at 582.

40. *Id.* at 582–83.

41. 295 F. Supp. 2d 996, 1000-01 (W.D. Ark. 2003).

42. *Id.* at 999.

43. *United States v. American Library Association,* 539 U.S. 194 (2003).

44. These statutes are codified at 20 U.S.C. § 9134(f)(3) and 47 U.S.C. § 254(h)(6)(D).

45. *American Library Association v. United States,* 201 F. Supp. 2d 401, 453 (E.D. Pa. 2002).

46. *American Library Association,* 539 U.S. at 209.

47. *Id.*

3

Libraries and the Internet

JUDITH F. KRUG

As Internet issues and problems consume more and more librarians' professional lives, the question arises, often in a humorous way, "What did we do before the Internet?" The truth is that we did the same thing before the advent of the Internet that we have been doing since, namely, bringing people together with the information they need and want.

The Internet has not changed that traditional role; it has not changed what librarians do. It has changed only, to some extent, how they do it.

What has not changed at all, however, is American librarians' commitment to intellectual freedom, or the place it holds in librarianship in the United States. In short, intellectual freedom is the heart and soul of the profession.

Intellectual freedom is based on the First Amendment to the U.S. Constitution, particularly the freedom of the press and the freedom of speech clauses. Librarians have interpreted these clauses to mean that all people have the right to hold any belief or idea on any subject and to express those beliefs or ideas in whatever form they consider appropriate. The ability to express an idea or a belief is meaningless, however, unless there is an equal commitment to the right of unrestricted access to information and ideas regardless of the communication medium. Intellectual freedom, then, is the right

Source: This is a revision of an article that was originally published in *IFLA Journal* 26, no. 4 (2000): 284–87.

to express one's ideas and the right of others to be able to read, hear, or view them.

With intellectual freedom as their core value, American librarians have assumed the responsibility to provide, within their collections, ideas and information across the spectrum of social and political thought. Library patrons can then choose what they want to read, or listen to, or look at.

In today's world, information is available in a variety of formats—books, magazines, films, videos, CD-ROMs, sound recordings, paintings, sculptures, and so forth. To this mix, electronic communication, specifically the Internet, has been added. In some key ways, the Internet has changed how librarians bring information together with people.

Previously, librarians, limited by money and shelf space, selected the items that went into their collections. To a large extent, this still holds true. But it is no longer totally true. The Internet is allowing libraries, for the first time, to make the vast array of ideas and information available to everyone—and to permit each library user to act as his or her own selector. This has caused great anguish in certain quarters because some people are convinced that if young people have unfettered access to the Internet, they will be drawn to websites featuring explicit sex. There does not appear to be evidence to support such beliefs, but this lack of evidence has not changed the minds of those who so believe.

These same people also find ALA's policies about children and young people to be misguided. ALA's policies urge librarians to provide all users, regardless of age, with the information they need and want. ALA's position has been willfully misinterpreted to mean that children not only do have—but also should have—access to what is termed inappropriate library materials. In this debate, the material that is allegedly inappropriate is not clearly defined. Indeed, it sometimes appears as if the definition is "I don't like it—therefore, it is inappropriate." Such a label has been applied to material as widely varied as the lingerie ads placed by Victoria's Secret, the images of starlets in bikinis found in *People* and movie star magazines, and information about medical matters (for instance, penile implants) and alternative lifestyles of which many people do not approve. There is no distinction made between "pornography," an umbrella term for material with sexual themes that some people would like to have censored—but, in fact, is legal and protected by the First Amendment—and materials believed to be obscene, child pornography, or harmful to minors, which are illegal. However, "obscene," "child pornography," or "harmful to minors" are terms of law, and only legal proceedings can determine if, indeed, a piece of material is illegal.

In many instances, these myths have been translated into legislative proposals. The first such proposal to become law was the Communications Decency Act (CDA), signed into law by President Clinton on February 8, 1996, as part of the Telecommunications Act of 1996.[1] The CDA was about keeping "indecent" material from anyone under the age of eighteen. It said that if "merely" access was provided to the Internet, there was no liability. But if anyone under eighteen was allowed to view "indecent" material, the provider was subject to fines up to $250,000 and/or up to two years in prison. The CDA put libraries and librarians at risk because the term "indecent," was not defined in the legislation, and without a definition, librarians had no guidepost.

In February 1996, two separate lawsuits were filed challenging the constitutionality of the Communications Decency Act. *American Library Association v. U.S. Department of Justice*[2] was filed after *American Civil Liberties Union v. Janet Reno;*[3] the cases subsequently were consolidated and decided under the title *ACLU v. Reno*. Both legal actions argued three main points:

1. The prohibition of material on the Internet that was "indecent" or "patently offensive" was unconstitutional because these terms were undefined, vague, and overbroad. The legislation made no distinction between material on the Internet appropriate for a five-year-old and that appropriate for a seventeen-year-old college student. In short, it was argued that government cannot limit adults (or nearly adults) solely to reading material that is appropriate for children.
2. There are alternative ways for parents to protect their minor children at home from materials on the Internet that the parents consider inappropriate. Such ways, filters, for instance, would not violate the First Amendment rights of adults and would be more effective than this law. These alternative measures, however, were not considered by Congress, which neither held

hearings nor invited any testimony on this issue before passing sweeping legislation.

3. The Internet is not a broadcast medium and thus is unlike television and radio, on which courts have imposed restrictions that control what content may be broadcast. Rather, the Internet is more like print—a newspaper, a bookstore, a library—because each member of the audience has control over what he or she can access; each has a choice. Accordingly, the Internet deserves the same First Amendment protection as books and newspapers, not the lesser protection granted to the broadcast media.

In June 1996, a lower court declared the CDA unconstitutional.[4] The government appealed, and on June 26, 1997, by a vote of 9 to 0, the U.S. Supreme Court declared the Communications Decency Act unconstitutional.[5]

The Supreme Court said:

1. Adults cannot be limited in their reading material to only that which is suitable for children.
2. There are alternative means to protect children, such as filters for parents to use at home.
3. The Internet is more like the print media than like the broadcast media and deserves the same First Amendment protection enjoyed by print. The Court, in fact, went a step further and said electronic communications may be entitled to even more First Amendment protection than print!

The American Library Association's lawyer called the decision the birth certificate of the Internet. It set the standard by which all future regulation of cyberspace communications would be judged by all other U.S. courts. By a unanimous Supreme Court decision, the freedom of expression on the Internet and access to that expression is protected in the United States.

In December 2000, Congress enacted the Children's Internet Protection Act (CIPA).[6] This act requires public and school libraries that wish to receive certain federal discounts or grants for Internet access (e-rate discounts, LSTA or ESEA grants) to certify that they have in place a policy of Internet safety that includes the use of technology protection measures such as filtering or blocking software to protect against access to illegal visual depictions accessible through the Internet.

In June 2003, the U.S. Supreme Court in *United States v. American Library Association* found CIPA to be constitutional.[7] The Court based its determination that CIPA is constitutional on the assumption that a library will disable the filter at the request of an adult without significant delay and without requiring a reason for the request. For more information about this decision, see "Public Libraries and the Public Forum Doctrine" (part 4, section 1).

The American Library Association recognizes that federal, state, county, municipal, local, or library governing bodies sometimes require that libraries use Internet filters or other technological measures that block access to constitutionally protected information. When this happens, librarians need to work with their governing bodies and attorneys to implement policies and procedures that will minimize the blocking of constitutionally protected information for both adults and minors. Decisions that should be made include:

1. At what level will the filter be set? The least restrictive level is the most efficient since it will limit the number of times the library will have to unblock erroneously blocked information.
2. How will adults request that the filter be disabled? The most efficient way is to provide an electronic means to make this request.
3. How will minors request that an erroneously blocked site be unblocked?
4. How will the library inform adults of their right to request unfiltered access and inform all library users of their right to request that an incorrectly blocked site be unblocked?
5. How will the library inform adult patrons that regardless of whether they have filtered or unfiltered access, it is illegal to use library computers to access sites that have been determined legally to be obscene or child pornography?

Contrary to popular belief, the American Library Association is not against filters. The Association believes that filters are appropriate devices for parents to use at home with their children. When filters are used at home, parents can program them according to their value system and the principles they wish to instill in their children. Providing library patrons a choice of filtered access also may be appropriate in some communities. However, ALA does not believe that it is appropriate for public institutions to require that filters be used to search the Internet. There are several reasons for this:

- Libraries are publicly supported governmental institutions and, as such, are subject to the First Amendment. The First Amendment forbids libraries from restricting information based on viewpoint or content.
- Libraries are places of inclusion rather than exclusion. Despite recent improvements in filtering technology, blocking/filtering software prevents access not only to what some may consider to be objectionable material but also to information protected by the First Amendment. The result is that legal, valuable, and useful information inevitably is blocked.
- The filter manufacturers consider their blockages to be proprietary information and, therefore, will not reveal what is being blocked or how it is being blocked.
- Software developers are making selection decisions based on their biases or beliefs, not on the norms and values of the community employing the filter.
- Filters cannot—and do not—block all of the material that many prefer not be accessible to children. Even the filtering manufacturers admit it is impossible to block all undesirable material. The Web is too vast and changes too quickly for filters to be effective. While research figures have varied widely, there is little debate that filters are not as effective as originally hoped. In truth, filters are merely mechanical devices—and mechanical devices have no judgmental capabilities or decision-making abilities. They are "things"!

For all of these reasons, then, mandatory filtering is not appropriate for libraries.

When all is said and done, how a library handles the Internet is a local decision. Strategies to help libraries manage the Internet in accordance with the First Amendment have been developed. They include:

- Internet use policies that provide parents with choices about how their young children access the Internet in the library

- Codes of conduct that define appropriate use of library computers and the Internet (e.g., no participation in illegal activities such as child pornography or gambling)
- Internet training classes for children and parents to teach them how to do an online search and other techniques that can ensure a positive online experience
- Links to preselected sites for children, such as the American Library Association's "Great Web Sites for Kids" (http://www.ala.org/greatsites/), and search engines specially designed for children, such as KidsClick! (http://sunsite.berkeley.edu/KidsClick!/)
- Links to information about online safety for children and teens, such as "Especially for Children and Their Parents" (http://www.ala.org/oif/youngpeople/children/), GetNetWise (http://kids.getnetwise.org), and safekids.com (http://www.safekids.com)
- Privacy screens on workstations or recessed monitors
- Time limits and other rules for computer use in keeping with the library's mission

For additional information on managing and communicating about the Internet see "Libraries and the Internet Tool Kit" (http://www.ala.org/oif/iftoolkits/internet/).

Librarians' main responsibility is to bring people together with the information they need or want. Neither the format in which the information appears nor the age of the user has much bearing on that responsibility. In fact, Article V of the *Library Bill of Rights* states, "A person's right to use the library should not be denied or abridged because of origin, age, background, or views." The librarian's role never has been, is not currently, and will not be in the future to keep people from the information they need and want.

In today's world, fulfilling our responsibilities presents librarians with a challenge and an opportunity. The challenge, of course, comes from the many people and organizations who have decided they, rather than parents, are better able to determine what information on the Internet is appropriate for all children. The opportunity lies in helping all of our users understand the Internet, its pitfalls, and the growing role it is playing in our lives as we move forward in the twenty-first century. It allows all people to access vastly more and more varied information than ever before in history. With librarians to help them, the public can harness this incredible resource and make it work for all of us.

NOTES

1. 47 U.S.C. § 233 (1996).
2. Decided sub nom. *American Civil Liberties Union v. Janet Reno*, 929 F.Supp. 824 (E.D. Pa 1996).
3. 929 F.Supp. 824 (E.D. Pa 1996).
4. *Id.*
5. *Reno v. American Civil Liberties Union*, 521 U.S. 844 (1997).
6. The provisions of CIPA are codified at 20 U.S.C. § 9134(f)(3) and 47 U.S.C. § 254(h)(6)(D).
7. 539 U.S. 194 (2003).

4
Privacy and Confidentiality in Libraries

CANDACE MORGAN, DEBORAH CALDWELL-STONE,
and DANIEL MACH

L ibrarians have a long history of advocating for the confidentiality of library records and the privacy of library use. Libraries
provide access to information on all subjects, from all points of view,
and library patrons make individual choices about the materials and
information they will access. A lack of privacy in intellectual endeav-
ors when using a library may have a significant chilling effect upon
library users' willingness to exercise their First Amendment rights.
Therefore, librarians recognize that if library patrons are to be truly
free to make individual choices, they must have a reasonable expectation that their library use will be kept confidential.

Definitions

For librarians, the *right to privacy* in a library is the right to engage
in open inquiry without having the subject of one's interest examined or scrutinized by others. *Confidentiality* exists when a library is
in possession of personally identifiable information about library
users and keeps that information private on their behalf.

Historical Basis for Privacy Rights

Recognition of a legal right to privacy is rooted in the experience of
the founders of this nation under British rule. Despite the fact that
British legal theory recognized that a man's house is his castle,

British policies authorized general searches of homes. The use of general warrants to gain evidence to maximize royal revenues and for political purposes outraged many colonial settlers. These writs of assistance could last forever and could be used by any officer on the basis of a mere suspicion. They did not need to be specific concerning the place to be searched or the person or things to be seized. They were, in fact, what we now call fishing expeditions.

Such abuses of authority prompted John Adams to draft Article IX, "Protection against Unreasonable Search and Seizure," of the 1780 Massachusetts Declaration of Rights,[1] the wording of which provided the foundation for the Fourth Amendment, which states:

> The right of the people to be secure in their persons, houses, papers, and effects, against unreasonable searches and seizures, shall not be violated, and no Warrants shall issue, but upon probable cause, supported by Oath or affirmation, and particularly describing the place to be searched, and the persons or things to be seized.

Although the Fourth Amendment guarantees a right to be free of unreasonable searches, the right to privacy is not among the rights specifically enumerated in the Bill of Rights.

It has taken judicial interpretation and legislative action to define the meaning of the right to privacy, which is seen as a penumbral right associated with the Bill of Rights, particularly the Fourth Amendment.

The Right to Privacy in Intellectual Activities

The Fourth Amendment refers to "houses, papers, and effects." In 1890 Samuel D. Warren and Louis D. Brandeis published an article entitled "The Right to Privacy," in which they argued that "recent inventions and business methods" called for extension of the right to privacy to include the protection of the "right to be left alone."[2] Thirty-eight years later, the Supreme Court ruled in *Olmstead v. United States* that wiretapping was not a physical invasion of the home and, thus, did not violate the Fourth Amendment. Brandeis penned a dissent to that decision based on "the right to be left alone—the most comprehensive of rights and the right most valued by civilized men."[3] This dissent marked the beginning of modern interpretation of the Fourth Amendment.

In *Griswold v. Connecticut* (1965), a case that established the right of married couples to obtain prescription contraception and the right of organizations such as Planned Parenthood to provide advice to married persons, Justice Douglas summarized previous cases implying that specific guarantees in the Bill of Rights have "penumbras, formed by emanations from those guarantees that help give them life and substance . . . making the express guarantees fully meaningful."[4] Thus, the First Amendment's protection of the rights to freedom of speech, freedom of the press, and freedom to peacefully assemble have been construed to include the peripheral rights to distribute, to receive, and to read; the freedoms of inquiry, of thought, and to teach; as well as the freedom to associate and privacy in one's associations. These guarantees create "zones of privacy" surrounding the First Amendment, the Fourth Amendment, the Fifth Amendment's guarantee against self-incrimination, the Ninth Amendment, and the Fourteenth Amendment's provision for due process.[5]

The Chilling Effect as a Deterrent to Free Speech

First Amendment rights are considered chilled when individuals seeking to engage in activities protected by the First Amendment are reluctant to do so because they fear the possible consequences. Societal loss and damage to our way of government may also occur when essential constitutional rights are not exercised because of the chilling effect of governmental action.[6]

Concern that government action would chill the exercise of First Amendment rights led the Supreme Court to overturn laws targeting alleged subversive activities in the 1950s and 1960s. For example, in *NAACP v. Alabama* the Court struck down laws requiring the unauthorized disclosure of member lists, recognizing the chilling effect on the right to association, including "economic reprisal, loss of employment, threat of physical coercion, and other manifestations of public hostility."[7] In *Lamont v. Postmaster General*, the Court struck down a law requiring individuals to consent to the delivery of "communist political propaganda" through the mails, upholding the right of individuals to receive publications through the mails without government interference.[8]

The Fourth Amendment and the Right to Privacy

Modern Fourth Amendment law relies on the Supreme Court's decision in *Katz v. United States*, when the Court held that the Fourth Amendment "protects people, not places" and what a person "seeks to preserve as private, even in areas accessible to the public, may be constitutionally protected."[9] The test most often used by the courts to determine whether a right to privacy may exist looks to whether a person has "exhibited an actual expectation of privacy and the expectation is "one that society is prepared to recognize as 'reasonable.'"

In the *Katz* decision, the Court also reiterated that "the person's general right to privacy—his right to be let alone by other people—is like the protection of his property and of his very life, left largely to the law of the individual states."[10]

The Right to Receive Information in a Library

In numerous cases, beginning in 1943 with *Martin v. Struthers*, the courts have ruled that there is a constitutional right to receive information because the value of free speech is diminished if a speaker does not have the right to be heard and listeners do not have the right to hear a speech.[11] The first Supreme Court decision concerning a right to receive information in a library was *Board of Education v. Pico* in 1982.[12] For more information on this topic see "Public Libraries and the Public Forum Doctrine" (part 4, section 1).

State Constitutions and Laws Protecting Privacy and Library Records

Ten state constitutions guarantee a right of privacy or bar unreasonable intrusions into the privacy of individuals.[13] Laws in forty-eight states and the District of Columbia currently declare that a person's library records are private and confidential; the remaining two states, Kentucky and Hawaii, have attorneys' general opinions recognizing the confidentiality of library records. The language contained in many of these laws prohibits any disclosure of a library user's personally identifiable information or information that links a user to the use of a library resource, unless the library is presented with an order requiring disclosure from a court of competent jurisdiction.

These laws provide compelling evidence that the states recognize an individual's right to privacy in records of their library use and that library users have a reasonable expectation that records of their library use will be kept confidential. For information on the current status of state laws see http://www.ala.org/oif/stateprivacy laws/. Librarians and library boards should consult with local legal counsel to determine their rights and responsibilities under state law.

Judicial Processes and Library Records

The confidentiality of library records is not an absolute privilege. There are circumstances when a law enforcement agency or a prosecutor may compel a library to turn over a user's records pursuant to subpoena or court order.[14] This possibility clearly affects fundamental speech and privacy rights protected by the First and Fourth Amendments and can threaten to chill library users' exercise of their constitutional rights.

The case of *Branzburg v. Hayes* established the principle that a threat to First Amendment interests can limit the government's ability to compel the surrender of information for an investigation.[15] In a later decision, *In re Grand Jury Subpoena to Kramerbooks and Afterwords, Inc.*, a lawsuit concerning a bookstore's challenge to a prosecutor's attempt to obtain an individual's book purchase records, the federal court established a balancing test to be applied when a threat to a First Amendment right is raised as a basis for quashing a grand jury subpoena.[16] In such cases, the government must demonstrate a compelling need for the information sought and must show a sufficient connection between the information sought and the investigation before it can obtain an order to compel a party to produce the information. This standard can be applied by courts to determine when libraries must produce user records in response to a subpoena or court order.

Library Court Cases

There are few recorded cases that document challenges to attempts to obtain library or bookstore records through the use of judicial process.

In *Decatur Public Library v. District Attorney's Office of Wise County*, the district attorney, investigating a child-abandonment case, subpoenaed the records of all libraries in Wise County, Texas, requesting the names, addresses, and telephone numbers of all individuals who had checked out books on childbirth within the previous nine months.[17] The police had no evidence indicating that the person who abandoned the child might have borrowed library books. The court quashed the subpoena on the grounds that the subpoena unreasonably intruded upon the library users' right to privacy.

Similarly, the Supreme Court of Colorado held that law enforcement officials could not justify a request for information about a customer's purchases from the Tattered Cover bookstore.[18] The court based its decision on the free speech and privacy rights assured by the Colorado State Constitution. In another case, the Kent, Washington, Police Department, acting without a warrant, seized computers from the Kent Regional Library of the King County Library System as a part of an investigation concerning child pornography.[19] The court, which found that the warrantless search violated the library users' right to privacy, entered a preliminary injunction prohibiting the police department from searching or otherwise tampering with the computers and issued a writ requiring the police to return the computers to the library.

Responding to Judicial Process

Another Washington State case illustrates how one library responded to an overbroad law enforcement request for user records. In June 2004, a patron of the Deming branch of the Whatcom County Library System notified the FBI after the patron noticed words that appeared to be a threat against the country penciled in the margins of the book *Bin Laden: The Man Who Declared War on America*, by Yossef Bodansky. (The note quoted Osama Bin Laden, who said, "If the things I'm doing is [sic] considered a crime, then let history be a witness that I am a criminal. Hostility toward

America is a religious duty and we hope to be rewarded by God.") Soon after, an FBI agent visited the library and asked for the names of all individuals who had borrowed the book. After the library district's attorney told the agent that the library would not release any information without a subpoena or court order, a grand jury subpoena was issued.

The library responded to the subpoena by filing a motion to quash with the court. The motion advanced three arguments: (1) the subpoena infringed on constitutionally protected rights; (2) there was no substantial connection between the information sought and the subject of the grand jury proceedings; and (3) the information was not readily available to the library district because the records were maintained by the Bellingham City Library. In mid-July, the FBI withdrew the grand jury subpoena.

Current Issues

The USA PATRIOT Act of 2001

Passed in the wake of the September 11 attack on the World Trade Center, the USA PATRIOT Act (PL 107-56; Uniting and Strengthening America by Providing Appropriate Tools Required to Intercept and Obstruct Terrorism Act) amended 15 federal acts and 831 federal statutes, providing broad new powers to the federal agencies and departments that investigate crime, terrorism, and foreign espionage.[20] Laws changed by the Patriot Act include the Computer Fraud and Abuse Act, the Foreign Intelligence Surveillance Act, the Electronic Communications Privacy Act, the Family Educational Rights and Privacy Act, the federal wiretap statutes, and the federal rules of criminal procedure.

The changes raising the greatest concern for the library community are the amendments to the business records provision of the Foreign Intelligence Surveillance Act (FISA) made by Section 215 of the USA PATRIOT Act. Pursuant to these changes, court orders and warrants issued by the special FISA court, instead of requiring a showing of probable cause, require only a showing that the materials identified in the warrant application are "sought for" an ongoing investigation to protect against international terrorism or clandestine intelligence activities.

The law permits the FBI to target "any tangible thing," a broad definition that sweeps in library circulation records, Internet use records, and all kinds of electronic media. Any court order issued under the Section 215 amendment automatically contains a gag order forbidding the recipient from disclosing the existence of the warrant or the fact that records or electronic communications were turned over to the FBI. Both the secrecy provisions of Section 215 and the lowered legal standard for the search stand at odds with the heightened legal protections traditionally accorded to library records by state governments.

Section 505 of the USA PATRIOT Act expanded the FBI's ability to use National Security Letters (NSLs), a form of administrative subpoena that is issued on the agent's authority alone, without any judicial review. Like the new FISA provisions, NSLs carry their own automatic gag rule and are issued when an FBI agent seeks user information from the library in its capacity as a "wire or electronic communication service provider."

In cooperation with the Campaign for Reader Privacy, the American Library Association worked to amend or repeal those portions of the PATRIOT Act that posed a threat to library users' civil liberties.[21] In addition, several lawsuits were filed challenging the constitutionality of the provisions of the USA PATRIOT Act that affect libraries. For an update on the status of this litigation see the American Civil Liberties Safe and Free website, http://www.aclu.org/SafeandFree/SafeandFree.cfm?ID=15543&c=262.

RFID and Libraries

Radio frequency identification (RFID) is a technology that uses various electronic devices, such as microchip tags, tag readers, computer servers, and software, to automate library transactions. This rapidly developing technology has the potential to increase the level of privacy for library users, increase the efficiency of library transactions, and reduce workplace injuries. However, consumers, consumer groups, librarians, and library users have raised concerns about the misuse of RFID technology to collect information on library users' reading habits and other activities without their consent or knowledge.

In response to these concerns, ALA Council adopted the Resolution on Radio Frequency Identification (RFID) Technology and Privacy Principles at the 2005 Midwinter Meeting.[22] This resolution incorporated the Book Industry Group's RFID Privacy Principles into ALA policy and urged libraries considering the adoption of RFID technologies to take the following steps to protect user privacy:

- Implement and enforce an up-to-date organizational privacy policy that gives notice and full disclosure as to the use, terms of use, and any change in the terms of use for data collected via new technologies and processes, including RFID.
- Ensure that no personal information is recorded on RFID tags, which, however, may contain a variety of transactional data.
- Protect data by reasonable security safeguards against interpretation by any unauthorized third party.
- Comply with relevant federal, state, and local laws as well as industry best practices and policies.
- Ensure that the four principles outlined above must be verifiable by an independent audit.

It is important that libraries and librarians keep up-to-date on the development of RFID and the privacy issues this emerging technology raises for libraries. The latest information can be found by regularly checking ALA's issue pages on radio frequency identification chips and systems at http://www.ala.org/Template.cfm ?Section=ifissues&Template=/ContentManagement/ContentDispl ay.cfm&ContentID=67766.

Other Current Privacy Issues

This section has covered only a few of the many privacy issues confronting libraries. To keep up-to-date regularly check ALA's intellectual freedom issues page at http://www.ala.org/ala/oif/ifissues/Default883.htm.

ALA Help for Libraries

The American Library Association has developed a series of policies, statements, guidelines, and other tools for libraries to use in developing and implementing privacy and confidentiality policies, procedures, and practices, and in coping with law enforcement inquiries. Useful information can also be found in "Policies and Statements Related to Confidentiality, Privacy, and Government Intimidation" (part 3, section 5 of this book), the Privacy Tool Kit at http://www.ala.org/ala/iftoolkitsprivacy.htm, and ALA's privacy pages at http://www.ala.org/ala/oif/statementspols/privacypages .html.

The Future of Privacy and Confidentiality in Libraries

The fundamental American right to be free from unreasonable search and seizure of personal and private information has been significantly altered by the USA PATRIOT Act, Homeland Security, the attorney general's revised guidelines, data collection and mining, and numerous other government initiatives to prevent terrorism by developing profiles based on the personal characteristics of potential terrorists. The prevailing opinion in the federal government today is that a reasonable expectation of privacy does not exist when an individual gives information to any third party. This attitude blurs the line between intellectual activities and behavior and between public and confidential records even though legislation and judicial interpretations have created and upheld federal and state laws protecting the privacy of many personal records held by third parties, including library, medical, and financial records.

If we agree to a lower standard for the protection of the confidentiality of library records, we face the risk of no longer being able to rely on the subjective test the courts have defined for records that should be confidential—"a reasonable expectation for privacy."

If the public's view of the appropriate balance between security concerns and the privacy of library records tilts too far toward security, we face the risk that the courts may someday determine that society no longer considers it reasonable for state law to protect the confidentiality of library records. This trend would undermine the ability of our nation's libraries to provide access to the information necessary for an informed populace and threatens the future of American libraries as we know them today. Now, more than ever before, libraries must become advocates for the privacy and confidentiality rights of library users. For ideas on how to become a library advocate, visit ALA's issues and advocacy site at http://www.ala.org/ala/issues/issuesadvocacy.htm.

NOTES

1. See http://www.billofrightsinstitute.org/article.php?sid=197.

2. Samuel D. Warren and Louis D. Brandeis, "The Right to Privacy," 4 *Harvard Law Review* 193 (1890).

3. 277 U.S. 438, 478 (1928).

4. 381 U.S. 479, 484 (1965).

5. *Id.*

6. For a comprehensive discussion of the chilling effect and the First Amendment see Frederick Schauer, "Fear, Risk and the First Amendment: Unraveling the 'Chilling Effect,'" 58 *Boston University Law Review* 685, 782 (1978).

7. 357 U.S. 449, 462 (1958).

8. 381 U.S. 301 (1965).

9. 389 U.S. 347, 350–52 (1967).

10. *Id.*

11. *Martin v. Struthers*, 319 U.S. 141 (1943). See also Susan Nevelow Mart, "The Right to Receive Information," 95 *Law Library Journal* 2 (2003).

12. 457 U.S. 853 (1982).

13. States whose constitutions include guarantees of privacy or provisions protecting against unreasonable intrusions into privacy include Alaska, Arizona, California, Colorado, Florida, Hawaii, Illinois, Louisiana, Montana, South Carolina, and Washington. See Timothy O. Lenz, "'Privacy Talk' about Privacy in the State Courts," 60 *Albany Law Review* 1613, 1631 (1997).

14. For information on types of judicial process requests that may be used by law enforcement to obtain library records see "Confidentiality and Coping with Law Enforcement Inquiries," http://www.ala.org/ala/oif/ifissues/confidentiality.htm.

15. 408 U.S. 665 (1972).

16. 26 *Med. L. Rptr.* 1599 (D.D.C. 1998).

17. No. 90-05-192, 271st Judicial District Court, Wise and Jack Counties, Texas, (Letter Opinion) Judge John R. Lindsey (1990). Slip opinion on file with the Office for Intellectual Freedom.

18. *Tattered Cover, Inc. v. City of Thorton et al.*, 44 P.3d 1044 (Colo. 2002).

19. Preliminary Injunction/Writ of Replevin: *King County Library System v. City of Kent and City of Kent Police Department*, Case No. 02-2-17484-1

(W.D. Wash. 2002). Slip opinion on file with the Office for Intellectual Freedom.

20. See http://www.ala.org/ala/oif/statementspols/usapatriotactpages .html, http://www.epic.org/privacy/terrorism/hr3162.html, and http:// www.ala.org/oif/ifissues/usapatriotact/. The newly revised *Attorney General's Guidelines on General Crimes, Racketeering Enterprise and Terrorism Enterprises Investigations* is also of concern to librarians. It can be found at http://www.usdoj.gov/olp/generalcrimes2.pdf. For background and an analysis of the guidelines see http://www.epic.org/privacy/fbi/.

21. http://www.readerprivacy.org.

22. The text of the resolution can be found at http://www.ala.org/oif/ ifissues/rfid/.

PART V

Preparing to Preserve and Protect Intellectual Freedom

I

Essential Preparation

BEVERLEY BECKER

Libraries play a unique role in society: they are the one and only place dedicated to serving the information needs of everyone in the community. As such, they collect a wide variety of materials and information representing the range of human thought and experience. With such a wide spectrum of ideas and information available, it is inevitable that library users will occasionally encounter materials they believe to be offensive or inappropriate. Nonetheless, it is the responsibility of libraries to meet the information needs of everyone in the community. To do so, they must promote and protect intellectual freedom. The best way to do so is by preparing for a challenge before it occurs. Being prepared entails developing formal, written policies and procedures; educating the library board, staff, and volunteers about them—and about intellectual freedom in general; and working to build and maintain a strong foundation of support in the community served.

The first step is to develop written library policies and procedures. Once established and adopted, policies should be reviewed regularly and updated as needed. Putting policies in writing is key for several important reasons. Written policies encourage stability and continuity in the library's operations while reducing ambiguity and confusion about procedures. They show everyone that the library is running a businesslike operation, give credence to the library's actions, and inform the community about the library's intent, goals, and aspirations. People respect what is in writing, even though they may not agree with everything in the library's procedures manual. Written policies give the public a means to evaluate library performance and prove that the library is willing to be held accountable for its decisions. A well-written, board-approved policy will help disarm critics: unfounded accusations seldom prevail when the library's operations are based on clear-cut and timely written procedures that reflect thorough research, sound judgment, and careful planning.

Five policies, at least, are vital for the good of the library and the defense of intellectual freedom: materials selection policy, including requests for reconsideration; privacy and confidentiality policy; Internet use policy; public relations policy; and appeals policy. These policies should have the endorsement of the library's governing body, which will provide even firmer support of intellectual freedom if a censorship dispute arises.

Developing a Materials Selection Policy

The primary purpose of a materials selection or collection development policy is to promote the development of a collection based on institutional goals and user needs. The basis of a sound selection program is a materials selection statement identifying specific criteria for materials to be added to the collection.

A materials selection statement should include both an overarching policy or mission statement describing the philosophy of collection development that will guide selection decisions and specific procedures for carrying out the policy.

Components of a Selection Policy

A good policy statement will discuss the library's objectives in acquiring materials and maintaining services. It will state in succinct terms what the library is trying to accomplish in its program of services and the specific objectives for individual areas of service.

The policy should be derived from the library's mission statement. It is helpful if the role of the library in society (or in the parent institution) is spelled out in the policy and related to the objectives of selection, collection development, and maintenance. The overarching goal may be expressed in the broadest terms. For example, a policy for a public library should include reference to the traditional function of the library in the marketplace of ideas. It could include language like the following: "The library serves a traditional role as a public forum for access to the full range of recorded information within the marketplace of ideas. Collection development shall be content-neutral so that the library represents significant viewpoints on subjects of interest and does not favor any particular viewpoint."

A school library may declare that its main objective is "to make available to faculty and students a collection of materials that will enrich and support the curriculum, meet the educational needs of the students and faculty, and support the intellectual growth, personal development, individual interests, and recreational needs of students."

This may then be broken down into more specific objectives, such as "to provide background materials to supplement classroom instruction," "to provide access to classics of American and world literature," and "to provide a broad range of materials on current issues of controversy to help students develop critical analytic skills."

The policy will precisely define responsibility for selection of all types of library materials. It will name, by professional position, those persons responsible in each area of selection. A public library's statement of responsibility might read, "The elected Library Board shall delegate to the Head Librarian the authority and responsibility for selection of all print and nonprint materials. Responsibilities for actual selection shall rest with appropriate professionally trained personnel who shall discharge this obligation consistent with the Board's adopted selection criteria and procedures." Depending upon the size and purpose of the library, the statement might continue by elaborating on any specialized selection responsibilities, the role of user input, and the like.

In addressing subject matter, the policy will identify the criteria to be considered in selection and how those criteria will be applied to support the library's stated objectives. The criteria may include artistic or literary excellence, appropriateness to level of user, authenticity, interest, cost, and circumstances of use. It is also appropriate to include technical criteria, such as clarity of sound in audio materials. To guide the professional staff responsible for selection, criteria should be spelled out as specifically as possible. Bibliographies, reviewing journals, and other selection aids to be consulted should be listed. Special criteria to be applied in exceptional cases should be clearly stated. For example, a public library that regularly purchases all books on the *New York Times* best seller list, even if these titles do not always meet other criteria, should state this clearly in the policy. A section should explain how the library will treat donated materials and specify that such materials will be subject to the same selection criteria as materials the library purchases.

The policy should directly address problems associated with the acquisition of controversial materials. For example, the policy might state, "Individual items, which in and of themselves may be controversial or offensive to some patrons or staff, may be selected if their inclusion will contribute to the range of viewpoints in the collection as a whole and the effectiveness of the library's ability to serve the community." The document should also include a statement on intellectual freedom and its importance to librarianship as well as an affirmation of the *Library Bill of Rights*.

The library's selection procedures should be described step-by-step from initial screening to final selection. The procedures should provide for coordination among departments and professional staff, for handling recommendations from library users, and for review of existing material. Any special procedures pertinent to collection development should be spelled out precisely in the materials selection statement. Some items to consider are sponsored materials, expensive or fragile materials, ephemeral materials, jobbers and salespersons, distribution of free materials, and handling of special collections. The document should review procedures for collection maintenance.

Finally, occasional objections to materials will be made despite the quality of the selection process. The procedure for review of challenged materials in response to expressed concerns of library users should be stated clearly. The procedure should establish a fair framework for registering complaints while defending the principles of intellectual freedom, the library user's right of access, and professional responsibility and integrity. Each specific step to be taken when a request for reconsideration is made, and all possible avenues of appeal, should be listed.

Preparation of a complete statement requires a great deal of work, but is well worth the effort. Having well-prepared, written policies and procedures will be invaluable should a challenge arise.

Procedures for Handling Complaints

All librarians must be aware that at some time there will be complaints about library service—and sometimes these complaints will center around a particular book, magazine, or other item that the library distributes. What should one do when a complaint of this kind is made? Handling any type of complaint about library operations requires a courteous and calm approach. Above all, complainants must know that their objections will be given serious consideration and that interest in the library is welcome. Complainants should be listened to courteously and invited to file a complaint in writing if the problem cannot be resolved through informal discussion. If the complaint comes by letter, it should be acknowledged promptly. In either case, the complainant should be offered a prepared questionnaire to be submitted formally.

There are a number of advantages in having a complaint procedure available. First, knowing that a response is ready and that a procedure is to be followed, the librarian will be relieved of much of the initial panic that inevitably strikes when confronted by an outspoken and perhaps irate library patron. Also, the complaint form asks complainants to state their objections in logical, unemotional terms, thereby allowing the librarian to evaluate the merits of the objections. In addition, the form benefits the complainant. When citizens with complaints are asked to follow an established procedure for lodging their objections, they feel assured they are being properly heard and that their objections will be considered.

As soon as the complaint has been filed, the objections should be reviewed. The review should consist of specific steps, although the number will vary somewhat according to the individual library involved. Simultaneous with the review, the governing body (i.e., board of trustees, school board, etc.) should be routinely notified that a formal complaint has been made.

First, the person or committee that selected the item, or an ad hoc committee, should evaluate the original reasons for the purchase. The objections should be considered based on the library's materials selection statement, the principles of the *Library Bill of Rights*, and the opinions of the various reviewing sources used in materials selection. If the materials selection statement is sufficiently detailed to function as a guide for selection decisions, it should not be difficult to make a logical, strong response to the objections.

Second, the objections and the response should be forwarded to the acquisitions librarian who has final responsibility for selecting materials, and who, in turn, should review the response and if necessary either add relevant comments or return the response to the individual or committee for further clarification. After the acquisitions librarian's review, the person designated in the library's policy can send a written response to the complainant.

It is critical that the review process be as objective as possible. If the challenged item does not meet the library's own criteria for selection, the library must be ready to acknowledge that the material is indeed unsuitable and withdraw it from the collection. If, on the other hand, as is most often the case, the material does meet the selection criteria and is deemed suitable for the collection, it is the responsibility of the library staff to respond to the complaint clearly and precisely. This response also should inform the complainant how to pursue the matter further. If the complainant is not satisfied, the person designated by library policy should respond to the complainant promptly with an explanation of the library's decision and information about the next step available.

If the complainant still feels that the problem has been dealt with inadequately, the complainant may make a final appeal (within the structure of the library) to the governing body of the institution. This body will take appropriate action—for example, conduct a public hearing—according to the established procedures for such appeals. It must be emphasized, however, that requests for action from the governing body should not be routine; such requests are best avoided by an adequate initial response to the complaint.

At each step of this process, the utmost courtesy toward and respect for the complainant should be maintained. There is no reason for a librarian to become defensive when a complaint is made. Not only is this counterproductive, but it runs counter to library efforts to encourage user involvement and the First Amendment's guarantee of the right to petition the government for a redress of grievances.

The review procedure, including the written questionnaire, should be designed not only as a defense against potential censorship but also as a means to facilitate constructive dialogue. While these procedures do offer the library a defense against arbitrary attacks, they should never be permitted to degenerate into a bureaucratic smokescreen. In other words, the library should welcome constructive input even as it maintains firm barriers against censorship.

For further information, see "Challenged Materials" (part 2, section 2.5) and "Dealing with Concerns about Library Resources" (part 3, section 7.1).

Conducting a Challenge Hearing

Challenges to materials only occasionally reach the stage of a full-blown administrative hearing; often they are resolved at an earlier step in the challenge resolution process. When a hearing is necessary, however, certain important dos and don'ts should be observed.

The challenge process begins when someone objects to materials in a library collection. At this point, providing (1) an explanation of selection procedures, (2) a copy of the selection policy, and (3) a copy of the reconsideration or complaint form will often resolve the concern. A complainant sometimes may not return the reconsideration form because he or she sees the logic of the selection process that emphasizes intellectual freedom and due process. The complainant tends to be satisfied in registering a concern and knowing the library is taking the concern seriously.

There are some, however, who will wish to follow through on the procedures established in the selection policy approved by the governing authority for handling complaints. To activate the reconsideration procedure, a complaint should be in writing. In fact, the written and approved selection policy should state that to best serve the interests of all concerned, anonymous or unwritten complaints are not honored and that action occurs only when the reconsideration or complaint form has been returned. When a written complaint is filed, the reconsideration committee, usually comprised of representatives of all library users and the librarian (often, all are library staff—the actual composition of the committee is up to the individual institution), is formed. The committee should then undertake the following:

1. Read, view, or listen to the challenged material in its entirety.

2. Review the selection process and the criteria for selection.
3. Check reviews and recommended lists to determine the opinions of experts and critics.
4. Meet to discuss the challenge.
5. Make a recommendation to the administrator on removal, retention, or replacement.

Before the Hearing

After a formal, written request for reconsideration has been submitted and reviewed and a recommendation for retention or removal has been made, the complainant should be notified of the committee's decision. At the same time, the procedure for appealing the decision also should be provided. The appeal may involve a hearing by a school board, a board of trustees, or a city or county board of commissioners or council. (The selection policy should clearly identify the chain of command.) The appeal also must be in writing in order for the chair of the governing authority to place it on the agenda for the next meeting. The librarian should follow up on this step to make certain the presiding officer is aware of the policies and procedures that should be followed, including open meetings laws and the agenda. Normally, the board conducts a challenge hearing that provides the forum for the complainant to air his or her objections to the title in the collection and the recommendation of the reconsideration committee. The library's attorney should be kept informed and, if appropriate, involved in this process.

A hearing on challenged material is serious and often lengthy. Decide in advance on a length of time for the entire hearing. Have definite beginning and ending times.

The hearing should be announced well in advance. Indicate in an announcement or news release that an open hearing is being held and that the public is invited. Try to obtain full coverage by the local press, radio, and television. Prepare a news release to ensure that the media have the facts correct. Deliver copies of the library's selection policies to them along with a copy of the *Library Bill of Rights*. These policies, of course, should include procedures for handling complaints.

Seek help and advice from your state intellectual freedom committee, local and state colleges and universities, educational groups, teachers' professional organizations and coalitions, and the ALA Office for Intellectual Freedom (OIF). In addition, many nonlibrary groups have committees on intellectual freedom, freedom of speech, or academic freedom. Even when representatives from these groups cannot be present, written resolutions of support can be helpful.

Find people who will be willing to speak in support of the freedom to read, view, and listen. The best spokespersons in hearings tend to be attorneys, ministers, people from the news media, educators, and, of course, librarians. The audience response is usually more favorable to persons from the local community than to people brought in from outside. Student speakers also are effective. They speak from the heart and have no vested interest other than maintaining their freedom of choice guaranteed by the Constitution.

Long before a hearing, the library's attorney and members of the advisory board, the reconsideration committee, and the governing board should have become well schooled in the principles and procedures of intellectual freedom. It is the responsibility of the librarian to accomplish this, and doing so will ensure board support when a challenge hearing is necessary.

The Hearing

As people arrive for the hearing, they should be given a copy of the selection policy and the *Library Bill of Rights*. One or more persons should be stationed at the entrance to sign in people wishing to speak. Request that they identify the side on which they will be speaking. If at all possible, attempt to ensure that there will be a balanced number of speakers on both sides.

Begin the hearing on time. The chair of the governing board should preside, as at any other business meeting. After calling the meeting to order, he or she should explain the procedures to be followed at the meeting and the process followed thus far for reconsideration of the material. The board should announce at the beginning of the hearing that it will issue its decision at the next regularly scheduled meeting and that the purpose of the current meeting is simply to hear all sides of the issue. Speakers should be allowed to speak in the order they signed in. Limit each speaker to a specific amount of time, and appoint a timekeeper in advance. No participant should be allowed to speak a second time until everyone registered has been heard once. It is extremely important to adhere strictly both to the order of the speakers and to the time limits.

After the Hearing

The board should announce its decision publicly at its next regularly scheduled meeting. The agenda should include an item showing that the board will announce its decision, but the decision itself should not be released before the meeting. The usual notices and publication of the agenda will alert the public; news releases also may be used to ensure coverage and attendance at the meeting, if desired. Whatever the board's decision, the principles of the *Library Bill of Rights* should be reiterated, and the agreement of the decision with those principles should be explained. A very brief statement of the reason for the decision also should be made (e.g., "We have concluded that the material meets our selection criteria and will be retained without restriction").

By following this advice, the library board will be able to conduct a successful challenge hearing and improve the library's image in the process.

Developing an Internet Use Policy

Libraries should adopt and implement written Internet use policies in the same way they adopt other library use and access policies. A brief set of suggestions for developing an Internet policy follows. Librarians also should review Guidelines and Considerations for Developing a Public Library Internet Use Policy (part 3, section 6.1), prepared by the Intellectual Freedom Committee in June 1998 and updated in March 2005.

The Internet use policy should be short, reflecting the library's mission statement, other access policies, and the community's needs. It may stand on its own or serve as an addition to existing library policy. Either way, it should incorporate the ideas in the *Library Bill of Rights* and speak to access for all.

Policies will vary according to the individual library's mission. A typical policy will include a purpose statement, a code of conduct

—including specific rules and consequences for violating those rules, and a statement of responsibility.

A purpose statement should clarify that the library provides Internet access in support of its mission to meet the information needs of its community. This statement should affirm the library's stand on intellectual freedom and support of the *Library Bill of Rights*.

The code of conduct should establish reasonable time, place, and manner restrictions. It should include specific dos and don'ts, and expressly prohibit any use of library equipment for illegal activity.

Penalties for violating the policy must be clearly stated. Those penalties may include loss of computer privileges or even criminal prosecution. It is important to consider the need for due process in handling violations. Patrons should be notified of alleged violations and allowed to respond as they would to any other charge of misconduct.

A statement on privacy should be incorporated into the code of conduct or presented on its own. It should remind patrons to protect their own privacy while online and to respect the privacy of other library patrons.

A statement of responsibility should communicate clearly that individuals are responsible for the information they access online and that parents are responsible for their children. It should note that the library cannot guarantee the accuracy of information on the Internet.

Legal counsel should review the policy. A general discussion of the legal considerations surrounding Internet access in public libraries is available on the Freedom to Read Foundation website (http://www.ala.org/internetfilteringmemo.html).

Finally, the governing board should approve the Internet use policy. Make sure the board understands why the policy is needed and its implications. Keeping the board informed will encourage its support in case of future controversy. As always, review the policy regularly and update it as needed.

It is important to keep the policy simple, avoid jargon, and make sure the language is easy to read and understand. It will be worthwhile to involve the library staff, board, and Friends group in the policy-writing process.

Communicate the relevant policies for use of Internet-access computers to all library users, and post notices on all Internet-access computers that use of library equipment to access the illegal materials specified in the Internet use policy is prohibited.

In addition to developing an Internet use policy, libraries may discourage controversy by implementing programs and policies that address community concerns about the Web. Libraries should teach children, young people, and adults how to use the Internet and how to be critical users of information. Consider offering Internet training classes for all library users. Classes should cover the importance of intellectual freedom, how to search the Internet effectively, how to judge the validity of a website, and privacy and safety issues related to online searching. A good reference page to use in this training is "Especially for Children and Their Parents" (http://www.ala.org/oif/youngpeople/children/).

Whether the library faces challenges to print materials, videos, Internet access, or any other library resource, making these essential preparations—having written policies and procedures in place; making the library staff, board, and community aware of those policies and the underlying philosophy; and educating the entire community about the importance of intellectual freedom—will discourage censorship and ensure the best possible outcome to any challenge.

2

Communicating the Intellectual Freedom Message

LINDA K. WALLACE with LARRA CLARK

Libraries are democracy in action. For people of all ages and backgrounds, they provide free and open access to a spectrum of ideas and viewpoints that is often taken for granted—until it is challenged. Communicating the library's role in upholding intellectual freedom for all people should be of central concern to every library and librarian.

Highly publicized concerns about Internet access in libraries, challenges to books like *The Chocolate War*, and encroachments on readers' privacy have added urgency to the ongoing need to communicate about this aspect of the library's mission. A proactive public relations program designed to educate about the role of libraries and to advocate the importance of free access to information is the best way to address such concerns. This effort should be a key component of the library's overall communications program.

Developing an effective communications plan on intellectual freedom begins with an analysis of social and political attitudes and forces at the local level and how these relate to national trends. Other key elements also need to be identified.

The Audience

Who needs to hear the intellectual freedom message? Examples of key audiences are parents, teachers, government and religious leaders, members of the media, and business and labor groups. Be sure to include internal audiences—library users, staff, trustees, and Friends groups. Do not assume that anyone knows or understands what intellectual freedom is or the role of libraries and librarians in supporting it. It is also important to identify those who are potential supporters of censorship. What are their principal concerns? Knowing the philosophies and beliefs that threaten intellectual freedom will help the library in developing effective messages and engaging in meaningful dialogue. Also be sure to identify potential allies—individuals and groups who support civil liberties, the library, and its role in ensuring intellectual freedom. Identifying target audiences can save time and money. It also can increase effectiveness by providing a clear focus for your public relations efforts. Although some key audiences will remain the same, others may vary with time and circumstance.

The Message

The essence of a successful communications effort is a clear and consistent message. Try to use simple, clear language that is easily understood. The key message may be adapted for various audiences with slight modifications in wording or by changing the talking points and examples used. For example, the words "intellectual freedom" may resonate with some well-informed audiences, but talking about the "freedom to read, hear, or receive information" may be more appropriate for others.

Once you have defined the message, develop a message sheet that includes the key message, supporting points, facts and examples, and also sample questions and answers. The message sheet is an essential tool for designated spokespeople and should be shared with library staff, trustees, and advocates to support them in communicating the intellectual freedom message to library users, friends, neighbors, and others. It also provides a basis for speeches, fact sheets, brochures, and other communications and helps to ensure consistency in delivering the message.[1]

In gathering and preparing information, it is important to avoid language that is negative or judgmental. The American Library Association discourages all practices that involve the prejudgment and labeling of groups or individuals as censors. Libraries do not blacklist. It is important to acknowledge concerns as genuine and to address with respect those who express concerns or raise challenges.

Spokespeople

Effective communications depends on effective spokespeople. Because intellectual freedom is a complex and sometimes sensitive issue, it is particularly important to have knowledgeable, skilled spokespeople. And it is critical for speaking engagements and radio and television shows, where personal appearance and vocal technique are key to delivering the message successfully.

Although the library director or board president is generally a library's official spokesperson, heads of departments, such as children's or collection development, may be called on in their area of expertise. The president of the Friends or library advocates network also may be asked for comment. All library staff, trustees, and Friends should know the procedures for dealing with questions from the media and public, whether it is referring questions directly to designated spokespeople or to the library's public relations staff.

Some people are gifted speakers, but they may not be comfortable in high-pressure situations. Role-playing questions and answers should be part of the preparation process. In some cases, particularly those involving controversy, professional media training for designated spokespeople is a wise investment. You may also wish to organize a network of local advocates who are willing to speak out on intellectual freedom issues.[2] Allies, particularly those from local businesses, churches, and community organizations, lend power and extend the reach of your message.

Delivering the Message

Once you have identified key audiences and defined your key message, the next step is to identify communications strategies. The mass media—newspapers, radio, and television—are generally considered the most powerful because of their effectiveness in reaching large numbers of people. But in every community and state, there are other opportunities that may, in fact, be equally or more effective. These include the Internet, speaking engagements, or community newsletters and other publications.

Speaking engagements and newsletters are particularly effective ways to reach key audiences who share particular interests and concerns. Many groups are looking for speakers to address timely topics and how they relate to their communities or campuses. Simply send a letter or make a phone call to program chairs of groups you wish to target. Proactive outreach about new library policies, the USA PATRIOT Act, or special events like Banned Books Week can provide a forum for getting out intellectual freedom messages in an educational, rather than crisis, mode. A draft script, which includes the library's key message and talking points, should be provided for speakers. The script should be tailored to address the concerns of particular audiences, such as business owners, clergy, teachers, or parents.

Be sure to include a section on the library's website about intellectual freedom and library policies. Make sure contact information is provided prominently as well, so members of the media can find the appropriate library staff quickly if they have questions. Ask partner groups to post articles or banners with links to the library's web page. Create an electronic mailing list for those who wish to receive action alerts and updates on intellectual freedom issues. The library's newsletter, annual report, and other publications provide additional opportunities for educating about intellectual freedom, as do brochures created for specific audiences.

Recruiting other organizations that share an interest in First Amendment issues as allies is another effective strategy. Potential supporters might include law, journalism, education, and other professional or advocacy groups. Building a coalition of groups focused on a joint concern can be particularly effective in gaining credibility and influence with legislators and other elected officials.

Although a coalition can be more powerful, it requires additional communication and coordination to make sure the library message does not become lost. Make sure everyone has consistent messages and determine which speakers might fit best with which audiences to maximize your group effort. If doing media in coalition, be sure different partners are not calling the same reporters or producers because this will make you look disorganized and undermine your case.

Special events or promotions, such as Banned Books Week: Celebrating the Freedom to Read, sponsored by the American

Library Association and other concerned groups during the last week of September, provide opportunities to promote public understanding at the local level. Posters and a resource guide are available (see the Banned Books Week website at http://www.ala .org/bbooks/). National Library Week in April and Freedom of Information Day on March 16 provide other opportunities.[3] Planning local events in connection with these national observances can help attract media interest.

Programs and workshops directed at students, parents, educators, and other groups are excellent ways to communicate and educate about intellectual freedom issues. These can be on a wide range of topics, such as guiding your child on the Internet, helping your child select good books, or the future of the First Amendment. Special workshops also may be held for trustees, staff, and Friends to familiarize them with the concept of intellectual freedom and the library's role.

When deciding which strategies to use, consider the following:

Who is the audience and what is the key message for that audience?

What is the best way to convey the information to the target audience—radio, television, direct mail, other? What kind of image do you want to project? Will that image be an effective part of your total communications effort?

When is the deadline? Will your message be distributed in time to be effective?

Why is this the best strategy for this audience?

How much will it cost? Is this the most effective use of available funds?

Working with the Media

Because of its omnipresence in our lives, outreach to the media must be a key element in developing a public relations program. Journalists, in general, understand First Amendment issues and readily cover challenges to the public's right of access to library materials. Their support should never be assumed, however.

Preparation is key to dealing successfully with the media on intellectual freedom or any other issue. Read, listen, and watch news coverage to get a feel for how First Amendment and access issues are covered, and look for opportunities to communicate your message. Note the names of contacts who are (or are not) receptive to the intellectual freedom message. Make a list of media in your community or state. Be sure to include producers of radio and television talk shows as well as news and feature editors of newspapers and news assignment editors for radio and television.

Remember, regardless of their sympathies, reporters are paid to ask the tough questions their editors/readers/viewers/listeners want answered. Make sure you have a clear message and spokespeople prepared to deliver it. Also be prepared to provide supporting documents, copies of the library's intellectual freedom policies, fact sheets, and other documents that provide background and support for your message.

In dealing with members of the media, an effort should be made to build relationships based on trust and openness. Reporters are far more likely to give the library's message fair treatment if they feel they are being treated honestly and respectfully. When contacted by the media, gather as much information as you can about what they need and what their deadline is, then be sure to get back to them as quickly as possible. Always make time, however, to prepare an answer. Taking ten minutes to review a message sheet can make a critical difference in how well the message is communicated. Tell the reporter that you or a spokesperson will call back at a given time, and do so promptly. Avoid the infamous words "No comment." If you truly cannot comment, give a brief explanation: "I'm sorry I can't answer that question. I'll let you know as soon as I can." Or, "I'm sorry I can't answer that. Our board is still discussing the issue."

Bridging—quickly answering a question and then transitioning to your key message—is an important media technique that you should be aware of and include in any professional media training. Many people think that media spokespeople are successful if they can dodge tough questions, but the best way to be successful is to answer questions simply and honestly and then move quickly back to your key message. Every question is an opportunity to restate your case and educate.[4]

There are many ways of reaching out to the media. The most common is the press release highlighting an event or announcement of wide public interest. Begin with the most critical information in the first paragraph, with facts of lesser importance placed in descending order. Make sure your contact name and telephone number are included prominently. Op-eds and letters to the editor provide opportunities for readers to express their views. Intellectual freedom advocates can use these forums to educate others about issues of concern in either national or local news. Op-eds are guest opinion columns that appear opposite a paper's own editorials. Call the editor of the op-ed or editorial page and explain your idea briefly. Ask about length—most op-eds are about 750 words.[5] Letters are generally 200 to 300 words and to the point. Many newspapers also provide editorial guidelines online.

The editorial board meeting is an opportunity to solicit the support of a newspaper. Call the editor of the editorial page to ask for an appointment and explain why. (Some radio and television stations may offer support, too.) Prepare ahead of time to make a fifteen-minute presentation and to answer difficult questions. Editorial board meetings generally run around an hour and include key members of both the editorial and the news staffs.

The media frequently look for local people who can comment with authority on issues in the news, such as censorship. Where appropriate, members of state intellectual freedom committees may make themselves known as such a resource. To do this, send a brief letter to city and feature editors of key media. Such a letter could simply say, "Intellectual freedom issues are much in the news. If you are interested in a local point of view, I would be happy to help." Include a short biography highlighting relevant experience, or enclose a list of contact names, brief credentials, and contact information.

Talk show producers are frequently looking for guest speakers. Send a letter or e-mail pitching your topic, its relevance to the producer's audience, and the qualifications of the guest you are proposing. Follow up with a phone call. Make sure that the spokesperson understands and is comfortable with the needs of the broadcast media and that he or she is prepared to adapt the message for a particular audience and to answer any difficult questions—particularly if the show includes listener call-ins.

Keep in mind that hosts of talk shows may not be trained journalists. Rather, they may be advocates of a particular point of view. In today's highly competitive media market, their goal may also be to boost ratings by fanning the flames of controversy, sometimes at their guests' expense. Be sure to research the nature of a program (or publication) before seeking or accepting an interview. If you do go on a show, let staff and friends know so they can listen and call in to support your message.

For more information on how to create a media plan or prepare press materials, visit the ALA Public Information Office website (http://www.ala.org/ala/pio/availablepiomat/commhandbook.htm).

Dealing with Controversy

An ongoing public relations program and good media relations may help avoid controversy, but you should still be prepared should a crisis arise. All the elements of a good communications program become even more critical when dealing with controversy. Those elements include a clear and consistent message, skilled spokespeople, a targeted audience, and effective communications strategies. Controversy, though generally not considered desirable, can provide a highly visible forum for educating the public about important intellectual freedom issues.

Every library also should have a crisis or controversy management plan, one that provides a clear road map for library staff, trustees, Friends, and advocates when dealing with high-pressure situations.[6] Some actions—an organized move to limit Internet access in the library, objections to the library's *Playboy* subscription, or protests over an exhibit with sexually explicit art—can be anticipated and prepared for in advance.

It is important to prepare but not to overreact in dealing with such situations. If, for example, a local television station runs a "Sex at the Library" story about pornography on the Internet, a statement should be prepared but not necessarily released until you gauge reaction to the story. Many librarians have discovered that the public's good sense and confidence in libraries can withstand such sensationalized reporting. On the other hand, that kind of story may signal a need to intensify the library's Internet education efforts and prepare for any further media contacts the story may generate.[7]

Be strategic in your use of the media. A letter to the editor or an op-ed piece clarifying the library's position can be helpful, especially if it is to correct a misrepresentation of fact. Engaging in a long, defensive battle of letters is neither productive nor a good use of advocates' energies.

Before accepting an appearance on a radio or television talk show, make sure you understand the nature and format of the program. Consider the size and nature of the audience and how receptive it is to your message. What is the format? Will there be someone from the opposition? Will there be call-ins? What is the host's position? If there is reason to believe the host will not provide a fair forum, it may be better to decline.

A crisis is not the time to build good media relations. Your library should have established relationships with key members of the media to call on at such times. If the library has a reputation for open and honest communication, journalists are more likely to be receptive and helpful in communicating the library's message.

The role of spokespeople becomes even more critical when a library is dealing with controversy. Designating two or more spokespeople, one to deal with the media and one to handle concerns from staff and the public, is advisable, if possible. All the staff should know to whom calls or other media inquiries should be directed, and a call tree should be in place to alert key staff and board members if a crisis occurs. In addition to message sheets and media coaching, spokespeople should receive prompt updates on new developments. All library staff and intellectual freedom advocates should be informed and involved in communicating the key message.

When a library must deal with hostile or negative situations, the following guidelines can be useful:

1. Anticipate difficult questions and develop answers ahead of time. Practice your answers with friends and colleagues. Also practice some easy ones so you will not be caught off guard.
2. Listen. Do not judge. Try to identify and address the real concern or issue being expressed.
3. Acknowledge. Pause to show that you have given the question serious consideration. Frame your answer with a positive. For

example, "You evidently have strong feelings about this," or "I respect your views, but let me give you another perspective," or "We share your concern for children, but our approach is . . ."

4. Be factual. Make sure you have the information you need available. It is better to say "I don't know" than to give inaccurate information. If faced with a claim or information you are not familiar with, simply say, "I hadn't heard that. I'll have to check," or "What I do know is . . ."

5. Do not repeat loaded or negative words. If asked, "Why do librarians let children look at smut?" do not repeat the word "smut" in your answer.

6. Keep your answers to the point. Do not volunteer more information than is asked. Silence is a well-known technique used by reporters in the hope that their subject will stray off message.

7. Be truthful. Speak from your own experience: "In our library, our policy is . . ." or "My experience is . . ."

8. Do not assume anything you say is off the record. It can and may be repeated.

9. Maintain an open, calm, and friendly attitude. Avoid crossed arms, tapping feet, and other body language that conveys stress. Appearing defensive, angry, or out of control undermines credibility.

10. Above all, stick to the high road. Do not criticize or get personal with an opponent. Stay focused on the key message.

Conclusion

The best way to promote intellectual freedom is to practice good public relations, which includes ongoing public education and being prepared for potential controversy. Evaluating the effectiveness of your communications efforts should be built into your communications program. Key indicators to consider include the number of challenges received by the library, the amount and extent of media coverage on intellectual freedom issues, the editorial support given the library, and expressions of public concern and support. To improve on future efforts, make note of which strategies worked and which did not.

Few institutions enjoy the credibility and goodwill that libraries have. Communicating openly, honestly, and with full understanding of the social, legal, and professional issues involved is the best way to promote intellectual freedom and uphold the image of the library and librarians. Those involved in the defense of intellectual freedom should work hard to avoid developing an adversarial relationship with individuals or groups involved in censorship activity. It is much more productive to work toward developing relationships based on mutual respect. The more librarians and their supporters understand the feelings and beliefs of those who do not share their views, the easier it will be to relate to them as individuals with serious concerns.

Building a reputation for receptivity, openness, fairness, and friendliness toward the entire community can only enhance the standing of libraries and the concept of intellectual freedom.

NOTES

1. For copies of ALA messages and talking points, please e-mail kmirkin@ala.org or call the ALA Public Information Office at 1-312-280-5044.

2. *The Library Advocate's Handbook*, which is available from the ALA Public Information Office, provides guidance on organizing an advocacy network. To obtain a copy, call 1-800-545-2433, extension 5041 or 5044, or see the ALA web page at http://www.ala.org/pio/ and select "Available PIO Publications."

3. For calendars of library and literacy events sponsored by the American Library Association and others, see the ALA web page at http://www.ala.org/pio/.

4. For more information on what to do when the media call, please visit http://www.ala.org/ala/pio/mediarelations/whatdowhenmedia.htm.

5. Copies of *First Freedom* op-ed pieces are available from the Office for Intellectual Freedom. Call 1-800-545-2433, extension 4225.

6. Tips for creating a crisis communications plan can be found online at http://www.ala.org/ala/pio/mediarelations/.

7. Tips and guidance for communicating about the Internet can be found in Libraries and the Internet Tool Kit, available on the ALA website at http://www.ala.org/alaorg/oif/internettoolkit.html.

3

Responding to Organized Challenges

BEVERLEY BECKER

Most challenges to library materials and services come from well-meaning individuals, often parents, who find something offensive or objectionable in their local school or public library. These complaints usually—but not always—involve access to information for children and young adults, and are designed to protect children and society in general from ideas and information the complainant finds offensive or dangerous. Although such challenges can be difficult and stressful, library staff can rely on their library's materials selection and review policies to respond to the complaint. In these cases, essential preparations the library has taken before the challenge will greatly increase the likelihood of retaining the challenged materials or protecting library services.

Sometimes, however, challenges are more organized and demand a specific and strategic response. In these circumstances the library will greatly benefit from being prepared and should follow its review policy and procedures exactly. Nevertheless, organized challenges are more likely to become public, engaging the library in a public debate about the library, its collections or services, and the role it plays in the community.

Essential Preparation

Long before any challenge arrives—organized or not—librarians should ensure that they have a materials selection policy in place and that it includes a reconsideration policy for controversial materials. The materials selection policy should include the *Library Bill of Rights* and the Freedom to Read statement. The library also should have policies on patron behavior, privacy and confidentiality of library use, Internet use, meeting rooms, and exhibit spaces. All library policies should be approved by the governing body. In addition, a communications plan will serve the library well in any crisis (see "Essential Preparations," part 5, section 1).

The library should ensure that its governing body, all library employees, regardless of title, as well as volunteers are aware of these policies and are trained on intellectual freedom. They should understand the library's position on access to information and should be able to respond appropriately to a concerned library user. In some cases, a proper response may simply be to refer the library user to a senior librarian on duty. Each staff member should understand the library's framework, operating principles, and policies, and know how and be able to respond to a complainant with respect and accuracy.

The library also will benefit from an ongoing public relations program. If the library is an active and trusted part of the community, it will have more credibility when a crisis erupts. It is much easier to reach an audience when you are already one of the good guys. Libraries should take and make every opportunity to build support for intellectual freedom before a challenge occurs.

Not every television or radio program and newspaper article will be automatically sympathetic, so be sure you have developed good relationships with members of your local media and be prepared to meet the media. Everyone should know who your library's designated spokespeople are. If you have been asked to serve as a spokesperson, make sure you know your message. (For more information, see "Communicating the Intellectual Freedom Message," part 5, section 2.)

Censorship Tactics

Organized attempts at censorship primarily come in two forms. Either an individual finds something objectionable and forms an ad hoc group to champion the cause, or an existing organization decides to challenge information available in the library. These groups and efforts can be local, regional, or national; can be very effective in exerting pressure on libraries; and may have significant impact on library collections.

In Fairfax County, Virginia, parents have formed a group called Parents against Bad Books in Schools (PABBIS) in an effort to influence the selection of curriculum and library materials in schools. The group's stated purposes are (1) to raise awareness and inform people of the controversial materials in schools, (2) to show book content, (3) to help protect parental rights, and (4) to let parents know what they can do about controversial materials in schools.[1]

On its website, http://www.pabbis.com/, PABBIS lists books—and their perceived controversial contents—that it believes do not belong in schools. It also gives parents instructions for challenging library and curriculum materials and identifies all the county school librarians, "Purveyors of Smut for Children." Although PABBIS does make use of the existing reconsideration procedures to challenge school and library materials, it is simultaneously waging a public relations campaign against the school district and its employees. Not only is PABBIS attempting to remove from the schools books its members find questionable, but it is also working to change school policy to require that parents sign off on all potentially controversial materials.

Groups like PABBIS can exert tremendous pressure on the school board, teachers, and library staff. This organization is dedicated solely to limiting access to information in the school library and curriculum. In cases like this, library staff should rely on the existing policies and procedures to respond to specific challenges while working to educate the school board, school administration, and local community about the library's selection and reconsideration policies. It is also imperative to operate the school or library in a transparent fashion to ward off accusations of conspiracy or a hidden agenda.

In some cases, an existing group will encourage its members to actively challenge books in their local communities. For example, the ALA Office for Intellectual Freedom noted an increase in challenges to Carolyn Cooney's *The Terrorist* after the Council on American-Islamic Relations (CAIR), an Islamic advocacy group based in Washington, D.C., issued a warning to parents about the book because, it claims, the book contains inaccurate, offensive, and stereotypical references to Muslims, Muslim women, Arabs, and Islam.

In this case, librarians successfully relied on existing policies and procedures. Many also used the opportunity to educate library users about intellectual freedom and to create bibliographies and exhibits to highlight additional information on Islam.

Books are not, of course, the only library materials to suffer under organized attempts to restrict access to information. The most organized and difficult challenges many libraries have faced in recent years have been to Internet access. In a politically savvy campaign, the Michigan American Family Association (MFA) led the fight to impose Internet filters on the Herrick District Library in Holland, Michigan. The local chapter, funded with $35,000 from the national American Family Association (AFA), succeeded in getting an AFA-authored ordinance requiring Internet filters on the ballot.[2] In response, the citizens of Holland, Michigan, formed a group called Families for Internet Access. On a shoestring budget, the group organized citizens in the community, educated voters on the issues, and successfully challenged a national organization to defeat the proposed ordinance.[3]

Organized attempts to remove or restrict access to information may include coordinated challenges; organized political campaigning, such as ballot initiatives or pressure on (or from) local elected officials; and public criticism of the library and its employees. Unfortunately, the message is often inflammatory and much easier to communicate in a few words than the value of intellectual freedom and free expression.

Response Strategies

The trick—and it is a trick—is to remain calm and composed and then get organized! Whether it is a book, Internet access, or any other library service being challenged, you are standing on firm ground. Libraries provide access to a wide range of information within an established legal framework. Countless libraries have successfully resisted efforts to censor their collections or services.

If a challenge comes, reach out to the local and library communities for support. Consider contacting

- community leaders and community organizations that would support the position of the library;

- local news media whose editorial support would
  be valuable;
- other librarians in the community and state whose
  support could be available if needed;
- all library staff and the governing board;
- the library's legal counsel;
- your state library association's intellectual freedom
  committee; and
- the ALA's Office for Intellectual Freedom.

You also will want to designate a spokesperson and develop talking points.

The role of the library staff will vary, depending on the specific situation. In some cases, staff may have to stand back and let the community debate the issues. Nonetheless, the library should always promote the importance of intellectual freedom and the unique role the library plays in the community. The library is the one and only place dedicated to meeting the information needs of the entire community. It has an obligation as a government institution to abide by the First Amendment and provide equal and equitable access to all library resources for all its constituents.

Many libraries see success when the community realizes it is under attack and steps up to show its support for the local public library. In Montgomery County, Texas, the local Republican Leadership Council (RLC) pressured the county commissioners to remove two sex education books from the library collection, arguing that they promote homosexuality to children. When the commissioners removed those two children's books, they were greeted with a tremendous public outcry, which led to a new review process and the return of those books to the library's collection. The organization Mainstream Montgomery County formed

> to preserve religious and personal freedom, to maintain
> the separation of church and state, and to counter the
> imposition through public policy of one religious tradi-
> tion over others. To carry out our purpose, Mainstream
> Montgomery educates voters about the true purpose and
> negative effects of the public policies promoted by religious/
> political right groups. We inform citizens how the goals

and tactics of religious/political organizations affect our local communities, motivating them to become more involved in the electoral process and local government.[4]

Community-based organizations can be extremely effective in dealing with organized censorship attempts, but do not underestimate the importance of maintaining a well-run library, with well-trained staff and written policies and procedures, to encourage this kind of support.

Libraries should keep the following tips in mind:[5]

- Keep library operations transparent.
- Keep policies up-to-date.
- Maintain written copies of library policies.
- Respond to reasonable requests for information respectfully, accurately, and promptly.
- Stress the positive, pro-family activities at the library.
- Encourage library users and the community to suggest materials for inclusion in the library.
- Respond to untrue charges and unfair criticism respectfully, accurately, and promptly.

Conclusion

Well in advance of any censorship attempt, appropriate policies, a materials selection program, a procedure for handling complaints, and a public relations program should be established. After the challenge comes, rely on those established policies and procedures, and reach out to the community for support.

Unfortunately, not every attempt to resist censorship will be successful. Nonetheless, there are countless examples of communities that have resisted the pressure from individuals and organized groups to restrict and limit access to information. Only a few such examples have been included in this section; for more examples, see http://www.ala.org/ala/ifrt/ifrtinaction/ifrtawards/ifrtaction-links/Default4283.htm. A well-prepared library will fare much better than an unprepared one, and the community will fight to protect an institution that it values and respects.

NOTES

1. Parents against Bad Books in Schools, http://www.pabbis.com/news.htm.

2. Brian J. Bowe, "High-Profile Crusade," *Holland Sentinel*, February 17, 2000, http://www.hollandsentinel.com/stories/021700/new_crusade.html.

3. Brian J. Bowe, "Group Forms to Fight Internet Filter Proposal," *Holland Sentinel*, December 22, 1999, http://www.hollandsentinel.com/sotries/122299/new_group.html.

4. Mainstream Montgomery: A Voice for Moderation in Montgomery County, Texas, http://www.mainstreammc.org.

5. Adapted from Rob Boston, "Religious Right Censorship Attempts," *Intellectual Freedom Manual*, 6th ed. (Chicago: American Library Association, 2002), 370–81.

PART VI

Working for Intellectual Freedom

I

Free People Read Freely

Knowing Where to Go for Help

DON WOOD

*Restriction of free thought and free speech is the most
dangerous of all subversions. It is the one un-American
act that could most easily defeat us.*

—Supreme Court Justice William O. Douglas

*Libraries should challenge censorship in the fulfillment
of their responsibility to provide information and
enlightenment.*   —ALA *Library Bill of Rights*

Intellectual freedom[1] is essential to being well informed, and thus
well equipped, to govern ourselves. Censorship[2] to restrict or suppress information for almost any reason (e.g., moral guardianship or
political purpose) is absolutely opposed to the principles of intellectual freedom. Censorship flourishes when intellectual freedom is not
promoted and safeguarded. To preserve intellectual freedom, it is
often important to know where to go for help to oppose censorship.

This section explains where to go for assistance in a censorship
challenge, how to oppose censorship at any level (local, state, or
national), where to volunteer in support of intellectual freedom, and
how to organize.

It begins with a brief but detailed overview of many groups that
promote and defend intellectual freedom in libraries, specifically

- The American Library Association (ALA)

- The ALA Intellectual Freedom Committee (IFC)
- The ALA Office for Intellectual Freedom (OIF)
- The Freedom to Read Foundation (FTRF)
- The LeRoy C. Merritt Humanitarian Fund
- The ALA Intellectual Freedom Round Table (IFRT)
- The Intellectual Freedom Action Network

It continues with an overview of how state library association intellectual freedom committees and intellectual freedom coalitions also support intellectual freedom principles. All of the groups discussed, except the intellectual freedom coalitions, may be contacted through the ALA Office for Intellectual Freedom (oif@ala.org). How to locate online information about these groups is found in the appendix of this book and at "Navigating the OIF Website" (http:// www.ala.org/ala/oif/navigatingoif.htm). In addition, the list of selected online resources at the end of the section supplies URLs for many of the organizations and resources identified.

American Library Association

The American Library Association is the first place to turn for librarians and library governing bodies wanting to preserve and protect intellectual freedom. The Association maintains a broad program for promoting and defending intellectual freedom. The four main ALA units that can assist people with intellectual freedom matters are

- The Intellectual Freedom Committee, which recommends policy to the ALA Council (ALA's policy-making body) and sponsors educational programs
- The Office for Intellectual Freedom, which implements ALA policy concerning the concept of intellectual freedom as embodied in the *Library Bill of Rights*[3] and provides advice and consultation (case support) to individuals involved in potential or actual censorship disputes
- The Intellectual Freedom Round Table, a forum for the discussion of activities, programs, and problems in intellectual freedom in libraries and for librarians
- The Intellectual Freedom Action Network, volunteers who support the freedom to read in censorship controversies in their communities

ALA Intellectual Freedom Committee

The Intellectual Freedom Committee was established "to recommend such steps as may be necessary to safeguard the rights of library users, libraries, and librarians, in accordance with the First Amendment to the United States Constitution and the *Library Bill of Rights* as adopted by the ALA Council. To work closely with the Office for Intellectual Freedom and with other units and officers of the Association in matters touching intellectual freedom and censorship."

To fulfill its charge, the IFC recommends policies concerning intellectual freedom to the ALA Council. The Council-approved policy statements (e.g., Interpretations of the *Library Bill of Rights*) not only provide librarians with policies to adopt in their own libraries but also establish a professional standard that ALA is committed to defend.

The IFC also writes and disseminates guidelines and other statements to assist librarians in promoting and defending intellectual freedom. Examples include Dealing with Concerns about Library Resources; Guidelines for Developing a Library Privacy Policy, found in the Privacy Tool Kit; and ALA Intellectual Freedom Policies and the First Amendment, written by Bruce J. Ennis, first published in *Freedom to Read Foundation News* 19, no. 1 (1994).

Educational Programs

At each ALA Midwinter Meeting and Annual Conference, the IFC sponsors an issues briefing session that educates attendees about current hot topics in intellectual freedom. In addition, the IFC cosponsors at least two programs at each ALA Annual Conference, one with the ALA Committee on Legislation, another with the Association of American Publishers and the American Booksellers Foundation for Free Expression. The Committee also schedules open hearings, as needed, on policies and statements to gather suggestions from other ALA members.

Office for Intellectual Freedom

The Office for Intellectual Freedom, the administrative arm of the IFC, implements ALA policies on intellectual freedom and educates librarians and the general public about the importance of intellectual freedom in libraries. Because the most effective safeguards for the rights of library users and librarians are an informed public and a library profession aware of repressive activities and how to oppose them, the OIF maintains a wide-ranging program of services (e.g., challenge support, opposing repressive legislation), educational programs (e.g., Lawyers for Libraries, discussed below), educational and informational publications (e.g., *Newsletter on Intellectual Freedom*), an intellectual freedom volunteer group and an educational news-only electronic list (see "Intellectual Freedom Action Network," below), and a website.

Challenge Support and the Challenge Database

CHALLENGE SUPPORT

Rarely does a day go by without the OIF receiving a request for assistance with a challenge to library materials or services. The OIF provides reviews and information about the author of the challenged material, applicable ALA policies, and advice about the implementation of reconsideration policies, and as well as other counseling specific to the situation at hand. If needed, the OIF will provide a written position statement defending the principles of intellectual freedom in materials selection or specific library services. As requested, the OIF provides the names of persons available to offer testimony or support before library boards, supplied from the ranks of the Intellectual Freedom Action Network and state library association intellectual freedom committees. The individual requesting assistance retains the right to choose the options that best apply to the specific situation.

When a censorship problem arises, librarians have at least three options:

- They can visit "Dealing with Challenges to Books and Other Library Materials" (http://www.ala.org/oif/challengesupport/dealing/), on which is found links to materials to help cope with challenges.
- They can visit "Reporting a Challenge" (http://www.ala.org/oif/challengesupport/reporting/), on which is found links and information on who to contact regarding a challenge.
- They can contact the Office for Intellectual Freedom (50 East Huron Street, Chicago, Illinois 60611; 1-800-545-2433, extension 4223; oif@ala.org).

CHALLENGE DATABASE

In 1990, the OIF established an electronic challenge database to record and report statistics on challenges to library materials across the country. The database is a useful tool for identifying trends in types of censorship cases and for documenting responses and solutions to these cases. Librarians are encouraged to document and report challenges and their outcome to the OIF. All identifying information is kept strictly confidential.

You may call in reports on attempted censorship of library and other materials, or you may send newspaper clippings, magazine articles, letters, or OIF's reporting form—the Office for Intellectual Freedom Challenge Database Form (http://www.ala.org/ala/oif/challengesupport/reporting/challengedatabaseform.html).

In 2001, the OIF published "The 100 Most Frequently Challenged Books of 1990–2000." The list was compiled from 6,364 challenges to library materials reported to or recorded by the Office for Intellectual Freedom from 1990 through 2000. (Over 8,000 challenges have been recorded from 1990 through 2004, for an average of over 500 challenges per year.)

Seventy-one percent of the challenges from 1990 through 2000 were to materials in schools or school libraries; another 24 percent were to materials in public libraries. Sixty percent of challenges were brought by parents, 15 percent by library patrons, and 9 percent by administrators (see "Challenges by Initiator, Institution, Type, and Year," http://www.ala.org/ala/oif/bannedbooksweek/bbwlinks/challengesinitiator.htm).

At the beginning of each year, the OIF also compiles a list of the top ten most frequently challenged books for the immediate past year. The press release announcing this list helps bring awareness to the next Banned Books Week, ALA's annual celebration of the freedom to read (see "Banned Books Week," below).

Opposing Repressive Legislation

Repressive legislation on such matters as material deemed harmful to minors can severely restrict the activities of librarians striving to provide service in accordance with the First Amendment, their state constitutions, and the principles of the *Library Bill of Rights*. When requested, therefore, ALA, through the IFC and the OIF, as well as through the Freedom to Read Foundation, acting singly or jointly, supplies testimony informing lawmakers of the potential effects of the legislation on the principles of intellectual freedom as applied to library service. Pending legislation in the U.S. Congress is frequently brought to the attention of these groups by the ALA Washington Office. With the assistance of legal counsel, the OIF will provide analyses of proposed state or local statutes affecting intellectual freedom brought to its attention.[4]

Educational Programs

BANNED BOOKS WEEK

The OIF designs and administers the annual Banned Books Week: Celebrating the Freedom to Read. Observed each year since 1982 during the last week of September, the event reminds Americans not to take their freedom to read for granted. For more information on the history and current celebration of Banned Books Week, visit http://www.ala.org/bbooks/.

LAWYERS FOR LIBRARIES

The need for local attorneys with the knowledge and skills necessary to defend the freedom to read continues unabated. To assist in educating attorneys, the OIF developed Lawyers for Libraries, an ongoing project designed to create a network of attorneys around the country involved in, or committed to becoming involved in, the defense of the First Amendment freedom to read and the application of constitutional law to library policies, principles, and problems. Visit http://www.ala.org/lawyers/ for information on the history and the latest institutes.

Publications

NEWSLETTER ON INTELLECTUAL FREEDOM

One of the Intellectual Freedom Committee's most important publications is the bimonthly *Newsletter on Intellectual Freedom* (NIF). The NIF was initiated in 1952 and has been edited and produced by the OIF staff since 1970. Addressed to both librarians and the general public concerned about intellectual freedom, the NIF provides a comprehensive, national picture of censorship efforts, court cases, legislation, and current readings on the subject. Through original and reprinted articles, the NIF offers a forum for expressing varying views about intellectual freedom and a means of reporting activities of the IFC, the OIF, and the Freedom to Read Foundation. Since 2003, the NIF also has been available as an online publication. It is available by subscription from ALA Subscriptions (1-800-545-2433, extension 4290) or by contacting OIF at oif@ala.org. Additional information about the NIF is found at http://www.ala.org/nif/.

MONOGRAPHS, RESOURCE GUIDES, TRAINING MATERIALS, AND MANUALS

In addition to the *Intellectual Freedom Manual*, the OIF produces the *Banned Books Resource Guide* and the Banned Books Week Kit; *Confidentiality in Libraries: An Intellectual Freedom Modular Education Program*; *Censorship and Selection: Issues and Answers for Schools*, 3rd edition, by Henry Reichman; and *Hit List for Children 2: Frequently Challenged Books*. The OIF consulted in the publication of *Hit List for Young Adults 2: Frequently Challenged Books* as well. The office also compiles press clippings, editorials, and public statements detailing the ways various libraries around the country have handled requests to remove specific materials and sends those resources to others dealing with similar problems. In addition, the office produces and distributes documents and articles concerning intellectual freedom to both librarians and the general public.

The General Public

One of the goals of the office is to educate librarians and the general public about the nature and importance of intellectual freedom in libraries. One way the OIF seeks to make the library profession's support and concern for intellectual freedom known to the general public is through the mass media and other forums, such as the OIF website, which either attempts to address specific concerns of the general public (e.g., the web pages "For Young People" and "For Children and Their Parents") or supplies information for anyone interested in intellectual freedom (e.g., the page "Intellectual Freedom Issues").

Working Together

With the assistance of the ALA Intellectual Freedom Committee and the ALA Committee on Legislation, OIF monitors current legislation activities and develops strategies to defeat legislation aimed at restricting access to information. Moreover, both the IFC and the OIF cooperate with other national organizations, such as the Association of American Publishers, the American Booksellers Association, the American Booksellers Foundation for Free Expression, Americans United for Separation of Church and State, GetNetWise, the Media Coalition, the National Coalition against Censorship, People for the American Way, and other state and regional First Amendment organizations in activities that support free expression.

Website

The Office for Intellectual Freedom's web pages are organized under eleven main headings:

- Basics (of intellectual freedom)
- First Amendment (advocates, court cases, resources)
- Statements and Policies (ALA)
- Intellectual Freedom Tool Kits (Internet, privacy, etc.)
- Challenge Support
- Intellectual Freedom Issues
- Banned Books Week
- For Young People
- IF Groups and Committees (IFC, FTRF, IFRT, etc.)
- Programs and Events (Lawyers for Libraries, NIF, etc.)
- About Us (history of OIF, website, how to contact OIF staff)

For how to find what you need, see "Quick and Easy Guide to the Office for Intellectual Freedom's Pages" (http://www.ala.org/ala/oif/quickeasyguide.htm), "Quick and Easy Links to the OIF Website" (http://www.ala.org/ala/oif/easylinks.htm), and especially "Navigate the OIF Website" (http://www.ala.org/ala/oif/navigatingoif.htm).

Freedom to Read Foundation

The Freedom to Read Foundation was incorporated as a separate organization in 1969 by the ALA to act as its legal defense arm for intellectual freedom in libraries. Therefore, the FTRF presents a report of its activities to the ALA Council at each ALA meeting. The purposes of the FTRF are to

- Promote and protect the freedom of speech and of the press
- Protect the public's right of access to information and materials stored in the nation's libraries
- Safeguard libraries' right to include in their collections and to make available to the public any creative work they may legally acquire
- Support libraries and librarians in their defense of First Amendment rights by supplying them with legal counsel or the means to secure it

The FTRF's work has been divided into two primary activities:

- The allocation and disbursement of grants to individuals and groups primarily for the purpose of aiding them in litigation
- Direct participation in litigation dealing with freedom of speech and of the press

The FTRF is devoted to the principles that the solution to offensive speech is more speech and that the suppression of speech infringes on the rights of all to a free, open, and robust marketplace of ideas. The FTRF opposes censorship through litigation of statutes or government actions that limit, or could have the effect of limiting, the availability and accessibility of constitutionally protected information in libraries. (A time line of FTRF activities is found at http://www.ftrf.org/ftrftimeline.html.)

Librarians affected by repressive statutes or official actions, those whose professional positions and personal well-being are endangered because of their defense of intellectual freedom, and library boards, librarians, and library employees threatened with legal action on such grounds should contact the FTRF (ftrf@ala.org)

In addition, Jenner & Block, the general counsel of the FTRF, provides memoranda to assist librarians in opposing censorship.

Although they are general discussions of issues and not opinion letters, these memoranda are posted to the FRTF website to help librarians understand the legal implications of issues affecting libraries and librarians.

Membership

In 2005, a regular FTRF membership cost thirty-five dollars. By joining FTRF, you

- Help defend the First Amendment in the courts, including the U.S. Supreme Court
- Support librarians around the country besieged by attempts to restrict library materials and services
- Expand the freedom to read by offering legal and financial help in cases involving libraries and librarians, authors, publishers, and booksellers
- Receive the quarterly *Freedom to Read Foundation News*, which includes articles and timely reports on censorship trends, current court cases, and more
- Vote for and are eligible to run for trustee in the annual board elections

For additional membership information, visit http://www.ftrf .org/joinftrf.html.

LeRoy C. Merritt Humanitarian Fund

Librarians requiring immediate financial aid should contact the LeRoy C. Merritt Humanitarian Fund. Established in 1970 as a special trust in memory of Dr. LeRoy C. Merritt, the Merritt Fund is devoted to the support, maintenance, medical care, and welfare of librarians who, in the trustees' opinion, are

- Denied employment rights or discriminated against on the basis of gender, sexual orientation, race, color, creed, age, disability, or place of national origin
- Denied employment rights because of defense of intellectual freedom; that is, threatened with loss of employment or discharged because of their stand for the cause of intellec-

tual freedom, including promotion of freedom of the press, freedom of speech, and freedom of librarians to select items for their collections from all the world's written and recorded information

For more information, contact the Merritt Fund at 1-800-545-2433, extension 4226, or merritt@ala.org.

Intellectual Freedom Round Table

The Intellectual Freedom Round Table, established in 1974, is a membership organization within ALA. Participation in the IFRT allows ALA members to maintain close contact with ALA's overall intellectual freedom program.

The IFRT sponsors an intellectual freedom program at ALA's Annual Conference, cosponsors other programs on various intellectual freedom–related subjects, and provides an online newsletter. The IFRT and individual IFRT members are available to assist the IFC, the OIF, and the FTRF in various joint activities.

Awards

The IFRT administers three awards: the annual John Phillip Immroth Memorial Award, which recognizes extraordinary personal courage in the defense of intellectual freedom; the annual ProQuest/SIRS State and Regional Intellectual Freedom Achievement Award, which honors the most successful and creative state project during the preceding year; and the biennial Eli M. Oboler Memorial Award, which recognizes the best work in the area of intellectual freedom published in the two calendar years prior to the presentation of the award. For more information on these awards, visit http://www.ala.org/ifrt/awards/.

Intellectual Freedom Action Network

The Intellectual Freedom Action Network (IFAN) is a grassroots, ad hoc group of volunteers who have identified themselves as willing to come forward in support of the freedom to read when censorship controversies arise in their communities. It was established by OIF in the fall of 1994.

In response to requests by members of the Intellectual Freedom Round Table for a more active voice in intellectual freedom issues, IFAN also was formed as a rapid-response force to counter the successful and widespread efforts of national censorship groups to organize and mobilize local chapters to work on restricting the availability of expressive materials with which they disagree or which they find offensive. Librarians attacked by such groups were encountering levels of organizational skill to which they, as individuals, could not respond. The IFAN works to address the need for support and to eliminate the sense of isolation that librarians feel when they find themselves involved in a censorship challenge.

The purpose of the IFAN is twofold. Participants are asked to submit to OIF information on groups attempting to censor materials in libraries. Members of IFAN also are asked to lend support (e.g., by writing letters to the editor, attending a school or library board meeting, or calling an affected colleague) when a controversy erupts in their community.

The information they provide about issues is very useful in helping OIF oppose censorship in its many forms. For example, IFAN members are effective in alerting OIF about local and statewide controversies involving book challenges, proposed changes in library policies and operations that would limit access to library materials, and state legislation that would restrict the availability of constitutionally protected expression.

Members themselves can stay informed by subscribing to IFACTION and IFFORUM (see below), by reading about recent developments, or by viewing or listening to local news.

All librarians and other intellectual freedom supporters should join IFAN by contacting OIF at 1-800-545-2433, extension 4223, or by e-mail at oif@ala.org.

IFACTION

The *Intellectual Freedom Action News* (formerly *Memorandum*) was published monthly by OIF for IFAN members and other interested persons. Publication ceased with the June/July/August 1999 issue and was replaced by IFACTION, the news-only, no-discussion e-list of IFAN and OIF.

IFACTION helps to fulfill OIF's goals "to educate librarians and the general public about the nature and importance of intellectual freedom in libraries" and to keep IFAN members informed. To that end, several intellectual freedom news items are posted daily.

IFACTION informs its subscribers—IFAN members and other interested persons—by posting

a wide variety of articles and information on intellectual freedom issues of interest to its subscribers, primarily librarians;

information on intellectual freedom issues that may not have another outlet; and

information that indicates intellectual freedom principles and concerns are held not just by the library profession but also by youth and others in the general public.

Visit http://www.ala.org/ala/oif/ifgroups/ifan/ifactionb/ifaction.htm for instructions on how to subscribe and unsubscribe from IFACTION, how to receive IFACTION in digest form, or to review the IFACTION archive.

IFFORUM

IFFORUM is a self-subscribing, unmoderated electronic list that OIF maintains as an avenue of discussion on various intellectual freedom topics. Information on subscribing to IFFORUM and other related e-lists is found at http://www.ala.org/alaorg/oif/elists.html.

State Library Association
Intellectual Freedom Committees

ALA and the OIF have formed close working relationships with the state library association intellectual freedom committees. Activities vary from state to state. In some states, the committees have worked with other organizations to build impressive state coalitions in defense of intellectual and academic freedom. Elsewhere they have concentrated on compiling and developing state intellectual freedom manuals and continuing education materials. The relationship of the ALA IFC and the OIF with the state committees is one of mutual cooperation and assistance. The OIF supports the work at the state level with information, coordination, and ideas. Like IFAN volunteers, the state committees can be the OIF's eyes and ears at the local level. And, of course, when incidents or other controversies arise, the state library association's intellectual freedom committee frequently mobilizes the troops and, in cooperation with ALA, provides embattled librarians with on-the-spot assistance.

Becoming involved and working together with colleagues and friends, librarians, library board members, and Friends of the Library can fulfill the state organizations' mission to oppose censorship and protect access to the broadest range of information.

Visit http://www.ala.org/ala/oif/ifissues/inthestates/Default 5103.htm for links to various state-related groups and activities, including how to contact elected officials, various resolutions passed by state library associations, state and regional library associations, state intellectual freedom committee chairs, state legislation affecting libraries, and state privacy laws regarding library records.

Please keep OIF informed about all state matters affecting intellectual freedom. Send your information to Office for Intellectual Freedom, American Library Association, 50 E. Huron Street, Chicago, Illinois 60611 or to oif@ala.org as soon as possible.

Intellectual Freedom Coalitions

Intellectual freedom coalitions[5] are other avenues of activism in support of intellectual freedom open to ALA members. Coalitions can be formed around one central issue (e.g., Bill of Rights Defense Committee or Mainstream Montgomery) or several issues (e.g., National Coalition against Censorship).

Such groups exist (or could exist) in almost every community. Very often, the formal and informal ties ALA members establish with these coalitions enable ALA to cooperate with and assist the groups in effectively opposing censorship.

To create these ties, libraries, librarians, and state intellectual freedom committees can join or cooperate with booksellers, publishers, artists, teachers, civil libertarians, journalists, authors, musicians, and other groups and individuals with First Amendment concerns in local, state, and regional coalitions in defense of intellectual freedom.

An intellectual freedom coalition is useful for a number of purposes, such as supporting intellectual freedom legislation, defeating legislation that would negatively affect libraries, and overturning board decisions removing or censoring library resources. Most important, by forming coalitions concerned citizens and organizations can learn who their friends are before an intellectual freedom crisis occurs, concentrate limited funds and personnel where they are most needed, and reach broader audiences. In short, coalition members can benefit from the collective prestige, resources, and contacts coalitions provide.

How to Organize and Manage a Coalition

The first step in organizing a successful intellectual freedom coalition is to learn about successful organizations.

The second step is to ask organizers of existing coalitions how they organized and how they maintain their coalitions. Remember that coalitions can differ greatly from one another. Some are highly structured, full-time organizations themselves. Others are closer to an informal network of communication and support. The same coalition that may function like a well-oiled machine at times of crisis may be minimally active during less critical times. Essentially, the level of organization and commitment should be appropriate to the needs of those involved and no more. If a coalition's needs can be met through a structure that simply facilitates regular contact and little else, this is fine. Indeed, the coalition may be a coalition of one. (A coalition is what its members make it or need it to accomplish.)

The third step in organizing a coalition is to identify state or regional organizations whose goals and objectives are consistent with ALA's intellectual freedom principles. Consider inviting local and regional chapters of the American Civil Liberties Union; booksellers and publishers groups; arts groups; religious organizations; civic groups; educational organizations, including the PTA, the National Education Association, the American Federation of Teachers, the National Council of Teachers of English, and groups of school administrators; lawyers' organizations; and societies of authors and journalists. Individuals also should be sought out and encouraged to participate, since they may be in the best position to do the kind of day-to-day coordination that will be necessary to keep the coalition functioning.

Develop a succinct letter of introduction to be sent to those invited to the organizational meeting. Spell out clearly your own conception of the proposed coalition, but make it clear that the final goals and objectives, as well as the structure of the group, are to be determined democratically.

At the first meeting, the coalition should draft a statement of its principles and, if desired, a constitution and bylaws. These can be more or less formal, depending on the desires of the constituent groups. Committees with concrete goals and specific projects should be organized immediately so the coalition does not become bogged down in sterile debate or bureaucratic busywork. Choose responsible officers who have the time and commitment to keep things going.

Possible projects for the coalition to take up include creating a website, designing a public relations brochure, publishing a news-letter, monitoring legislation, organizing an information network to mobilize support during times of crisis, creating a speakers' bureau, and organizing statewide conferences on intellectual freedom. In addition, librarians and the general public interested in defending and preserving intellectual freedom must be able to deal effectively with the media and to communicate effectively with concerned parents and would-be censors, who may be well organized and well financed.

Summary

Opposing censorship is worthwhile work, and for Americans, it is also necessary work. To have the information needed to be self-governors, we must provide the means to protect the freedoms to read, speak, view, and access all constitutionally protected ideas and information.

The need to oppose censorship will never end until censorship from all sides—the left and the right—ends, so be prepared, stay informed, and be counted:[6]

Make intellectual freedom in all of its forms a central part of your library's mission.

Educate others about the importance of intellectual freedom and how the changing information and technological environment is making the need for intellectual freedom in libraries even more critical.

Advocate support for the library's role in preserving intellectual freedom. Talk to local library and school boards, the media, and elected officials at all levels of government.

Monitor the news and your community for incidents of censorship in your area and report them to the American Library Association's Office for Intellectual Freedom.

Lend your support to others who are facing censorship challenges.

Respond to requests for support from the Office for Intellectual Freedom on controversies in your area.

Stay up-to-date on legislation and court cases that could affect intellectual freedom in libraries.

Network with civil liberties groups and other organizations in your area that are dedicated to intellectual freedom principles. Your support for them will mean increased support for libraries.

Be a leader. Start a local group dedicated to ensuring that intellectual freedom in libraries is preserved.

Get involved professionally. Join ALA's Intellectual Freedom Action Network or volunteer to work with intellectual freedom committees at the state and regional levels. Become a member of ALA's Intellectual Freedom Round Table so your voice can be heard. Join the Freedom to Read Foundation or donate to the Merritt Humanitarian Fund.

As many have noted, the best way to oppose censorship is with education. After all, censorship is neither a satisfactory substitute for nor a complement to effective education and learning. To succeed in school and throughout their lives, children must be educated to access information efficiently and effectively, evaluate information critically and competently, and use information accurately and creatively.[7]

A quality education such as this—one that provides us the greatest possibility of both safety and achievement, regardless of circumstance—is achieved only if we protect our right—and everyone else's right—to seek, receive, hold, and disseminate information from all points of view.

> If all mankind minus one, were of one opinion, and only one person were of the contrary opinion, mankind would be no more justified in silencing that one person, than he, if he had the power, would be justified in silencing mankind. Were an opinion a personal possession of no value except to the owner; if to be obstructed in the enjoyment of it were simply a private injury, it would make some difference whether the injury was inflicted only on a few persons or on many. But the peculiar evil of silencing the expression of an opinion is, that it is robbing the human race; posterity as well as the existing generation; those who dissent from the opinion, still more than those who hold it. If the opinion is right, they are deprived of the opportunity of exchanging error for truth: if wrong, they lose, what is almost as great a benefit, the clearer perception and livelier impression of truth, produced by its collision with error.[8]

NOTES

1. "Intellectual freedom is the right of every individual to both seek and receive information from all points of view without restriction. It provides for free access to all expressions of ideas through which any and all sides of a question, cause or movement may be explored. Intellectual freedom encompasses the freedom to hold, receive and disseminate ideas." American Library Association, "Intellectual Freedom and Censorship Question and Answer," http://www.ala.org/alaorg/oif/intellectualfreedomandcensorship.html.

2. Defined in 1986 by the IFC as "a change in the access status of material, based on the content of the work and made by a governing authority or its representatives. Such changes include exclusion, restriction, removal, or age/grade level changes." American Library Association, "Support for Dealing with or Reporting Challenges to Library Materials," http://www.ala.org/ala/oif/challengesupport/challengesupport.htm#definitions.

3. "The *Library Bill of Rights* is a policy statement adopted by the American Library Association to protect the right of all library users to choose for

themselves what they wish to read or view. The policy is more than 60 years old and has been adopted voluntarily by most libraries as a way of ensuring the highest quality library service to their communities." American Library Association, "Coping with Challenges," http://www.ala .org/ala/oif/challengesupport/dealing/copingchallengesstrategies.htm.

4. See also American Library Association, "Pending Internet Legislation," http://www.ala.org/ala/oif/ifissues/issuesrelatedlinks/pendinginter- net.htm; "State Legislation," http://www.ala.org/ala/oif/ifissues/ inthestates/statelegislation.htm, which links to state legislation affecting libraries; and "News Sources for Information about Censorship, the Internet, Filters, Filtering, Intellectual Freedom, and the First Amend- ment," http://www.ala.org/ala/oif/basics/basicrelatedlinks/ newssources.htm, which links to news and other relevant sources. In addition, see "Contacting Elected Officials about Issues/Legislation Related to Intellectual Freedom," http://www.ala.org/ala/oif/basics/ basicrelatedlinks/contactingelected.htm, which includes links to the ALA "Take Action!" page, the *Library Advocate's Handbook* (English and Spanish editions), the "ALA Washington Office Legislative Alert" page, and vari- ous ways to contact state and federal legislators.

5. Article IV of the *Library Bill of Rights* states, "Libraries should cooperate with all persons and groups concerned with resisting abridgment of free expression and free access to ideas."

6. From ALAAction No. 2, "Intellectual Freedom," revised April 2005, http:// www.ala.org/ala/oif/basics/intellectualfreedom.htm, and "What You Can Do to Oppose Censorship," http://www.ala.org/ala oif/basics/ whatcandoopposecensorship.htm.

7. See "The Nine Information Literacy Standards for Student Learning," http://www.ala.org/ala/aasl/aaslproftools/informationpower/ informationliteracy.htm, excerpted from American Association of School Librarians, "Information Literacy Standards for Student Learning," in *Information Power: Building Partnerships for Learning*, 2nd ed. (Chicago: American Library Association, 1998), 8–47.

8. John Stuart Mill, *On Liberty*.

Selected Online Resources

The URLs for the online resources mentioned in the preceding text are listed below in alphabetical order.

- ALA Intellectual Freedom Policies and the First Amendment
  http://www.ala.org/ala/oif/basics/alaintellectual.htm

- ALA Washington Office
  http://www.ala.org/washoff/
- Awards Administered by IFRT
  http://www.ala.org/ifrt/awards/
- *Banned Books Resource Guide* and Banned Books Week Kit
  http://www.ala.org/bbooks/resource.html
- Bill of Rights Defense Committee, http://www.bordc.org
- Challenges by Initiator, Institution, Type, and Year
  http://www.ala.org/ala/oif/bannedbooksweek/
  bbwlinks/challengesinitiator.htm
- Coalition of One
  http://www.ncac.org/action/action.html;
  http://www.ncac.org/action/suggestions.html
- Dealing with Challenges to Books and Other Library
  Materials
  http://www.ala.org/oif/challengesupport/dealing/
- Dealing with Concerns about Library Resources
  http://www.ala.org/alaorg/oif/dealingwithconcerns
  .html
- For Children and Their Parents
  http://www.ala.org/ala/oif/foryoungpeople/
  childrenparents/especiallychildren.htm
- For Young People
  http://www.ala.org/ala/oif/foryoungpeople/
  youngpeople.htm
- Freedom to Read Foundation
  http://www.ftrf.org
- *Freedom to Read Foundation News*
  http://www.ftrf.org/ftrfnews.html
- FTRF Reports to the ALA Council
  http://www.ftrf.org/ftrfreports.html
- Guidelines for Developing a Library Privacy Policy
  http://www.ala.org/oif/iftoolkits/privacy/guidelines/
- History and Current Celebration of Banned Books Week
  http://www.ala.org/bbooks/
- History and Latest Institutes for Lawyers for Libraries
  http://www.ala.org/lawyers/

- IFACTION Subscription Information and Archive
  http://www.ala.org/ala/oif/ifgroups/ifan/ifactionb/
  ifaction.htm
- IFC Guidelines and Other Statements
  http://www.ala.org/ala/oif/statementspols/
  statementspolicies.htm
- IFC Reports to the ALA Council
  http://www.ala.org/oif/ifcreports.html
- Information about Membership in FTRF
  http://www.ftrf.org/joinftrf.html
- Information about Successful Coalitions
  http://www.ala.org/alaorg/oif/coalitions.html
- Intellectual Freedom Action Network
  http://www.ala.org/ala/oif/ifgroups/ifan/intellectual.htm
- Intellectual Freedom Committee
  http://www.ala.org/ala/oif/ifgroups/ifcommittee/
  intellectual.htm
- Intellectual Freedom Issues
  http://www.ala.org/oif/ifissues/
- Intellectual Freedom Round Table
  http://www.ala.org/ifrt/
- Interpretations of the *Library Bill of Rights*
  http://www.ala.org/oif/policies/interpretations/
- Jenner & Block Memoranda Discussing Censorship Issues
  http://www.ftrf.org/jbmemoranda.html
- LeRoy C. Merritt Humanitarian Fund
  http://www.ala.org/alaorg/oif/merritt.html
- Links to State-Related Groups and Activities
  http://www.ala.org/ala/oif/ifissues/inthestates/
  Default5103.htm
- Mainstream Montgomery
  http://www.mainstreammc.org
- National Coalition against Censorship
  http://www.ncac.org
- Navigating the OIF Website
  http://www.ala.org/ala/oif/navigatingoif.htm
- *Newsletter on Intellectual Freedom*
  http://www.ala.org/nif/

- Office for Intellectual Freedom
  http://www.ala.org/oif/
- 100 Most Frequently Challenged Books of 1990–2000
  http://www.ala.org/ala/oif/bannedbooksweek/
  bbwlinks/100mostfrequently.htm
- Other National Organizations Interested in Intellectual
  Freedom
  http://www.ala.org/ala/oif/firstamendment/
  advocates/advocates.htm
- Privacy Tool Kit
  http://www.ala.org/oif/iftoolkits/privacy/
- Quick and Easy Guide to the Office for Intellectual
  Freedom's Pages
  http://www.ala.org/ala/oif/quickeasyguide.htm
- Quick and Easy Links to the OIF Website
  http://www.ala.org/ala/oif/easylinks.htm
- Recent Developments in Intellectual Freedom
  Controversies
  http://www.ala.org/ala/oif/basics/basicrelatedlinks/
  newssources.htm
- Reporting a Challenge
  http://www.ala.org/oif/challengesupport/reporting/
- Source for ALA Publications
  http://alastore.ala.org
- State Library Association Intellectual Freedom Committees
  http://www.ala.org/alaorg/oif/stateifc.html
- Subscription Information for IFFORUM and
  Related E-lists
  http://www.ala.org/alaorg/oif/elists.html
- Time Line of FTRF Activities
  http://www.ftrf.org/ftrftimeline.html
- Top Ten Most Frequently Challenged Books for the
  Immediate Past Year
  http://www.ala.org/ala/oif/bannedbooksweek/
  challengedbanned/challengedbanned.htm#mfcb

2

Lobbying for Intellectual Freedom

ALA WASHINGTON OFFICE

Lobbying is the process through which citizens seek to persuade elected officials to a particular course of action. It is the most effective way for citizens to express their opinions and interest in particular causes to their elected representatives. Lobbying for library interests is a long-term and ongoing effort, and is usually most effective when it involves the joint efforts of professional lobbyists as well as individual librarians and library supporters. Supporters of intellectual freedom will find advice and guidelines for library advocacy and library lobbying from the American Library Association, its Office for Intellectual Freedom, its Washington Office, its Public Information Office, and its state chapters.

When lobbying on intellectual freedom issues raised by local, state, or federal legislation, keep in mind that First Amendment and censorship issues tend to generate controversy and strong emotions, particularly in the post–September 11 world. Lobbying in these arenas requires sensitivity and diplomacy in working with elected officials to develop policies supportive of intellectual freedom.

Library Lobbying: A History of Good Relationships

For many years, the library community has enjoyed productive working relationships with members of Congress on both sides of the aisle. Just about everyone loves libraries, and members of

Congress will often share stories of their childhood experiences in public and school libraries. Most members also understand how valuable libraries are to their communities.

But that does not mean that lobbying for libraries, intellectual freedom, or First Amendment issues will be easy. Legislators have countless competing interests that fight for their time and attention, and library issues may seem less pressing to them than other things. But librarians bring to the table a number of particular skills and abilities that help make them very effective lobbyists.

Librarians are naturally skilled at assembling information—like statistics and anecdotes—and turning disparate facts and stories into a cohesive message. Legislators respond best to logical and succinct arguments, and librarians are very effective creators and ambassadors of well-presented messages. Legislators also are primarily interested in supporting legislation that will demonstrably help their own constituents—the voters in their congressional districts. Libraries exist in every single congressional district in this country. They employ thousands of workers, provide information to hundreds of thousands of citizens each day, and contribute in a variety of ways to state and local economies. Because of libraries' broad reach and because we share a number of concerns with other coalitions and groups, we have many friends and allies, some of whom may weigh more heavily than we do on the political scales. These powerful friends are invaluable lobbying partners. Keep them in mind when you need to mobilize support for a key issue, and follow the next series of steps to become an informed, effective lobbyist for intellectual freedom.

Know the Issues and Stay Informed

One of the easiest and most effective ways to stay informed on legislative issues is to follow the electronic information published by the ALA Office for Intellectual Freedom and the ALA Washington Office. Both offices manage e-lists—ALAWON (Washington Office) and IFACTION (OIF)—that offer up-to-the-minute breaking news on legislation and issues relating to intellectual freedom and the First Amendment. The Office for Intellectual Freedom website (http://www.ala.org/oif/) and the Washington Office website (http://www.ala.org/washoff/) offer a wealth of information on key issues as well as links to other useful electronic material. Often the Washington Office e-list, ALAWON, will direct readers to the Legislative Action Center (http://www.capwiz.com/ala/home/), an online gateway to the U.S. Congress. Users can look up names and contact information for members of Congress, send prewritten e-mails to Congress on key issues, or compose and send original e-mails or faxes to federal representatives.

The ALA Office for Intellectual Freedom tracks state-level legislation through its relationship with the Media Coalition (http://www.mediacoalition.org). The Media Coalition is an association that defends the First Amendment right to produce and sell books, magazines, recordings, videotapes, and video games. It also defends the American public's First Amendment right to have access to the broadest possible range of opinion and entertainment. Other sources for news and action alerts regarding state-level activity include state library associations and school library media associations, and their legislation and intellectual freedom committees.

Organize and Mobilize Intellectual Freedom Supporters

When lobbying for federal or state support in the legislature, the more people and groups you have on your side of the issue, the better your chances are to make a difference. Work to mobilize supporters by contacting your state library association's legislation committee. Ask to speak with any lobbyists, government relations coordinators, or political consultants associated with the state library association, and offer your help to these lobbyists. Many state library associations may not employ full-time professional lobbyists. If that is the case, ask the association's legislation committee for help in organizing a group of intellectual freedom supporters to contact state or federal legislators. E-lists are a great way to keep in touch with like-minded and politically interested librarians, friends of libraries, and trustees, and a terrific way to mobilize support when action is needed. Work to develop a core group of individuals knowledgeable about intellectual freedom issues and willing and able to speak on short notice.

Also, stay in touch with ALA's Washington Office. The Washington Office can provide you with helpful information on the issues as well as tips on communicating with legislators and their staffs. Tell ALA's lobbying staff if you are planning to meet with members of Congress in Washington, D.C. After your meetings, fill them in on whom you talked with and what was said. This will help ensure that ALA's lobbyists can keep the momentum from your meeting going and ensure that members of Congress and their staffs keep intellectual freedom issues front-of-mind.

Build Strong Coalitions

The nature and diversity of librarians' work both in libraries and in the communities, campuses, or organizations those libraries serve make librarians highly capable coalition builders. Librarians can work with groups representing educators and educational institutions, for example, or with groups representing children or parents, or with scholars and news reporters, or with publishers and chambers of commerce, or with citizens' and public-interest groups. Library interests relating to the public's access to needed information cross over levels of education, industry concerns, and the many content-related issues of public-interest groups.

A wide variety of groups either share library objectives or can be persuaded to do so. These groups may work with library supporters on many issues or on only one particular measure. Some organizations or industry groups may join librarians on one bill and be on the other side of the table for the next piece of legislation. Groups representing publishers, for instance, are frequently ALA's partners on censorship issues, but they are often on the opposing side when it comes to copyright legislation.

For the most part, American politics is coalition politics rather than confrontation politics. Candidates and elected officials strive to satisfy as many elements of their constituency as possible. It is helpful to demonstrate to legislators that many nonlibrary organizations support library efforts. If a library group takes a position on a bill, that position is strengthened if the statement is signed by many other organizations.

Work to Nurture and Seed Coalition Relationships

Library advocates should make contact and keep in touch with the leadership and the legislative activists of organizations with similar objectives. Coalition building and nurturing should be organized to develop clear lines of communication and action, to avoid duplication of effort, and to avoid conflicting messages. Keep a current list of coalition contacts so they can be called upon to help when the need arises.

Use the Media

It is important to remember how valuable the media can be in helping to shape public opinion. In addition to regular communications with legislators, timely and concise letters to the editor as well as op-ed pieces should be sent to local newspapers and other publications. The public relations programs of individual libraries can be called on to help with composing letters and op-eds, as can ALA's Public Information Office and Washington Office. ALA's online Media Relations Tool Kit will be an invaluable resource for intellectual freedom lobbyists (http://www.ala.org/ala/pio/mediarelations/mediarelations.htm). If your local newspaper publishes an editorial that calls for lower government expenditures, write a letter to the editor that points out the effects of a cutback on your community's library users. If a newspaper columnist supports removing Harry Potter from school library shelves, write a letter to the editor that addresses the dangers of censoring library collections. If a pending bill is endorsed, or opposed, by the editors of the local newspaper, write a letter that presents the library position.

Work to develop good working relationships with the publications and media outlets of greatest influence in your area. Do not wait until a time of desperate need to get your voice heard—an ongoing relationship with a key reporter could prove invaluable in a crisis situation. The ALA's Library Advocacy Now! materials and training packages provide excellent tips and advice on getting the library message across to both opinion shapers and decision makers.

Get Familiar with the Legislative Process

It is important to know how state and federal legislatures work, when they are in session, what the committees are, where relevant legislation will be referred, and what steps a bill must go through to be enacted. If you are getting involved in legislative advocacy for the first time, learning about the legislative process and the intricacies of committees, subcommittees, power and politics may seem daunting. Do not hesitate to draw upon the knowledge of your state library association and staff at the ALA Washington Office to find out who is powerful in the legislature, and who among library friends might have influence over those with power. Also, it is a good idea to keep in mind the priorities of the party currently in power, as well as what other issues are on the agenda of the committee that has jurisdiction over library or intellectual freedom issues. The more you know about the competing interests legislators face in their committees, the better equipped you will be to explain why your issues should not be pushed to the side in favor of other priorities.

Get to Know Legislators and Their Staffs

In general, only a few federal legislators will take a strong and detailed interest in library legislation—because they have a personal interest; or because they have a concerned relative, friend, or vocal constituent base; or because they are on a committee or subcommittee handling bills of this type.

Every member of Congress and U.S. senator has an office in the home district as well as in Washington. It is just as important, and often easier and more convenient, to get to know local congressional staff as it is to get to know staff in Washington. Go to see these local staffs and bring them information on intellectual freedom issues. Invite local congressional staff to your library when you have scheduled a good program or event. Introduce them to your patrons and brief them on matters important to your library.

Long before a library measure is being promoted, or before a crisis erupts, it is important to identify sympathetic individuals in the political structure. Keep a current contact list of library and intellectual freedom supporters in the state and federal legislatures and a current file of library and intellectual freedom advocates in the community, and keep in touch with both groups. These friendly legislators and their staffs can become sources of information and advice regarding effective strategy and timing, positions to be taken in hearings, the nature of the testimony that will be most effective, the kinds of witnesses to be secured, and the sources of opposition to a particular measure.

Personal Contacts with Legislators Work Best

Considerable contact between library supporters and legislators (and their staffs!) is essential during the process of lobbying. All people who are active in legislative affairs will be seeing legislators frequently and in time will get to know many legislators well as individuals. Often, the most useful visits are in the home district rather than at the state capitol or in Washington, D.C. Work to become familiar with your member of Congress's district staff, and learn from them when your member of Congress will be home in the district and available to meet with citizens.

To meet with a legislator, make an appointment and then leave little to chance. Before the meeting plan what you will say, and be sure you are well versed on the issue or bill being discussed. Bring some one-page fact sheets or leave-behinds with you that cover all the relevant points, and leave these handouts with the legislator when your meeting is complete. A fact sheet on the local library and its services to users also would be valuable. During the meeting give the legislator ample opportunity to ask questions, and before leaving ask which staff member to keep in touch with when the legislator is unavailable and request to be kept informed of progress on the measure under discussion. Similarly, it is important to keep legislators informed of the library's activities. Invite legislators and staff to functions or special activities (particularly those with media presence) or ask them to join a board or advisory group, if appropriate.

A small-group visit to a legislator is particularly effective, especially if the group includes a trustee or Friend of the library as well as representatives from community groups or library-user constituencies. A good way to gain experience in this type of lobbying is to participate in the annual National Library Legislative Day event organized each May by ALA Washington Office and the D.C. Library Association (http://www.ala.org/ala/washoff/washevents/events.htm). On National Library Legislative Day, library delegations from each state visit congressional offices in teams, preceded by briefings and followed by a reception on Capitol Hill. Many state library associations also sponsor state legislative days or special events in the state capital.

Library supporters have discovered during their visits to Washington that often twenty minutes spent with the key legislative assistant for a member of Congress may be more productive than five minutes spent with the member. At the federal level, personal or committee staff draft bills, develop floor statements, brief the legislators, and convey constituent opinion to their bosses. Good relationships with legislative staff are essential to all lobbying efforts.

Face-to-face meetings with legislators need not be frequent. Usually one meeting before a legislative session begins, preferably in the home district, and perhaps one more visit during the legislative session when an important measure is at a decisive point will be sufficient. Of course, new legislators should be visited early, even before they are elected, to ascertain their viewpoints, their interests, and their potential positions regarding library and intellectual freedom issues.

Follow-up Is Key

Whenever possible, meet your legislator or your legislator's staff before calling or sending letters, e-mails, and faxes on library issues. Correspondence is much more powerful when the sender is known to the legislator and the staff. Ideally, each legislator should have a series of contacts with one or more library supporters from the home district or state, a number of letters each year, and at least one personal visit during each legislative session. Always follow up with a letter of thanks after meeting with your legislator or with legislative staff.

The ALA Washington Office can offer many effective tips and guidelines for communicating with members of Congress. In addition, ALA's "Issues and Advocacy" web page offers a wealth of helpful information about contacting, meeting, and following up with legislators (http://www.ala.org/ala/issues/onlinetools/actionkit/legislators.htm).

Be Persuasive, Professional, and Persistent

Legislative strategies and tactics require frequent adjustment to changing conditions. Today's minority party might be next year's majority, and vice versa. Be flexible and adjust to the style of a key legislator; facts and figures may work with one chair of a committee, while the sponsor in the other chamber may need homey library stories to recount to colleagues or in floor statements. Politics is called the art of the possible, and democratic politics is often the art of compromise. Progress must often come one small step at a time. Library groups should not think in terms of winning or losing but of how to move forward, even if it involves three steps to the side first.

It is important to stay professional in demeanor with enemies as well as friends. Stay alert to the moral and philosophical attitudes of candidates and officeholders. Recognize that those on opposing sides may have legitimate concerns. Sometimes those concerns can be addressed through other means without harmful effects on libraries or the First Amendment. Make library concerns known early, and where possible, get commitments in support of intellectual freedom before controversy erupts.

Each step in the process of achieving rapport with legislators is simple in itself. The power of these efforts is in their cumulative impact and their multiplication when performed by many others. Each participant in the process and each step in the process is significant. There may be many decision points and calls for action on the way to enactment. There may also be a few times when the process falls short and must be started all over again. Once ALA's Washington Office was established, it took ten years before the first federal library legislation was enacted. Persistence pays off, so keep at it!

NAVIGATING THE OIF WEBSITE

DON WOOD

Background and History

The OIF website (http://www.ala.org/oif/) links to every ALA intellectual freedom policy, statement, and guideline, and encompasses the websites of the Committee on Professional Ethics, the Freedom to Read Foundation, the Intellectual Freedom Action Network, the Intellectual Freedom Committee, the Intellectual Freedom Round Table, the LeRoy C. Merritt Humanitarian Fund, the Office for Intellectual Freedom, and the state intellectual freedom committee chairs. The OIF home page was created in 1996.

The OIF program officer/communications (dwood@ala.org) is responsible for creating, mounting, and maintaining the pages on the OIF website. However, the author would be all staff members of the Office for Intellectual Freedom and all groups associated with OIF (e.g., the ALA Intellectual Freedom Committee, the Intellectual Freedom Round Table, and the Committee on Professional Ethics).

The website provides information and resources for librarians and the general public and helps fulfill the ALA Office for Intellectual Freedom's mission:

> The Office for Intellectual Freedom is charged with implementing ALA policies concerning the concept of intellectual freedom as embodied in the *Library Bill of Rights*, the Association's basic policy on free access to libraries and library materials. The goal of the office is to educate librarians and the general public about the nature and importance of intellectual freedom in libraries.

The primary audience is composed of librarians and the general public.

Where to Begin

How this chapter—and the OIF website—is organized is explained under the heading "All These Sites Are Interrelated." If you have visited the OIF website before or if you are ready to navigate the pages, skip this brief introduction and go directly to the next heading, "Topics, Policies, and Groups." Otherwise, learn here how to find the website as well as intellectual freedom topics, policies, and groups.

The OIF website (http://www.ala.org/oif/) is found from the American Library Association's home page (http://www.ala.org). Once there:

1. Click on "Our Association" (http://www.ala.org/ala/ourasso-ciation/Default262.htm) on the top-level navigation bar (be-tween "Awards and Scholarships" and "Issues and Advocacy");
2. Click on "Offices" (http://www.ala.org/ala/ourassociation/offices/offices.htm) on the left-hand navigation bar (between "My ALA" and "Other Groups and Organizations"); and
3. Click on "Intellectual Freedom" under that heading on the left-hand navigation bar or on "Office for Intellectual Freedom" (http://www.ala.org/oif/) on the retrieved page.

Topics, Policies, and Groups

Here are three quick ways to find an intellectual freedom topic, policy, or group:

To find a topic of interest, such as "Censorship," "USA PATRIOT Act," or "Privacy and Confidentiality," click on "Intellec-tual Freedom Issues" (http://www.ala.org/oif/ifissues/) on the left-hand navigation bar.

To find a policy, such as the *Library Bill of Rights* or the Code of Ethics, click on "Statements and Policies" (http://www.ala .org/oif/policies/) on the left-hand navigation bar. See also information under the heading "Special Navigational Aids" to find "Quick and Easy Links" and "Redirects."

To find the seven groups associated with the Office for Intellectual Freedom, click on "IF Groups and Committees" (http://www.ala.org/oif/ifgroups/) on the left-hand navigation bar or at the heading on the top of the OIF home page. Doing so retrieves the seven groups directly associated with the OIF as well as a link to a page of other intellectual freedom advocates. Of course, each site can be found by pointing to its URL:

- Committee on Professional Ethics
  http://www.ala.org/oif/ifgroups/cope/
- Freedom to Read Foundation
  http://www.ftrf.org
- Intellectual Freedom Action Network
  http://www.ala.org/oif/ifgroups/ifan/
- Intellectual Freedom Committee
  http://www.ala.org/oif/ifgroups/ifc/
- Intellectual Freedom Round Table
  http://www.ala.org/ifrt/
- LeRoy C. Merritt Humanitarian Fund
  http://www.merrittfund.org
- Other First Amendment Advocates
  http://www.ala.org/oif/first/advocates/
- State Intellectual Freedom Committee Chairs
  http://www.ala.org/oif/ifgroups/stateifcchairs/

Note: To retrace the steps taken, click on each heading and subheading to obtain a bread-crumb trail, such as Home . . . Our Association . . . Offices . . . Intellectual Freedom . . . Statements and Policies . . . Other Policies and Guidelines, or Home . . . Our Association . . . Offices . . . Intellectual Freedom . . . Statements and Policies . . . *Library Bill of Rights* . . . Interpretations.

Special Navigational Aids

Quick and Easy Links to the OIF Website
(http://www.ala.org/ala/oif/easylinks.htm)

The page "Quick and Easy Links to the OIF Website" provides links to key subject areas on the OIF website. Each link takes visitors to a page with a combo box of options, leading them to, for example, the

Library Bill of Rights; Interpretations of the *Library Bill of Rights*; other ALA policies, resolutions, and guidelines; intellectual freedom issues; and intellectual freedom tool kits, as well as to programs such as Banned Books Week. The five links are

- Basic ALA Policies
- Intellectual Freedom Basics
- Censorship Pages
- Privacy Pages
- USA PATRIOT Act

Redirects to the
Office for Intellectual Freedom's (OIF's) Website
(http://www.ala.org/oif/redirects/)

The page "Redirects to the Office for Intellectual Freedom's (OIF's) Website" provides shorter URLs to some of the OIF's most sought-after pages.

All These Sites Are Interrelated

All the intellectual freedom websites are interrelated and adhere to similar designs. It is best to begin by learning how to navigate the Office for Intellectual Freedom's site, which at first glance appears to be the most complicated. It is hoped, however, that it is as easily navigable as the least complicated of the sites, especially after this introduction. Introductions to other sites follow alphabetically, beginning with the Committee on Professional Ethics, followed by the Freedom to Read Foundation, the Intellectual Freedom Action Network, the Intellectual Freedom Committee, the Intellectual Freedom Round Table, the LeRoy C. Merritt Humanitarian Fund, and the State Intellectual Freedom Committee Chairs.

Office for Intellectual Freedom
(http://www.ala.org/oif/)

The Office for Intellectual Freedom's home page includes its charge; links to navigational aids, hot topics and alerts, and other intellectual freedom organizations; references; and sites of information to help visitors learn what they can do to oppose censorship and support intellectual freedom. Its pages are found under eleven major headings.

Basics
(http://www.ala.org/oif/basics/)

The "Basics" page provides links to "Intellectual Freedom and Censorship Questions and Answers," "First Amendment Basics," "International Intellectual Freedom Basics," "American Library Basics," "International Library Basics," "Censorship Basics," "Internet Censorship," "What You Can Do to Oppose Censorship," "What You Can Do to Celebrate Your Freedom to Read!" "ALA Intellectual Freedom Policies and the First Amendment," "Intellectual Freedom, ALAAction No. 2 in a series," and "Lester Asheim in Cyberspace." Most of these pages provide links to basic intellectual freedom documents, such as the *Library Bill of Rights*, The Freedom to Read, and Libraries: An American Value.

First Amendment
(http://www.ala.org/alaorg/oif/first.html)

This page provides links to other "First Amendment Advocates," "First Amendment Resources," and "Notable First Amendment Court Cases," along with links to related topics on non-ALA sites.[1]

Statements and Policies
(http://www.ala.org/ala/oif/statementspols/statementspolicies.htm)

This page provides links to various ALA intellectual freedom policies arranged under topical headings such as "Academic Libraries," "Access," "Basic Intellectual Freedom Policies," "Behavior," "Destruction of Libraries," "Diversity," "Ethics," "Evaluating Library Collections," "Exhibit Spaces and Bulletin Boards," "Expurgation of Library Materials," "Governmental Intimidation," "Internet," "Labeling," "Library Resources," "Media Ownership," "Meeting Rooms," "Minors," "Privacy," "Public Forum," and "Torture." The left-hand navigation bar provides links to the "*Library Bill of Rights*," the "ALA Code of Ethics" (including its history and the Spanish version), the "Freedom to Read Statement," "Intellectual Freedom Resolutions" (e.g., "New FCC Rules and Media Concentration"), "Other Policies and Guidelines" (e.g., "Policy on Governmental Intimidation" and "Policy Concerning Confidentiality of Personally Identifiable Information about Library Users"), ALA's "Core Values Statement," and "Related Links."

Intellectual Freedom Tool Kits
(http://www.ala.org/oif/iftoolkits/)

The Office for Intellectual Freedom, with the ALA Intellectual Freedom Committee and others, develops tool kits on a variety of topics to assist librarians and the general public. Tool kits under "Intellectual Freedom Tool Kits" on the left-hand navigation bar include the "Intellectual Freedom Manual," "Libraries and the Internet Tool Kit," "Outsourcing and Privatization," and "Privacy." The page "Intellectual Freedom Manual" provides both related links and links to chapters that could not be published in the current edition of the *International Freedom Manual* due to space limitations.

Challenge Support
(http://www.ala.org/oif/challengesupport/)

In addition to a link to "Definitions to Clarify Terminology Associated with Challenges," the "Challenge Support" page provides links to two pages: "Dealing with Challenges to Books and Other Library Materials" and "Reporting a Challenge." "Dealing" provides links to "The Censor: Motives and Tactics," "Checklist and Ideas for Library Staff Working with Community Leaders," "Conducting a Challenge Hearing," "Coping with Challenges: Kids and Libraries," "Coping with Challenges: Strategies and Tips for Dealing with Challenges to Library Materials," "Dealing with Concerns about Library Resources," "Developing a Confidentiality Policy," and "Workbook for Selection Policy Writing." "Reporting" provides information on how to report a challenge, either with the Challenge Database Form (online or print version)[2] or by contacting Beverley Becker, associate director of the Office for Intellectual Freedom, at 1-800-545-2433, extension 4221, or bbecker@ala.org.

Intellectual Freedom Issues
(http://www.ala.org/ala/oif/ifissues/intellectual.htm)

This page provides links to various intellectual freedom issues, such as "Book Burning," "Censorship and Challenges," "Censorship in the Schools," "Confidentiality and Coping with Law Enforcement Inquiries," "Destruction of Libraries," "Freedom of Information Act," "Media Concentration," "Privacy and Confidentiality," "Radio Frequency Identification Chips and Systems," "Surveillance in America," and the "USA PATRIOT Act." The left-hand navigation bar provides links to "In the States." This page provides links to "Contacting Elected Officials," "Resolutions of State Library Associations Supporting Legal Action by the American Library Association to Challenge CIPA in Federal Courts," "State and Regional Library Associations," "State Intellectual Freedom Committee Chairs," "State Legislation," "State Privacy Laws regarding Library Records," and "USA PATRIOT Act Resolutions of State Library Associations."

Banned Books Week
(http://www.ala.org/bbooks/)

September 23–30, 2006, will mark the twenty-fifth annual celebration of Banned Books Week: Celebrate the Freedom to Read. The page "Banned Books Week" provides links to "Background" (history of Banned Books Week and Banned Books Week sponsors), "Challenged and Banned Books" (Why Are Books Challenged? Who Challenges Books? What's the Difference between a Challenge and a Banning? How Is the List of Most Challenged Books Tabulated? The Most Frequently Challenged Books, The Most Frequently Challenged Authors, and the Top Ten Challenged Authors, 1990 to Present), and "BBW Kit" (how to order the Banned Books Week Kit of posters, bookmarks, and resource guide). In addition, there are links to "The 100 Most Frequently Challenged Books" and to the ALA Public Information Office's "BBW Press Kit." Most pages also provide links to related topics on ALA and non-ALA sites.

For Young People
(http://www.ala.org/oif/youngpeople/)

Young people have First Amendment rights, and the "For Young People" page provides information and links to explore these rights, particularly as they apply in school. Links lead to "What You Can Do," "Court Cases," "School: Intellectual Freedom for Young People," "Hot Issues," and "Especially for Children and Their Parents." Once again, most pages provide links to related topics on ALA and non-ALA sites. The left-hand navigation bar provides a link to "The One Un-American Act," by William O. Douglas.

IF Groups and Committees
(http://www.ala.org/oif/ifgroups/)

This page provides links to the pages of the Committee on Professional Ethics, the Freedom to Read Foundation, the Intellectual Freedom Committee, the Intellectual Freedom Round Table, the LeRoy C. Merritt Humanitarian Fund, and the State Intellectual Freedom Committee Chairs. These pages include links to the groups' rosters and other related pages. "IF Groups and Committees" also provides links to the Intellectual Freedom Action Network and IFACTION, and other First Amendment advocates.

Awards, Institutes, Programs, and Publications
(http://www.ala.org/oif/programsandevents/)

The page "Awards, Institutes, Programs, and Publications" provides links to "Intellectual Freedom Programs at the ALA Annual Conference," "Lawyers for Libraries," "Intellectual Freedom Publications," and "Banned Books Week." The page "Intellectual Freedom Publications" includes links to "Freedom to Read Foundation News," "Intellectual Freedom Action News," "Newsletter on Intellectual Freedom," and "Order OIF and Banned Books Week Materials."

About Us
(http://www.ala.org/alaorg/oif/aboutoif.html)

The "About Us" page provides links to "How to Contact OIF Staff" and "History, Authorship, and Purpose of the OIF Website."

Committee on Professional Ethics
(http://www.ala.org/oif/ifgroups/cope/)

The Committee on Professional Ethics' home page includes its charge and contact information for its OIF staff liaisons. Its pages are found under three major headings:

Roster (http://www.ala.org/oif/ifgroups/cope/roster.html)

The "Roster" page is automatically generated and formatted by ALA's iMIS membership system. Contact information, including e-mail addresses, is always current.

COPE in Action (http://www.ala.org/oif/ifgroups/cope/copeaction.html)

The "Cope in Action" page provides links to ALA's Code of Ethics. On the left-hand navigation bar under the heading "Cope in Action" are links to "Skits" (scripts that explore ethical issues, performed by the Committee on Professional Ethics at past ALA Annual Conferences) and "Explanatory Statements" (explanatory statements written by the Committee on the ALA Code of Ethics).

Related Links (http://www.ala.org/oif/ifgroups/cope/related.html)

The "Related Links" page, in addition to supplying links to other intellectual freedom groups, links to "Intellectual Freedom Issues," "Codes of Ethics from Library Associations Worldwide," "Ethics Links to Librarian and Information Manager Associations WWW Pages," "ProfessionalEthics.ca," and "Creating a Code of Ethics for Your Organization." It also links to "Code of Ethics for Special Collections Librarians" (October 2003), prepared by the Association of College and Research Libraries' Rare Books and Manuscripts Section. It is an update to the 1993 Standards for Ethical Conduct for Rare Book, Manuscript, and Special Collections Librarians.

Freedom to Read Foundation
(http://www.ftrf.org)

The Freedom to Read Foundation's home page includes its mission and contact information for its staff liaisons. Its pages are found under four major headings:

Organization (http://ftrf.org/organization.html)

The "Organization" page provides links to "FTRF Board of Directors" and "How to Join the Freedom to Read Foundation."

FTRF in Action (http://ftrf.org/ftrfaction.html)

The page "FRTF in Action: provides links to "Elections," "First Amendment Court Cases," "First Freedom Op-ed Service," "FTRF News," "FTRF Endorsements," "FTRF Time Line," "Status of Recent Cases," "Jenner & Block [FTRF's counsel] Memoranda," "Reports to ALA Council," and "Roll of Honor Award."

Related Links (http://ftrf.org/related.html)

The "Related Links" page provides links to the "Office for Intellectual Freedom" and "Intellectual Freedom Issues."

About FTRF (http://www.ftrf.org/about.html)

The "About RTF" page describes the purpose and activities of the Freedom to Read Foundation and how to contact the foundation.

Intellectual Freedom Action Network
(http://www.ala.org/oif/ifgroups/ifan/)

The Intellectual Freedom Action Network's home page describes its purpose and how to volunteer. Its pages are found under two major headings:

IFACTION (http://www.ala.org/oif/ifaction.html)

The "IFACTION" page describes the news-only, no-discussion e-list of the Intellectual Freedom Action Network and the Office for Intellectual Freedom. There is also a brief description and link to the now-defunct *Intellectual Freedom Action News* (formerly *Memorandum*), which was published monthly by the OIF but ceased publication with the June/July/August 1999 issue. IFACTION replaced *Intellectual Freedom Action News*.

Related Links (http://www.ala.org/oif/ifgroups/ifan/related.html)

"Related Links," in addition to providing links to other intellectual freedom groups, links to "Intellectual Freedom Issues."

Intellectual Freedom Committee
(http://www.ala.org/oif/ifgroups/ifc/)

The Intellectual Freedom Committee's home page includes its charge and contact information for its OIF staff liaisons. Its pages are found under three major headings:

Roster (http://www.ala.org/oif/ifgroups/ifc/ifcroster.html)

The "Roster" page provides links to the rosters of the IFC and its subcommittees. Each roster is automatically generated and formatted by ALA's iMIS membership system. Contact information, including e-mail addresses, is always current.

IFC in Action (http://www.ala.org/oif/ifgroups/ifc/ifcaction.html)

The "IFC in Action" page provides links to "IFC Reports to Council" and "Intellectual Freedom Manual."

Related Links (http://www.ala.org/oif/ifgroups/ifc/related.html)

"Related Links," in addition to providing links to other intellectual freedom groups, links to "Intellectual Freedom Issues."

Intellectual Freedom Round Table
(http://www.ala.org/ifrt/)

The Intellectual Freedom Round Table's home page includes its mission. Its pages are found under four major headings:

Organization (http://www.ala.org/ifrt/organization.html)

The "Organization" page provides links to the rosters of the IFRT Executive Committee and other IFRT committees. Each roster is automatically generated and formatted by ALA's iMIS membership system. Contact information, including e-mail addresses, is always current. In addition, this page provides links to the contact information of the IFRT liaisons and representatives and for the OIF staff liaison to the IFRT. This page also provides links to "Forms for IFRT Ballot," "IFRT Bylaws," "How to Join IFRT (membership information)," "IFRT Chairs," "ALA Round Table Coordinating Assembly," and "ALA Round Table Handbook."

IFRT in Action (http://www.ala.org/ifrt/ifrtaction.html)

The "IFRT in Action" page provides links to "Awards" (Eli M. Oboler Memorial Award, John Phillip Immroth Memorial Award, SIRS-ProQuest State and Regional Intellectual Freedom Achievement Award), "E-List," "Program," "IFRT Report," "IF Competencies," "IF Syllabi," and "Merritt Fund and IFRT."

Related Links (http://www.ala.org/ifrt/related.html)

"Related Links," in addition to providing links to other intellectual freedom groups, links to "Intellectual Freedom Issues."

About IFRT (http://www.ala.org/ifrt/about.html)

The "About IFRT" page describes the purpose and activities of the Intellectual Freedom Round Table and how to contact the OIF staff liaison to the IFRT.

LeRoy C. Merritt Humanitarian Fund
(http://www.merrittfund.org)

The LeRoy C. Merritt Humanitarian Fund's home page includes its mission. Its pages are found under five major headings:

Trustees Roster (http://www.merrittfund.org/roster.html)

The "Trustees Roster" page provides contact information for the Merritt trustees.

Who Was Leroy C. Merritt? (http://www.merrittfund.org/ leroycmerritt.html)

The "Who Was. . . ?" page provides information about LeRoy C. Merritt.

How to Donate to the Merritt Fund
(http://www.merrittfund.org/donations.html)

The "How to Donate" page provides information about how to donate to the Merritt Fund. (The Merritt Fund is supported solely by donations and contributions from concerned groups and individuals. Contributions to the Merritt Fund are not tax-exempt because they are used to give direct aid to individuals without reference to Internal Revenue Service requirements regarding tax-exempt organizations. Hence, contributions do not qualify as personal tax deductions for donors.)

Application for Assistance (http://www.merrittfund.org/assistance.html)

The "Application for Assistance" page provides links to the Word and PDF versions of the Merritt Fund's application for assistance.

Merritt Fund in Action (http://www.merrittfund.org/merrittaction.html)

The "Merritt Fund in Action" page provides links to "Application for Assistance," "Merritt Fund Three-Year Report" (August 2003), and "Merritt to the Rescue" (an interview with someone assisted by Merritt).

State Intellectual Freedom Committee Chairs
(http://www.ala.org/oif/ifgroups/stateifcchairs/)

The State Intellectual Freedom Committee Chairs' home page includes information on contacting the OIF staff liaison to the state IFC chairs, how chairs can be subscribed to the state IFC business e-list, and how to provide updated contact information, terms of office, and so forth. Its pages are found under three major headings:

Roster (http://www.ala.org/oif/ifgroups/stateifcchairs/roster.html)

The "Roster" page provides contact information for the state IFC chairs. (New state IFC chairs are asked to provide change-of-address information to the Office for Intellectual Freedom, American Library Association, 50 E. Huron Street, Chicago, Illinois 60611, or oif@ala.org, as soon as possible. They may use either the Change of Address Form, which can be mailed or faxed, or the Online Change of Address Form, which is e-mailed directly.)

State IFC in Action
(http://www.ala.org/oif/ifgroups/stateifcchairs/stateifcchairsaction.html)

The "State IFC in Action" page provides links to "State and Regional Library Associations" and "ALA Conference Planning Calendar, 2002–2012" as well as to pages related to activities and actions of the state intellectual freedom committees.

Related Links (http://www.ala.org/oif/ifgroups/stateifcchairs/related.html)

The "Related Links" page, in addition to providing links to other intellectual freedom groups, links to "Intellectual Freedom Issues" and "In the States" (links to important state pages on the ALA website). This page provides links to "Contacting Elected Officials," "Resolutions of State Library Associations Supporting Legal Action by the American Library Association to Challenge CIPA in Federal Courts," "State and Regional Library Associations," "State Intellectual Freedom Committee Chairs," "State Legislation," "State Privacy Laws regarding Library Records," and "USA PATRIOT Act Resolutions of State Library Associations."

NOTES

1. Links to non-ALA sites have been provided because these sites may have information of interest. Neither the American Library Association nor the Office for Intellectual Freedom necessarily endorses the views expressed or the facts presented on these sites; and furthermore, ALA and OIF do not endorse any commercial products that may be advertised or available on these sites.

2. Since 1990, the American Library Association Office for Intellectual Freedom has maintained a confidential database on challenged materials. The Association collects information from two sources: newspapers and reports submitted by individuals, some of whom use the Challenge Database Form. All challenges are compiled into a database. Reports of challenges culled from newspapers across the country are compiled in the bimonthly *Newsletter on Intellectual Freedom*; those reports are then compiled in the *Banned Books Week Resource Guide*. Challenges reported to the ALA by individuals are kept confidential. In these cases, ALA will release only the title of the book being challenged, the state, and the type of institution (school, public library). The name of the institution and its town will not be disclosed. A list of most frequently challenged books is compiled from these challenges for each annual Banned Books Week.

GLOSSARY

arbitrary distinctions   Inappropriate categorizations of persons, classes of persons, conduct, or things based upon criteria irrelevant to the purpose for which the distinctions are made. For example, a rule intended to regulate the length of time an item may be borrowed should not be based on an irrelevant consideration (arbitrary distinction) such as a personal characteristic of the borrower (height or age).

challenge   A formal, written complaint requesting that library materials be removed or restricted. In 1986, in response to inquiries from librarians facing book or material challenges for the first time, the Intellectual Freedom Committee developed the following list of definitions to clarify terminology associated with challenges:

expression of concern   An inquiry that has judgmental overtones.

oral complaint   An oral challenge to the presence and/or appropriateness of the material in question.

written complaint   A formal, written complaint filed with the institution (library, school, etc.), challenging the presence and/or appropriateness of specific material.

public attack   A publicly disseminated statement challenging the value of the material, presented to the media and/or others outside the institutional organization in order to gain public support for further action.

censorship   A change in the access status of material, based on the content of the work and made by a governing authority or its representatives. Such changes include exclusion, restriction, removal, or age/grade level changes.

compelling government interest   A term used by courts when assessing the burden of government regulation or action upon the exercise of a fundamental right such as freedom of speech. For such a rule to withstand constitutional challenge, the government must show more than a merely important reason for the rule. The reason for the rule must be compelling; that is, it must be so important that it outweighs even the most valued and basic freedom it negatively affects.

equal and equitable access to information and services   Approach to operating that ensures that everyone the library serves is entitled to the same level of access to information and services and that all have the opportunity to avail themselves if they so choose. *Equal* access refers to uniform access to information and services. *Equitable* access refers to just and fair access taking into consideration the facts and circumstances of the individual case. Access to information and services is equal and equitable when there is a level playing field. For more information on these terms, see "Equality and Equity of Access: What's the Difference?" prepared by Nancy Kranich (http://www.ala.org/ala/oif/iftoolkits/ifmanual/)

extralegal pressure   Threat of legal action or pressure by community members or organized groups that results in the banning of library materials. Lester Asheim used this meaning of the term in his September 1953 *Wilson Library Bulletin* article "Not Censorship, but Selection" (http://informatics.buffalo.edu/faculty/ellison/Syllabi/580/NotCensor.html). The term also refers to requests from law enforcement without a proper court order and actions taken by persons in positions of authority (e.g., mayors, elected officials, school officials) to remove or restrict access to library materials or services without following library policies and procedures.

limited public forum   A public place purposefully designated by the government, or established through tradition, as a place dedicated to a particular type of expression. As in a traditional public forum, only reasonable content-neutral time, place, and manner restrictions on speech within the scope of the designated purpose of the forum may be imposed. The government may exclude entire categories of speech that do not fall within the designated purpose of the forum but may not discriminate against particular viewpoints on subjects appropriate to the forum.

materially interfere   A term used by courts to describe the necessary level of intrusion, inconvenience, or disruption of an accepted or protected activity caused by certain conduct in order to justify regulation of that conduct. A material interference is much more than mere annoyance—it must be an actual obstacle to the exercise of a right.

substantial objectives   Goals related to the fundamental mission of a government institution and not merely incidental to the performance of that mission. Providing free and unrestricted access to a broad selection of materials representing various points of view is a substantial objective of a public library.

SELECTED BIBLIOGRAPHY

Becker, Beverley C., and Susan Stan. *Hit List: Frequently Challenged Books for Children*. Rev. ed. Chicago: American Library Association, 2002.

Boghosian, Heidi. *The Assault on Free Speech, Public Assembly, and Dissent: A National Lawyers Guild Report on Government Violations of First Amendment Rights in the United States*. Great Barrington, MA: North River Press, 2004.

Bollinger, Lee C., and Geoffrey R. Stone. *Externally Vigilant: Free Speech in the Modern Era*. Chicago: University of Chicago Press, 2002.

Boss, Richard W. "RFID Technology for Libraries." *Library Technology Reports* 39, no. 6 (November/December 2003).

Cole, David, and James X. Dempsey. *Terrorism and the Constitution: Sacrificing Civil Liberties in the Name of National Security*. New York: New Press, 2002.

Curtis, Michael Kent. *Free Speech, the People's Darling Privilege: Struggles for Freedom of Expression in American History*. Durham, NC: Duke University Press, 2001.

Davis, Charles N., and Sigman L. Splichal, eds. *Access Denied: Freedom of Information in the Information Age*. Ames: Iowa State University Press, 2000.

Doyle, Robert P., comp. *Banned Books: 2004 Resource Guide*. Chicago: American Library Association, 2004 (updated every three years).

Foerstel, Herbert N. *Banned in the U.S.A.: A Reference Guide to Book Censorship in Schools and Public Libraries*. Westport, CT: Greenwood Press, 1994.

———. *Refuge of a Scoundrel: The Patriot Act in Libraries*. Westport, CT: Libraries Unlimited, 2004.

Haynes, Charles, et al. *The First Amendment in Schools: A Guide from the First Amendment Center*. Alexandria, VA: Association for Supervision and Curriculum Development, 2003.

Hentoff, Nat. *The War on the Bill of Rights and the Gathering Resistance*. Rev. ed. New York: Seven Stories Press, 2004.

Hollingsworth, Peggie J., ed. *Unfettered Expression: Freedom in American Intellectual Life*. Ann Arbor: University of Michigan Press, 2000.

Jones, Barbara M. *Libraries, Access, and Intellectual Freedom: Developing Policies for Public and Academic Libraries*. Chicago: American Library Association, 1999.

Kranich, Nancy. *Libraries and Democracy: The Cornerstones of Democracy.* Chicago: American Library Association, 2001.

Leone, Richard, and Greg Anrig, eds. *The War on Our Freedoms: Civil Liberties in an Age of Terrorism.* New York: Century Foundation, 2003.

Lesesne, Teri S., and Rosemary Chance. *Hit List for Young Adults 2: Frequently Challenged Books.* Rev. ed. Chicago: American Library Association, 2002.

Minow, Mary, and Thomas A. Lipinski. *The Library's Legal Answer Book.* Chicago: American Library Association, 2003.

O'Harrow, Robert. *No Place to Hide.* New York: Free Press, 2005.

Peck, Robert S. *Libraries, the First Amendment, and Cyberspace: What You Need to Know.* Chicago: American Library Association, 2000.

Rabban, David M. *Free Speech in Its Forgotten Years.* Cambridge: Cambridge University Press, 1997.

Robbins, Louise S. *Censorship and the American Library: The American Library Association's Response to Threats to Intellectual Freedom, 1939–1969.* Westport, CT: Greenwood Press, 1996.

Smith, Robert Ellis. *Ben Franklin's Web Site: Privacy and Curiosity from Plymouth Rock to the Internet.* Providence, RI: Privacy Journal, 2004.

Stone, Geoffrey R. *Perilous Times: Free Speech in Wartime from the Sedition Act of 1798 to the War on Terrorism.* New York: Norton, 2004.

Strossen Nadine. *Defending Pornography: Free Speech, Sex, and the Fight for Women's Rights.* New York: Scribner, 1995.

Symons, Ann K., and Charles Harmon. *Protecting the Right to Read: A How-to-Do-It Manual for School and Public Librarians.* New York: Neal-Schuman, 1995.

Symons, Ann K., and Sally Gardner Reed, eds. *Speaking Out: Voices in Celebration of Intellectual Freedom.* Chicago: American Library Association, 1999.

U.S. Children's Online Protection Act Commission. *Final Report of the COPA Commission Presented to Congress, October 20, 2000.* Washington, DC: Government Printing Office, 2000.

Wachsberger, Ken, ed. *Literature Suppressed on Political Grounds, Literature Suppressed on Religious Grounds, Literature Suppressed on Sexual Grounds, Literature Suppressed on Social Grounds.* Banned Books Series. New York: Facts on File, 1998.

INDEX

Composition in ATLisbon and Palatino using QuarkXpress 5
on a PC platform

Printed on 50-pound white offset, a pH-neutral stock, and bound
in 10-point cover stock by Victor Graphics